Cooperative
and
Collective in
China's Rural
Development

SOCIALISM AND
★ SOCIAL MOVEMENTS ★

Series Editor: Mark Selden

FREEING CHINA'S FARMERS
Rural Restructuring in the Reform Era
David Zweig

DANWEI
The Changing Chinese Workplace in
Historical and Comparative Perspective
Edited by Xiaobo Lü and Elizabeth J. Perry

**COOPERATIVE AND COLLECTIVE IN
CHINA'S RURAL DEVELOPMENT**
Between State and Private Interests
*Edited by Eduard Vermeer, Frank N. Pieke,
and Woei Lien Chong*

**THE DISTRIBUTION OF WEALTH IN
RURAL CHINA**
Terry McKinley

CHINA AFTER SOCIALISM
In the Footsteps of Eastern Europe
or East Asia?
*Edited by Barrett L. McCormick
and Jonathan Unger*

CHINA IN REVOLUTION
The Yenan Way Revisited
Mark Selden

DILEMMAS OF REFORM IN CHINA
Political Conflict and Economic Debate
Joseph Fewsmith

THE HIGHLANDERS OF CENTRAL CHINA
A History, 1895-1937
Jerome Ch'en

CHINA'S TRANSITION FROM SOCIALISM
Statist Legacies and Market Reform,
1980-1990
Dorothy J. Solinger

BUKHARIN IN RETROSPECT
*Edited by Theodor Bergmann,
Gert Schaefer, and Mark Selden
Introduction by Moshe Lewin*

REINVENTING REVOLUTION
New Social Movements and
the Socialist Tradition in India
Gail Omvedt

**THE POLITICAL ECONOMY OF
CHINESE DEVELOPMENT**
Mark Selden

**THE CHINESE STATE IN
THE ERA OF ECONOMIC REFORM**
Edited by Gordon White

**MARXISM AND THE
CHINESE EXPERIENCE**
Issues in Contemporary Chinese Socialism
Edited by Arlif Dirlik and Maurice Meisner

**STALINISM AND THE SEEDS OF
SOVIET REFORM**
The Debates of the 1960s
Moshe Lewin

★ *Socialism and Social Movements* ★

Cooperative and Collective in China's Rural Development

Between State and Private Interests

Edited by
Eduard B. Vermeer, Frank N. Pieke,
and Woei Lien Chong

An East Gate Book

M.E. Sharpe
Armonk, New York
London, England

An East Gate Book

Copyright © 1998 by M. E. Sharpe, Inc.

Library of Congress Cataloging-in-Publication Data

Cooperative and collective in China's rural development : between
state and private interests / edited by Eduard B. Vermeer, Frank N.
Pieke, and Woei Lien Chong.
     p.   cm. —(Socialism and social movements)
"An East gate book."
Includes bibliographical references and index.
ISBN 0-7656-0093-5 (hc : alk. paper)
  1. Rural development—China.
2. Rural development—Government policy—China.
3. Privatization—China. 4. China—Rural conditions.
5. Economic stabilization—China.
I. Vermeer, E. B. (Eduard B.) II. Pieke Frank N.
III. Chong, Woei Lien. IV. Series.
HN740.Z9C6323   1997
307.1′412′0951—dc21
97-26792
CIP

Printed in the United States of America

∞

BM (c) 10   9   8   7   6   5   4   3

Contents

Acknowledgments

The editors of this volume are indebted to many participants in the "International Conference on Chinese Rural Collectives and Voluntary Organizations: Between State Organization and Private Interest" at Leiden University in January 1995 of which this volume is the result. We have greatly benefited from their lively discussions and scholarly comments. We also gratefully acknowledge the financial support for the conference by the following organizations: the Ford Foundation (Beijing); The CNWS Research School for Asian, African and Amerindian Studies (Leiden); The Faculty of Arts, Leiden University; The International Institute of Asian Studies (Leiden); The Royal Netherlands Academy of Arts and Sciences (Amsterdam); and the Stichting voor de Bevordering van de Studie van het Chinees aan de Rijksuniversiteit Leiden.

Summary of the Chapters

Eduard B. Vermeer and Frank N. Pieke

The contribution of **Mark Selden** puts contemporary developments in the historical perspective of farmers' cooperatives, which were destroyed by forced collectivization in the 1950s. Now, as then, the government has little tolerance for
pluralism and autonomous organizations, yet an urgent need for voluntary organization exists, and the goals of mutual help and democratic management continue to be worthy of state support. Recently, farmers have shown impressive
success both in private and cooperative economic undertakings in more dynamic
regions. Cooperatives have the potential to integrate the useful collective elements of the past and mediate between the state and local needs and interests.
The question remains how well cooperative institutions will fit in the rapidly
changing rural economic structure.

Examining the different definitions of the village as a settlement and a community, **Stephan Feuchtwang** discusses rural organization from a social perspective. Traditionally, farmers conceptualized their village community's relation to
the natural and social environment through geomancy (*fengshui*), local territorial
cults, and the bonds of kinship and friendship. Collectivization in the 1950s
strove to replace these with definitions of the village as a socialist collective
which was part of a vertically integrated administrative hierarchy. Depending on
the larger political, social, and economic context, definitions of the village and
the village community currently draw on all of these very diverse sources. The
question "What is a village?" will therefore be answered differently from one
village to the next. By problematizing and investigating a category of Chinese
social structure which is usually taken for granted, Feuchtwang draws our attention to the negotiated and adaptive nature, not only of the village, but of Chinese
social structure in general.

Margaret McKean discusses the recent Chinese experience in light of the international literature and debate about how to organize common property resource management (CPRM) regimes. A core feature of effective CPRM regimes is excludability, which limits the number of users who are entitled to the utilization of a given resource. This should put an end to the evil effects of "free-riding." However, exclusion may be incompatible with maintaining shared community values, and monitoring and sanctions are needed.

Jean C. Oi argues that the often spectacular economic growth achieved in the Chinese countryside cannot simply be credited to the free forces of the market and the entrepreneurial spirit of individual farmers and private businesses. No independent economic elite has emerged from the market reforms. As in the Newly Industrialized Countries of East Asia, the state in China plays a crucial role in initiating and facilitating enterprise. There is, however, a crucial difference. In China, it is not the central state, but rather local governments and their cadres which have taken the lead. Villages and townships have grasped the opportunities offered by decentralization to restyle themselves as "local state corporations," using their organizational strength and superior access to resources and markets to become a dominant factor in rural industrial growth and allocation of investments and profits.

Pei Xiaolin stresses the continuity of the collective and post-collective periods, during which the village remained an integrated organization with administrative, managerial, and economic functions. Village cadres behave as business administrators rather than as government officials. Their personal connections are most important not only in township and village enterprises, but also in all other fields of management. Strong community relationships reduce transaction cost. The recognition that at least the cohesive-type villages, with their well-defined administrative and economic boundaries, behave like competitive firms has important implications for the common preposition that Chinese enterprises tend to have fuzzy boundaries and soft budgetary constraints. Of course, not all villages are of the cohesive type, and in some TVEs property rights reside mostly with management or the village leader.

Eduard B. Vermeer describes the consequences of the disbanding of collective organizations in the early 1980s, and the quick and largely adequate reactions of the local CCP and the Chinese government. From 1987, the CCP gave high priority to irrigation, and together with local government, reasserted control over local water conservancy stations and the direction of peasant corvée labor. Management was revitalized and became more pluriform. As a result of widespread privatization, and the increased economic power of the farmers, the new systems operate differently and more democratically than the old ones. However, the degree of autonomy of irrigation districts is closely linked with their budgetary position. At the village level, collectively organized or private irrigation services are mainly found in well-developed communities, while poor communities depend on the state or have completely abandoned such services. Vermeer sees a need for new regulations of the duties of village government and the rights of water users.

John Morton and **Robin Grimble** describe the changing role of institutions and households in an irrigated oasis settlement in western Inner Mongolia, with particular reference to the most crucial resource, groundwater. Here, a growing colony of farmers has been maintained on arid land with shrinking ground water resources, and high, but subsidized costs of irrigation. The Yao Ba irrigation district is responsible for most of the district's agricultural income. The fate of two levels of organization under this system is discussed, only one of which proved to be effective. The authors conclude that because of political opposition from both the government and farmers, the Water Bureau of the Banner has been unable to raise water fees or take other measures which would reduce water use and make irrigation more economical.

Peter Ho demonstrates the difficulties of proper land management in pastoral areas. Most post-1949 grassland control measures in Ningxia Autonomous Region have had detrimental effects, because they were founded on collective or individual property right structures which were defective as well as based on fundamental misconceptions about CPRM. Another major reason was that the state pushed relentlessly for increased production. Overgrazing became extremely serious, fencing failed, and penalty rules were not enforced. Ineffective controlling institutions and regulations, as well as insufficient manpower to realize implementation persist today. Farmers continue to use the pastures at will. One should not be optimistic about the solution offered by a self-regulatory CPRM regime: it needs a proper framework of state support, excludability, and a transfer of a significant part of the herding population to other economic activities.

Wang Zhenyao describes how, since 1988, direct and democratic elections of village committees have been introduced by the Ministry of Civil Affairs. This new system of democratic self-government aims to enfranchise new social groups, such as private entrepreneurs, and to fight power abuse and corruption of long-incumbent cadres. Wang acknowledges that the system is still far from perfect or universal. For instance, in Fujian Province, ballots were given to households, not to individuals. However, the democratic election of village leaders is increasingly embraced by villagers, and the second and third rounds of elections have shown improvement over the first and second ones. The gradual introduction of rural democracy under the guidance of the state and with the support of the local CCP is believed to be the most feasible and effective way forward for the democratization process in China.

Frank N. Pieke contrasts the cases of two villages, one poor and one relatively rich, in Raoyang county, Hebei Province. To understand the highly specific social and political consequences of the Chinese reforms in these two villages, the theories of market transition, civil society, and local state corporatism are all found lacking because of their structuralist and normative assumptions. Pieke argues for a more flexible approach focusing on certain key processes whose interaction can lead to vastly different outcomes in places that can be as near as two villages in the same county. More attention should also be paid to the economic plans and policy preferences of higher levels of the state which continue to shape the behavior of local economic and political actors.

John Flower and Pamela Leonard use a case study of a village in western Sichuan to explore further Stephan Feuchtwang's stress on the complexity of villages' self-definitions. Flower and Leonard show the relevance of religion in creating the village as a localized imagined community which includes the local cadres and government institutions, and argue against the simple view that everything that is beyond the reach of the state must be regarded as resistance against the state. Rooting their power in local practices and organizations, the cadres not only become more effective leaders, but are also able to coopt such practices and organizations for their own and the state's purposes.

About the Editors and Contributors

Eduard B. Vermeer teaches history and economy of China at Leiden University. He is the author of *Economic Development in Provincial China: The Central Shaanxi Since 1930* and *Chinese Local History: Stone Inscriptions from Fukien in the Sung to Ch'ing Periods,* and editor of *Development and Decline of Fukien* and *From Peasant to Entrepreneur: Growth and Change in Rural China.* With the CASS Institute of Economics, he is preparing the fourth rural household survey of Wuxi and Baoding.

Frank N. Pieke is University Lecturer in the Modern Politics and Society of China and Fellow of St. Cross College, University of Oxford. He is author of *The Ordinary and the Extraordinary: An Anthropological Study of Chinese Reform and the 1989 People's Movement in Beijing* (London: Kegan Paul International, 1996).

Woei Lien Chong is Chief Editor of the academic journal *China Information: A Quarterly Journal on Contemporary China Studies*, published by the Documentation and Research Center for Contemporary China, Sinological Institute, Leiden University, The Netherlands. Her field of research is contemporary Chinese thought.

Stephan Feuchtwang is head of the China Research Unit at City University, London, which specialises in research on rural China. He is author of *The Imperial Metaphor; Popular Religion in China*, Routledge, 1992. Currently he is working with Dr. Wang Mingming of Beijing University on a book about political and religious authority in two townships, one in northern Taiwan, the other in southern Fujian.

John Flower is Assistant Professor of East Asian history at the University of North Carolina at Charlotte. Flower lived in Sichuan Province, China, from 1991 to 1993. His thesis, written at the University of Virginia, explores alternative constructions of Chinese cultural identity in the "two worlds" of city and countryside by focusing on intellectuals' attitudes toward villagers, and rural and urban viewpoints on economic development, morality, and "traditional Chinese culture."

Robin Grimble has a Ph.D in Agricultural Economics from the University of London (Wye College) and has worked as a natural resource economist/socio-economist at the Natural Resources Institute in the UK since 1976. His interests include natural resource management, environmental policy, and water management, including the socio-economics of small-scale irrigation. He has worked on these issues as a researcher and consultant in Thailand, China, and other developing countries in Asia, Africa, and Latin America.

Peter Ho is a Ph.D candidate at the Sinological Institute of the University of Leiden, The Netherlands. He graduated in Social Forestry (1990) and Sinology (1993). He has done research and consultancy work in China in the fields of common property resource management, agricultural extension, and rural economics. He is currently involved in research on the impact of the Rangeland Law, as well as rangeland policy formulation and implementation in the Ningxia Hui Autonomous Region.

Pamela Leonard is a social anthropologist specializing in environment and development issues. She completed her Ph.D. in 1994 at the University of Cambridge after two years of fieldwork in rural China. Her thesis, "The Political Landscape of a Sichuan Village," details the changing economy and landscape of a Sichuan village through the lens of the historical memory of its inhabitants. Leonard is currently teaching anthropology at the University of North Carolina at Charlotte and is a practicing farmer.

Margaret McKean is attached to the Department of Political Science, Duke University in Durham, North Carolina.

John Morton has a Ph.D in Social Anthropology from the University of Hull, and has worked as a Social Anthropologist at the Natural Resources Institute, UK, since 1993. His interests include socio-economic aspects of irrigation and drainage, livestock development, and the analysis of indigenous and local government institutions. He has worked on these interests in Pakistan, China, and a number of African countries.

Jean C. Oi is Associate Professor of Political Science, Stanford University, having previously taught at Harvard and Lehigh universities. She is author of *State and Peasant in Contemporary China: The Political Economy of Village Government* and has forthcoming *Rural China Takes Off: Incentives for Industrialization*. Her recent articles have appeared in *World Politics, Journal* *of Development Studies*, and *The China Quarterly*. During 1995–1997 she was Visiting Associate Professor of Social Science, Hong Kong University of Science and Technology.

Pei Xiaolin is attached to the Department of Economic History at Lund University, Lund, Sweden. He has published in *The European Journal of Development Research*, and has co-authored an article on "Agrarian Structures, Property Rights and Transition to Market Economy in China and the Former Soviet Union" (forthcoming).

Mark Selden teaches Sociology and History at Binghamton University. His recent books, *China in Revolution. The Yenan Way Revisited* and the co-authored *Chinese Village, Socialist State* are scheduled for publication in translation in China in 1997.

Wang Zhenyao is a member of the Rural Work Committee of the China Research Society for Basic-Level Governance, Beijing.

Cooperative
and
Collective in
China's Rural
Development

Introduction

China's New Rural Organization

Eduard B. Vermeer

In recent years, economic reforms have increasingly been studied, both in China and the West, from the perspective of institutional change. The high costs and partial failure of the rapid transition from the old socialist order to more democratic and market-oriented political and economic institutions in Russia and Eastern Europe have been a warning to Chinese policy-makers and a lesson to economists. Privatization and free elections did not result in genuine market capitalism, economic growth, and democracy. Rather, they produced new interest groups of insiders over which the weakened government and disillusioned population could exert little control, often to the detriment of the national economy and society (see e.g., Frydman and Rapaczynski 1994; Daviddi 1995; Naughton 1995; and Ye Yuansheng 1994).

During the same period, the more gradual reforms in socialist China presented a striking contrast. They produced a tremendous economic success, while maintaining social (and by and large, also political) stability in spite of rapid economic growth and the opening of the country to Western and capitalist influences. While economists may disagree about the origins and major causes of China's economic successes since 1978, few will dispute that its growth started, and much of its growth and stability continue to be rooted, in the non-state, non-urban sector: the rural areas which provide for almost three-quarters of China's population. Unlike urban residents, the state has provided them with little if any social security, and acknowledges only indirect responsibility for their well-being. By 1996, in spite of their continued official categorization as "peasants" (*nongmin*), the rural laborers were responsible for almost half of China's large and small rural communities, *xiang* and *cun*, showed themselves highly responsive to the opportunities offered by the government's relaxation of political and economic controls and the local decentralization since the early 1980s.

The Chinese farmers should be credited for their responsiveness to improved agricultural prices and new labor opportunities. However, because of their small size and limited financial and organizational capacity, rural households quickly reached the limit of their economic possibilities. Beyond a certain size, for political and fiscal reasons most private enterprises took the form of collective enterprises. For this reason, the fast-growing sectors of rural industries and services were, and still are, dominated by old or new collective and cooperative rural organizations and enterprises. This raises the question of their contribution to the reform process and China's economic success. The role of these and other intermediate organizations between state and private interests was the focus of a conference held at Leiden University, The Netherlands, in January 1995—the "International Conference on Chinese Rural Collectives and Voluntary Organizations: Between State Organization and Private Interest." This volume contains a selection of revised papers which were originally presented and discussed at this conference.

China's experience of decollectivization is unique and complex. After liberalization, a great variety of organizational forms arose which reflected not only socio-economic differences but also different responses of local communities to new political and economic opportunities. At the same time, and partly in response to a bewildering local multiformity which was inexplicable to orthodox Marxist planners, the Chinese government set up, or actively monitored, a number of local experiments in organizational models. National and local governments instituted laws and regulations meant to define the boundaries of village authority and the scope for rural autonomous organizations. However, the decreasing legitimacy of Communist Party leadership, political indecision and the uncertainties of the cycles of tightening and liberalizing political control all created considerable room for local political and economic actors to take initiatives of their own.

Until 1983, China used rural collective organizations as units of administration, production and consumption. They dominated most aspects of rural politics, administration, economy and society, while staying within the narrow limits set by the Chinese Communist Party. The "household responsibility system" (basically a restoration of the family farm) changed all this. The local administrative structures of communes, brigades and teams were changed into townships and administrative villages which were initially only supposed to carry out limited and mainly administrative functions. Nevertheless, the collective tradition did not die. The townships and villages maintained their ownership and management of land, most of the collective enterprises, and many services.

In most areas, rapid economic growth provided local government and managerial cadres with ample financial means and a strong economic power base, on which they have continued to build. Township and village administrations, often with the active involvement of current and former cadres, now play a crucial role in the coordination of local economic life and its integration into the regional

economy. The collective period has left an important legacy of leadership structures relevant to modernization in the context of a market economy.

The pressures of economic growth and social change have destroyed the
uniformity of Chinese village organization, and in most cases profoundly
changed the pre-reform fabric of village society. Pre-revolutionary lineages and
other traditional organizations have re-emerged, albeit in adapted forms. Nevertheless, unlike Eastern Europe, in most places the transition to greater autonomy
and market orientation has been gradual and incomplete. It has remained within
a government-determined social framework, and has been guided, if not controlled, by existing rural political elites. Moreover, state-imposed obligations in
grain and cotton production, birth control, taxes, and state monopolies of essential supplies and services have continued to limit the farmers' freedom. Similar
constraints and obligations have been imposed on rural entrepreneurs in non-
farm sectors.

Has the market sector generated a second, economy-based hierarchy in rural
society which parallels the bureaucratic hierarchy, as described by Szelenyi for
Hungary (Szelenyi 1988) or has this new economic stratification even replaced
the old political one? The answer of most scholars, including the contributors to
this volume, seems to be in the negative. In China, the two hierarchies are
intertwined, and stratification is by no means clear. The present economic elite
depends heavily on favors, permits and support of the local cadres. The political
hierarchy, moreover, has changed beyond recognition. Most of the traditional
cadres who were "red" but not "expert" lost their status and high positions to
new Party and government cadres whose rise is linked to, and who take pride in,
their cooperation with the economically successful farmers and entrepreneurs, or
who have become managers of enterprises themselves.

A rural community's elite may consist of people from different sectors or
backgrounds: Party and government cadres, rural entrepreneurs, and rural intellectuals and professionals (teachers, technicians). Many of these people have
taken on new roles and responsibilities; for instance, in the early 1980s, many
teachers were given political positions. Various contributions in this volume
show that the newly emerged class of rural entrepreneurs has close connections
with, and partly consists of, traditional political leaders. This gives rise to interesting questions about the functioning and self-conception of local Communist
Party cadres and entrepreneurs. A recent Chinese survey team concluded that the
development of private businesses in China has been largely based on active
relations between government, state enterprises, and private enterprises. The
owners of private enterprises do their utmost to create a network of relationships
with cadres of all kinds and at all levels. In contrast, contacts between entrepreneurs themselves are rather limited, and "at present the prerequisite conditions
are not yet fulfilled for them to create a form of self-consciousness and independent organizations" (ZSQJYK 1994). The so-called "Individual Business Associations" have been created and are run by the local state bureaus for industry and

commerce; like other so-called "mass organizations" and technical associations, they have a potential for becoming more than executive branches of government and Party, but they have not progressed very far in that direction.

Naturally, mass organizations and technical and credit associations represent clearly defined interests, but at our conference, opinions differed on the viability or even the desirability (from the point of view of democratization) of such government-supported rural organizations. This is not simply a question of working within or against the bureaucratic system of government and Communist Party (the interests of which do not necessarily run parallel). Because of the system's ill-defined boundaries and responsibilities, it is not immediately obvious whether the activities of individual actors and organizations circumvent, complement, strengthen, or weaken the existing political structures. Most cadres and entrepreneurs chart their course cautiously somewhere in between circumvention and support, and go for those institutional and personal goals which seem feasible in view of the political wind and local currents of the moment.

Competition between rural entrepreneurs and contractors who bid for collective enterprises or goods may stop them from forming interest groups, but only as long as rural government succeeds in keeping competition open and fair. The tradition of self-sufficiency and the multiple economic and social functions of the village and township work against such competition, and in small districts with few competitors it becomes almost an impossibility. More often than not, entrepreneurs, cadres and officials have entered into open or covert alliances, which are controlled by neither government nor Party institutions. They thrive on monopolies and further their self-interest, ultimately developing into intermediate organizations between the state and private sectors which, even if their activities are not technically illegal (although many are) do defy the spirit of the law, Party ideology and popular opinion. The numerous examples from press reports and some individual village studies suggest a clear correlation between rural economic (particularly industrial) growth and the emergence of new village elites (e.g., Wang Hongsheng 1995; Yan Yunxiang 1992). The corrupting tendencies of official-entrepreneur alliances are most pronounced in the construction sector.

Responding to societal pressures, the functions of local government are subject to change. First, the state has to trim its apparatus for budgetary reasons. Secondly, economic reforms, industrialization of the country and a much-increased flow of labor and goods have called many government functions into question. Thirdly, political relaxation, eroding official salaries, and economic opportunism have created the conditions for officials to enrich themselves individually or as a group, at the expense of the state or the communities they are supposed to serve. How to reassert political control over corrupt local officials and village cadres is a major problem for the Chinese government.

Opinions differ on the role which village democracy could play. One of our contributors, Wang Zhenyao of the Ministry of Civil Affairs, expresses his conviction that the creation of a democratic system in China may well start from the villages, because the farmers are economically more independent and the government is less dominant in the villages than in urban areas. However, the democratic system which now exists in about one-half of China's villages, that of an elected villagers' committee under the control of an assembly of villagers' representatives, has some fundamental flaws.

In the first place, Communist Party members make up the majority of the appointed or elected village leaders. Many Chinese officials and some scholars believe that the efficiency of the implementation of national and local policies is served by one person functioning both as village committee chairman and village Party secretary (see e.g., Gao Jie 1994). Moreover, few people are both willing and capable of fulfilling positions in village government, so that it may indeed be the case that a combination of functions is politically the most effective. However, CCP members are also subjected to the higher authority of the Party, which means that those who combine functions have a dual allegiance which may result in conflicting obligations. In the villages, the problem of separation between government and Party is more difficult than at township or county levels, because the village committee and leaders lack formal government authority. In the second place, sometimes (particularly in South China) the chief cadres of the villages draw their salaries from the township, and also, in conformity with the Organic Law, village leaders are seen by the township government as the executives of state policies under their own authority. Third, the village electorate depends for much of its income on contracts with the village committee it is supposed to control, and may well be concerned about the personal consequences of opposing local leaders. Fourth, the formal creation of village democracy in 1987 did not come from below, but was instituted from above. Its purported goals were to increase the accountability of village cadres, define township authority within villages more clearly, and reaffirm state control—goals not necessarily shared by the village communities.

During the drafting process of the Organic Law in 1987, there was optimism that increased rural participation could be combined with, and even contribute to, a more successful implementation of state policies in the countryside, even unpopular ones regarding taxation and birth control. At the same time, some people realized that popular participation and greater village autonomy could be inimical to the interests of the state. At all levels of government, but mainly in counties and townships, Party leaders and government executives had strong reservations about the creation of autonomous political organizations which could subvert their power and resist their demands. Entrenched political interest groups were prone to resist any genuine change in a power structure which protected their economic or social interests. The result was a compromise law, to be implemented on a trial basis, which defined village committees as "mass organizations of self-government" which receive "guidance, support and assistance" from the government. They were to have a head and two to six members, and be in charge of the fulfilment of state duties and policies, management of village lands and collective property, mediation, and other village affairs. They were to be elected and controlled by villagers' councils (O'Brien 1994).

These councils, however, were much too large to be effective organs of democratic control. The subsequent creation of much smaller village representatives' meetings made day-to-day village representation less unwieldy, but also brought the new and old political organizations closer together. Therefore, even if village committees were established in most villages during the 1990s, in many cases they have remained a superficial cover for conflicting interests of several pre-existing functional organizations of power in the villages: the Communist Party, the state apparatus, local cadres' interest groups, clans, etc. Mediation between these interests and resolution of conflicts continues to take place in the village Party branch (though some hold "enlarged sessions" with village representatives) or through the township government.

For many of these institutions or groups, a greater degree of village democracy is undesirable because it conflicts with their own legitimacy or goals. Some villagers have tried to use the new elective structures to their own advantage, while others react by shirking all political and administrative duties. It seems that active leaders, pre-existing patterns of social organization and perceived economic opportunities within the village are important determinants of popular participation.

Kevin O'Brien has made a typology of four possible outcomes of the combination of participatory goals (such as free elections, active councils, public accounting) with the fulfilment of unpopular state-assigned tasks (such as birth control, tax collection, and grain procurement). Village committees that score high on both counts are "up-to-standard," while those that are low on both counts are called "paralyzed." According to Chinese estimates of 1990, 15 percent of the village committees fell into the first category and 20 percent into the second. "Authoritarian" committees score low on participation but high on fulfilment of state tasks; conversely, "run-away" committees score high on participation but low on state task fulfilment.

The contributors to this volume have found a great diversity of management situations in the township and villages they studied. The range is from villages which are run like a firm by the village head or Party secretary to villages which are not merely "paralyzed," but totally empty shells. The authors offer various explanations for this diversity, for example differences in what the "village" as a community and a place means to the villagers themselves; the level of economic (or industrial) development; the location of the village and its previous social structure; etc.

Unfortunately, little is known about the methods used by "run-away" committees to resist successfully pressures from above. For obvious reasons, neither they nor their *xiang* government wish to publicize open or hidden conflicts rooted in run-away democracy. However, the Chinese authorities appear to be much more concerned about the "paralyzed" villages. A 1990 survey showed that in such villages, a lack of development programs caused poverty. There was neglect not only of state-imposed duties but also of readjustment of land holdings, purchase of fertilizer, product sales, irrigation, and education. Their cadres embezzled village funds, and the social order broke down (Guo Qingsheng 1992). Some Chinese researchers do not hesitate to note the negative feelings of farmers towards the village cadres. In Sishui in Shandong, farmers say, "they take down our homes, snatch our grain, catch our pigs and sheep, and grasp our girls [for sterilization]." "They are 'three-demands cadres': they demand our grain, our money and our [infant's] lives." "The good ones don't come, and those who come are no good." The cadres are scolded for pursuing the governments' interests instead of being responsive to peasant needs (Guo Qingsheng 1992, pp. 253–257).

In many areas, management of the economic functions of village government has been put in the hands of so-called rural community cooperatives. These are economic, not legal entities, and one of their functions seems to be to maintain control over village collective economic interests against encroachment by township government, corrupt cadres and private entrepreneurs. Their legitimacy and acceptance by the villagers critically depend on their economic performance. As long as employment in industries and services increases and incomes grow, conflicts of interests between villagers and managerial cadres (not a few of whom are from outside the village) who control enterprise assets and usurp part of their profits may remain dormant. The real test will come when, for whatever reason, the village economy stops growing. Especially in developed areas with many collective assets, farmers and lower-income groups may then demand a more equitable distribution of resources and income, and a new class struggle may appear.

Policies directed at a devolution of ownership of collective enterprises to *xiang* or *cun* economic committees, and of actual management to contractors or appointed managers have been implemented with enthusiasm in areas with profitable collective industries. Divestment of collective assets, many of which were acquired at little or no cost by private contractors or Party cadres, has reduced the political and economic power of the township and village as collective institutions. Since 1992, some townships established semi-independent asset management companies which took over all collectively-owned enterprise assets from the township economic committee (from which they drew most of their staff). Now these companies appoint the enterprise managers and represent the (often majority) share held by the company at share-holders' meetings. Not being governmental institutions, their accountability towards the political representative organizations is, at best, indirect and more often than not almost zero. They do not have to follow the general regulations on distribution of collective enterprise profits (such as the 6:2:2 or 5:3:2 ratios for collective accumulation, welfare, and pay-outs to the employees), but can distribute profits solely on the basis of shares (Vermeer 1996).

Yet, in the eyes of many of the new elite of local politicians, managers and contractors, such cosmetic divestment of collective industrial property does not go far enough. Comparisons with the almost completely privatized agricultural sector, and with private enterprises and partnerships in the township and village are easily made. Privatization has proven to be a powerful stimulus to labor productivity and profitability. In view of the cut-throat competition between local industrial enterprises on the Chinese market, going against that trend could be disastrous. Therefore, most township governments and many village economic committees have supported enterprise privatization schemes. A politically acceptable compromise, which remains within the favorable tax category of "collective enterprises," has been the share-holding cooperative system. Experiments with this were started in 1987, and it became more flexible and widespread in 1992, after the trial company law had been adopted. By selling off part of the township or village collective industrial assets to the employees of TVEs, often in the form of non-marketable shares, part of the original collective ownership was maintained, and new collective ownership was created at the lower level of the enterprise as a collective of workers.

Because of the high interests on savings during the recent years of inflation, only guaranteed high dividends on purchased shares or distribution of shares for free or at reduced prices have been able to convince the employees to take part in share-holding schemes. Thus, shares in the TVEs had to be sold off cheaply. On the face of it, this should be a popular policy. However, at the same time that shares were sold or given to the staff and common workers, the managers also took a share. The size of the latter depended on several factors: their previous financial involvement as a contractor for or founder of the enterprise; their present willingness to invest; and last but not least their ability to negotiate a good deal with the authorities. Thus, their share can be very substantial, even a majority share.

Local administrators want to divest of collective property primarily because of the positive effects of an injection of private and employee capital into the collective enterprises. Many have already jumped on the bandwagon of entrepreneurship. The village Party secretary is often a major if not *the* major village entrepreneur. The grey zone between administration and business, and between collective and private, varies per area, but its scope is generally increasing. The initiative comes from both private entrepreneurs who further their business interests by "wearing the red hat" of manager of their so-called collective enterprise, and from local cadres who convert the collective government institutions into so-called companies (such as in the example given above) which are almost completely beyond political control. The latter tactic may be easier to apply wherever township and villagers' committees of representatives are very weak or even absent. Most likely, the power of the local CCP branches over appointments and policies has also been affected by this trend. Because most managers and higher administrators are also Party members, it is very difficult to distinguish personal power from the institutional power of the Party branches. The number of "hats" which a township or village cadre may wear is growing: Party secretary, head of the Economic Committee or United Cooperative, president of the asset management company, general manager/contractor of a combined enterprise, head of a branch factory. The combining of these roles is an open invitation for local dictatorship and corruption.

The farming sector is still the mainstay of the rural economy, even if its relative importance is declining in some industrializing areas. A number of agriculture-related services (such as irrigation, extension work and marketing) are still organized by the collective or some sort of cooperative, with or without state support, for sound financial, political or organizational reasons. However, there is a considerable distrust of government and collectively organized activities. With the diversification of agriculture and rural industrialization, government officials and farmers perceive the need for cost-effective service organizations, which should be as self-supporting as possible. In response to these needs, a wide variety of corporations and voluntary associations has been promoted by the government, or has sprung up by themselves. It is generally realized that government functions have not kept up with rural economic and social changes. Basically, China has emphasized liberalization, i.e., abolishing policies and regulations which inhibit growth. While this approach is far from having reached its limits in major sectors such as prices and cropping policies, there is an obvious and growing need at present for the establishment of organizations which actively promote agricultural development.

A State Council study recommended that the present marketing and supply cooperatives be transformed from extensions of the Ministry of Commerce to organizations run by rural share-holders, which can represent their own interests instead of those of the state. Furthermore, farmers should be encouraged to respond to market demands, and be allowed to establish direct links with trade and industry. In addition, more attention should be paid to quality, standardization and inspection of agricultural products. The government should increase its financial support for improvement of production conditions (water conservation, forestry, agro-industry), technical change (science and technology, education, extension), and the increasing of the potential value of agricultural products (processing, storage, transport, marketing). It should be directed primarily at grain and cotton, the intermediate and poor areas, and other weak links (Guowuyuan 1994). This view of the functions of government in agriculture is much more selective and concentrated than before. It anticipates different capabilities and needs of local village organizations, depending on local economic and social structures and levels of development. In response to such different priorities set by government for its own activities, the functions of intermediate village organizations have become much more diverse. One cannot but note that not only Chinese villages, but also local government organizations have adopted very different goals and methods. While part of this may be explained by differences in the local situation, the functioning and orientation of local organizations are shaped to a considerable extent by the personal views, priorities and working style of their leaders.

The study of the present functions and authority of the semi-autonomous voluntary associations provides valuable test cases of and insights into the scope for autonomous political action. In many cases, there may be a win-win situation, but the effectiveness of new services or institutions has to be demonstrated to the farmers first. Peter Ho and John Morton and Robin Grimble, in their analyses of local natural resource conservation, demonstrate the difficulties, political and legal, in organizing and institutionalizing village management structures which require short-term sacrifice for long-term benefits. In pastoral and mountain areas, the privatization of collective or state-owned grassland and forest resources has largely failed, which brings the authors to question whether common property resource management leading to sustainable utilization is an alternative, more viable option.

Almost all contributions in this book are based on recent fieldwork in China. The variety of views to a certain extent reflects the different localities, but is primarily based on the differences in approach and interpretative frameworks. Together, in their exploration of the newest social and organizational developments in China and their summing up of our state of knowledge of this rapidly expanding field, they cover a significant part of present-day China research. The focus of this volume is explicitly on organizational change in the Chinese countryside, and its implications for rural society and politics. Thereby, it hopes to contribute to a better understanding of the position and role of intermediate organizations between state and private interests during the process of reform of the socialist state and collective village.

References

Daviddi, R., ed. 1995. *Property Rights and Privatization in the Transition to a Market Economy: A Comparative Review.* Maastricht: European Institute of Public Administration.

Frydman, R., and Rapaczynski, A. 1994. *Privatization in Eastern Europe: Is the State Withering Away?* Budapest: Central European University Press.

Gao Jie. 1994. "Cunmin weiyuanhui zuzhi jianshede beijing, xianzhuang he zhengce daoxiang" (Background, Present Situation, and Political Direction of the Establishment of the Organization of Villagers' Committees). *Faxue yanjiu,* no. 2, pp. 11–15.

Guo Qingsheng. 1992. "Guanyu tanhuan bantanhuan cunde zhuanti diaocha" (Investigation of the Topic of Paralyzed and Semi-paralyzed Villages). In Li Kang, ed. *Zhongguo nongcun jizeng shequ zuzhi (xiangcun) jianshe xin tansuo* (New Explorations into the Establishment of Basic-level Community District Organizations [*xiang* and *cun*] in China's Villages). Beijing: Zhongguo kexue jishu chubanshe, pp. 282–287.

Guowuyuan. 1994. Guowuyuan yanjiushi ketizu. "Jianli yu nongcun shichang jingji yaoqiu xiangshiyingde zhengfu zhineng tixi" (State Council Research Office Study

Group, "Establish a System of Governmental Functions Which Meets the Demands of the Rural Market Economy). *Jingji yanjiu cankao*, no. 136, pp. 2–26.

Naughton, Barry. 1995. *Growing Out Of the Plan: Chinese Economic Reform 1978– 1993*. New York: Cambridge University Press.

O'Brien, Kevin J. 1994. "Implementing Political Reform in China's Villages." *The Australian Journal of Chinese Affairs*, July, pp. 33–61.

Szelenyi, Ivan. 1988. *Socialist Entrepreneurs: Embourgeoisement in Rural Hungary*. Madison: University of Wisconsin Press.

Vermeer, Eduard B. 1996. "Experiments with Rural Shareholding Cooperatives: The Case of Zhoucun District, Shandong Province." *China Information*, vol. 10, nos. 3/4 (Winter 1995/Spring 1996), pp. 75–107.

Wang Hongsheng. 1995. *From Revolutionary Vanguards to Pioneer Entrepreneurs: A Study of Rural Elite in a Chinese Village*. Ph.D diss., University of Amsterdam.

Yan Yunxiang. 1992. "The Impact of Rural Reform on Economic and Social Stratification in a Chinese Village." *The Australian Journal of Chinese Affairs*, no. 27, January, pp. 1–23.

Ye Yuansheng, ed. 1994. *Zhongguo jingji gaige lilun liupai* (Schools of China's Economic Reform Theory). Zhengzhou: Henan People's Publishing House.

ZSQJYK. 1994. "Zhongguo siyou qiyezhu jieceng yanjiu" ketizu. "Woguo siyou qiyede jingying qingkuang yu siyou qiyezhude qunti tezheng" (Project Group for "Research on the Stratum of Private Entrepreneurs in China," "The Management Situation of Private Enterprises and Group Characteristics of the Owners of Private Enterprises in China"). *Zhongguo shehui kexue*, no. 4, p. 71.

The author wishes to thank Frank Pieke and Tak-wing Ngo for their useful comments on an earlier draft to these introductory comments.

Part I

The Cooperative Heritage and the Rural Framework

1

Household, Cooperative, and State in the Remaking of China's Countryside

Mark Selden

"Change, even fundamental change, of the social world," David Stark observes, "is not the passage from one order to another but rearrangements in the patterns of how multiple orders are interwoven. Instead of *transition* we examine *transformation* in which new elements emerge through adaptations, rearrangements, permutations, and reconfigurations of existing organizational forms" (Stark 1996). Through an analysis of changing patterns of household, redistributive economy and state, this chapter similarly assesses the logic, limits and potential of cooperation in China's rural economy and society.

The demise of communism in Eastern Europe and elsewhere, together with the startling changes in the political economies and societies of China, Vietnam and other countries since the 1970s, have led many analysts to focus on what is radical and new, notably the private sector and the market. The present chapter, too, highlights dimensions of significant rural transformation in recent decades. But it seeks the roots of change in the institutions and practices of the former collective regime and social structure, pays close attention to little noted but crucial continuities in the salience of the organizational and redistributive economy, and rejects facile assumptions concerning the inevitability of the triumph of a Smithian market economy.

In *Governing the Commons* (1990, p. 29), Elinor Ostrom poses a question that is central to the present inquiry: how a group of principals who are in an interdependent situation can organize and govern themselves to obtain continuing joint benefits when all face continuing temptations to free-ride, shirk, or otherwise act opportunistically.[1] Like Ostrom, eschewing universal solutions, this study seeks to comprehend the specificity of social and political milieux which give rise to successful and failed cooperative solutions in order to clarify workable solutions to problems of fragmentation and cooperation that confront post-collective rural China.

Paradoxically, perhaps, the emergence of a complex, market-driven economy pivoting on the mesh of contracted family micro farms and private firms, an organizational economy featuring township and village enterprises (TVEs), and businesses driven by foreign capital and regional networks, has occurred together with the reification and resurgence of old and new forms of cooperation rooted in three decades and more of Chinese cooperative and collective experience.

Household Contracts and Patterns of Rural Cooperation

Under the household contract system that has structured Chinese agriculture since 1982, formal ownership and substantial redistributive power over land remain in the hands of village officials and villagers must fulfill contractual obligations ranging from grain quotas to corvée labor. Villagers have nevertheless regained substantial control over their labor power, choice of crop, mobility, and the right to engage in sideline, industrial and commercial activities and to market many of their products. The direct exercise of state power at all levels has been reduced, as has that of collectives whose leaders formerly exercised monopoly power over the agricultural economy, the allocation of labor, income and resources. Yet village authorities retain significant power even as the autonomous realm of villagers has grown.

Local authorities in the 1990s continue to shape and circumscribe ownership rights over family farms, private capital, and the market in the following ways:

(1) Land use rights are contracted to households by the village for specified periods, officially authorized for 15 years in 1984 and 30 years in 1992, in return for payments of grain, cash and labor. By one 1994 estimate, farmers' obligations were 52 billion *yuan*, that is 41 *yuan* per person (Bowles and Dong 1994, p. 52; *Nongmin ribao*, April 14, 1995). Village officials retain the authority to redistribute village lands to adjust for population shifts. Households are authorized to rent out their contracted land for the duration of the contract but not to sell it (Selden and Lu 1993; Jiang 1994).

(2) The state, working through a chain of command and a distribution network reaching down to the village and the household, controls the supply and price of critical inputs such as fertilizer, seeds, and oil.

(3) Many villages provide a range of services to farmers such as tractor plowing, fertilizer and seed distribution, and irrigation.

(4) The state creates and restricts markets primarily through imposition of compulsory crop sales quotas on grain, cotton and other crops at state prices. These quotas were substantively reduced but not eliminated in the early 1990s. A legacy of the collective era is that local authorities have far more power to shape economic and social life than their predecessors had on the eve of land reform in the 1940s.

The imprint of the revolution is also evident in land tenure patterns. Among the features which distinguish conditions in rural China from those in many countries with comparable income and technological levels are the roughly equal per capita land distribution within each village and the limited alienability of land. Universal access to land provides the rural poor with a safety net that assures subsistence and limits the growth of large inequalities in wealth and power that are rooted in skewed land concentrations such as those found in India, the Philippines, Indonesia, Brazil and elsewhere (Matson and Selden 1992; Sen 1982).[2] Yet the plots of land are so small, and the price, contractual terms and marketing structures so unfavorable to farmers that the great majority who cannot obtain off-farm jobs face the prospect of achieving bare subsistence. According to a 1989 sample survey, the average household received 9.7 plots of land totaling .62 hectares, figures consistent with my own local data on rural Hebei in the nineties (Smil 1993, p. 148).

If land ownership equity remains an important subsistence guarantee, off-farm employment or other income is essential to prosper in China's countryside. Coastal and suburban areas have boomed precisely as a result of their ability to generate industrial and commercial jobs and income. Widely (if inequitably) shared rural income gains of the last fifteen years are directly attributable to the fact that some 120 million rural residents obtained industrial and commercial jobs (the largest employment expansion experienced in any part of the world economy in these decades).

This chapter considers some of the forms of cooperation and the redistributive economy in China's countryside, including their impact in reducing the poverty and vulnerability of rural households, both those whose income depends on farming and those participating in small and medium sized industrial and commercial enterprises. For if the market and the household economy have surged in recent decades, the considerable power of village and local government authorities continues to shape China's rapid economic growth in the 1990s.

Much of the Chinese and Western literature on rural development since the 1980s has posed the policy alternatives starkly in terms of the triumph of the family farm and the market on the one hand, or the collective, the state and the plan on the other (Nee 1989 and 1996; Oi 1992; Walder 1995; Zhou 1996). Authors typically champion either private entrepreneurs and the market or the local state and its collective enterprises as the explicandum and harbinger of hope for China's dynamic rural development. This chapter finds that intermediate forms of cooperation, mutual aid, and common property regimes—both those that rest on foundations of the family farm and those rooted in township and village entities or their subsidiary enterprises and building on the strength of local networks—shape rural economy and society. It explores the diverse forms of the cooperative and redistributive economy with an eye to their contributions and potential contributions to economic development and their implications for the empowerment of immediate producers in a mixed economy. It considers historical problems and prospects for achieving effective cooperative practices responsive to and supportive of the employment and social welfare needs of family farms functioning in a market milieu. The issue of cooperation is politically sensitive since recollectivization, threatening the initiative and vitality, indeed the very existence of family farms and the autonomy of rural producers, has been actively discussed and even implemented in a few well publicized areas, while certain elements essential to a flourishing cooperative movement have been slow to develop.

Following discussion of the historical evolution and consequences of a broad range of cooperative and collective approaches in rural China from the 1940s through the late 1970s, I consider examples of cooperation since the dissolution of collective agriculture and the communes in the early 1980s.

By "cooperation" I refer to group social and economic mutual-aid activities initiated and sustained by producers, and "cooperative economy" refers to the range of economic activities conducted by cooperatives. The principles of cooperation can be summarized in the following three points (Cf. Bi and Guan 1991; Vanek 1971 and Pestoff 1991)[3]:

(1) The primary aim of cooperatives is to contribute to the welfare of their members, that is, they are self-help or mutual-aid organizations;
(2) Cooperatives embody principles of democratic management in which members share in decision making;
(3) Cooperatives are open and autonomous organizations based on voluntary participation and freedom of withdrawal.

Cooperative potential—and obstacles to its realization—is assessed in three types of organization that have emerged in rural China since the transformation of the collective-commune system in the early 1980s. The first and most important is the township and village enterprises (TVEs) that provide the institutional basis for China's rapid rural industrialization and export boom. The second is small-scale mutual aid and cooperation illustrative of farmer self-organization at the level of production. The third is a range of voluntary associations and cooperative commercial, service and technical support organizations known as Specialized Production Technology Associations (SPTAs) that serve the interests of private producers by promoting rural development. To what extent do these cooperatives and proto-cooperatives function as business enterprises? As redistributive or welfare agencies for local communities? As common property regimes? To what degree are they subordinate to or autonomous from the state? Do they constitute voluntary associations serving, and responding to, the interests of their members?

In addressing these questions, it is fruitful to review briefly the historical origins and growth of cooperation from the 1920s and 1930s when cooperatives emerged in China as a means of securing financial and technological assistance, particularly in specialized farming enterprises (Vermeer 1988, pp. 290–323). From the early 1940s, cooperatives appeared both in the Communist-led anti-

Japanese resistance base areas and in regions under Guomindang control (the *gonghe* or *gungho* movement). In the Communist-led resistance areas, these were mainly service cooperatives, including consumer cooperatives, supply and marketing cooperatives, and credit cooperatives, with significant financial and organizational resources provided by the state. Some temporary production cooperatives were also organized, mainly in the form of seasonal mutual aid involving small groups of farmers. From 1943, the Communists promoted diverse forms of mutual aid and small-scale cooperation in the base areas, building on and refining traditional patterns of mutual aid (Selden 1993a and 1995; Friedman, Pickowicz, and Selden 1991; Keating 1994). From their inception, however, a tension emerged between the autonomous and democratic tendencies of these cooperatives on the one hand and a proclivity for the state to dominate rural economy and society on the other. Stated differently, tensions emerged between priorities of members and those of the state, between economic and political goals, and between enterprise profits and member welfare.

Land reform in the late 1940s and early 1950s eliminated tenancy and hired labor, broke the power of the rural rich, and resulted in roughly equal per capita land holdings within each village. This produced equitable land distribution patterns that constitute perhaps the most enduring legacy of the revolution. The average farm after land reform was just under one hectare. Given the shortage of tools, equipment, and draft animals, many households, sometimes with official prodding, organized seasonal or year-round mutual-aid teams to exchange labor and coordinate the use of farm tools and draft animals. In China in the 1920s through the early 1950s, as in Europe, North America and Japan, farmers joined cooperatives primarily to win security, obtain financing and technology, and improve their competitive positions in the market and in bargaining with the state while preserving important elements of autonomy in family farms which remained the basic units of production (Bergmann and Ogura 1985). In the early 1950s, however, the state restricted and then virtually eliminated off-farm employment and private marketing activities that had provided farm families important supplementary income sources (Friedman, Pickowicz, and Selden 1991).

In the years 1953–55, larger and organizationally more ambitious elementary agricultural producers' cooperatives (APCs) replaced mutual-aid teams. The APCs practiced year-round unified management, while individual members received remuneration both on the basis of their investment of land, draught animals and labor contributions. As the movement to form APCs accelerated, the state promoted ever larger and more comprehensive units, reduced the scope of the private sector and the market, and slighted questions of farmers' willingness to join. From late 1953, when only 0.3 percent of peasant households had joined elementary APCs, a nationwide cooperativization campaign began. In 1955, elements of choice and democratic management disappeared in the drive that basically completed collectivization within one year (Selden 1993). From 1950 to 1955, China's state-run supply and marketing cooperatives (SMCs), as well as credit cooperatives (CCs), expanded more rapidly than production cooperatives. By summer 1955, SMCs embraced more than 90 percent of rural households (Bi and Guan 1991) and CCs were extended to every township (Huang, Liu, and Zhang 1990). Small farmers, who faced difficulties in obtaining supply, marketing, and credit services, as well as access to new technology, benefited from group purchasing, marketing, and credit services. In the early 1950s, however, these service organizations developed as an arm of the state and not as autonomous cooperatives organized by, or responsive to, member farmers. They eventually replaced rather than supplemented the market, establishing, for example, state monopoly pricing on both purchase and sale of farm inputs and crops.

In the 1950s, the Chinese state promoted the multiplicity of service organizations to facilitate a transition from household to collective and from market to plan. East Asian socialist as well as corporatist states have frequently fostered cooperation as a means both to promote and control agriculture. In Japan, as well as in Taiwan and South Korea, for example, the state has long encouraged, as well as exercised significant controls over, cooperative organizations in ways that restricted but—in contrast to China—left intact significant elements of the autonomy of family farms and rural markets (Kojima 1993).

Against Cooperation: The Triumph of the Collective

Despite sprouts of farmer-centered cooperation that preceded and continued in the early years of the People's Republic, autonomous democratic farmers' self-help organizations did not flourish. Particularly from the curbing of markets in 1953 and collectivization in 1955, and with state-run supply and marketing and financial cooperatives as the institutional basis for resource centralization in the service of industrialization, farmer-centered and autonomous cooperatives were overwhelmed. Collectivization eliminated smaller, semi-voluntary cooperatives and subordinated farmers to the state, the countryside to the city, and agriculture to the state's industrial and military priorities. Collectives, presiding over a regime of compulsory labor and sales to the state, provided vehicles for state-centered accumulation featuring the transfer of the rural surplus to the cities and to industry.

In the high collective years, 1955–1978, rates of accumulation, defined as taxes + public accumulation/net income, ranged, by one informed calculation, from 13.4 to 27.8 percent, among the highest levels in the world (Zhou 1991). This was the key to China's heavy industrial growth which, together with the building of urban and rural infrastructure, absorbed the agricultural surplus leaving little to improve the livelihood of most rural producers. "From each according to one's ability, to each according to one's work," in practice meant more or less equal distribution of subsistence within each village (brigade), a practice closely associated with the campaigns to Learn from Dazhai in the 1960s and 1970s. Collectives, as the agents of the state directing this urban- and industrial-centered accumulation process, established redistributive processes and elemental welfare systems that were predicated on maintaining low levels of rural income. For nearly a quarter of a century after recovering from the Great Leap famine that brought death to tens of millions, the Party exercised tight controls over the countryside and policed the urban-rural divide via the *hukou* system of population control (Cheng and Selden 1994; Friedman, Pickowicz, and Selden 1991).

Under the collective-commune system, the state's compulsory sales quotas at low fixed prices, together with its high prices for fertilizer, pesticide, fuel and other supplies, provided the primary vehicles for extraction and transfer of the rural surplus. The income available for distribution to collective farmers was the remainder after taxes and after deductions for the team's own public accumulation fund, public welfare fund, administrative expenses, and reserve food grain. Income distribution, accumulation and resource allocation were controlled by the state working with and through local officials. High levels of investment of labor in agricultural infrastructure, such as irrigation and soil improvement over a quarter century of collective agriculture (1955–80), together with a green revolution based on high yielding varieties and chemical fertilizer from 1964, produced significant increases in grain yields while per capita rural incomes remained virtually stagnant (Selden 1993).

With the passage of initiative from farmers to cadres, with rural incomes stagnant over a quarter century of collective agriculture, and with most market opportunities proscribed, farmers had ever less incentive to work hard or creatively in the aftermath of the Great Leap famine. Moreover, in the absence of a birth control program prior to the 1970s, the remunerative structure of collectives that provided rewards based on the number of laborers per household actually served as an incentive for population growth, thus increasing pressures on China's densely populated arable land.[4] Villagers who were barred from nonagricultural or off-farm employment and from supplementing their farm incomes in the market remained strapped for resources, particularly cash that was essential for observing marriages, funerals and important holidays as well as building homes. Studies stressing the egalitarian features of the Mao period often forget two important dimensions of rural life. First, substantial parts of the rural population lived in chronic poverty and experienced food grain shortages, or produced little surplus for sale. For example, in the years 1973–80, an estimated 330–440 million Chinese consumed less than 2,100 calories per day. This was 43–58 percent of the population, and nearly all of them were rural people. Similarly, the available evidence suggests that nearly all deaths associated with the Great Leap famine were rural (Zhou 1991; Friedman, Pickowicz, and Selden 1991). In the years 1977–79, at the end of the collective era, 221 counties and 27 percent of China's 5 million teams had per capita collective incomes that were consistently below the official poverty level of 50 *yuan* (Vermeer 1982, pp. 14, 28, 29). Second, with collective incomes virtually frozen over twenty-five years and villagers barred from migration or from seeking off-farm employment, the income gap between city and countryside grew, as did the gap in cash income and welfare benefits (Selden 1993, pp. 21–22, 169–70). Not only did collectives entrench bare subsistence for a large portion of China's rural producers, most households experienced declining income measured as a return to labor hours as a result of substantial population growth pressing at the limits of China's arable land, large-scale mobilization of women to work in the fields, and the longer season for agricultural labor extended by multi-cropping and winter capital construction.

Collective production was arranged on the basis of state-mandated targets and compulsory crop sales to the state. Agricultural inputs and marketing also came under state monopoly control. In the years 1955–78, moreover, whatever autonomous character the SMCs and CCs may have had earlier disappeared. While still formally termed "cooperatives" (*hezuoshe*), in essence they had become branches of state commercial departments and state banks respectively, serving the interests of the center and beyond the control of rural producers among whom autonomy and initiative passed to the collectives.

Mutual-aid and cooperative organizations based on the family farm vanished so quickly in the early 1950s that they never established strong traditions of voluntary participation and democracy. Control over land, labor and the harvest passed from the household to collective units under state control. Mobilizational collectivism transferred authority and initiative from farmers striving to survive and prosper in the market to cadres exercising absolute power over the lives and livelihoods of villagers bound to the collective and the land.

This section has noted several important consequences of collectivization for China's countryside in general and the prospects for cooperation in particular. It suggests that collectives were instrumental in raising accumulation rates, in transforming a significant rural surplus to the cities and industry as well as contributing to rural infrastructure such as irrigation and soil improvement. At the same time, the passage of initiative from farmers and small-scale cooperatives to cadre-driven collectives and the state, and the association of collectives with frozen incomes over a quarter of a century, struck at the fragile roots of cooperation that had barely begun to grow in the 1940s and early 1950s and gave rise to deepening contradictions between households and collectives.

After Collectivization: Household, Market, and the Organizational Economy

In the early 1980s, the driving force for abolition of the communes, brigades, and teams came from villagers seeking greater autonomy (Zhou 1996; Kelliher 1992). The redistributive economy did not, however, simply disappear to be replaced by the unfettered autonomy of household and market. The township government, the village committee, and the villagers' group assumed important administrative functions and in more dynamic areas increased their strength by playing leading roles in rural industrialization. At the same time, land rights, labor processes, and patterns of marketing, income distribution, and consumption were transformed with the resurgence of the household economy and the market.

Throughout the collective era, the rural household was preserved not only as a consumption, reproductive and cultural unit, but also as a productive unit at the margin of the collective economy with private plots supplementing consumption and income. This was one important foundation for the post-collective transformation. With restoration of family farms as the basic units of agricultural production in the early 1980s, farmers regained substantial control over their labor and their harvest including the right to consume, sell, or invest a larger share of their products and income. Important production, savings, and consumption decisions passed from the direct control of the collective and the state to the household and the market.

However, China's embrace of market principles and practice over nearly two decades has involved more than privatization. A 1991 Ministry of Agriculture report states that since the early 1980s, 2.1 million villages and sub-village groups, some 26 percent of former teams, maintained or reinstituted cooperative activities, accounting for machine-ploughing more than 35 percent of farmland, irrigating 70 percent of irrigated areas etc. (Bowles and Dong 1993).[5] Village and township maintenance and provision of the majority of irrigation services is a particularly critical element of the persistence of the organizational economy at the heart of agriculture, one that functions on the foundations of the family farm. Since the 1980s, while collectives have lost their monopoly power in agriculture, not only has the state continued to play an important role, but the organizational economy of village and township has shown new vitality, notably in the form of TVEs that have spearheaded China's rural industrialization and rapid export growth. TVEs, joint enterprises (*lianheti*), and diverse new forms of the organizational economy link autonomous households with common interests and goals such as access to technology, markets, and capital.

The literature on TVEs has emphasized their contributions to industrial growth, employment, exports, and income generation. But TVEs also play important roles in promoting agriculture and, indeed, state regulations require allocations of substantial portions of their profits for this purpose. For example, in the years 1978–87, TVEs directly subsidized agriculture in the form of a contribution of 15 billion *yuan* out of a total of 72.8 billion *yuan* of profits that were provided in the form of investment in rural infrastructure, agricultural operating expenses and transfers to farmers. This was approximately half the total provided by the state for basic construction in agriculture in the same period (Wen and Chang 1994).

Issues of cooperation constitute contested terrain in China's dynamic rural economy. In contrast to proponents of cooperatives that resemble the associations of independent producers that have spread throughout Europe, the United States, or, in corporatist versions, to parts of East and South Asia, some Chinese analysts conflate the former collective economy with an emerging new cooperative economy, and some view cooperatives as organizations that will eventually replace family farms. For example, widely publicized experiments with re-collectivization in a few counties in the late 1980s and early 1990s raised fears among rural households that state-promoted cooperatives might be a step toward reimposed collectivization and elimination of the market (Friedman 1990).

Following the reestablishment of family farms in the 1980s, most villages sold, leased or distributed productive assets such as machinery, equipment, and storehouses to households that contracted to farm the land or to run a variety of sideline or industrial enterprises. However, not all economic activity reverted to the household. Instead, many villages and townships, notably those in more prosperous regions such as coastal and suburban areas, building on collective industrial foundations, expanded or initiated a range of enterprises including factories and workshops. As the 1980s and 1990s advanced, some of these firms took the form of joint enterprises in conjunction with Chinese or foreign investors. Others subcontracted work from private or foreign firms.

The TVEs, notably those with ties to foreign capital, have been central to the surge in China's industrialization and its export of manufactures since the 1980s. As recently as 1980, rural industry, 95 percent of which then operated by local governments including collectives, accounted for 10.4 percent of China's gross industrial output. By 1992, the share of industrial output provided by state enterprises had dropped from 76.0 to 48.1 percent as rural enterprises increased their share to 38.7 percent, including 24.8 percent generated by township and village enterprises, 6.8 percent by private enterprises, and 7.1 percent by other, mainly joint, enterprises. Nearly all of the above is classified as TVE production in Chinese government data, making the TVE a hybrid category that conceals much concerning the complex and fluctuating social relations of rural industry (State Statistical Bureau 1993, p. 414).

TVEs are at the center of the debate over China's changing economy. Are they a new form of capitalist enterprise? Are they simply the former collectives re-christened? Are they a new local corporatist institution that extends the state's domain in the context of a growing market economy? Are they the bridge to a free market capitalism? Who "owns" and who "controls" TVEs? What is certain is that they have become the most rapidly growing sector, the largest source of new employment and income generation, and the cutting edge of China's booming exports, trade surplus ($45 billion in 1993), and growing foreign exchange reserves ($50 billion in December 1994) (Kaifang reference room 1995, pp. 45–46).

The TVEs can be understood in light of multiple rearrangements in the patterns of the former collectives. The collective and the TVE have foundations in the township and village economy and both are subject to directives from Party and state. Yet the TVEs should not be conflated with the state and particularly not with state sector or national industry. Analysis of the primary features that differentiate TVEs both from the former collectives and from state sector industry is central to an understanding of the recombinant features of China's contemporary political economy.

TVEs function in a milieu of burgeoning market activity in which profit and loss determine survival. In Janos Kornai's terms, their behavior contrasts with that of state sector enterprises and the former collectives since they are subject to hard budget constraints as indicated by large numbers of bankruptcies, mergers, and takeovers (Kornai 1990; Walder 1995). In 1990, a national survey found that 31 percent of state enterprises ran a deficit, many of them for years on end. By comparison, 8 percent of TVEs operated with a deficit (Wong, Ma, and Yang 1995, p. 4). In 1989, a year of sharp financial contraction, some three million TVEs went bankrupt or were taken over by other enterprises and employment in TVEs fell from 48.9 million in 1988 to 45.9 million in 1990 (Che and Qian 1994, p. 7). Budgetary constraints, and the response to them, may nevertheless take different forms in TVEs than in most capitalist enterprises. For example, there is evidence that township and village officials place lower emphasis on profits than on assuring remunerative employment and welfare for a significant group of villagers and local workers (Weitzman and Xu 1994; Naughton 1994, p. 268; Oi 1992, p. 119; Walder 1995).

TVE ownership is multilayered, involving not only township and village but at times also various levels of the state as well as private capital.[6] This complex intertwined character of multiple overlapping layers of public and private is vividly captured in Zhiyuan Cui's metaphor of "moebius strip ownership" to describe the blurring of boundaries between state, private and collective in the TVEs, a moebius strip having the "topological feature that it is impossible to distinguish their insides from their outsides" (Cui 1995). TVEs include enterprises run by the township, by the village, by partnerships of private investors (*lianheti*), by individuals, and by combinations of any of the above as well as in conjunction with higher levels of government and private as well as foreign investors. Important spatial differences denote the characteristic ownership patterns of enterprises classified by the Chinese state as TVEs. In greater Shanghai and southern Jiangsu, for example, most TVEs are owned by the local government and are relatively capital intensive; in Guangdong's Pearl River delta there is a particularly eclectic mix of ownership forms, with a growing portion of private Chinese and foreign capital often linked with local government investment; in northern Jiangsu and in Wenzhou district of Zhejiang, nearly all enterprises are family or jointly owned (Che and Qian 1994, pp. 9–10).

Table 1.1 conveys, but imperfectly, a sense of the complexity of TVE ownership and employment patterns and the direction of change over time. Absent in particular is the important relationship between foreign capital and TVEs that has spurred China's export performance, and the hybrid nature of many TVEs. The table does indicate, however, the explosive growth of joint and private enterprises in the 1990s, showing that by 1992 these accounted for 90 percent of

Table 1.1

Categories of Township and Village Enterprises, 1978–1993

| Year | Total | % | Collective | | | | Private | | | |
			Township	%	Village	%	Partnership	%	Private	%
TVEs										
1978	1,524	100	319	20.9	1,205	79.1	0	0	0	0
1985	12,224	100	419	3.4	1,430	24.1	1,121	9.2	9,253	75.7
1992	20,792	100	397	7.9	1,131	5.4	902	4.3	18,487	88.4
1993	24,529	100	434	1.8	1,251	5.1	NA	—	NA	—
Employment										
1978	28,266	100	12,576	44.5	15,689	55.5	0	0	0	0
1985	69,790	100	21,114	36.1	22,157	31.7	7,714	11.0	18,806	26.9
1992	106,246	100	26,289	24.7	25,469	24.0	7,710	7.3	46,778	44.0
Workers per enterprise										
1978	18.5		39.4		13.0		0		0	
1985	5.7		50.4		15.5		6.9		2.0	
1992	5.1		66.2		22.5		8.5		2.5	
1993	5.0		66.3		23.0		NA		NA	

Source: John Wong and Mu Yang, "The Making of the TVE Miracle—An Overview of Case Studies," in John Wong, Rong Ma, and Mu Yang, eds., *China's Rural Entrepreneurs. Ten Case Studies.* Singapore: Times Academic Press, 1995, p. 19.

enterprises and 52 percent of employees, though a much smaller percentage of the output value.[7] It reveals too the larger scale of enterprises run by the township, averaging 66.2 employees in 1992, and village, with 22.5 employees, compared with just 8.5 in partnerships and 2.5 in private enterprises. Between 1978 and 1993 the number of employees in TVEs grew from 28 million to 123 million, the fastest growing sector of the Chinese economy whether measured by employment, output value, profits, or exports.

TVEs, while operating on a much smaller scale and with a fraction of the number of employees of state enterprises, spanned the full range of Chinese industrial firms, closely mirroring the subsectoral composition of state enterprises in such diverse areas as coal, chemicals, machine building, food and textiles (State Statistical Bureau 1986; Che and Qian 1994, p. 8).

Making sense of the TVE phenomenon requires refining and recasting concepts of ownership and management in order to capture the range and complexity of the social relations linking individuals, communities, multiple layers of the state and corporate capital in the realms of labor, land, income, subsistence and much more than can ever be captured by formal title.

TVEs, like many rural industries in the late collective years, and like their counterparts among small industries in Japan, Taiwan and other parts of East Asia, frequently subcontract work from larger enterprises.[8] In suburban Shanghai and Tianjin, TVEs regularly subcontract to state enterprises; in coastal Guangdong and Fujian, subcontracting is frequently to Hong Kong, Taiwan or U.S. firms (Cf. Ka 1993; Arrighi, Ikeda and Irwan 1993; Gereffi 1993).

It is common practice for state officials at the relevant levels to appoint (and to fire) TVE enterprise managers. But who controls the enterprise? The long continuing debate over capitalist vs. managerial control of the contemporary U.S. corporation has resonances in China's TVEs. The evidence thus far available suggests that TVE managers enjoy wide powers including authority to hire and lay off workers, and it is believed by many that managers routinely siphon off large portions of the profits.[9] The fact that managers in many TVEs are subject to dismissal by the township or village authorities is not sufficient to support the conclusion of Chang and Wang (1994) that township governments control the TVEs. The evidence is rather of a symbiotic relationship between TVE and local government with power shifting to and fro between poles of autonomy and control over time.

In contrast to the collective era, labor is no longer assigned by township (commune), village (brigade) or sub-village (team) officials, nor is the labor pool restricted to residents of the locality in which the enterprise is located or owned, though locals often constitute the core labor force. Desirable positions are routinely reserved for local residents while other jobs often go to residents of nearby communities and the least desirable jobs to migrant workers. The close congruence between enterprise and local community that was a hallmark of Maoist self-reliance—or involution—is thus broken at least partially. More dynamic zones are no longer constrained by limited labor supplies, and poorer areas, that have few if any TVEs but export abundant labor, benefit from worker remittances.

Workers who had guaranteed work but little choice under the collective can now seek alternative employment, but they also face layoffs and enjoy little security, particularly migrant workers. In contrast to state enterprises that once guaranteed lifetime employment, free or subsidized health care, and generous pensions, TVEs typically provide few benefits and no security, although wage levels in some TVEs approach or occasionally even surpass those in state enterprises.

In contrast to most state sector workers who receive a monthly wage and benefit package, virtually all TVE workers, especially unskilled workers, are paid piece rates; in the 1990s, however, the practice of TVEs is making itself felt in many state enterprises which have also adopted piece rates.

The redistributive character of TVEs owned by local government differs significantly from that of the former collective. One reason for this is the partial disjuncture between workers and residents. While TVE workers receive wages, dividends may be distributed to community residents whether or not they work in the enterprise. This opens the possibility of the employment of an underclass of migrant workers while the lion's share of the rewards go to residents as shareholders.

The relative institutional uniformity of collectives in the years 1955–78 contrasts in other respects to the diversity of TVEs. While collectives blanketed the entire countryside, TVEs concentrate in the richer coastal and suburban areas as well as in prosperous model villages. Most poor regions, particularly those lacking water, rail or highway linkages, have few if any TVEs or other non-agricultural or cooperative enterprises, though some, Zhejiang's Wenzhou being the most famous, have overcome these disadvantages and produced flourishing industry and commerce. A 1985 World Bank survey of four counties, for example, reveal in Table 1.2 the range of gross value of industrial output ranging from localities boasting some of China's most industrialized localities to some of the most industrially backward areas (Svejnar and Woo 1990, pp. 63–64).

Whatever the gains enjoyed by poorer rural communities from remittances by residents working in more prosperous areas, spatial income differentials between

Table 1.2

1985 Gross Value of Industrial Output (million yuan)

Wuxi (Yangzi river delta, Jiangsu)	3,650
Nanhai (Pearl river delta, Guangdong)	1,518
Jieshou (inland, North China plain, Anhui)	104
Shangrao (Inland, north of Wuyi mountains, Jiangxi)	27

prosperous and poor regions have grown apace and TVEs and foreign investment have played important roles in these differentiating processes.

TVEs and some cooperatives, more than the former collectives, exemplify what Philip Huang (1993) has called the third realm and Janos Kornai (1990) the third way, referring to an intermediate position between state and society. They occupy positions in the interstices between the state and the household in ways that distinguish them from the former collectives and from ideal type models of free market capitalism. From the perspective of cooperation, they embody elements of the redistributive economy in the provision of benefits to residents of their communities who further gain by access to secure jobs. At the same time, cooperative members—whether members of the community or workers in the TVE—have little if any share in decision-making which is generally delegated to a manager with powers comparable to those exercised by cadres under the collective system. Unlike the collectives, however, workers in TVEs and other enterprises do have the right of exit, that is to seek other employment either locally or outside.

The rural employment- and income-generating capacity of TVEs is particularly noteworthy in contrast to the previous collective performance. Having created an average of 6.5 million new jobs each year in the 1990s, the 123 million people employed in 24.5 million TVEs constituted 28 percent of the total rural labor force. TVEs cut deeply into the vast reservoir of 100–300 million villagers whose agricultural jobs disguised their massive structural underemployment in the late collective years. The total output value of TVEs increased from 66.5 billion *yuan* in 1980, accounting for 35 percent of the gross value of agriculture, to 3.15 trillion *yuan*, 2.9 times the value of agriculture, in 1993. The association of agriculture with the rural economy was transformed in more dynamic areas into one of agro-industry with industry leading the way and agriculture frequently in decline as in much of Guangdong's Pearl River delta. In 1993, TVEs accounted for 45 percent of China's total exports (Wong and Yang 1995, pp. 16–17; Liu 1995, p. 154). In sum, in the course of little more than a decade, driven by the dynamic expansion of TVEs and by foreign capital infusion, the fundamental character of the coastal rural areas and some inland regions shifted from the overwhelming predominance of agriculture to industrial and commercial activities. This achievement was made possible by the opening of the market, the increased mobility of villagers previously bound to their communities, who now moved in and out of jobs in towns and cities, and the end of "agriculture first" policies which proscribed most non-farm efforts as "the capitalist road."

Since the 1980s, numerous enterprises, ranging from family farms to partnerships to joint ventures, have flourished independent of village ownership and control. In prospering townships and villages, diversified agricultural, industrial and commercial activities display multiple forms of ownership including foreign and joint Chinese-foreign ownership. In the former collective system, members working in different units, whether in agriculture, sidelines, or industrial work, often including those working outside the community, all received income under a unified distribution system in which a single accounting unit dispensed workpoints. There was virtually no experienced link for most people between individual work performance and remuneration, and little personal incentive to excel.

The collective system produced inequalities of power and privilege between cadres and villagers while highly egalitarian household income distribution patterns prevailed within village communities (teams and brigades). In Wugong village, Hebei, the largest formal income differentials depended on the ratio of laborers to dependents within the family, producing a cyclical pattern that appears to have been widespread in rural China (Selden 1993a). This cycle contrasts with more stable forms of differentiation in societies with substantial intra-village or class differentials of land and other forms of wealth. Since the 1980s, with household contracts, growing labor mobility, and the rapid growth of TVEs and other enterprises, incomes rose and their sources grew more diversified, spatial and class differentiation increased, and new conflicts surfaced among households, lineages and third realm enterprises.

TVEs, the prototypical third realm enterprises, continue significant elements of the former collectives under conditions of an expansive market economy yet in ways consistent with certain cooperative principles, particularly those of redistribution and of open and autonomous organization. At the same time, the legacies of mobilizational collectivism and of the Party state, together with current prioritizing of the search for profit, constitute formidable obstacles to the realization of democratic managerial ideals that are central to the cooperative vision.

The Logic and Limits of Cooperation: Intra-Village Mutual Aid

A decade after the transformation of the collective system, which, together with increased purchasing prices for agricultural products, market reopening and relaxation of controls on population movement, energized the rural economy giving rise to substantial increases in agricultural productivity, diversification, commodification and widely shared gains in rural per capita incomes, there was consensus that serious obstacles confronted agriculture but wide differences of opinion about solutions to the problem. A 1991 survey conducted by the Rural Economic Research Center of the Ministry of Agriculture covering 7,448 rural households in 274 villages throughout the country highlighted the following problems facing farm households: (1) shortage of funds to purchase inputs; (2) lack of know-how; (3) insufficient supply of improved seed varieties; (4) inability to purchase sufficient chemical fertilizers and pesticides; and (5) shortage of resources for farmland capital construction (Rural Economic Research Center, Ministry of Agriculture 1991).

This brief list of problems only hints at central issues that are the product in part of state policies and priorities in the wake of decollectivization (Sicular 1993;

Kojima 1993). Other problems include the growing scissors gap since the early 1980s in which the price of state-controlled inputs from chemical fertilizer to oil has risen at rates many times those of grain prices and investment in agricultural infrastructure has declined with the drop in state and collective support. Small farmers, particularly the poor, lack the wherewithal to invest in agricultural infrastructure and equipment, and given the unfavorable price situation confronting agriculture, few who possess the necessary resources are choosing agricultural investment. These problems are a function of insecurity of tenure and markets and of relatively low return on agricultural investment compared with actual and anticipated returns in commerce and industry. They are also a product of political problems associated with the lack of any effective organized farmer representation as well as arbitrary taxation policies and the state's frequent refusal to pay farmers for their crops (the problem of I.O.U.s rather than cash).

Small farmers in market economies everywhere confront certain problems comparable to those now facing Chinese farmers. One promising approach to problems of security, equity, and technological advance has been the organization of cooperatives responsive to the needs and interests of farmers and other rural producers. These cooperatives can be classified into two broad groups: specialized and comprehensive cooperatives. Specialized cooperatives include credit cooperatives, supply and marketing cooperatives for specific branches of production (such as dairy, grains, vegetables, and flowers), housing cooperatives, and consumer cooperatives. Such organizations have flourished in Europe and North America and can be found in Asian societies including India, Bangladesh and the Philippines (Fulton 1993).

Farmers' associations in Japan, South Korea and Taiwan, by contrast, are comprehensive nationwide cooperative organizations resting on the foundations of the family farm. They not only provide technical services, but also directly represent the economic and political interests of farmers and negotiate with the state on their behalf to establish prices and subsidies for agriculture. For example (Ohno 1987),

> virtually all farmers in Japan belong to Nokyo, and Nokyo activities cover practically every aspect of its members' lives. Nokyo markets the farmers' produce, supplies necessities for agricultural production and farmers' everyday life, provides guidance, banking services, mutual aid (insurance) services, wedding and funeral services, as well as operating a big supermarket chain . . . City, town and village cooperatives form the base; above these are the prefectural level organizations; and at the top is a national-level organization.

These cooperative associations, positioned between the state and rural households, are based in varying degrees on principles of voluntary participation, autonomy and democratic management. Indeed, cooperatives in these East Asian countries at their best not only protect the interests of small farmers, but may help to lay the foundations for building a democratic polity.[10]

Farmer-centered cooperative practices, whether in specialized or comprehensive cooperatives, remain rare in China where farmers face continued difficulties in creating effective institutions representing their long-term interests independent of state power. The Chinese state, which created peasant associations at the time of land reform, and poor-and-lower middle peasant associations during the Four Cleanups movement of 1964, demobilized these organizations as soon as they had served the state's specific purposes. Chinese farmers, and rural people generally, have lacked even the weak representation at regional and national levels that industrial labor has enjoyed through the All-China Federation of Labor and women have had through the Women's Federation (Bernstein 1995). Similarly, farmers have been consistently among the least represented groups in the National People's Congress and other government organs from the village to the center—*even* if one accepts the view that rural officials represent the interests of farmers (O'Brien and Li 1993–94, p. 26).

What then of various state-sponsored collective and cooperative organs such as SMCs and CCs? Despite reform efforts since the 1980s, far more than their counterparts in Japan, South Korea and Taiwan, where similar tensions between the state and farmers exist, these organizations remain de facto instruments of the state. One important source of resistance to reforms that would enhance their cooperative and autonomous character and strengthen ties to their village constituents is the officials who administer SMCs and CCs and fear the loss of their status and power as state employees. This is hardly surprising since the existing state-dominated system guarantees officials important privileges that are unavailable to others outside the state sector, particularly farmers. Most important, state employees and their families have cash income and benefits such as urban household registration which entitle even those who work in rural areas to receive food at subsidized prices, priority access to non-agricultural employment, and government pensions. So long as nominal cooperatives and their administrators remain part of an unaccountable and privileged state sector, farmers will neither identify with nor control their operations and the potential of the third realm for autonomous action serving the interests of the rural population or its own members will be limited.

Prior to the 1980s, these statist cooperatives generally provided low quality services to collective farmers while retaining their monopoly position on supplies, marketing and credit. In the 1990s, they continue to function as government agencies controlling distribution of scarce resources and maintaining closer ties to local officials and to the state than to the farmers they ostensibly serve. This is among the reasons for the emergence of new and thus far fragile mutual aid and cooperative alternatives: small-scale mutual aid within the village and specialized cooperatives with a regional or national organization.

To what extent do these new cooperatives represent the interests of their members? Or are they rather "transmission belts" subordinate to state interests? Most significant are the semi-independent specialized cooperatives that foster trade and provide technical support with respect to a range of commodities. Members of specialized cooperatives have been drawn primarily from the ranks of entrepreneurial and specialized households. Most small subsistence farmers, whose family holdings rarely exceed an acre or two, however, lack the information and the resources to join specialized cooperatives. As in many other countries, members tend to be drawn from the ranks of the best educated and most entrepreneurial farmers. The cooperative movement struggles to survive and grow, striving simultaneously for official recognition and support and to protect its autonomy, while most farmers either work with the state's organizations or go it alone.

Of the households in the previously cited 1991 survey, 55.3 percent relied entirely on family resources for the purchase of improved seed varieties and chemical fertilizer, cultivation, irrigation, plant protection, threshing and marketing; 32.8 percent benefited from services provided by village government, and just 11.9 percent looked to cooperative forms of mutual aid or private services. There remains a broad area in which cooperatives could contribute to the dissemination of technical and market expertise and support at a time when services at the village level have disappeared or are in disarray following dismantling of collectives and numerous small farmers face both the state and the market with little or no institutional support.

The financial and technological weakness of most family farms constitutes a barrier to the development of autonomous cooperatives. Many rural families who do not have industrial or commercial incomes remain strapped for cash. With abundant underutilized labor and low opportunity costs, they frequently choose self-exploitation of family labor over the purchase of services from existing nominal cooperatives. Together with the tiny scale of land and resources available to micro farms, this constitutes an incentive barrier to the emergence of cooperatives that serve the interests of farmers.

Despite these difficulties, a variety of forms of mutual aid and cooperation have emerged. In some villages, small informal organizations similar to the mutual-aid teams of the 1940s and early 1950s, or reviving much older forms of labor exchange, have reappeared to pool land, labor, technology and knowledge. In others, village-sponsored cooperative enterprises provide unified services for households. The latter, where successful, reduce household costs and assure access to all members of the community of scarce inputs in timely, equitable ways.

One example of the new mutual aid in the 1980s is seen in Huaili village in western Shandong where cooperation has been facilitated by the local pattern of land distribution (Judd 1994). Blocks of land are allocated to self-selected groups of approximately one dozen households, often lineage members, relatives, or neighbors, whose adjacent land facilitates pooling of productive resources and inter-household cooperation. The division of land and of some productive resources provides the basis for a variety of provisional mutual-aid arrangements.

In Zhangcun village, Raoyang county, Hebei, a similar land distribution pattern involving groups of households has thus far produced no significant labor pooling of a mutual-aid type. The small group (*zu*), embracing approximately a dozen households with adjacent land, does, however provide one important service: the provision of irrigation to member households. In addition, a few member households of the *zu* exchange agricultural labor during peak seasons. In Zhangcun, significant growth in agricultural yields following the contracting of land permitted households to purchase their own draft animals and equipment, thereby reducing the need for mutual aid. In general, it appears that the collective experience has made villagers wary of mutual aid beyond the scale of kin and close friends.

Frank Pieke, in his chapter in this volume, finds diverse forms of inter-household cooperation in two other Raoyang county villages, Liuman and Niucun. He too singles out irrigation, particularly the sharing of wells among several households, as the most important form of long-term interhousehold cooperation. This pattern of cooperation centered on irrigation is surely among the most important in the agricultural sector. Irrigation cooperation involves both small groups of households who share existing wells, and village governments that regulate the distribution of water from surface sources as well as planning, facilitating, and in some instances helping to finance well drilling and other capital construction.

Stephan Feuchtwang, in his contribution to this volume, notes instances in Huairou county in suburban Beijing of villages that facilitate cooperative farming among groups of specialized agricultural households. Examples of this type are frequently found in suburban households in areas that have abundant access to industrial jobs and where many prefer not to farm their own land. Sometimes this approach rests on the use of hired, particularly migrant, agricultural labor. These examples by no means exhaust the range of cooperative agricultural enterprise, but are emblematic of some of the most important types of agricultural mutual aid and cooperation that have emerged within rural communities since the 1980s.

Rural cooperation takes numerous other forms in industry and commerce. Among the most important kinds of autonomous pooling of labor, capital and expertise in the countryside since the 1980s are partnerships (*lianheti*) that have been particularly prevalent in commercial and industrial activities but that also include orchards and commercial crops and some forms of animal husbandry. Further research seems likely to reveal diverse new and old forms of mutual aid and cooperation emerging in numerous localities.

The creation of micro farms of the household contract type has created pressures for new forms of small-scale mutual aid and cooperation within communities. If farmers, newly freed of many collective constraints, have not raced to organize mutual aid, our discussion has indicated several ways in which small groups of villagers, sometimes with the active encouragement of local government, have begun to cooperate while preserving the prerogatives of the family farm and control over their labor and resources.

The Logic and Limits of Cooperation: Regional and National Forms

Some of the most significant and innovative forms of cooperation transcend the village and local community. Technical services to agriculture and the countryside are provided by the state, by the community (village), and by technical associations which embody cooperative elements. In animal husbandry and cash crop production, where direct state control ended, both specialized and comprehensive cooperatives have been increasing. By 1988, there were an estimated 100,000 specialized production technology associations (SPTAs) with 2.5 million members (Research Department, Chinese Association of Science and Technology 1988). A 1991 report puts their numbers at 120,000 (Zhang 1992). By 1994 SPTAs provided 140 kinds of professional services ranging from animal breeding to fisheries to cash crops. Particularly active provinces such as Sichuan, Shandong and Heilongjiang boasted more than 10,000 associations each (Yao 1994).

The SPTAs are loosely organized associations with few if any controlling hierarchical structures. At the same time, they lack horizontal ties with one another and most are relatively small and weak (Popularization Department, Chinese Association of Science and Technology 1991). The initiators and most members are specialized farmers who seek the participation or the guidance of university teachers, researchers and technicians. SPTAs, in short, while open to all, tend to self-select and promote the interests of the most energetic and entrepreneurial sectors of the rural population. They provide technical assistance and facilitate information dissemination in pig-breeding, chicken farming, orange and tangerine growing, edible mushroom production and other specialties while generally retaining independence from the state and its institutions. Most leaders of the SPTAs are elected by and from the members.

SPTAs resemble service cooperatives. One popular type of SPTA focuses on the extension of applied technologies and expertise through study groups in which members learn from one another and by organizing seminars and short-term training courses taught by professionals from the official extension system or universities. SPTAs collect small fees to finance these activities, sometimes with local government financial assistance.

Another type of SPTA provides production services. Hybrid rice growers' SPTAs help members improve rice breeding techniques and market their seeds through the seed company of the county agricultural bureau. Orange growers' SPTAs extend services for purchasing inputs and marketing fruit. They also provide non-member farmers with grafting and other technical services on a fee basis. These functions are extremely modest compared with those provided previously by collectives or those provided by comprehensive coops elsewhere such as Japan's Nokyo.

To what extent have SPTAs created autonomous organizations? To what extent have they been absorbed or coopted, collective or corporatist style, by the state? While not enjoying the status of state organizations, some SPTAs invite state officials to lead their organizations or subordinate themselves to appropriate governmental departments in order to obtain official resources. Indeed, less than 7 percent of the SPTAs, according to the 1991 survey, are independent economic entities with members' investment related to services provided. Given close formal and informal ties, it is frequently difficult to distinguish the boundaries between the SPTA and the state.

SPTAs, for all their present limitations in number, size, resources and autonomy, constitute sprouts of a potential cooperative movement. Together with TVEs, they suggest important space for the emergence of a third realm in agriculture with the capacity to represent and strengthen the position of farmers. Their close ties with government constitute both a strength (in terms of resources and legitimation) and a danger (in terms of autonomy) from the perspective of building a thriving cooperative movement capable of representing the interests of their members and, ultimately, of the rural population. However, with membership limited to the technically advanced and prosperous, those most in need of technological, informational and financial support remain beyond their purview. This opens the possibility that even a flourishing cooperative sector may exacerbate already growing intra-rural income differentials by serving the prosperous and the technically advanced while the poor and the uneducated remain without access to new technology. Precisely such an outcome has been reported by Hatti and Rundquist (1989) with respect to Indian cooperatives. They conclude that cooperatives in the state of Karnataka seem "geared towards serving the needs of the traditionally wealthy and economically powerful groups of the society."

The demand for applied technologies has increased greatly with the diversification of the rural economy and the proliferation of small and medium size enterprises for which technical assistance is critical. When former collective members became independent producers responsible for family farms, many lacked technical and market expertise. Demand for services from the agricultural extension system quickly mushroomed beyond the capacity of the system. SPTAs emerged as networks through which farmers could help one another to obtain technical, market and other information.

SPTAs constitute a response to growing diversification, specialization, and commodification of the rural economy. Unlike the former collectives, SPTAs often extend across the territorial limits of such administrative boundaries as township, county, and provincial borders. A fundamental tension remains. The SPTAs may represent grassroots initiatives by farmers and entrepreneurs seeking technical assistance and services, but their growth frequently is a product of state initiative and many remain or become subordinate to state authority. At their best, they suggest important elements of a third realm: autonomous but benefiting from government support while organizationally serving member needs. Examination of SPTAs, TVEs and other organizational and cooperative or community-based forms reveals the multiple and sometimes contradictory economic roles of the state at the national, regional and local levels.

Conclusion

New forms of cooperation have emerged in response to the household contract system, market resurgence, and rural industrialization. Cooperatives formed at the initiative of rural producers or of local government, and including specialized and comprehensive cooperatives as well as TVEs, have the potential to combine the institutional strengths of the household and village-centered enterprise with a regional and national structure that could empower and represent farmers, provide technological and managerial expertise, and help stabilize markets. In many countries cooperatives contribute to improved economic performance, security, income, information dissemination, and services for their members. A similar potential and need exists for the range of cooperatives and proto-cooperatives, including those serving specialized farmers as well as intra-village, village-wide, and national service organizations. This need grows in the context of China's diversifying rural economy with its mix of mini farms and township and village enterprises. The state at all levels can contribute to the viability of cooperatives and the flourishing of the rural economy. The danger exists, however, that the state or local officials, with their historic proclivity to favor the command economy, will restrict the growth of autonomous cooperatives and other farmer representatives either by curbing their spread and activities or by subordinating them to the state.

The local state in particular can make important contributions to rural development, including support for TVEs, autonomous cooperatives and other local organizations. Yet official intervention through the administrative hierarchy down to the villages threatens the autonomy of cooperatives and other non-governmental organizations. Cooperatives can contribute to the prosperity of the countryside if the state is willing to accept autonomous growth and a future in which the family farm plays an important role, and if farmers succeed in pooling resources to overcome their vulnerability to the market, the state, and their own infringements on natural resources.

In the 1990s we observe in various forms of cooperation sprouts of inter-farm household organization with the capacity to coordinate and construct agricultural infrastructure, spur rural industrialization, and minimize environmental destruction. China can learn selectively from the experience of irrigation cooperatives on Taiwan that raise funds from both members and the government to invest in the construction of irrigation systems. These autonomous cooperatives strengthen the ability of small farms to overcome the limits of isolation, lack of expertise, and capital shortage in order to compete effectively in the market. It can also learn diverse lessons from the experiences of comprehensive cooperatives in Japan, Europe and North America that provide effective market outlets for farmers and represent their interests in negotiations concerning subsidies, quotas and prices with the state.

A serious constraint on cooperation in China today is the political tendency that takes the collective system as superior to the cooperative and views the rise of the family farm and diverse independent cooperatives as dangers to be curbed. This perspective strongly influences some local party branches, leading some village officials to seek to restore the monopoly powers of the collective economy rather than to strengthen and link family farms and autonomous cooperatives. The rise of voluntary, farmer-initiated cooperatives can enhance the performance of family farms and village enterprises including their ability to adapt to the market. Similarly, the expansion of villagers' capacity to control the TVEs can enable these dynamic third realm enterprises to realize more fully their cooperative potential.

Member participation is the essence of a healthy and thriving cooperative movement. This requires multiple patterns of organization responsive to diverse local, regional and national needs and interests. If administrative measures are instead taken to compel farmers to accept a unified pattern and state control, based on a corporatist or collectivist vision of unitary organization, the result will be the pyrrhic victory of state organs and the withering of cooperatives to the detriment of the countryside and the nation.

China confronts a policy conundrum: state support in the form of resources, facilities, and encouragement is essential to the promotion and expansion of a cooperative movement that can overcome problems associated with micro farms seeking to thrive in a market economy. At the same time, cooperation is threatened by the specter of commandism, by the conviction that a single correct structure and approach must be applied universally (*yi dao qie*), and by a perception of cooperation as, at best, a station on the road to collectivization. Under favorable conditions, cooperation, expanding the scope of activity in the third realm between household and state, offers an approach applicable to a range of problems facing China's countryside.

Acknowledgments:

I am grateful for critical comments, suggestions and sources to Paul Bowles, Xiao-yuan Dong, Edward Friedman, Carl Riskin, Eduard Vermeer and Zhu Ling.

Notes

1. While Ostrom and much of the literature focus on common pool resources, such as fishing grounds and groundwater basins, the analytical tools are here applied to a broader range of social and economic issues that confront local households, communities and nations.

2. Equal land distribution and curbs on land sale alone, while protecting subsistence

rights, cannot, of course, prevent substantial income inequality based on industrial, commercial, financial and other income sources.

3. This is an ideal type definition. In the real world, cooperatives stand at various points along a spectrum with respect to the embodiment of democratic principles and voluntary participation. The definition used here is framed so as to accommodate both autonomous cooperatives with open membership and cooperatives operated by local governments, in some instances in collaboration with private interests whose membership is defined by residence in a community. This permits us to explore and evaluate the cooperative elements in contemporary post-collective local government, in TVEs, and so forth.

4. Eduard Vermeer rightly notes that China's population growth rate was lower than that of many poor agrarian countries even prior to the birth control drive of the 1970s and suggests that part of the reason for this may have been the subsistence guarantees provided by collectives (Personal communication, September 1995). It is nevertheless true that China's population grew substantially over these decades, placing great pressures on the land, and that birth rates were sharply reduced once the state implemented a thoroughgoing birth control program.

5. These figures probably exaggerate the extent of village-organized agricultural production. Yet numerous examples attest to the possibility of the resurgence of various forms of group farming, including those organized at the village or sub-village level. This area merits further research.

6. Private entrepreneurs frequently register their enterprises as TVEs for purposes both of security and to obtain benefits denied to private enterprises (Nee 1989; Young 1995, pp. 96–97). Registration of a private firm as a TVE, however, risks loss of autonomy and may increase the likelihood of state control.

7. The fact that TVEs include private and joint venture enterprises has received insufficient attention from analysts stressing their statist character. Andrew Walder (1995), for example, correctly notes the important redistributive aspects of TVEs, many of them falling under government jurisdiction. His analysis does not, however, capture the surge of joint venture, private and foreign-funded enterprises that are included under the rubric of TVEs.

8. It is worth noting that, simultaneous with the acceleration of growth of foreign trade from 1970, China's rural industries also increased rapidly. 1970 was the year when the North China Agricultural Conference established Zhou Enlai's course of conservative modernization opening the way to a surge of rural industry. Commune and brigade enterprises grew at average annual rates of 25.7 percent with output value rising from 9.3 billion yuan in 1970 to 27.2 billion *yuan* in 1976, and then further accelerated to 49.3 billion *yuan* by 1978 (Byrd and Lin 1990, p. 14; State Statistical Bureau 1992, pp. 389–90; Friedman, Pickowicz, and Selden forthcoming.)

9. One informant summed up a widely held view: when the enterprise loses money, the township or village picks up the tab; when there are profits, managers illegally pocket them.

10. Critics frequently paint them as corporatist institutions that serve the state at the expense of their constituents. In contrast to Chinese collectives and to such organizations as the SMCs and CCs, however, they appear to exercise greater autonomy from the state in representing their constituents' interests. The National Association of Farmers, organized in South Korea in 1987, for example, coordinated demonstrations from the county to the national level, pressuring government to end agricultural imports and to increase price supports (Hart-Landsberg 1993, p. 258). In the collective era in China, no organization even ostensibly spoke on behalf of farmers. And when farmers did wield power to transform the collectives in the early 1980s, they did so without organization and without ideological appeals (Zhou 1996).

References

Arrighi, Giovanni, Satoshi Ikeda and Alex Irwan. 1993. "The Rise of East Asia: One Miracle or Many?" In Ravi Palat, ed. *Pacific Asia and the Future of the World-System*. Westport: Greenwood.

Bergmann, Theodor, and Takekazu Ogura, eds. 1985. *Cooperation in World Agriculture. Experiences, Problems and Perspectives*. Tokyo: Food and Agriculture Policy Research Center.

Bernstein, Thomas. 1995. "Proposals for a National Voice for Agricultural Interests: A Farmers' Association." Unpublished paper presented at a conference on "Rural China: Emerging Issues in Development," East Asian Institute, Columbia University, March 31–April 1.

Bi Meijia and Guan Aiguo. 1991. *Yazhou nongcun hezuoshe jingji* (The Rural Cooperative Economy in Asia). Beijing: Chinese Commercial Publishing House.

Bowles, Paul, and Xiao-yuan Dong. 1994. "Current Successes and Future Challenges in China's Economic Reforms." *New Left Review*, no. 208, pp. 49–76.

Byrd, William, and Qingsong Lin. 1990. "The Nature of the Township Enterprise." In Byrd and Lin, eds. *China's Rural Industry: Structure, Development and Reform*. New York: Oxford University Press.

Chang, Chun, and Jijiang Wang. 1994. "The Nature of the Township Enterprise." Unpublished paper.

Che, Jihua, and Yingyi Qian. 1994. "Understanding China's Township-Village Enterprises: Boundaries of the Firm, Governance, Monitoring, and Capital Market." Unpublished paper presented to the International Conference on Property Rights of TVEs in China. Hangzhou, August 7–9.

Cheng, Tiejun, and Mark Selden. 1994. "The Origins and Social Consequences of China's Hukou System." *The China Quarterly*, no. 139, pp. 644–66.

Cui Zhiyuan. 1995. "Moebius Strip Ownership and Its Prototype in Chinese Rural Industry." (manuscript).

Friedman, Edward. 1990. "Deng Versus the Peasantry: Recollectivization in the Countryside." *Problems of Communism*, vol. 39, no. 5, pp. 30–43.

_____, Paul Pickowicz and Mark Selden. 1991. *Chinese Village, Socialist State*. New Haven: Yale University Press.

_____, Paul Pickowicz and Mark Selden. Forthcoming. *The Agony of Village China*.

Fulton, Murray. 1993. "Cooperatives in Rural Development. Theory and Observations." Unpublished paper presented to the International Conference on China's Rural Reform and Development in the 1990s, Beijing.

Gereffi, Gary. 1993. "International Subcontracting and Global Capitalism: Reshaping the Pacific Rim." In Ravi Palat, ed. *Pacific Asia and the Future of the World-System*. Westport: Greenwood.

Hart-Landsberg, Martin. 1993. *The Rush to Development. Economic Change and Political Struggle in South Korea*. New York: Monthly Review Press.

Hatti, Neelambar, and Franz-Michael Rundquist. 1989. "Cooperatives in Rural Development in India. Modern Inputs, Production Structure and Stratification in Sirsi Taluk, Karnataka State." In Bjorn Gyllstrom and Franz-Michael Rundquist, eds., *State, Cooperatives and Rural Change*. Lund Studies in Geography 53. Lund: Lund University Press.

Huang Da, Liu Hongru, and Zhang Xiao, eds. 1990. *Zhongguo jinrong baike quanshu* (The Chinese Financial Encyclopedia). Beijing: Economic Management Publishing House, pp. 244–45.

Huang, Philip. 1993. " 'Public Sphere'/'Civil Society' in China? The Third Realm Between State and Society." *Modern China*, vol. 19, no. 2, pp. 216–40.

Jiang Bing. 1994. "The Emergence of a Land Market in China. Issues in the Reform of the Planned Land Management System and the Development of a Land Market with Chinese Characteristics." Ph.D thesis, Department of Economics and Centre for Asia Studies, University of Adelaide.

Jiang Zhongyi. 1991. "Wo guo nongcun jingji gaige zhong de hezuo jingji zhidu" (The System of Cooperative Economy during the Rural Economic Reform in China). *Nongcun shehui jingji xuekan* (Academic Journal on Rural Socio-economy), no. 1.

Judd, Ellen. 1994. *Gender and Power in Rural North China.* Stanford: Stanford University Press.

Ka Chih-ming. 1993. *Taiwan dushi xiaoxing zhizaoye de chuangye, jingying yu shengchan zuzhi* (Market, Social Networks, and the Production Organization of Small-Scale Industry in Taiwan: The Garment Industries of Wufenpu). Nangang, Taipei: Institute of Ethnology, Academia Sinica.

Kaifang reference room. 1995. "Situation in China's Economic Reform for 1995—Zhu Rongji's Closed-Door Speech at End of December 1994." *Kaifang* (Open Magazine), February, in FBIS-CHI 95-007, May 19, pp. 44–52.

Keating, Pauline. 1994. "The Ecological Origins of the Yan'an Way." *The Australian Journal of Chinese Affairs*, no. 32, pp. 12–53.

Kelliher, Daniel. 1992. *Peasant Power in China. The Era of Rural Reform 1979-1989.* New Haven: Yale University Press.

Kojima Reiitsu. 1993. "Agricultural Organization: New Forms, New Contradictions." In Kueh and Ash 1993, pp. 97–122.

Kornai, Janos. 1990. "The Affinity Between Ownership Forms and Coordination Mechanisms: The Common Experience of Reform in Socialist Countries." *Journal of Economic Perspectives*, vol. 4, no. 2, pp. 131–47.

———. 1990a. *The Road to a Free Economy.* New York: Norton.

Kueh, Y.Y. 1993. "Food Consumption and Peasant Incomes." In Kueh and Ash 1993, pp. 229–72.

Kueh, Y.Y., and Robert Ash, eds. 1993. *Economic Trends in Chinese Agriculture. The Impact of Post-Mao Reforms.* Oxford: The Clarendon Press.

Liu, Xiao Meng. 1995. "Garment Factory" in Wong, Ma and Yang 1995, pp. 153–75.

Matson, Jim, and Mark Selden. 1992. "Poverty and Inequality in China and India." *Economic and Political Weekly*, April 4, pp. 701–15.

Mearns, Robin. 1993. "Pastoral Institutions, Land Tenure and Land Policy Reform in Post-Socialist Mongolia." Research Report 3, Policy Alternatives for Livestock Development in Mongolia (PALD).

———. 1995. "Community, Collective Action and Common Grazing. The Case of Post-Socialist Mongolia." Institute of Development Studies Discussion Paper 350, Institute of Development Studies.

Naughton, Barry. 1994. "Chinese Institutional Innovations and Privatization From Below." *American Economic Review. Papers and Proceedings*, vol. 84, no. 2, pp. 266–70.

Nee, Victor. 1989. "A Theory of Market Transition: From Redistribution to Markets in State Socialism." *American Sociological Review*, no. 54, pp. 663–81.

———. 1996. "The Emergence of a Market Society: Changing Mechanisms of Stratification in China." *American Journal of Sociology*, vol. 101, no. 4, pp. 908–49.

O'Brien, Kevin, and Lian Jiang Li. 1993–94. "Chinese Political Reform and the Question of 'Deputy Quality'." *China Information*, vol. 8, no. 3, pp. 20–31.

Ohno Kazuoki. 1987. "Nokyo: The 'Un'-cooperative." *AMPO. Japan-Asia Quarterly Review*, vol. 19, no. 2, pp. 25–28.

Oi, Jean. 1992. "Fiscal Reform and the Economic Foundations of Local State Corporatism in China." *World Politics*, vol. 45, no. 1, pp. 99–126.

Ostrom, Elinor. 1990. *Governing the Commons. The Evolution of Institutions for Collective Action*. Cambridge: Cambridge University Press.

Pestoff, Victor. 1991. *Between Markets and Politics. Cooperatives in Sweden*. Boulder: Westview.

Popularization Department of the Chinese Association of Science and Technology and the Popularization Department of the Sichuan Provincial Association of Science and Technology (Zhongguo kexue pujibu and Sichuansheng kexue pujibu). 1991. *Nongcun zhuanye jishu xuehui de lilun yu shijian* (The Theory and Practice of the Rural Specialized Technology Associations). Chengdu: The Southwest Financial and Economic University Publishing House.

Research Department, Chinese Association of Science and Technology (Zhongguo kexue jishu xiehui diaoyanshi). 1988. *Nongcun zhuanye jishu xiehui wenti tantao* (Explorations on the Rural Specialized Production Technology Associations). Beijing: The Chinese Science and Technology Publishing House.

Runge, Carlisle. 1986. "Common Property and Collective Action in Economic Development." *World Development*, vol. 14, no. 5, pp. 623–35.

Rural Economic Research Center, Ministry of Agriculture. 1991. *Development in the Countryside*, nos. 14–24.

Schmitter, Philippe. 1974. "Still the Century of Corporatism?"In Frederick Pike and Thomas Stritch, eds., *The New Corporatism: Social-Political Structures in the Iberian World*. Notre Dame: University of Notre Dame Press.

Selden, Mark. 1995. *China in Revolution. The Yenan Way Revisited*. Armonk: M.E. Sharpe.

———. 1993. "State, Cooperative and Market: Chinese Developmental Trajectories." In Louis Putterman and Dieterich Rueschemeyer, eds., *The State and the Market in Development*. Boulder: Lynne Rienner.

———. 1993a. *The Political Economy of Chinese Development*. Armonk: M.E. Sharpe.

——— and Aiguo Lu. 1993. "The Reform of Land Ownership and the Political Economy of Contemporary China." In Mark Selden, *The Political Economy of Chinese Development*. Armonk: M.E. Sharpe.

Sen, Amartya. 1982. "How Is China Doing?" *New York Review of Books*, vol. 29, no. 30, December 16.

Sicular, Terry. 1993. "Ten Years of Reform: Progress and Setbacks in Agricultural Planning and Pricing." In Kueh and Ash 1993, pp. 47–96.

Smil, Vaclav. 1993. *China's Environmental Crisis. An Inquiry into the Limits of National Development*. Armonk: M.E. Sharpe.

Stark, David. 1996. "Recombinant Property in East European Capitalism." *American Journal of Sociology*, vol. 101, no. 4, pp. 993–1027.

State Statistical Bureau. 1986, 1992, 1993. *Statistical Yearbook of China*. Beijing: State Statistical Bureau.

Svejnar, Jan, and Josephine Woo. 1990. "Development Patterns in Four Counties." In William Byrd and Lin Qinsong, eds., *China's Rural Industry. Structure, Development and Reform*. Oxford: Oxford University Press, pp. 63–84.

Taylor, Jeffrey. 1993. "Rural Employment Trends and the Legacy of Surplus Labour." In Kueh and Ash 1993, pp. 273–310.

Unger, Jonathan, and Anita Chan 1996. "Chinese Corporatism: A Developmental State in an East Asian Context." In Barrett McCormick and Jonathan Unger, eds., *China After Socialism: In the Footsteps of Eastern Europe or East Asia?* Armonk: M.E. Sharpe.

Vanek, Jaroslav. 1971. *The Participatory Economy. An Evolutionary Hypothesis and a Strategy for Development*. Ithaca: Cornell University Press.

Vermeer, Eduard. 1982. "Income Differentials in Rural China." *The China Quarterly*, no. 89, pp. 1–33.

————. 1988. *Economic Development in Provincial China: The Central Shaanxi Since 1930.* Cambridge: Cambridge University Press.

Wade, Robert. 1987. "The Management of Common Property Resources: Collective Action as an Alternative to Privatisation or State Regulation." *Cambridge Journal of Economics*, pp. 95–106.

————. 1992. "Common-Property Resource Management in South Indian Villages." In D.W. Bromley *et al.*, eds., *Making the Commons Work*. San Francisco: Institute for Contemporary Studies, pp. 208–28.

Walder, Andrew. 1995. "Local Government as Industrial Firms: An Organizational Analysis of China's Transitional Economy." *American Journal of Sociology*, vol. 101, no. 2, pp. 263–301.

Weitzman, Martin, and Chenggang Xu. 1994. "Chinese Township Enterprises as Vaguely Defined Cooperatives." *Journal of Comparative Economics*, vol. 18, April, pp. 121-45.

Wen, Guangzhong James, and Gene Chang. 1994. "The Nature of TVEs' Policy to Subsidize Agriculture: Reinternalization of Externalities." Paper presented to the International Conference on Property Rights of TVEs in China, Hangzhou, August 7–9.

Whyte, William. 1985. "Working with Small Farmers and Agricultural Cooperatives in Latin America." In Bergmann and Ogura, 1985.

Wong, John, and Mu Yang. 1995. "The Making of the TVE Miracle in Asia. Overview of Case Studies." In Wong, Ma and Yang 1995, pp. 16–52.

Wong, John, Rong Ma and Mu Yang, eds. 1995. *China's Rural Entrepreneurs. Ten Case Studies*. Singapore: Times Academic Press.

Yao Jianfu. 1994. "Zhongguo nongcun feizhengfu zuzhi—nongcun zhuanye jishu xiehui" (China's Rural NGOs—Rural Science and Technology Associations). Manuscript.

Young, Susan. 1995. *Private Business and Economic Reform in China*. Armonk: M.E. Sharpe.

Zhang Xiaoshan. 1992. "Chinese Rural Cooperatives—New Areas of Activities" (manuscript).

———— and Yuan Peng. 1991. *Hezuo jingji lilun yu shixian—Zhongguo bijiao yanjiu* (The Theory and Practice of Cooperative Economy—China-Foreign Comparative Studies). Beijing: Chengshi chubanshe.

Zhang Yunqian. 1991. "Shuangceng jingying, shehuihua fuwu, he shequ hezuo zuzhi" (Double-Level Management, Socialized Services, and Community Cooperation). *Zhongguo nongcun hezuohua lishi ziliao* (Materials on the History of Chinese Rural Cooperation), no. 4.

Zhou Binbin. 1991. "Renmin gongshe shiqi de pinkun wenti" (The Problem of Poverty During the Period of the People's Communes). *Jingji kaifa luntan* (Forum on Economic Development), no. 3.

Zhou, Kate Xiao. 1996. *How the Farmers Changed China. Power of the People*. Boulder: Westview.

Zhu Ling. 1991. *Rural Reform and Peasant Income in China*. London: Macmillan Press.

Zhu Ling and Mark Selden. 1993. "Agricultural Cooperation and the Family Farm in China." *Bulletin of Concerned Asian Scholars*, vol. 25, no. 3, pp. 3–12.

2

What Is a Village?

Stephan Feuchtwang

A place of residence can be described purely geographically, as a dispersed or a nucleated settlement. But the singular which identifies it as "a settlement" comes first. It has been identified as a place to be described. Indeed its identification as a place usually entails a name and a history. They combine with the geographical features of the description to make it a place. They make it a bounded place, an "inside" within which there is a sense of co-residence, however subdivided by kinship and neighborhood it is. Such an "inside" will itself be included in a greater bounded space. It is in a hierarchy of orders of inclusion. A settlement is, in short, a place which is a territorial definition of belonging. In beginning to pose the question in the title of this chapter, let "village" be understood simply as a second-order place, beyond neighborhoods of household and family. But since its name and boundaries are historical, the same name can have different stories attached to it by different sets of residents, and of course the name may be one of a succession of names in a story told of the same or a similarly bounded place.

We should not assume that there is only one such definition, nor that the different definitions are congruent. For different purposes, or according to different institutions, residents may refer to different boundaries to define the place in which they live. We should be alert to the possible coincidence or near coincidence of different identifications of a place of residence. Where there is a strong coincidence it is likely that the place so defined will have a strong sentience for the residents, and the more this definition is shared by the other residents the more solidary that sentience will be. On the other hand, there may be different senses of the place in which they live, the boundaries of the place may not be clear or agreed, and as a place it may have more sentience for some of them than for others. I will seek to show two things. The first and more theoretically important is to highlight the question of sentience: that the sense of what is the bounded space in which they live, its sentience, varies. The second follows from this and is more a descriptive fact, that a "village" is a different thing in different localities and a different thing according to different residents and purposes in any one locality.

The main empirical base on which I will build is a set of ten investigations of administrative villages in the People's Republic of China conducted by Chinese colleagues under my overall direction in 1991–1993.[1] Despite the existence of a national government and its regulations, the variation between local political cultures and economic conditions, particularly since the dissolution in the early 1980s of nearly all team, brigade and commune organizations of collective production, makes generalization about contemporary China either superficial or unreliable. Instead of trying to say what is similar to all named villages and village governments, it is better to attempt an account of the range of differences.

In doing so, I shall distinguish the following sets of institutions, each of which have produced senses of bounded place. Firstly, the traditional, in which there is an archaic sense of duration, which is frequently referred to as "natural" as in "natural village" (*ziran cun*). By "traditional" and "natural" I refer to villagers' senses of what is local and long-standing, whatever the documented evidence of actual continuity, and not to any objective or scientifically arbitrated knowledge of the natural environment. Secondly, the administrative, which refers to the political organization of a state and of government, which has a history of revolutionary, secular change. For a village the administrative is what is called the "collective" or sub-governmental institutions.

A third set of institutions, which are conventions of association by kinship and friendship linking households or units of government and economic activity, will also be introduced, but only briefly and merely as a corrective to the salience of any of the senses of place produced by the above two sets of institutions.

The definitions of these sets of institutions, and a discussion of what "traditional" implies—which is certainly not some unchanging and unadaptive constraint—will be treated in the following sections. The whole of my argument about salience stems from their elaboration. But first some formal features of the distinctions between them should be understood.

The distinctions between the three sets of institutions are imperfect in two ways. They are not exclusive sets. Their distinction relies on observable, historical and discursive separations—not theoretically conceptual ones. The economic reforms of the seventies and eighties have been working on precisely a separation between administered and autonomous economic organization, but of course, they are not separated. Not only are they interdependent, but to some extent they coincide. Indeed, the Chinese village as a so-called collective institution is a form of articulation between autonomous and administered economic organization. It is also an articulation of "traditional" and administrative institutions.

But generation of a sense of place is different in the two sets. The "traditional" place order builds upwards and outwards to higher orders from below in inclusive or segmental identifications. The "collective" place combines definition by government, i.e., from a center downwards, with a bottom-up competitive and associational order of economic organization. I will argue that in different parts of China, one or other of these sets of institution is more salient than the others in defining senses of place and their associated senses of history. Much more conceptual work is required, however, and the distinctions I am making are provisional. If they obscure important senses of shared space, they should be rejected.

Theoretical Orientations

I am addressing the following question. With what strength and shared sense of definition do rural residents treat where they live as a place of shared or common identity? The answers have implications for those interested in political culture and in environmental issues. Identification with a place is a preliminary condition for taking joint responsibility, and joint responsibility for a locality is the political pre-condition for managing the combination of conditions which constitute an ecological environment.

There are several different ways in which this question could be conceived. One way would be to concentrate on control over means of production and units of consumption: it would involve description of rights and forms of property, legal and customary, and seeing how they combine, after distinguishing outright from multiple rights to land or water, use rights from residual rights, tenancy from sub-tenancy, and so on. The answer would lie in the relations of dependency, control and exclusion which these rights and forms defined: whether there was a discernible boundary of shared dependency, control of, or exclusion from, means of production and livelihood beyond the household.

Another way of addressing the question of common identity would be to focus upon political and administrative organization, both governmental and non-governmental, defining territorial and functional spheres of power, distinguishing agents from principals, estimating the nature and extent of political participation, the resource basis and character of leadership and access to the holders of these powers, for instance over irrigation or the organization of forceful defense. The answer here would come from any hierarchical and lateral boundaries of leadership (followership), patronage (clientage), authority (respect) and government (subjection) beyond the household.

Both the property-related and the political answers are indispensable and I will not ignore them. But either framework of analysis taken too strictly might omit villagers' own senses of shared identity, interest and responsibility. In order to make sure they are included, I shall concentrate on institutions and discourses which provide collective subject positions: forms of shared identity which distinguish "internal" rivalries or senses of common conditions from "external" responsibility.

Political and economic institutions could be disaggregated in different ways. They include over-lapping agencies whose boundary definitions differ from each other. The areas of jurisdiction of water control, for instance, differ from areas of transport control, and both from those of military command. It is true that a person will define place and social identity according to situation and to its point of immediate interest: irrigation, road maintenance, or defense against theft. These are functional situations. I am concerned with multi functional senses of shared space, a general sense of bounding an inside from an outside. That is what "traditional" and "collective" places provide, even if each in its different ways contains affiliations which relate that place to different, third-order focuses, the "collective" leading off into different administrative definitions of functional jurisdiction. I am here confining attention to only one level of place, which I have called "second-order," and to inclusive orders only insofar as they affect the sense of identification with that place.

In principle, shared subject positions of place contain sub-divisions and offer different interpretations and claims to belonging which can conflict. Their boundaries are also, in principle, porous; they are crossed from above and from the sides. The placing and nature of these boundaries may differ according to different institutions and discourses. They may not coincide. But the condition of finding that a second-order place exists amounts to finding that there is some coincidence of definitions within a set of institutions and in any one discourse. Beyond that, the greater the coincidence, the greater is the salience of the place.

Modern and Traditional Institutions of Rural China

In the course of this century, a critical institutional distinction has been established, creating a dichotomy which has been a fetish of social sciences, the dichotomy of the modern and the traditional. "Modern" refers to relatively recent institutions with a secular and positive political and governmental history and its attendant forms of administration, discourse, property and ideology, which are part of the formation of nation-states. They distinguish themselves from older institutions reflexively. The very designation "traditional," and others like it (such as "backward" and "superstitious" or less pejorative ones such as "religious" or "customary") is one of the effects of this separation. It is a separation of institutions which are predicated upon objectives in a secular history, breaking from institutions of kinship, property and worship which had formally also been political and juridical. This separation is one of the most important structural effects of the long-term social transformation which for convenience we can, in the context of Chinese history, call the republican revolution, although it is a longer process of transformation than the date of the fall of dynastic rule marks out.

From the village perspective, "traditional" institutions are those through which resistance or at least defensive reaction to an agrarian state was organized and upon which the same state was built. They were institutions which were themselves formed through (but not necessarily by) the agrarian states' cultural and coercive powers, even though they were never entirely or at any one time congruent with its administration and its reproduction. Now they are "revived" under another kind of state and its politics, separated from it by another kind of historical project.[2] Inevitably, what I write here is in the modern, secular historical mode, but with discursive sensitivity to other senses of time and place, and without an evolutionary or developmental agenda. What, then, has continued, or been "revived," and what not?

In rural China, the most common basic unit of both property and identity has for very many centuries been a household, its family name and ancestral line, and its private, heritable property. Beyond the household, collective property in late imperial and early republican China was religious or ancestral when it was not that of a commercial organization or of the imperial state. Religious property was either that of monastic foundations, such as those of the sacred mountains, of cult centers on mountains or in cities, and of temple or ancestral cults in towns and villages. Less common were their equivalents for Islam and Christianity. Temple and ancestral trusts consisted in land as well as buildings, and their income was the revenue and rent from these two kinds of property and the activity which took place on them, such as temple fairs. The land of temples and ancestral trusts were a major kind of village corporation, renting their land exclusively to villagers or descendants, using their income for ancestral or temple ceremonies. In places in which much land was owned by landlords from other places and little owned by village residents, such trust lands were the main or the only basis for speaking of "village land."

Republican governments have introduced another kind of collective property altogether, the co-operative or collective identified by a "public" or an administrative, rather than a religious or ancestral unit. Even more radically, they have sought to join the village traditional settlement into the administrative hierarchy as a unit of self-government. I shall explore the variable success of this innovation and of the new kind of collective property at the village level. To do this, I think it is necessary to establish the preceding and now separated senses of place which I have labelled "traditional," into which and out of which the new "public" and "collective" ones have been introduced.

I do not think it is useful to ask whether survivals or revivals of traditional institutions are genuine repetitions of what was. Nor does it make much sense to ask whether they are entirely new in content if not in form. For Helen Siu (1990) the revival of Chrysanthemum Festivals in the Pearl River delta has accommodated itself so entirely to the activities of socialist market economic reform and their political institutions that they should be considered as part and parcel of the same one history. Certainly this is a preferable conclusion to one which simply says that they are a revival, a return of the historically suppressed. The separation to which I have referred must be a prior consideration to either conclusion. The separation itself is new, and in saying so I side with Helen Siu. But at the same time, it demands an account of two (or more) sets of institutions each with their own cyclical rhythms of time and secular moments of change, whose effects upon each other have to be argued, rather than by taking for granted a single historical moment and a totality of effect.

In the narratives by which villagers identify their ancestral past and what has happened in it and to it, different sets of institutions and senses of history and identity are brought into contact with one another. I shall consider only one way in which they are combined: the sense of second-order place. But we are also dealing with a more theoretical enterprise, one implied by the fact that historians can write histories in the plural of what is at the same time named as the same population or place, such as China. A history of Chinese demographic change, or of the Chinese economy, or of ecological events, or of the Chinese state, or of Chinese Buddhism is in each case marked by significant cycles and transformative events which do not necessarily coincide chronologically or in their number with the rhythms and events of the other histories. For instance, a rhythm of state suppression and revival of the same set of institutions—those which for convenience we can label "traditional" and "religious"—has itself a far longer history than that of the republican state. The transformative event which produced the republican state is for the religious institutions a significant moment in that rhythm, but it is not a total transformation as it is in Chinese political history. It is not a replacement by an entirely distinctive set of religious or ideological institutions.

On the other hand, the fact that their suppression was by a new set of ideological and governing institutions, with new determinations of authority, history, education and knowledge, means that the suppression and revival in this case has had a distinctive effect. It has separated or alienated them. Subsequent accommodation turns their archaic sense of time into one of regional or local custom and tradition within a larger national identity of a people, its localities and their biographies. From the perspective of the religious institutions themselves, however, there are places where their continuity is still very strong as a determinant not only of second-order identities but also of a second-order political leadership and the economic organization of commodity production and consumption. In such places, writing their history as part of late imperial China is also the history of the present day, even while another history of a new state and of capitalist labor markets and organizations on a larger scale must be told alongside it (e.g., Wilkerson 1990).

A Traditional Place

"Places" are inscribed in ways by which they can be recognized and linked to other places beyond. A genealogy links a household to other households in branching lines of descent. A gazetteer or local record (*difang zhi*) links a place to larger places, including the whole of China, not just geographically but also by reference to classics or orthodoxies of ceremonial order and of virtuous conduct and accomplishment.

Within this inscription of a place, I want to single out the idea of a shared environment which is both social and physical. This is a well-established idea in ordinary Chinese custom and practice. It is an idea of an environment which can be enhanced or changed to the detriment of others by a social actor, from the head of a household to the emperor. This idea is formalized in the art of site selection called *fengshui*. Disputes about the *fengshui* environment frequently occur, and a comparison with property boundary disputes is a good way of understanding what is the sense of shared environment implied in *fengshui*.

Many disputes have arisen in village neighborhoods over the addition of a building such as an out-house, a pigsty extending into what other households deem to be the space of a common property such as a path. Paths are boundaries as well as connections, and I shall return to them shortly. Apparently similar are disputes about the visual encroachment involved by the same act of building. The neighbors consider how this might affect their well-being and if they conclude that it will harm them they object. But the common property in this case is not a border between private properties. It includes both. It bears the same relation to the parties concerned as does noise or other kinds of pollution. Because *fengshui* is always a matter of vision we can say that its practice, texts, experts and instrument (the magnetic compass and its rings of symbols) are a method of arbitrating visual pollution. It is also a method of improving the visual outlook and well-being of a client, since it is the art of finding places where the inner energies (*qi*) of earth can be gathered.

Energy flows are visible as raised formations or as depressions of land and as watercourses. They are always depicted in cartography as lines and profiles of slopes which can be traced as branches from more central masses, on the largest scale back to the Kunlun range of mountains for the whole of China. The patterns made by these branches differ and signify different fortunes, but as patterns they are always drawn and conceived in a double perspective: from above and from the point of view of a selected position within them. They are patterns within a horizon of survey. What is seen and mappable is itself a sign of inner flows seen both from an objective or high perspective, and from a point of view within it. The seen surface can be treated like a body by means equivalent to traditional Chinese medicine. *Fengshui* experts can impair a site by injecting poisons into a chosen spot or improve it as a gathering point by modifying the visual aspect, advising where to plant trees, dig pools or erect pagodas, or where to put up shields to ward off malign influences. But these actions affect the same environment as seen from other points of view.

The notional horizon defines an inner and an outer territorial circumference. The inner one defines the point of view, but it is also a space with its own "inside" called a "lair" (*xue*), within which everyone is affected according to their shared position in relation to the flows and the forms of the outer circumference. This inner space may be a grave, a house, a neighborhood, a township. In this environmental diagnosis and treatment there is an assumption of common property structured in two ways. One is by territory and the other by descent. Its residents are defined as families. Their place of permanent residence is not just in the here and now. It is a place of origin, however recently established. The residents include with their own the fortunes of their descendants in the male line. The line of origin is the social equivalent of the perspective which defines a point within a territory as the point of view and it is of course both temporal and spatial.

As with pollution, the common good in this reckoning is land, water, atmosphere and outlook including that of the built environment. They are shared as a common condition, but they can also be used to individual advantage. Any circumference can be reconceived as containing different advantages from the same flow of energies, according to different territorial or genealogical positions within it. Each brother and his descendants may reap a different fortune from the grave of his mother. There is jockeying for advantage within and by means of the shared condition, such that it is itself changed. On the other hand, the shared condition can be good or bad for all within it as a neighborhood. For instance, one street of a small town in Taiwan in the sixties was thought to have bad *fengshui* because so many households in it had been reduced to selling their daughters into prostitution.

A place in the collective person of its resident households can know its destiny (*yun*) through *fengshui*. At the same time, as with other Chinese ways of divining destiny, remedies can be found. Destiny can be changed. The aspects and dispositions of buildings and natural features within the horizon are malleable.

In sum, although they are both about the physical forms and visible demarcations of the built and the natural environment, the conception of shared environment displayed in boundary disputes differs from what is displayed in *fengshui* disputes. Both pit the interests of parties to a common property against each other. But boundary disputes are either about borders between private properties or about the common domain between them. The boundaries are a common domain or line between properties. In *fengshui*, the common domain includes the private properties even while their owners dispute on the basis of their ownership. Both are part of a shared environment. *Fengshui* reasoning is more inclusive, less definite and fixed, but equally prone to disputation. Paths and roads are sites of dispute and of definition, in which both kinds of reasoning occur, concerning family property, neighborhood, as well as shared environment.

Much of the cosmology used in *fengshui* is evoked by Taoist ritual and local festivals. I am therefore including them in the one "traditional" set of institutions. Taoist rituals, including those of local festivals, are indeed ways of improving or maintaining collective destinies. But though it is a set, the institutions in it differ from each other. Annual festivals of guardian gods are minor versions of the great rite of renewal (the *jiao*) which is performed at much less frequent intervals, when the local temple is refurbished. This rite and its minor versions demarcate a place clearly in a territorial definition. The households of the territory are united through sub-territorial representatives of each neighborhood, and one of these sub-territories may be responsible in rotation for the festival and rite, but the stress is on unity. Division, angry words, negative sentiments are dangerous, just as they are at New Year. The temporary or temple altar space for the occasion is the only focal point, and in it the whole universe and its genera-tion are evoked. The relation of the local place to the larger forces of the whole is readjusted and harmonized by invitation, entertainment and seeing of gods and ghosts in their proper order and place. The borders—shores, roads, streams—are margins from which the outer gods of heaven and the lower earthbound ghosts are invited and beyond which demons are thrust. Every area of China has had this definition of itself as a set of territories linked through pilgrimages, rotations and tours of borders (Feuchtwang 1992). The cosmological place is here a bounded place of origin. It is a subject in relation to other such places and it has subdivisions, but unlike the *fengshui* concept, it has no further subject positions within it from each of which the whole is a different place.

A unified place is, however, still a place to which there can be rival claims of origination. The principle of descent can be said to act on the principle of territorial unity to construct a hierarchy of privileged claims to it. As with *fengshui*, the two principles are always there, though in a varying balance. All over China there are settlements in which one or two surnames are dominant. In southeastern China, descent was frequently the organizing principle of whole nucleated settlements; villages are often also lineage segments. But even in the lineage villages of south-eastern China, where ancestral halls are the focal points of the sense of place, the territorial principal still has its own ceremonial focus in shrines to guardian gods, or on occasions when a founding or legendary ancestor is celebrated as a territorial guardian. In settlements where there is no dominant surname, territorial guardian gods are the principle focus of the definition and identity of a traditional place, but ancestral worship, genealogy and the care of graves do not for that reason cease to function as foci for a sense of origin and belonging.

A traditional place, including a so-called natural village or hamlet (*ziran cun*), is, in short, a ritual and historical unit whose residents are divisible into those who claim descent from an original settlement, however recent it was in fact, and those who were later immigrants. It is common property in being a shared environment and a shared destiny which can be remedied by cosmogonic ritual adjustment or by *fengshui* treatment. It contains the boundaries of private and corporate properties. But in *fengshui* discourse alone, each subdivision is an alternative focal point for the shared environment, whereas in the ancestral hall and temple rituals there is subdivision of a place with a single focal point.

The discourse of *fengshui* and the rituals of ancestral and of territorial guard-ian festivals are means by which a settlement is identified. Each operates the two principles of territorial bounding and descent in quite different ways, but the boundaries of the place identified by a *fengshui* horizon may be exactly the same as those of the territory of a guardian god.

Paths, watercourses and bridges are boundaries and links, as well as being common property. Their construction and upkeep are often organized in the same way, by whatever is the local focus for second-order place definition—traditionally a system of territorial and ancestral leadership and patronage for their construction, or a system of rotation of responsibility for their upkeep. They fix the horizons as well as being key features of the *fengshui* landscape. Local temples and ancestral halls, or halls in the oldest residence, contain the altars which mark the point of view of the second-order lair, which is the traditional second-order subject position beyond domestic altars.

Modern administrative institutions have in most places replaced or overlaid these traditional institutions. But the underlying principles of traditional definition compose a different place, with a different temporality—genealogical and microcosmic—which can subvert the modern institutions. This is beautifully illustrated by the series of incidents in which shared pathways were sabotaged in a vendetta between the families of Guangxin and Guangjun who formed local segments of the same line in a Sichuan village studied by Pamela Leonard (1994, pp. 182–183).[3] Each accused the other and the local government of using official privilege for their own ends. Guangjun or his allies expressed his grievance twice through blocking paths. First he closed the public path between his and his rival's house, forcing visiting officials to pass through his kitchen or find another route. Then, after the reforms, when his rival Guangxin had been selected as a model farmer, an ally of Guangjun extended the front line of her house so that it blocked a path connecting Guangxin's courtyard to the road, forcing official delegations to choose more definitively than before which part of the village and which of the two sides they were visiting.

These paths defined borders within a village. The landscape of the place beyond them was defined by a temple which stood in the village but was the focus for a much larger territorial definition of local cosmic forces, known symbolically in the idiom of both *fengshui* and the consecration of temples as dragons of rain, flood and mudslide whose control was celebrated in the figure of the temple's deity. His festival was revived after a particularly bad flood and mudslide, simultaneously attributed to bad political leadership, disruptive exploitation of the stones and trees of the land, and to the cosmic forces which determine phases of fortune. The temple had been taken over for the offices of the township government. Later, when some of its materials were used for a new township office, the remaining part was used for the team grain store. But its incense was guardedly burned throughout these appropriations of the temple building. In the mid-eighties the temple was rebuilt and the revived festival of its deity effectively stood at the center of another discourse and definition of a place equivalent to, but not the same as, the township, with its own sense of authority and moral rectitude.

How the two were combined is the subject of the chapter in this book by John Flower and Pamela Leonard. What I wish to add here is the passage by which Pamela Leonard concludes her own account: "the reborn temple is more than a traditionalist reaction against environmental degradation, political corruption, economic stagnation, social disintegration and moral decay; it is the creation of new expressions of values derived from historical memory and speaking to the present"

(1994, p. 260). In other words, there is more than one historical memory involved: the combination of simultaneous discourses and institutions is also a combination of different histories and reckonings of place and change. Protest and negative judgment in one account, endorsement of change and the acquisition of a better life in another. Both can indeed be spoken by the same person, as Leonard illustrates by quoting villagers speaking about former times as hardship and yet about its institutions such as the temple with pride and as a focus of moral good. Each is a differently told and reckoned social memory.

Because they are both borders and means of communications, paths are of crucial interest in another respect: transformation of place. Their reconstruction as roads and the construction of new roads where there were no paths are sites for dispute and redefinitions of place. The building of a road mobilizes both modern and traditional historical memories, even as it changes the definitions of places. It cuts into and divides a place, or causes it to become less well defined by increasing communication with a higher level of inclusion so that the higher level becomes more salient for its inhabitants.

At the side of the new county and township roads which in the last few years have cut through one of the villages in Fujian included in our survey, new workshops, retail outlets, multi-story buildings and houses have been built. In them live new settlers from the county capital and from other villages. Many of the new households are those of villagers who have been resettled to make way for a water supply scheme. The new residents are mixed with the older single-surname settlers of two natural villages. Of their two ancestral halls, one is entirely surrounded by the new multi-story blocks. You can see the tiles of its slightly curved roofs past market stalls and pool tables which crowd the concrete space between the concrete pillars of the ground level of the blocks surrounding it. Through the central gate of the hall where there had once been fields and a view beyond them to a river, there is now a stinking pool of rubbish.

The multi-story blocks are part of a development project promoted by the village's official leaders including a member of this local section and its lineage. The name of the natural village, North Stone, is now the name of the development project. The whole nature and definition of the place is changing into a section of a city, much appreciated by the young. But the name contains a memory. The elders of the lineage segment say it was their ancestors who gave the settlement its name. The same elders have fought for proper accommodation of the ancestral hall and they continue the fight, despite their lack of success until now. Reconstruction of the rear hall from the disrepair into which it had fallen during the Cultural Revolution continued even while the development project's scaffold and concrete surrounded it. On its new, red lacquered wooden columns are sentiments inscribed in gold which, so we were told, address the treacherous types (*bai lei*) who are the village cadres: "If you want good children, accumulate merit; To raise a family, read books." This silent rebuke to political leaders for neglect of filial duty to their history and descent group is not the only sign of traditional redefinition of authority. Overseas members of the same surname from this village are being contacted to use whatever influence they have to support a claim for compensation beyond what the government has already agreed (but not paid). The claim is for a piece of open land in the hills behind the street, where an entirely new ancestral hall can be built. If it succeeds, North Stone will have two definitions. But the size, boundaries and nature of the two will be dramatically disparate, even though the ancestral hall retains the claim to a longer social memory. Place definitions, both traditional and administrative, have been transformed by their markers which are also lines of communication.

In late imperial and early republican times, the fact that much village land could have been owned by absentee landlords, and the fact that a village manufactory such as a silk reeling mill had outside shareholders, reminds us that the horizons of *fengshui* and the boundaries of temple festivals did not and probably never did coincide with all the links of interest in village property. Even the links from village temples themselves or from villages without temples to the temples in larger villages and towns, and further to regional centers of pilgrimage, may have provided more powerful foci of belonging than the named settlements marked by the lowest order of ancestral and territorial markers beyond households. Furthermore, in most villages at any time there will be residents who are not included in its festivals except as guests, because they are still considered to be (or consider themselves to be) temporary residents or outsiders. Nevertheless, through diverse lines of reference and interest, horizons and the marking of the borders of the nearest temple area did define and continue territorially to define a place and its named identity alongside administrative or collective institutions.

Government administration introduces a second principle which has historically, in imperial as well as republican China, cut across the boundaries of place defined according to the principles of territorial identity and descent. But the republican revolution has wrought a radical separation, and its institutions are far more co-ordinated and consolidated than the sub-governmental institutions of the imperial regime. The salience of administrative place is a powerful and sometimes overwhelming challenge to the salience of traditional place.

An Administrative Place

The organizing principle of administration is, of course, government from a center. It is the reverse of reference from a traditional place to a more inclusive conception of nature or universe. The capital is the center of the universe, cosmological or political. Traditional places are loci defined from below and outwards, whereas administrative places are defined from the inclusive order, which is outside, and downwards. The traditional may imply a different and potentially disruptive order. For the administration of both border and inland control, military garrisons and patrols were imposed from a higher center. For revenue collection, labor service, and mutual surveillance, the periodic institution of registration deliberately cut across the boundaries of traditional settlement (Dutton 1992, chapter 3). But eventually, as with military garrisons, the units of the register encouraged or imposed from above might be naturalized or absorbed into the institutions of the local elite and the places of their patronage. In one direction, from below, the process of naturalization will have included the ritual inscription of the formerly imposed boundaries by festivals. In the other direction, from above, naturalization will have inserted some of the exemplars and definitions of moral authority of state orthodoxy through a local elite.

The impositions of administrative boundaries under a Communist government bear some similarities to the imperial system of registration. They too deliberately cut across the boundaries of identified settlements, combining traditional places which had not been united by descent or territorial origin. Between the imperial and the Communist came the registration and taxation system of the warlord and Nationalist republican periods, and it is this which changed the relationship of administrative order to villages.

Duara provides evidence that the late imperial relation of the state to villages and their land was transformed during the warlord and Nationalist periods. It had been a relation of what he describes as brokerage. Tax brokers and protectors, as well as local gentry, mediated at several levels between the county administration and the village (Duara 1988, chapter 2). But at the beginning of this century, the village became more than a unit of tax registration and protection from extortionate levies. Under the new, republican regimes it became a collector of levies for its own investment projects. What previously had been organized by local patrons, such as militia and crop-watching associations, was replaced by state-sponsored public associations for the same purposes (Duara 1988, chapter 5). In addition, republican government encouraged new associations hostile to the older ones. A widespread instance was the formation of village school associations opposing backward superstitions and promoting a new, forward-looking or modernizing education, the school funds financed in part by taxing the offerings at local festivals. In other words, local leaders who would previously have been brokers, exploiters, protectors, and patrons now added to these the new role of state-recognized village authority for economic, educational, and infrastructural improvement according to whatever were the local government's criteria of development.

Nationalist republican administration was patchy, depending a great deal on local governors. In famous reformers' counties like Ding in Hebei Province, the organization of village public associations (*gongyi hui*) went much further than elsewhere. But a County Reorganization Act was promulgated nationally in 1929, instituting township and village governmental and sub-governmental organization (as a *bao* with *jia* sub-units). We found in the records and old villagers' testimonies several local government initiatives reaching to village level in Anxi county, southern Fujian. They included not only the taxing of festivals for schools but also the organization of boat transporters into an association, and the appointment of a village head who was poor but educated and was not the leader of the village lineage or its segments. In the northern Yunnan county of Yongsheng we also found from the same mix of sources that the head of the *bao* had been active in raising funds from wealthy villagers and labor from the poor to build bridges and tracks.

For tax administrative purposes, the early republican governments sought to establish clear territorial boundaries on villages, marking land out as adhering to each village whether or not it was owned by village residents (Duara 1988, pp. 203–207). Land reform under Communist government completed the process of territorial consolidation, unifying village land and village residents. Exertion of strict state controls on migration furthered the consolidation. But land reform also began the process, carried on through collectivisation, of dismantling the property base and cutting through the principles of previous village leadership and organization.

There may have been a period of five to ten years until the formation of advanced producers' cooperatives in 1955 when residence, land, and administration coincided in the clearest ever definition of the village as a unit from the households upwards and from the government administration downwards. But in this very period new public associations, the mass organizations of peasants, youth and women, replaced the older ones, and the larger villages and small towns became the lowest level of rural Party organization and of state-organized credit and marketing. The Party became and remains the center-down means of recognizing public and political authority at village level. In the economy, the state-organized system of marketing and distribution became the unified mechanism of tax collection.

Above the villages, the boundaries and units of government administration changed from military regions to provinces, prefectures and counties, and then collectivisation brought what had been a distinct hierarchy of marketing centers into congruence with administrative centers and boundaries. The new lowest level of unified administration was the commune, the lowest level of Party organization the brigade, and the lowest level of production and distribution the team. A great deal of re-naming and redrawing of boundaries was involved. Villagers learned to use these new words and names for residential and economic units while remembering and continuing occasionally to use the old ones. Of the ten villages included in our research project only one bears a name given during collectivisation. The rest retain their pre-Communist names, although some of them are only as old as the Nationalist reorganizations of village boundaries. On the other hand, the administrative boundaries of only two are definitely (and two others are possibly) the same as the traditional places currently given that name. In all cases the administrative village, and before it the brigade, included units which were not part of the village as defined before Communist government. I have already mentioned the Fujian case of the two single-lineage villages being joined. The smaller lineage was used, with temporary and partial success, to destroy the influence of old loyalties. In all the villages, not only were the territorial temples and ancestral halls themselves destroyed or used for other purposes and their rituals forbidden, but the territorial units of new political ceremony, meeting and mobilization combined territories in different boundaries than the traditional rituals had marked. The period of collectivisation was a new period, longer than the land reform period, of congruent definition of village boundaries.

Now, however, the administrative divisions which have inherited the collectives' boundaries have lost the collective monopoly of production and distribution. More than that, administrative divisions are once again only one among other definitions of place. The redistribution of land to households and the reintroduction of capitalist relations have once again generated marketing hierarchies. The revival of temples and their regional systems have generated other inclusive levels in which a household and a village places itself and is placed.

Administrative, marketing, property and ritual hierarchies of definition are diverging from each other again. The naturalizing ritual and local historical and genealogical definitions of place have been renewed. But one unreversed and in my opinion irreversible fact of republican life for villagers is the transformation of state brokerage into state inclusion of village authority and territorial definition. State inclusion is more than a matter of taxation. It is also an institution of village economic powers, among which are powers of contract, commission, permission and management of resources defined as its own, acting as a "collective." Could this become a new way of sensing place as "traditional"?

Villages or the smaller units of residence which are neighborhoods or separate hamlets are frequently still known by residents according to the collective designation. They are often called "teams" (*xiaodui*) rather than "small groups" (*xiaozu*) as they should be according to current administrative parlance, and the larger units of which they are administrative parts are called "brigades" (*dadui*), not villages (*cun*). Most of this is the inertia of memory. The recent past of collectivisation itself took some getting used to. It was installed into everyday usage by political urgency, and by villagers' caution and in some cases enthusiasm. It lasted some twenty or more years in a relatively stable fashion. The new administrative designations of small group and administrative village will take years to become ordinary and universal because there is far less political urgency to adopt them. In addition, there is also some remaining truth in the collective designations, and it is endorsed in Party and state usage itself. Villages are called "collective" (*jiti*) as well as "public" (*gongyi*) institutions, and so are the enterprises registered as those of the village and township. The state endorses villages as units of self-reliance with their own responsibilities for welfare below the lowest level of ministerial administration, which is the township (*xiang* or *zhen*).

The "collective" is official, included in Party policy implementation. That does not mean that it will always be so. But the institution of the village as a unit of government is surely here to stay. By that definition, in addition to the other definitions—of descent, territory, and property—it is recognized as a place. But the extent of its economic powers, how they are organized, and what is done with them vary greatly.

A Collective Place

An administrative village (*xingzheng cun*) in the People's Republic of China in the 1990s has an administrative office (*cun gongsuo* or *banshi chu*) with jurisdiction over a number of settlements or neighborhoods called villagers' small groups (*cunmin xiaozu*), each with its village-appointed head. The core of the official leadership of the village is a trio consisting of a general director (*zhuren*), a Party secretary (*shuji*) and a bookkeeper (*wenshu*). Frequently they, with the possible addition of other village administrators, are members of the village Party committee.

A central document of August 1990 entitled "Summary of a National Forum on the Work of Constructing Organization at the Village Level" (Zhonggong zhongyang 1991) declared the strengthening of the village office as the state's fundamental organization in rural society to be an important task. In 1991 that strengthening included, at least in some areas, putting village officials onto the payroll of the township.[4] In our two Yunnan villages it also meant that the three main village officials should serve three-year terms of office and not come from the village in which they are posted. Other salaried cadres may be added, such as a director of the village economic co-operative society (*jingji hezuo she*), who is in fact usually in charge of its agriculture. But whether township budgets will stand this, and whether their officials impose it must be a matter for local investigation. In February 1992 central government issued a document (Number Two) which further strengthened township government, this time at the expense of the county level (Leonard 1994, p. 159). At the same time, the strengthening of village organization is officially interpretable as an encouragement to reinforce political participation in the election of the village residents' committee (*cunmin daibiaohui*) (see the chapter in this volume by Wang Zhenyao). Village officials are electable or appointable from this committee, but it was not evident in function or conversation in any of the villages in our survey. Plainly, the township and the village as agents of central government are deemed to have important parts in furthering reforms which have encouraged the production of commodities and market exchange as incentives of material development. The great success of township and village enterprises has without doubt had much to do with this. But we should remember that their success has been very uneven and is geographically concentrated. As for the strengthening directives themselves, they are nationwide, but they contain possibilities of almost contradictory interpretations. Which interpretation is adopted locally will depend upon the efforts of central reformers—themselves divided—and on the resources and political inclinations of local officials.

The township government treats the village office as its outpost. But the stipends of small-group leaders and other cadres, such as the family planning woman and most of the primary school teachers are usually paid by the village from levies of the village households, as are various infrastructural investments, utilities and welfare provision. So their number, quality and extent depend upon the resources at the village's disposal. The "collective," which is to say the administrative village, remains the prime institution of responsibility for social security after households themselves. The resources for these responsibilities are dependent on its powers of levying revenue or gaining income in its own right as manager of economic production.

The two great resources over which village administrations have powers are land and industrial or other commercial enterprises. Legally, an administrative village as agent of the state is the owner of the land distributed to households. In effect this now amounts to a residual power. When land is vacated because a household, through age, illness, infertility or inability to adopt heirs, has abandoned farming the land it has contracted from the village, the land reverts to the village. The village coming to the rescue of the unfortunate household also disposes of its land. The same residual power has, in the past decade in most villages, been used once or twice to re-adjust the distribution of land to all households according to changes in their size. But there is no indication of a political will for further large-scale readjustment as distinct from piecemeal administration of reverted land, except where more central pressure of advice and aid is in favor of land consolidation for production efficiency. The residual power entailed in collective ownership of the land is realized chiefly through the levying of fees from enterprises for the use of the land and from households as part of their contract.

Every village Party committee and the cadres in village administration through which it works also has the power of implementing policy handed down most immediately from the township capital. One strand of policy concerns the use of seed, new crops, water and fertilizer on land managed by households. Agricultural extension points exist in most if not all administrative villages but the extent of activity varies enormously, and the sanctions at their disposal may not be great. Village administrations help to manage the irrigation system and to arbitrate the inevitable disputes over water shares. But maintenance of the irrigation system is very variable, well kept in some villages and not at all in others, even though irrigation fees are collected in them all. Similarly, most villages have fertilizer stations, and the richer ones have tractor stations. But for all these services households are charged fees.

The usual stories of ambivalence can be told about the implementation of policy. In the northern Yunnan basin where two of our villages were placed, subsistence rice was the chief preoccupation of farmers. But the township tried to implement a policy of introducing a cash crop, tobacco, which would increase the local tax revenue base. The township assigned each village a target of land to be planted with tobacco. In the two villages investigated, to reach the target would have meant transferring some paddy to tobacco-cropping. Households had been willing to use hillside but not irrigated valley-land. Cadres had to go out in teams and tear up the paddy in the fields which they had required for tobacco. Even so, the targets were not met in either village and the cadres stood to lose the bonus promised for reaching the targets. The local village cadres felt particularly ambivalent about implementing the policy, since they shared the village priority which puts the growing of rice for their own use first over any other agriculture. But in the last resort their loyalty or interest was in Party or government employment. This is yet another illustration of the position of team and brigade leaders caught between protecting or leading fellow-villagers and relaying more central political and administrative orders (Chan *et al.* 1992; Oi 1989). The "collective" is at the same time a local authority, an accumulation of resources for its own investment and for the personal reputation and private advantage of its officials, and an outpost of central government.

In the southern Fujian village which includes North Stone and its ancestral hall, like all villages on the edge of urban development, the village administered the selling of land to the county government for the building of apartment blocks, a school and industrial enterprises. The households to whom the land had been contracted were paid a part of the proceeds. But the village kept a third for its collective funds, some of it used for building a new village office which also houses a private village enterprise.

On the other hand, the retention of land for collective management by the administrative village is far less frequent than are administrative interventions in the use of land. None of the ten villages in our 1991–3 survey ran a collective agricultural enterprise. Elsewhere, the collective is active in organizing specialist households into farming cooperatives on consolidated land, as in two villages I visited in Huairou county, Beijing, in 1988. This is a possible extension of village administration in many villages, once industry is well developed and if the tradition of collective management has been maintained. But piecemeal subsistence and cash-cropping seem to be more usual. In all ten villages of our 1991–3 survey there was some private cash-cropping enterprise, least in the Yunnan and Gansu villages, most in the Fujian and Jiangsu villages. But in only two of them was it on a large and consolidated scale. One was the richest of the villages, on the coast of southern Fujian. Most villagers had left the land. They were engaged in their own or relatives' industrial (garment manufacturing) enterprises producing in whole or part for export through Hong Kong. But another source of their exceptionally high income was the cultivation of prawn beds. These were private shareholding cooperatives of village households. Village cadres had no administrative part in organizing them or the other villagers' industrial enterprises. On the contrary, they were themselves involved in setting up private enterprises of their own, including one in the office of the village administration, as in the other Fujian village, and in privatizing and running the electricity supply station.

Whereas in southern Fujian village administration and its cadres are dispersed into private enterprises and non-governmental collective organization, the cross-over from public office to private interest takes a completely different form in one of the two villages surveyed in southern Anhui. There the village administration has been effectively taken over by a village company. When farm land was contracted to households, huge tracts of forest which had belonged to the commune were offered to households (the forests controlled by higher levels of government were not on offer). Two households, one from one of our villages and one from another which we did not study, took up the offer. Both have turned their contracted responsibilities into large businesses. One markets the timber. The other is the Party secretary of the village we studied. A traditional domestic craft of the village had been the manufacture of paper. Most village households were engaged in it. Under the administration of the commune in 1968, a small factory for hand-made paper was set up, supplanting the domestic sideline activity of former times. The Party secretary incorporated this factory into his forestry firm and sold shares to households in his own and surrounding villages to raise money for investment in paper-making machinery and a new building. Since then, with bank loans and county involvement, the mill has expanded into an industrial complex in the village with a branch in the county town. While in other villages, enterprises have grown and dispersed under separate management and investment, here the one enterprise has grown into several factories.

As is the case with other villages' enterprises, the village itself is given privileged access to employment. Indeed, villagers expect to be employed in it as a collective right. But of this they are soon disabused. Qualifications for employment include a skill needed by the enterprise, connections with the managers, and an investment of cash. But if employment is not a universal benefit to the villagers, the reservoirs and irrigation schemes built by the company are. Moreover, the Party secretary is spreading the benefits of his village company to a far poorer neighboring village, further up in the mountains. This poor village has only a small crochet workshop as a collective enterprise, and a few households are engaged in making charcoal and selling timber. Otherwise all households farm for subsistence, and the product is insufficient. Casual and migrant labor to earn cash with which to buy state grain keeps them above the poverty line. In 1992 the Party secretary started a forestry cooperative there, and in 1993 his company invested in the building of a narrow track which will make the village accessible to motor transport and to a new packaging plant of the company in which residents of the village will be employed. Here we have a distinctly public service enterprise which is a private share-holding company. It is politically endorsed. As the company began to develop the poor village, the Party secretary was appointed as joint secretary of both villages' Party committees. By both this corporate reorganization and the building of the track, a new place is being formed.

As his company grows, it may be that the two villages will merge as a place identified by the resident households as "their" village. In the meantime, the residents of the relatively wealthier village depend on the company's payments to the village; they pay no levies themselves. Schooling, the care of the old without family support, and the treatment of the sick and the injured are all supported by the village welfare fund and therefore by the company's "management" fees for use of the land. There are other kinds of employment and private enterprise pursued by residents of this village, but as by far the largest employer and investor not only in industry but in irrigation, as well as in the village's social funds, the presence of the company as a village company in so many senses is overwhelming and its leadership identified firmly as collective and with the Party. The company's management and higher-level employees constitute a village elite.

We move on, now, to a further contrast. In southern Jiangsu, the tradition of collective management has been maintained in a more administration-centered way. The administrations of both of the villages we surveyed retained substantial powers of management over the village industrial enterprises. They appoint their managers, determine their wage fund, oversee their reproduction plans, as well as take a share of their profits. The managers are themselves members of the village Party branch, and the Party secretaries are the managers of the largest enterprises of each village. Although all households farmed, the majority of the economically active were employed in industry. Industry was more linked to agriculture in one of the two villages than it was in the other. In this administrative village the biggest enterprises are silk textile mills, one run by the township and two run by the village. A third village enterprise is a small liquor refinery. Since mulberry is one of the main cash crops, a portion of the household farms' income depends on the silk enterprises. But the rest of the cash-cropping (orchards and fishponds) does not. In the other village, the enterprises are entirely industrial, unrelated to agriculture. They also produce more revenue.

Apart from their reserving employment for villagers, the main sense of dependence on the enterprises is the result of their profit-sharing with the village administration. Out of the village's share of enterprise profits, the installation of utilities (water and electricity in both villages, gas in the more industrial one), the building and staff of the school and a number of social security schemes are funded. Villagers were saved from having to pay levies either for these utilities and securities or for the village cadres and teachers. But in the first village, initial pride and pleasure in the village enterprises and village leadership has waned, whereas in the more industrial village they remain high. The villagers in the one considered the enterprises were being run for the benefit of their managers more than for the village, whereas the other villagers retained faith in their village leadership and the management of the enterprises.[5] But in both, as in the wealthier of the two Anhui villages, the administrative village and its enterprises were identified as "the village." In these three places, the administrative village seems to have acquired sentience.

In the poorer Anhui village, in the very rich southern Fujian village, and indeed in the other five villages we surveyed, "the village" was described by respondents in terms of natural and economic conditions, including the beauty of the landscape, and the possibilities of making a livelihood, without mention of the village leadership. In the two Yunnan villages, the only enterprises were small construction companies, recorded in village statistics as village enterprises, but entirely private in investment and control, and their management fees have little impact. For the two Gansu villages, the only enterprise of great importance is a nearby plastic fiber mill which employs some women from each village. Its original investment was from the township, but it has become virtually autonomous. Its manager makes all decisions and enterprise profits fund its expansion and diversification. Even so, one of his decisions was to retain and not replace with more productive machinery the labor-intensive reels in one of the plants. He professes a public concern to provide employment for the poorer residents of the township. But to villagers this and other such services are remote, identified either with the state or with the company itself and its manager, not with a place or with any sense of collective or common property.

In sum, what gives substance to the new collective and focuses villagers' identification with it as a place which is an administrative village is a combination of two things: industrial enterprise and the involvement of cadres in it as a Party or village "collective." But this only happens in some of the local political cultures of the many which exist in China.

Households and Their Networks

> "The patrilineally structured rural household has not merely retained its corporate character but has also used its intrinsic flexibility to meet new possibilities in the 1980s" (Johnson 1993, p. 119).

With increased migration of various kinds, households extend their sense of important relations and ideas of important places to other locations through personal networks of social support. In both the poorest and in the richest of the villages in our survey, half or more of the households have members living in other provinces.

We have found in our surveys that kinship is more important than friendship for entrepreneurs and cadres, although they are as often through mothers, sisters and daughters as they are through male descent lines. Only for the households of factory workers was friendship more important than kinship.

Some villages near urban centers are effectively disappearing, as more of their households transfer to urban registration. On the other hand other villages, even while they industrialize, consolidate a village identity and the networks of the more powerful and resourceful households, ranging great distances, still refer back to them.

These personal networks include relations which have been described as client-age. As a political scientist, Oi (1989) focused attention upon hierarchical relations rather than horizontal relations of personal connection and sympathy. One point I would make about these relations is that since the writing of her book, they have dispersed. Their dispersal is part of the same process which has produced dis-junctures of different kinds of hierarchy, administrative, governmental and non-governmental accumulations of economic resources, and separations of governmen-tal and non-governmental criteria and hierarchies of respect and authority. There has been a pluralizing of village and township elites along these lines. A further point I would want to add is that patronage, or clientalism, is always a relation dependent upon the institution in which it occurs. It cannot therefore by itself define relations of power and authority. The institutions and discourses in which such relations operate and are defined must be described. The institutions of rural China are not a fixed feature, as Oi's book makes abundantly clear.

There are contrary tendencies in personal networks as far as village definition is concerned. On the one hand, there is a blurring and decreasing of the importance of the village evident in the extension of kinship and friendship networks such that different village households have different paths and extensions of interdependency which do not coincide in range and definition with those of other households. On the other hand, there is a firming of village boundaries in the tendency noted in all ten villages, and reported in other village studies (e.g., Chan *et al.* 1992, pp. 188ff), to narrow the range of marriage partners, which is to say increasing village endogamy. Reference back to the village in the networks of the most economically and politi-cally powerful is also evident. I would think that the salience of village definition is to a large extent independent of the personal networks of households. It can focus the dispersal of networks. Its clarity and coincidence in one or the other sets of institu-tions will entail not just a strong sense of place but also a strong sense of authority and of leadership recognized according to that sense, and therefore of having a direction, a future and being a place of return or at least reference. As strong temple or ancestral hall leadership and festivity can bind the otherwise divisive *fengshui* perspectives and rivalry between lineage segments or between surnames, rendering them internal divisions within a unit, so can it or the collective authority or both hold a center for otherwise blurring and dispersing networks.

The Collective and the Traditional Place

There has been a craze of housebuilding in the last decade. In all the ten villages, rituals of protection and orientation are performed for some households, employ-ing a local expert in *fengshui*. The movable definition of territory according to the visual perspectives of *fengshui* are still available, and occasionally used. But in none of the three villages with strong enterprises and collective management have the ritual definitions of the past been revived. Nor have those of the poor Anhui village. We found a range in the ratio of traditional and collective definitions of place that was extreme, from traditional dominance and its virtual substitution of administrative definition, to the collective or administrative extinction of traditional definitions.

Where temples and ancestral halls have been reconstructed, they only have the land on which they are built, including a yard. Temple and ancestral trusts have not been revived. The rebuilding and festivals rely on public subscription. Collections from every household, rather than land and its revenue, are the vital manifestation of these two foci of naturalized places.

In the rich coastal Fujian village, the administration has presided in the last ten years over a great deal of public work and welfare: paving roads and paths, rebuilding the primary and secondary school, rebuilding two ancestral halls which double as old people's recreation centers. In fact, however, the fundraising and management of these works lie in another organization. The village head frankly acknowledges that the power is not in his committee's hands but in another committee, which is a combination of the school management committee, the village lineage committee, and the village overseas committee. The school of this village was founded in 1921 by the local lineage, funded by overseas emigrants, but with strong republican aims of promoting a new, national culture. Today, the school management committee meets in the office of the village's Philippine emigrants' association. All three committees' members include both ex-cadres and overseas villagers. All this needs formal government approval, but has no trouble in acquiring it. Here we have a merging of administrative into traditional place. It is certainly "public," but the content is a mixture of agencies, many of which are designated "private," whether they are the households of cadres and ex-cadres or those of overseas Chinese. But none of this has any organizational connection with the organization of the villagers' industrial and commercial enterprises. Kinship is the primary relation among the managers and agents of these enterprises. Half the registered households are in fact resident in Hong Kong and overseas, working as agents of their enterprises. Other enterprises are shareholding cooperatives of groups of friends. They come together in their subscriptions to the school, halls, temples and the other public works.

This village is a complement to the new village corporation in the forests of southern Anhui. Where the Anhui village is a new shareholding corporation into which village officials have been subsumed, in this coastal Fujian village the traditional institutions provide the organization into which some of the resources of private enterprises are drawn through donations for public works and from which village leaders in their official roles have been sidelined.

In the other southern Fujian village in our survey there is no such munificence of overseas connection and no merging of administrative and natural organization, although village cadres are involved in both. As everywhere in Fujian and Guangdong, temples and ancestral halls have been built and their festivals are maintained by public subscription. Their building in this village is organized by informal committees whose leading authority is an ex-cadre, who has moved from being a poor and illiterate peasant without lineage status to being a Party cadre in charge of the district when he was caught in a losing faction twice, in the fifties and in the Cultural Revolution, and is now the local manager of a joint enterprise. Not the traditional type of leader, he nevertheless leads the traditionalizing process of his village, in particular the building of its temple and ancestral hall. On the other hand, the village administration's public works, its office building and the broadening and hardening of village tracks were organized and paid for by administrative levies of money and labor on the residents. The school comes somewhere in between. It was founded in 1932 by lineage heads but with encouragement and a curriculum approved by the republican government county and *bao* authorities. Now, however, it is not funded by voluntary donations but by the government and villagers' fees, while receiving the traditional support from lineage elders whose status has been ritually renewed by the rebuilding of their ancestral hall. It is a state school with a partially pre-republican and a partially modernizing village history.

In this village, there are several natural settlements which are segments of the two lineages, each of which had been a separate village. I have already mentioned the transformation of one of these segments, and the ancestral hall of the smaller of the two traditional, lineage villages. The administrative village with its residual powers and revenue from levies and sale of land to the county government still unites the two traditional villages. It joins township and county governments in a number of development projects, including the one called North Stone. The villagers benefit from the location of industries on its administrative border as employers, but there is no special quota for them. The borders themselves are shifting. But the temple and festivals of the territorial guardian of the larger traditional village have become the most vivid collective activity and identification of the place, and the rotation of responsibility for them defines sub-units corresponding to pre-republican definitions. Compared with the coastal Fujian village, here the economic resources available to village officials through their administrative powers and contacts are possibly greater because of the proximity to a growing town. But they are not fed into either the traditional institutions or into collective organizations of the administrative village. Between them, the county, township and village administrators with their road construction and development projects are urbanizing parts of the traditional villages, displacing and reseparating the two lineages, while they in their turn retain or gain their own authority by redefinition and revitalization throwing up a leadership with its own authority.

There are three aspects of village administration as such. The first reflects the tax-collecting and other duties assigned by higher government and Party. The second reflects the career prospects and personal interests of its cadres, in both of which economic performance is the main indicator of success. The third reflects public service and leadership appreciated by fellow villagers. In both the villages in southern Fujian the first two heavily outweigh the third. The third has been redefined in terms of the traditional villages and their ritual definitions.

In the northern Yunnan basin and the Gansu valley there are far fewer possibilities of advancement in any one of these aspects of village administration and leadership. The settlements of two of the villages, one in each location, are small and scattered and include many households whose family history there is only four generations old. The definitions of even the two more compact and old villages are less sentient than the four villages we surveyed in southern Jiangsu and southern Fujian. The village administrations and small group leaders have more presence in Yunnan than they have in the two Gansu villages, but the initiative and power comes from the township or county. In Gansu, the administration of the villages was dormant. The traditional or naturalizing definition of place in some of its settlements was focused on the slow reconstruction of small territorial temples. But a more vivid point of focus was an annual mountain gathering in a complex of temples being rebuilt with contributions from the whole valley, and from visitors as far off as the provincial city. Here a multi-village region seems to be a more important place than a village as a traditional unit of small natural settlements. Similarly, in the Yunnan basin, the sentient place seems to be the whole basin and the rebuilt Buddhist temples on its containing slopes, where women gather for the chanting of scriptures and the sharing of a feast several times a year.

The range of possibilities of what is a village to be found in just the ten included in our survey is as disconcerting as it is interesting. The only constant is the administrative village, the so-called "collective." But its substance and sentience for villagers depends on the size of its industrial enterprises and the way they are managed. In the two southern Jiangsu villages, the Communist tradition of collective management has been successful and the benefits expected from it include the provision of utilities and social insurance, as in none of the other villages. In the wealthier Anhui village, a village company is similarly identified with the collective but is a mix of private shareholding and administrative investment, of private management and local, public interest where "public" means a village collective which is far narrower than the dispersal of shareholders and the higher levels of administration which have invested in it. The poor neighboring village will soon be incorporated into it. Could this be a pioneer of what since 1992 has been heralded as the new form of shareholder village enterprises, and will they retain their local public service loyalties?

Whether or not they do retain a local public meaning in the fast-moving economic transformation of the Chinese countryside, these modern collective villages are the only ones of the ten in which there has been no renewal of traditional institutions. In them ancestral memories are celebrated domestically but not in public ceremonies. The temples and halls of their pre-republican past, though recorded in local histories and remembered by older villagers, have not been rebuilt.

In the two villages of southern Fujian, on the contrary, village temples and halls have been rebuilt and their festivals renewed. They now provide the most sentient definition of the village as a place, but the other "collective" definition has the substance of residual powers and opportunities for village cadres which it has in every village. The disparity between the two kinds of definition and activity of the village is also a disparity between two kinds of authority and two means of mobilizing material resources. The gap between the two is the space of informal power strategies and the ethics of human relations and responsibilities judged by the criteria of reciprocity and face. Informal power which uses these criteria for the gaining of authority works everywhere in administrative and other hierarchies, including the most substantial collective villages. But it appears more openly in places like southern Fujian where there are distinct sets of village institutions, only one of which is that of the administrative "collective" village.

In southern Jiangsu and southern Fujian, village definition of either kind was vivid. But in the villages we studied in northern Yunnan and eastern Gansu, beyond the small nucleated settlement there was a much weaker sense of "village," even where the administrative village was one of close settlements. No important village enterprises, but a close market town which is also the township capital, or else the ritual centers on mountain slopes which encompassed a region larger and more vaguely defined than the township were of rival importance to the "village." The same appears to be true of the village in Sichuan studied by Pamela Leonard. A large township enterprise was yet another local focus of support and opportunity for the Gansu villagers.

But if the village is always a two-faced administration, representing for villagers both their own place and the state, other relations to township, market and ritual locality spread these definitions of place into an even greater disjunction. The local offices of central government, branches of central banks, and state grain and tax warehouses are the foci of what villagers say is not their own responsibility but that of the state. These are funded by involuntary levies and controlled by higher authorities, whereas the ritual events and buildings are funded by voluntary donations. Villagers are more active in remedying their own destinies than they are in relation to what most of them and village and township cadres see as higher government business, before which they act negatively or passively. Negatively, villagers usually expected little help from and wanted to be left alone by agents of the state. Passively, they expected to be taxed, but complained if they saw the taxes as unfair or ill-used. Again passively, they expected to be helped, particularly in the construction of roads, sanitation, irrigations systems and large-scale environmental improvements and responsibilities. Even a group of township cadres, eating and working in their compound said such things were the business of government (*zhengfu*): "if the government has no money to invest, what can we do about it?"

Conclusion

I do not want to conclude with this note of ambivalence in relation to the state. Preoccupation with the question of whether a civil society might be emerging in China has tended to ignore the countryside and has fixed attention on the extent to

Table 2.1

Second-order Multifunctional Place Definition

	Traditional		Modern collective (strong township connection)	Corporate (weak township connection)	Convergence of T & M	Divergence of T & M
	Village	Region				
1.	+		−			!
2.	+			−		!
3.		−	−			!
4.		−				!
5.	−	−			!	
6.		−	−		!	
7.			+			
8.						
9.				+		
10.				−		

+ = strong sentience. − = weak sentience ! = yes.
1 = inland Fujian village, 2 = coastal Fujian village, 3&4 = Gansu villages, 5&6 = Yunnan villages, 7&8 = Jiangsu villages, 9&10 = Anhui villages

which society has been penetrated by the state. The state-society symbiosis which others have described is I think still too fixated upon the question of how much the "state" is involved and ensconced in emergent economic relations and organizations, or conversely how autonomous of state government they are becoming.

I hope I have shown that at the level of second-order senses of place and their institutional or discursive definitions beyond households there are two sets of institutions in which place and its leadership is identified, only one of which is that of sub-government administration. The other is a bottom-up hierarchy of "traditional" authority and reputation for cultural knowledge and status. Both are undergoing transformation by processes of political change and economic growth. Politically aided private enterprise is generating hierarchies of central places of marketing, contracting and credit. Horizontal relations of personal connection are more important for the great majority of households, touching hierarchies which reach into these state and other institutions at various points. They co-exist with impersonal claims upon or complaints about government and with other equally impersonal relations of sale and purchase. They also enter the more personal institutions of celebration and enjoyment of organized activities, in particular those of local festivals and sports.

I hope I have also shown that there is a great, perhaps surprising range of possibilities, which can be summarized in Table 2.1.

In presenting this table, let me state its worth. It is a scheme only, a shell with far less of the substance which my own introductory orientation requires and the illustrative examples I have cited themselves suggest. More particular studies of leadership, authority, and respect from below, such as those by Leonard and

Flower and from above at township and county level such as those by Oi must be consulted and undertaken to provide a fuller picture of any one "village" and its places. When this is done it may be that this table will have to be modified, perhaps beyond recognition. In the meantime, however, the table does suggest a range of possibilities, not only in the cells which are filled by the villages in our survey, but also by the unfilled cells.

Notes

1. This was a project financed by the UK Economic and Social Research Council to enquire into rural social support arrangements and the transformation of local traditions. I am most grateful to the ESRC and to my colleagues in the research, Chang Xiangqun, Guo Xiaolin, Lu Feiyun, Pan Jianxiong, Qian Wenbao, Shen Guanbao, Wang Mingming, and Zhu Weimin. The villages were in five different provinces: Gansu, Anhui, Jiangsu, Fujian, and Yunnan.

2. The distinction between two kinds of history is a subject requiring far more elaboration than I can offer here. I have started such an elaboration based on Joseph Levenson's distinction between absolute and relative histories, in Feuchtwang (1992).

3. I am indebted to John Flower and to Pamela Leonard for showing me a copy of the latter's dissertation. It is an ethnography which with marvelous detail and direct quotation demonstrates the way in which political, moral and physical environment must be jointly treated, as they are in the villagers' stories as they themselves tell them.

4. My thanks go to Guo Xiaolin for this information.

5. Our surveys were samples randomly selected from the household records of administrative villages. They included a question "Are you proud of the village?" followed by asking for reasons. The answers to this question are the source for these and other comments on how the villagers felt about their village, and whether or not they identified it with the administrative leadership.

References

Chan, Anita; Madsen, Richard; and Unger, Jonathan. 1992. *Chen Village under Mao and Deng.* Berkeley: University of California Press.

Duara, Prasenjit. 1988. *Culture, Power, and the State; Rural North China, 1900–1942.* Stanford: Stanford University Press.

Dutton, Michael. 1992. *Policing and Punishment in China: From Patriarchy to "the People."* Cambridge: Cambridge University Press.

Feuchtwang, Stephan. 1974. *An Anthropological Analysis of Chinese Geomancy.* Vientiane: Vithagna.

Feuchtwang, Stephan. 1992. *The Imperial Metaphor; Popular Religion in China.* London: Routledge.

Johnson, Graham E. 1993. "Family Strategies and Economic Transformation in Rural China: Some Evidence from the Pearl River Delta." In Deborah Davis and Stevan Harrell, eds., *Chinese Families in the Post-Mao Era.* Berkeley: University of California Press.

Leonard, Pamela. 1994. *The Political Landscape of a Sichuan Village,* D.Phil. dissertation, University of Cambridge, England.

Oi, Jean. 1989. *State and Peasant in Contemporary China; The Political Economy of Village Government.* Berkeley: University of California Press.

Siu, Helen. 1990. "Recycling Tradition: Culture, History and Political Economy in the Chrysanthemum Festivals of South China." In *Comparative Study of Society and History*, pp. 765–794.

Wilkerson, James Russell. 1990. *Other Islands of Chinese History and Religion.* Ph.D. dissertation, University of Virginia.

Zhonggong zhongyang wenxian yanjiushi and Guowuyuan fazhan yanjiu zhongxin, eds. 1991. *Xinshiqi nongye he nongcun gongzuo zhongyao wenxian* (Important Materials on Agricultural and Village Work in the New Period). Beijing: Zhongyang wenxian chubanshe.

3

The Role of Common Property Regimes in Managing Common-Pool Resources in China Today

Margaret A. McKean

Socialist China collectivized the ownership of many kinds of goods and resources, but China is now going through a process of de-collectivization and privatization of ownership over some of these goods and resources. China's experience raises crucial questions for us all—not just for China, not just for economies moving from socialism toward the market—about what kinds of property rights institutions are appropriate and desirable for what kinds of resources. There is also debate within China about what to de-collectivize and how fast this process should occur, raising at least the theoretical possibility that China, and others, may make serious mistakes in remapping property rights institutions. Indeed, "privatization," whatever that means, is a world-wide fad right now, not just in former socialist economies. And as with all fads, there is a risk of misdiagnosing past errors and overextending our application of the lessons we think we are learning.

My own fear is that shared ownership of some resources is indeed appropriate but we leave this possibility out of our discussions of de-collectivization and privatization. That is, we often misconstrue what "privatization" ought to include—we say "privatization" when we mean "individuation" and thus overlook the possibility of shared (collective!) ownership that is also private. I believe there is a category of resources—called "common-pool resources" (Ostrom 1990; McKean and Ostrom 1995; McKean 1992; 1996a)—for which shared private ownership is often quite appropriate. Several chapters in this volume deal specifically with such resources—Vermeer on irrigation, Morton and Grimble on groundwater management, and Ho on grazing lands—and it is the purpose of this chapter to comment on the arrangements China applies to such resources. However, many of the terms used in the literature about China as if they have distinct meanings—collective, communal, cooperative, common—have still other technical meanings in the literature on property rights, and to confound matters further we treat these in our everyday usage essentially as synonyms with little distinction at all among them. So I feel compelled to begin with a discussion of definitions, simply to ensure that my own usage is clear in the discussion to follow.

Definitions

I will begin by illustrating the distinction between types of goods (inherent characteristics of resources) and types of property rights (institutions that humans create to define and defend our claims to goods). Unfortunately, we routinely speak of private, collective, and public *goods, and* of private, collective, and public *property*, and this practice of using the same troika of adjectives to refer to types of goods and to types of property manages to keep all discussion about goods and property seriously confused. It would not be so bad if we always created private property rights for private goods, collective rights for collective goods, and within that larger category public property for public goods, but we are not this tidy in our habits. Indeed, since many resources carry the attributes of both private and public goods, it is impossible for us to map our property rights institutions onto resources as neatly as we might want to. Goods are messy, so property rights are necessarily messy, and because we invent property rights institutions and can argue about what is desirable or appropriate, we make property rights even messier than they need to be. Worst of all, economists—who really should know better—are among the worst offenders in using the term "common property" (which ought then to refer to a kind of property rights arrangement) for "collective goods" (either "common-pool goods" or "public goods" in the typology below), particularly collective goods to which *no* property rights at all are attached. They thus simultaneously commit three sins: the confusion of property with goods (rights with resources), the confusion of property with the absence of property, and the conflation of common-pool goods with public goods.

Types of Goods or Resources

Economists have long agreed that the two most important attributes of goods are the degrees of *"excludability"* and *"subtractibility"* with which they can be used. If we allow both of these attributes to vary along a continuum we automatically get the following four-way typology. There is strong consensus on the significance and accuracy of this four-way division, although there has been some debate as to the best labels for each of the four cells, and there has also been an evolution in perception of where actual examples of resources fall in the typology as we learn more about the limits in different resource systems.

Excludability refers to the ease with which one can exclude potential users

	Exclusion easy	Exclusion difficult or costly (collective goods)
Subtractible (rival in consumption)	Private goods trees, sheep, fish chocolate cake	Common <-> pool goods forest, pasture, fishery air quality, water quality any environmental sink over time geo <-> stationary orbits
Non <-> subtractible (non <-> rival in consumption)	Club or toll goods Kiwanis club camraderie	Pure public goods defense, TV broadcasts lighthouse beams an environmental sink at a given instant a given level of public health a given level of inflation a given level of noise

Chart 3.1 **Type of Goods, by Physical Attributes**

from consuming a good (note that "goods" include unattractive or negatively valued "bad goods," which we often call "bads"). Items that are small, portable, and easily locked up are obviously excludable. Goods that are large and have fuzzy boundaries (both stationary goods like a forest and mobile or fugitive goods like a fish population) are much more difficult to exclude potential users from. Some non-excludable goods are in fact ubiquitous (air quality, public safety, educational level in the labor force) and consumption of them may actually be involuntary; that is, it is both impossible to exclude someone else from consuming it, and it is also impossible to prevent oneself from consuming it. Non-excludable goods are problematic because there is very little incentive to provide or maintain goods that can be consumed by people who do not have to contribute to (or pay for) producing them to get them.

Subtractibility refers to the degree to which consuming a good leaves less behind for others to consume. Subtractible goods are rival in consumption—whatever I consume is no longer available to you or any other of my rival consumers. Non-subtractible goods are those that do not diminish in supply even when consumed. We once referred to air and water as "free" goods or as "infinite" goods because we thought they were non-subtractible; and in fact any environmental sink (an ecosystem used as a receptacle for pollution) is self-cleaning up to some point. But we have since learned that environmental sinks have limited capacity, that air and water and soil have varying quality levels, and that it is possible to "use up" nature's cleaning services. Subtractible goods are problematic because they can be depleted. Increasingly we discover that goods that are non-subtractible at a given moment are in fact subtractible over time.

The four cells of this two-by-two typology contain four different kinds of goods. *Private goods* are excludable and subtractible and thus non-problematic: those who do not pay for them cannot have them, those who produce them can charge a price for them and get it so they will produce them, and thus those who want them and can pay for them can have them. Private goods get produced and maintained. *Toll goods* are non-subtractible but because they are also excludable they are non-problematic: those who want them will arrange for their production and consume them gleefully. I prefer to call all of the non-excludable goods *collective goods*, but as the chart shows these come in two major types. *Pure public goods* are non-excludable and thus pose serious problems of provision and maintenance. But because they are non-subtractible, we can rest assured that whatever does get produced does not disappear. The most worrisome category of goods is *common-pool goods*, which are non-excludable and thus may not get produced or maintained, and which are also subtractible, meaning that whatever we do manage to produce is rapidly beset with problems of depletion. If life were all private goods and toll goods, we would have few problems. But in fact, many of the things we want are pure public goods or common-pool goods and are difficult to produce. Worst of all, as we reach resource limits in many areas, we are finding that many things we thought were pure public goods (non-subtractible in consumption) are in fact subtractible, so the most problematic set of common-pool goods is steadily growing.

Types of Property Rights

The nature of a good is an inherent physical characteristic regardless of the institutions humans devise for allocating that good.[1] We must remember that all four types of goods exist in abundance in all societies, regardless of the property rights institutions those societies choose to create. Thus private *goods* abound in China, always have and always will, even if private *property rights* were virtually extinguished at certain points. A log, a toothbrush, a fish, a dumpling, a printing press—these are excludable and subtractible and thus private goods by their very nature even if a regime insists on having five thousand people own them jointly or on having the government own them in trust for future use. Similarly, groundwater basins, grazing lands, forest ecosystems, and irrigation systems are common-pool goods (subtractible in consumption but with difficulties in exclusion) by their very nature, regardless of the property rights arrangements we create (or fail to create!) for them. Whether a regime assigns parcelled individual rights to plots of forest or holds a forest as state property, the forest itself remains a common-pool resource by its very nature.

But property institutions are human inventions. The "privateness" of property rights refers to the clarity, specificity, and especially the exclusivity of the rights, and not to the identity of the rights-holder (see Locke 1965; De Alessi 1980; 1982; Libecap 1989). Rights that are unclear or non-specific can be considered vague, at most as private rights-in-the-making, inchoate. Rights that are clear and specific but still non-exclusive can be regarded as public rights.[2] Scholars who have designed taxonomies to classify property rights arrangements usually come up with a four-fold division: open access (no property rights arrangements at all), private property, common property, and public property (Berkes *et al.* 1989; Feeny *et al.* 1990; Bromley and Cernea 1989; Ostrom 1990). This four-way taxonomy creates the regrettable impression that common property and private property are mutually exclusive, and I believe it conflates property rights arrangements with property owner. I prefer instead the following list that separates these two dimensions (adapted from McKean 1992):

No Owner

> (a) unowned non <-> property (or open <-> access) to which no one currently has rights and from which no potential user can be excluded (such as the high seas, the upper atmosphere, or unclaimed lands);

Public Owner (Government)

> (b) public property held in trust for the public by the state to which the general public has some access (national parks, national forests, public buildings, municipal parks, city streets, highways, a nation's territorial seas, and many of its waterways);

> (c) [private] state property is essentially the exclusive and therefore *private* property of government bodies, to which the general public does *not* have access: many government office buildings, typewriters and desks in government offices, lands off limits to the public, and state <-> run enterprises that sell their products.

Private Owner

> (d) jointly owned private property whose individual co <-> owners may sell their shares at will without consulting other co <-> owners (some agricultural cooperatives, business partnerships, joint stock corporations);

> (e) common property, or jointly owned private property that all co <-> owners may simultaneously agree to sell by an agreed <-> upon voting rule but whose individual co <-> owners can sell, trade, or lease their shares to others only in accordance with rules laid down by the group (this provision creates the possibility that individual co <-> owners may be unable to sell their shares, or may forfeit their shares upon change in residence, or may acquire shares through application but without purchase);

> (f) individually owned private property whose individual owners have full and complete ("fee <-> simple" or "freehold") ownership except as attenuated by government regulation.

Chart 3.2 Type of Property Rights, Categorized by Type of Owner

The scheme above distinguishes between jointly owned private property and common property with greater restrictions on the transferability of shares only because there is so much variety in the real world on this particular feature, and because systems that restrict transferability of shares are often very insistent about it. But obviously the more flexible the rules placed on transferability of shares, the more closely common property begins to resemble jointly owned private property. This is tantamount to saying that well-defined common property regimes with flexible arrangements about transferability of shares are essentially business partnerships or firms. We frequently find that people think in evolutionary terms about property rights arrangements and assume that common property is a pre-industrial form, simpler than individual property and destined to be replaced by private property. But in fact, common property regimes often exist alongside individual property regimes, indicating that people have made careful choices about what kinds of resources are best managed in common and which ones are best managed individually. Rather than thinking of common property regimes as quaint traditional arrangements for nomadic pastoralists and other benighted pre-industrials who will "modernize" and eventually adopt individual property, then, we must acknowledge that common property regimes are fundamentally similar to quintessentially industrial and complex forms.

What is important in acknowledging these distinctions is to recognize that most of the permutations and combinations of resource types, property rights types, and rights-holders theoretically exist. We have to recognize these distinctions in order to think freely and creatively about new combinations. In particular, public entities can own private goods, private entities can produce public goods (and public bads in great abundance), private owners can recognize public rights in their property, and public owners can treat their property as private and ban public access and claims. Surprisingly, there is very little agreement about which of these combinations and permutations are wise or efficient. There is overwhelming consensus on only two points: (1) that private goods are best held as private property, and (2) that individually parcelled private property is an inadequate arrangement for non-excludable goods/bads (common-pool goods and pure public goods). There is also consensus, though weaker, on the efficiencies and potential for corruption that inevitably follow from vesting ownership in any entity other than a single individual with a central nervous system (e.g., collective or government ownership). Thus there is considerable controversy over when it improves matters (whatever one uses as the criterion for improvement) to vest ownership in collectivities or public entities. And we are left with a gnawing problem: what kind of property rights institution do we design when we *know* that individual private property is inadequate—that is, when we are concerned with common-pool goods or public goods rather than with private goods?

Common property regimes may be an important part of the answer. They offer a way of privatizing the rights to things without dividing the things into pieces, and are thus a way to divide and allocate the flow of skimmable or harvestable "income" (interest) from a capital stock (principal) without parcelling the stock itself. Thus common property offers us a way to leave an interactive resource system intact and apportion individual rights to the resource flows produced by that system. Leaving the stock whole is obviously desirable when the resource system in question is more productively managed as an intact whole rather than in uncoordinated bits and pieces. There is ample evidence that societies with both common and individual property use common property arrangements to give many individuals use rights but to manage the whole resource system as a single ecological unit (see McKean 1996b). Similarly, wherever coordination of individual use is important to maximizing long-term productivity of a resource—e.g., wherever competing and congested use patterns produce multiple negative externalities—common property regimes can be used to institutionalize mechanisms to allow for necessary coordination. We need to remember that industrial societies make very heavy use of environmental resources, not only as inputs but also as receptacles and buffers for the noxious byproducts of production and final waste—as environmental sinks. The overuse of an environmental sink should be thought of as equivalent to depletion of natural cleaning services, and thus as the depletion of a common-pool resource over which careful coordination is highly desirable. The logical conclusion here is that as industrialization and population growth produce more externalities in resource use, we should find more, not less, need to resort to common property arrangements (see McKean 1996a, for more).

Logically, then, common property arrangements would make sense both in over-crowded pre-industrial countries under serious resource pressure, and in industrializing and industrial countries where externalities abound. In both such situations, there is great need for coordinating competing resource uses, and for negotiating mutual restraints on the extent of resource use. China offers all of these circumstances simultaneously, suggesting that common property arrangements would often be appropriate. But needing something does not mean that people do it. We could easily anticipate two very different outcomes in China. One is that the rich recent experience with collective forms of ownership and management might equip the Chinese to make "better" (more socially efficient) decisions about which goods should remain in government hands, which ones should be individualized, and which ones should be privatized but held in common by groups of individuals. If this is so, then we would predict that China will have lots of common property regimes in the making. The other possible outcome is that because collectivization was overused and handled so badly, people have reacted with a backlash against it and fear using it even when it might make a lot of sense. To an outsider like me, the last couple of decades in China look like a gigantic and very creative experiment in institutional design of all types, but I fear the results may not be undergoing systematic cataloguing or evaluation. Moreover, I fear that little of the discussion in China is inspired by a sensitivity to the distinctions among types of goods, property rights, and owners, and to the value of improving the "match" between property rights institutions and types of goods.

Collectives and Cooperatives As Property Rights Arrangements in China

For Production of Private Goods

In the lexicon of Chinese studies, collectives are government-directed enterprises that were the building blocks of the people's communes and remained after the dissolution of the communes. Cooperatives, in contrast, are locally-owned by shareholders (these can range from local residents, employees of the cooperative, municipalities and other government units, and even foreign investors as well) whose returns are commensurate with the size of their investment and whose investments can be withdrawn at will. They are fairly recent inventions, and in any case smaller and more likely to invite participation and possibly control by beneficiaries of the cooperative venture involved. Voluntarism is the crucial thing that makes cooperatives work where collectives did not, as many of the authors in this volume have noted (Stephan Feuchtwang, Pei Xiaolin, and Mark Selden in particular). Even if collectives rewarded contributions of labor with work points commensurate with the effort invested, that labor was not contributed voluntarily and workers did not have the option to work elsewhere. But both investors and workers in the new cooperatives possess what Hirschman (1970) calls the right of exit—both capital and labor are available to these cooperatives only on the basis of willing consent. Thus the cooperatives must produce returns and wages that satisfy their shareholders and workers or lose them.

Because collectives are government-directed, they would be comparable to state-owned enterprises elsewhere. And in fact, regardless of who owns the land on which they are built, the productive machinery, and the products they yield, collectives (and cooperatives for that matter) in China today are generally engaged in the production of private goods: subtractible excludable items that are usually regarded elsewhere as most efficiently produced by private entrepreneurs and firms. Thus most observers would see collectives as appropriate targets for privatization (though in fact many have resisted, and the state is not willing to have all of them disappear).

But shareholder cooperatives, on the other hand, are already a form of private property akin to the private firm, or to jointly owned private property or common property as identified in Chart 3.2. The cooperatives, then, do not contradict the general trend toward the liberalization of the economy and the growth of private property rights. Pei Xiaolin (elsewhere in this volume) makes the intriguing and convincing argument that the village unit—which has in fact been responsible for the creation of most of the highly successful cooperatives accounting for rapid growth in China in recent years—is a firm. Even though there is no reason to think that residents in one village have any particular comparative technical advantage over another (skills in, say, the making of long-lasting light bulbs or the thoughtful design of leather handbags are not likely to be geographically concentrated), the village as a natural social unit (see Feuchtwang in this volume) does have a comparative advantage over some other assortment of persons in terms of social relations that minimize transaction costs. Thus the village can be transformed into a firm because of its comparative advantage as an organization.

China's experience with collectives, though unpleasant in many ways, may well have contributed to the ease with which villages can launch successful business operations. It appears from the case studies recounted in this book that most Chinese have learned quite selectively from their bad experience with collectivization. The idea of joint production or collaboration to capture economies of scale is still reasonable to most people even though people's communes demonstrated that one can go beyond the point where there are economies of scale. Rather, today's complaints and difficulties about collective approaches have to do with the continued involvement of government officials who will not suffer from the consequences of bad decisions (so continue to make decisions that are bad for others), and the failure to delegate sufficient control and jurisdiction to the lower layers of the organizational hierarchy. If the cooperatives are in need of further privatization it might only be to buy out shareholders who are government entities or to withdraw investments and labor from the cooperatives that government entities sponsor and to launch new ones without government involvement (see Selden in this volume). Cooperation without government interference remains a lively possibility in China, but cooperation in the shadow of probable government interference is something people do not feel enthusiasm for.

For Production of Common-Pool Goods

There are also collectives and cooperatives that own and manage common-pool resources rather than private goods. I am perfectly in favor of private ownership of common-pool goods if this means converting from ownership by public (government) entities to ownership by private *self-governing groups* of individuals (e.g., jointly held private property or common property). But because it is either physically impossible or will generate massive externalities to parcel a common-pool resource system into segments, it would not be appropriate to convert their ownership to *individual* private property. Shareholders' cooperatives on common-pool resources are in effect common property regimes (those at the "jointly owned private property" end of the scale). And China clearly possesses an organizational legacy of past experience with collaborative arrangements, both in pre-1949 China and under socialism, that could be valuable in designing successful common property arrangements for common-pool arrangements today.

China has some of the world's longest experience with irrigation, both in arid areas where scarce water needs to be widely distributed and in wet areas where wet-rice agriculture requires that water be in the right place in the right time in the right quantities. China thus has some of the largest and oldest irrigation systems on the planet, and much familiarity with the need to nest or layer small systems within the larger systems that they draw from (Ostrom 1992; Tang 1992). Cooperation among individuals is efficient here—individuals can make their own arrangements only at the cost of great duplication in equipment and possibly not at all—so collectivization under socialism need not have been a bad idea where irrigation was concerned. But socialism undermined sensible water pricing, concentrated at too high a level the authority over different layers in the system, and pursued an ideologically driven and uneconomic enthusiasm for infrastructure (e.g., irrigation) even where it was not needed. Another very serious problem, one that predates socialism but persists in spite of market reforms today, is the use of compulsory corvée labor (paid, but at pitifully low rates) rather than market-rate wage labor freely volunteered (Vermeer, this volume).

The current arrangements under de-collectivization for irrigation and groundwater management (Vermeer, and Morton and Grimble, this volume) continue to be confounded by either inability or unwillingness to raise user fees to anything like the levels that would reduce overuse and pay for investments and maintenance or to punish non-paying water users. There is heavy local pressure not to raise fees sufficiently to cover costs (the 1985 Water Fee Law seems to carry no force against this rent-seeking), and water managers are reluctant to deny water to people who pay no fee at all. But without enforcement of penalties for violators, no system will work. By refusing to penalize cheaters, the current arrangement manages to *undo* one of the most important advantages that common property arrangements can bring to the management of common pool resources. Mutual agreements to exercise restraint in resource use and punish overuse are a way to create exclusion where otherwise there would be a serious problem of non-excludability. That is, this system creates the opportunity to convert non-excludability into excludability—but the managers of the system, no doubt in collusion with the cheaters, do not utilize this opportunity. Unless they do, nothing will work.

Local water users are happy with low fees, of course, only because government subsidies are readily available to take care of costs not covered by those fees. I suspect that local water users would be considerably more willing to pay higher fees that cover costs and provide precious irrigation water if subsidies were not forthcoming. And in that case they would suddenly become much more militant enforcers of penalties against the free-riders in their midst, cutting off water supply to irrigators who do not pay their fees. With increased fees, water users would also become more discriminating in their use of water and might discover more ways to conserve water. They would support only the irrigation systems that were actually worth having. Socialism was certainly responsible for instituting state subsidies for water projects, but China will have the same difficulties getting rid of these subsidies as all countries that have them. People who have to pay user fees would much rather have most of the costs of provisioning covered by the public treasury, and once those subsidies are in place it takes a heroic act of political will to overcome well-organized lobbies of rent-seekers and their political friends, whether in China or in California's central valley or Idaho's potato plantations. Water projects seem to produce this political dynamic more readily than almost anything else.

The irrigation system fed by groundwater from boreholes in Inner Mongolia (Morton and Grimble) seems to be plagued with similar problems: the farmers who receive water apparently do not have control over volume or frequency, and although they pay very high electricity fees for pumping, the progressive schedule for water fees that was scheduled to be enforced in 1993 (and might have encouraged water conservation) was "frozen" and water fees have not risen to appropriate levels. Fees are charged per *mu* of land, which may be an appropriate surrogate for amount of water received, and may even be high enough to induce conserving behavior, but if farmers have no control over volume or frequency of water received, then they cannot calibrate their own demand for water to the price they must pay. Again, shareholder cooperatives and common property systems need to be able to control both the use/production of their product and the contributions in fees or labor that their owners/beneficiaries/customers (who are mostly the same people) contribute.

There are some promising developments in the recent experience of reform. First, decollectivization seems to have promoted a differentiation between irrigation systems that were never needed in the first place (or badly done) and allowed to fall into disrepair, and irrigation systems of such importance to their beneficiaries that they began cooperating on their own to restore them. Indeed, in the current atmosphere of reform it is permissible for people to form their own shareholder cooperatives without government involvement (e.g., without government entities owning any of the shares). Thus owner-investor-beneficiary-customers who are impatient or dissatisfied with enterprises sponsored by the collective or higher units of government sometimes get desperate enough to launch their own wholly private enterprises. In some instances these private enterprises produce public goods (roads, reservoirs, railway tracks) that benefit far greater numbers of people than just the owner-investors, by becoming the foundation for additional economic development in the region (Feuchtwang and Selden in this volume).[3] Vermeer, and Morton and Grimble tell us about arrangements for irrigation and groundwater that display growing local independence: many voluntary shareholding cooperatives for irrigation and newly independent *gachas* which have in some sense recaptured Mongolian-style village rule. Of course, it is the private shareholding cooperatives that most closely resemble the kind of common property arrangement that could be expected to work here.

Many of us appreciate quickly that water—irrigation systems, groundwater basins, river systems and the like—are appropriate settings for common property management, but we are less inclined to think this way for resources on the land that are fixed in place and ought to be amenable to subdivision or fencing just as cultivated fields are. What we need to recognize where land is concerned is that where the location of use must move around within a resource system, we need cooperative arrangements to govern those rotations, and the extent of resource extraction at any one point. Animals cannot graze in one fixed location forever but must move from season to season and from year to year on a very large pasture system. In arid lands, variable rainfall will add further uncertainty and movement to the arrangement. We want trees every year but it takes a forest

20–50 years to grow trees, so our point of use must change from year to year. In effect, wherever we must use fallowing and rotations on land, we need arrangements similar to those that help us with rotations and calibrated removal of water in irrigation and groundwater management too. This is why many landed resources are also common-pool goods amenable to governance through common property arrangements.

At first glance, the story of changing property rights arrangements on the grasslands (Ho, this volume) suggests that both collectivization and decollectivization were failures, leading one to wonder what is left that might possibly improve the quality and productivity of these lands. In fact, collectivization of the grasslands during the 1950s was bad not because collective approaches to grazing are wrong-headed—they are not—but because ownership was transferred to too high a level to give local users any sense of control over their resources. Both their lands and their decision-making prerogatives were essentially confiscated by the state. Collectivization was also damaging because it destroyed the fabric of functional traditional arrangements for resource use where these had existed. Environmental degradation occurred on these lands because much acreage was converted to cultivation, an entirely inappropriate use based on ideological preference rather than sound economic or ecological analysis.

As part of market reforms sweeping China, de-collectivization was then tried. In 1985 a new rangeland law permitted grasslands-owning collectives to issue long-term leases to small collectives or groups of households or individuals. This was expected to arrest desertification by giving lessees increased incentives to restore the land, but it failed to produce this outcome. On paper it would appear that the policies are in place to create vibrant shareholder cooperatives in grazing —common property systems that ought to work very well if they incorporate traditional practices on these lands (with modifications and new restraints made necessary by increased population in the area). There are private property rights in land use, enforcement institutions (grassland police!), and even rules of resource use now. And grassland management stations (agricultural extension offices, really) have been restored, which might help with the monitoring of both behavior and environmental conditions, thus improving the quality of information upon which successful collective action depends (Hardin 1982). But desertification continues because in fact none of these new institutions are credible. The *de facto* arrangement on the Ningxia grasslands is still no property rights at all: unfettered open access by herders who are not convinced that they can rely on these new institutions, and who are not free in any case to create their own resource management rules.

It is in forest management that reform seems to have led to the most promising common property arrangements. The Chinese seemed to have learned fast that forests are not private goods but are really common-pool goods where parcelled and fragmented management is inefficient.[4] The Chinese first experimented with applying the household responsibility system of long-term lease-holds to forests, expecting that the new individual near-owners of forest plots would afforest and maintain their forests in healthy condition. But they soon discovered that continued deforestation was the result. Of course, in addition to too much fragmentation creating externalities and coordination problems, another fundamental flaw in this policy was the uncertainty of it all. Uncertain or insecure property rights are little better than none at all and produce short-term maximizing behavior rather than long-term maximizing behavior. So of course the new owner/lessees, who were not sure they could trust their leases to last, cut all the timber that they could for quick sale. The Chinese reaction to this is a return to collective management of forests but this time through shareholder cooperatives. It is fascinating to me that the slogans used here—"distributing benefit, no distributing forest," "distributing share, no distributing hill"—correspond precisely to the way in which common property systems allocate individual rights to resource flows without parcelling the resource stock that produces those flows. As with the other common property cooperatives, though, problems concerning the autonomy of the cooperative over its activities persist.

The major problems in all four of these cases are similar. The fundamental difficulties are continued government interference (thus a lack of autonomous control) in resource use rules, user fees, and treatment of free riders, and lack of serious support for enforcing the property rights in resources that now exist on paper. As a group, the contributions in this volume create the distinct impression that the Chinese people have not reacted to their vacillating experiences with collectivization with an unwise or undiscriminating backlash against all forms of collective effort. Rather, they do seem to know when cooperation can improve results, when villages can act as firms, when shareholder cooperatives can produce private goods and also manage common pool natural resources. The problems that remain, it seems to me, are those that government causes and that people will have to demand that government solve: the government needs to enforce rather than ignore the property rights it acknowledges on paper, and to stop interfering in production and pricing decisions.

Notes

1. The nature of a good is susceptible to human manipulation in one way, in that techno-logical change can alter our ability to exclude people from using the good or enhance our ability to monitor use. Thus infra-red photography enables us to discover drift-net fishing fleets operating at night on the high seas, sophisticated chemical analysis permits us to fingerprint oil spillage and trace the offending bilge to its ship of origin, and scramblers and descramblers can convert television broadcasts from non-excludable goods into excludable ones.

2. Thus when the owning entity grants members of the general public some sort of a claim that might range from entry to brief occupancy and sometimes even to unconditional use, the owning entity is creating some sort of public right. Yet those rights can be revoked, or the criteria for eligibility altered, by the owning entity. Thus a restaurant or a store that is

entirely privately owned grants the general public the right to wander in and out to examine the menu and merchandise and becomes in some sense a public space just as much as any government-owned museum that is open to the general public with or without an admission fee. Thus regulations in the United States that limit smoking often apply not just to publicly owned buildings but often to privately-owned public spaces like restaurants and movie theaters.

3. Russell Hardin (1982) would call these groups of investors "k-groups"—with "k" being the number within a latent group of "n" individuals all sharing the same interest who are so interested in producing a certain outcome that they take on the task themselves even without the support of the rest of the group, knowing that the outcome will also benefit the "n-k" individuals who did not contribute.

4. The program for the auctioning of barren lands has resulted in individual rather than cooperative purchase, for a song, of very large amounts of land that the individual buyer and employees then afforest, usually with fruit trees. Individual ownership works here because the lands bought are large, large enough to internalize the externalities that would result from smaller plots. And the lands can be large only because the land is so degraded that it is very cheap. Once the new fruit orchards take hold, this land will become a very valuable asset to its owners, but at the same time the fact that it will be covered in vegetation means it will also provide public goods in the form of watershed management, erosion control, and even microclimate protection; see Meng Yongqing (1995).

References

Berkes, Fikret, *et al.* 1989. "The Benefits of the Commons," *Nature*, no. 340 (July), pp. 91–93.

Bromley, Daniel W. and Michael M. Cernea. 1989. "The Management of Common Property Natural Resources: Some Conceptual and Operational Fallacies." Washington, DC: World Bank Discussion Papers no. 57.

De Alessi, Louis. 1980. "The Economics of Property Rights: A Review of the Evidence." *Research in Law and Economics*, no. 2, pp. 1–47.

———. 1982. "On the Nature and Consequences of Private and Public Enterprises." *Minnesota Law Review*, no. 67 (October), pp. 191–209.

Feeny, David, *et al.* 1990. "The Tragedy of the Commons: Twenty-Two Years Later." *Human Ecology*, no. 18, pp. 1–19.

Hardin, Russell. 1982. *Collective Action*. Baltimore and London: Johns Hopkins University Press for Resources for the Future.

Hirschman, Albert O. 1970. *Exit, Voice, and Loyalty*. Cambridge: Harvard University Press.

Libecap, Gary D. 1989. *Contracting for Property Rights*. New York: Cambridge University Press.

Locke, John. 1965. "On Property: Chapter V in the Second Treatise (An Essay Concerning the True Origin, Extent, and End of Civil Government)." In *Two Treatises of Government* (any edition), paragraphs 25–51.

McKean, Margaret A. 1992. "Success on the Commons: A Comparative Examination of Institutions for Common Property Resource Management." *Journal of Theoretical Politics*, no. 4 (July), pp. 247–282.

———. 1996a. "Common Property: What Is It, What Is It Good For, and What Makes It Work?" In Clark Gibson; Margaret McKean; and Elinor Ostrom, eds., *Communal Management of Forest Resources*, chapter 2. Community Forestry. Forests, Trees, and People Programme Phase II, Working Paper #3. Food and Agriculture Organization of the United Nations.

————. 1996b. "Common Property Regimes as a Solution to Problems of Scale and Linkage." In Susan B. Hanna; Carl Folke; and Karl-Göran Mäler, eds., *Rights to Nature*. Washington, DC: Island Press.

McKean, Margaret and Elinor Ostrom. 1995. "The Importance of Common Property Regimes for Managing Forest Resources." *Unasylva*, vol. 46, no. 180 (January), pp. 3–15.

Meng, Yongqing. 1995. "China's Collective Forest Tenure Reform and Barren Land in Auction." Paper delivered at the International Conference on Chinese Rural Collectives and Voluntary Organizations, Leiden University, January.

Ostrom, Elinor. 1990. *Governing the Commons: The Evolution of Institutions for Collective Action*. Cambridge: Cambridge University Press.

————. 1992. *Crafting Institutions for Self-Governing Irrigation Systems*. San Francisco: Institute for Contemporary Studies.

Tang, Shui Yan. 1992. *Institutions and Collective Action: Self-Governance in Irrigation*. San Francisco: Institute for Contemporary Studies.

Part II

Economic Relations and Organization

4

The Collective Foundation for Rapid Rural Industrialization

Jean C. Oi

Whether an independent economic elite will emerge in China's countryside with market reforms is at the heart of debates about the re-emergence of civil society and peasant-state relations. Those who argue that there has been a major shift in power from redistributors (cadres) to producers foresee the rise of a new economic elite of private entrepreneurs (Nee 1989). The rise of an independent economic elite is also implicit and sometimes explicit in the view that China's rural economic growth is due to privatization or "hidden privatization." Writing about the spectacular growth of China's rural economy, a number of observers have lumped all rural firms together as "non-state firms," (e.g., McMillan and Naughton 1992), portrayed them as "semi-private," or used them to indicate a "capitalist revolution" in China (this view is most clearly articulated in Minxin Pei 1994, especially Chapter 3).

Without question, a growing private sector exists; some township and village enterprises are indeed "fake collectives"—using only the collective label for protection and economic benefit (Liu Yaling 1992). But to suggest that all rural industry is partially or secretly "private" misses the essential character of the process that has spurred China's rapid rural industrialization. Such characterizations misrepresent the character of these enterprises and misidentify the crucial actors in the process of China's economic reforms. Especially in the early to mid-1980s, when China's rural economy started its rapid growth, prospective private entrepreneurs—with the memory of the persecution of private enterprise during the Maoist period still fresh in their minds—were still unsure of the political winds and whether policies would change. As in other countries, when the risks or costs are too great for private individuals, it was the state, in this case, China's local governments, that had to step in and assume the entrepreneurial role and start rural industry (the classic statement is by Alexander Gershenkron, 1962). Rather than following the path of privatization, China's government-led industrial growth suggests an alternative to privatization for successful economic reform in Leninist systems.

It is similarly misleading to suggest that there has been no shift in the distribution of power and therefore that cadres retain a monopoly on power in China's country-side. Some may associate the term *local state corporatism* with this view, but such characterization misunderstands the intent of the term (for a short statement of local state corporatism see Oi 1992). In areas where there is local state corporatism, the cadres tend to be powerful, and in some places they may be quite authoritarian, such as in Daqiuzhuang. However, *local state corporatism makes no assumptions about cadre power; nor does it preclude successful private enterprise.* On the contrary, as the reforms progress, particularly after the later 1980s, in areas that were previously based on the growth of collectively owned rural enterprises, cadres have started to encourage private enterprise as well. Local state corporatism highlights the *corporate nature of management*, not the issue of who has power. Control over resources determines power, not any particular political configuration.

Cadres no longer *automatically* exercise a monopoly on power nor can they command obedience. Both now depend not on office, but on whether that office still has resources to control, and the ability of individual cadres to mobilize resources. Those that still control resources, such as those who run successful village enterprises, can use that power. Those that do not have resources can still give orders, but it is unclear whether they will be obeyed or whether they will be viewed as powerful. It can no longer be assumed that cadres have power, but it can also not be assumed that with the market reforms, cadres will automatically lose power. As the following article makes clear, ". . . the shift to market allocation per se has no predictable consequences for the allocation of power and income . . . " (Walder 1996).

Local state corporatism describes *one arrangement* of economic and political power that has led to successful rural industrialization. It does not claim to be the only model of China's growth nor does it assume to be the best. It is simply an analysis of the experience of those areas in China's countryside that have industrialized with collectively owned industry, where the collective has remained strong, and where local officials take an activist role in directing development. It does not describe the situation where there are no village enterprises, where the economy is still predominantly agricultural. In such circumstances, it is likely that the cadres control few resources because the rights to the income from the agricultural harvest now belong to individual households. As a result, the cadres are likely to be relatively weak. The concept is also likely to need modification to describe adequately those villages where there is a strong private sector and few collectively owned enterprises.

There is more than one development model. Different areas have been able to develop rural industry with different types of management systems. Moreover, as time goes on, new forms are emerging that may depart from the descriptions presented here.[1] Nonetheless, while temporal, geographic, ethnic, as well as economic variations must be taken into account when trying to make generaliza-tions, it is useful to examine closely the pattern of development where local governments have played a leading role in the rapid growth of rural industry. This pattern is only one of many, but it is one that has been found in a significant number of rural areas in China, in the north as well as in the south.

This paper is an analysis of the role of the collective in the development of rural industry. The argument is that corporate management and use of communal funds and resources have allowed township and village enterprises to develop rapidly. Instead of operating as independent enterprises dependent on private funds and resources to engage in market production, township and village enterprises take advantage of community and governmental resources to create their competitive advantage.

A counterargument might be that China's rapid rural industrialization could just as easily have come from external reasons such as increased demand, mobility of labor, higher prices, etc. While that is possible—and my analysis does not preclude these factors—one must still understand how a locality is able to take advantage of a favorable market environment. One cannot assume that all rural areas have the resources and knowledge to participate in the market and interpret demand. Unlike agriculture, starting a factory requires considerable capital outlay, technical exper-tise, as well as access to and knowledge of the market. Elsewhere I have examined the different ways that producers in China obtain information and technology for market production (Oi 1994). One finding is that, while there is variation depending on product type and also the resources of individual factories, in almost all cases, the local government bureaucracy can facilitate development.

My intent here is to show how the local state can take external factors and maximize them to give local enterprises the greatest competitive advantage to make the best possible use of whatever conditions may happen to exist. My argument is that like the East Asian NICs, the state, in this case, local government, can be an activist state that *selectively* intervenes to guide and assist local industry to take maximum advantage of market opportunities.

Local state action may distort the market, but that is exactly the point. As Alice Amsden has noted, some East Asian NICs purposely get the prices wrong, in order to gain competitive advantage and gain the largest market share. Local state corpo-ratism is not about cadre power, but about how local governments can assist their enterprises and how they can use their bureaucratic positions to further their local economic interests in a *market context*.

I will begin by making clear who owns important rural industries, what this ownership means, and how key resources are obtained by these producers.

I. Collective Ownership of Township and Village Enterprises

The term rural enterprises (*xiangzhen qiye*) encompasses four types of enter-prises: township, village, joint, and private. Of these, township- and village-owned rural enterprises led China's industrial growth during the reform period. They number less than privately owned enterprises, but are more important in terms of output value and in terms of the number of employees per firm. Township- and village-owned enterprises are *collectively owned (jiti suoyou)*, but the meaning of "collective" has been complicated by the post-Mao reforms.

Collective ownership means government ownership: the difference is that the government or state is the *local* state, i.e., governments at the township and village levels, not the national state. The crucial difference between township and village enterprises and those that are commonly referred to as "state-owned" enterprises has to do with whether they are part of the original planned economy —whether their inputs and products were allocated under the plan and perhaps the benefits that accrue to their workers, not whether they are owned by government.[2] Township and village enterprises are government-owned, but they are not and never were part of the centrally planned economy, their inputs and products were never allocated under the plan; they produce for the market.[3]

Property rights over the profits from township and village enterprises are held by the collective, which in this case means the township and village, respectively. However, collective ownership of township and village enterprises does not mean that every member of the township or village has shares in these enterprises. In some areas, such as in Guangdong, there is movement toward a share system, but this is still rare. Contrary to the implications of some recent writing, the members of the "collective" do not actually get dividends from their shares.[4] In most cases, members of the collective benefit from the income of these enterprises through the provision of welfare and other services and goods by the government to the community as a whole. It is normally the township or village *government* that decides the disposition of the residual and the use of these collective funds. In this sense, local governments are the *de facto* owners of these enterprises, but in the local corporate sense. This is not hidden privatization. The income belongs to the collective and is used for collective purposes, not as the private income of individuals.[5]

The confusion over the status of township and village enterprises has been caused in large part by the institution of "the contract responsibility system." This may be one key reason why observers underestimate the role of local government and think that township and village enterprises are private or semi-private. The term "contracting" masks the heavy involvement of local officials in the crucial decision-making concerning these still collectively owned rural enterprises. It suggests that decollectivization had the same impact on collectively owned industry as it did on agricultural land where property rights over the residual did revert to the household. Contracting suggests a degree of autonomy and allocation of property rights that simply is not present with regard to industry. In contrast to agriculture and land, the property rights of township and village firms remain in the hands of local governments. Those who have contracted to run the collective enterprises are not an independent economic elite.

Those who run the enterprises are still largely dependent on the local government officials who appoint them. There is competitive bidding to win contracts, and in many cases, the contract goes to the highest bidder. Yet local officials ultimately have the authority to decide to whom the contract is awarded. Trust, reputation, and loyalty are as important as promises of high returns.

The contract responsibility system for collective industry decentralized the day-to-day management and provided incentives for factory managers to be efficient and increase production.[6] There is local variation, but most lessees remain employees of the local government, that is, the collective. Those who contract are provided with lucrative incentives, bonuses, housing, and other perks to encourage efficiency and increase production. The factory managers make recommendations and those who run factories targeted for expansion play an active role in the development process, but the local officials, most importantly the village Party secretary or the township economic commission and township heads, have the final say in major decisions regarding these collectively owned enterprises.[7]

In contrast to administrative guidance in Japan where governments rely on the "carrot," i.e., preferential allocations as an inducement for independently-owned firms to conform to certain strategies of economic growth, local governments in China are able to maintain direct influence and intervene in the internal affairs of a key portion of the economy—the township and village enterprises. By maintaining ownership, local governments may limit management autonomy, use of enterprise profits, access to credit, and allocation of investment opportunities and key inputs.[8]

Individuals who contract to operate collectively owned enterprises are, by definition, renters. Unlike private entrepreneurs, contractors will seldom, if ever, invest in these ventures with their own funds. All investment in collectively owned enterprises is made by the collective, whether managed by the collective or by individual contractors. In this sense, the collective, personified by the local cadres, is the entrepreneur who takes the risks, makes the investment decisions, and, when necessary, finds ways to bail out of financial problems.[9] When factories want to expand production or buy new machinery, the contractor or manager approaches the village or township government, not the bank. Depending on the size of the investment or loan required, the village or township will either provide it from its accumulation fund or arrange for a loan from the local savings cooperative, or, if the amount is large, from either the local branch of the Agricultural Bank, or try to secure loans from the finance and tax offices. When factory managers do approach the banks for loans, especially in the case of large loans, it is either together with the township or village head or after the arrangement has already been set up by the village or township head.

Also in contrast to private enterprise, these township and village enterprises and those who contract them are subject to local government regulation through plans and targets, which are still commonplace at the local levels, even though

China has been moving away from central planning.[10] Targets for profit, output, and revenue are formulated and transmitted by the bureau for the management of rural enterprises. The county finance bureau issues to its townships quotas for revenue, with built-in growth rates based largely on the number and performance of the township and village industries.

The continued ability of local governments to intervene directly and monitor the internal management and operation of township and village enterprises explains why local governments are willing to invest so much time and effort in promoting these enterprises. The risks for local governments are less when they channel resources to their preferred enterprises. County governments, for example, deal with their subordinate levels, not with independent entrepreneurs. This differs from other developing countries, where there are two separate elites, each with a separate basis of power. The contract responsibility system charges factory managers with the burden of running the factory efficiently and profitably— but with only limited control over the factors of production. Those who lease the collective factories are dependent on executive management (that is, the local officials who are sometimes, concurrently, the chairmen of the village industrial corporation), to make key decisions. The factory manager may have control of routine day-to-day management of the factory, but major decisions about personnel, investment, and product line require official approval and intervention.

II. Collective Ownership and Economic Growth

The owner of township and village enterprise is the collective, defined as the township or the village, respectively. The level that owns the enterprise is the one that is most intimately involved in decision-making and management of these firms. Each enterprise constitutes part of a collective's resources and directly contributes to the economic well-being of all township or village members. Local governments, in turn, treat enterprises within their administrative purview as one component of a larger corporate whole. The relationship is similar to that within a business corporation, with local officials acting as the equivalent of a board of directors or chief executive officer.

Local authorities mobilize all existing resources to maximize economic growth within their community. By contracting management of enterprises to individuals and promoting the private sector, an increasingly diversified, industrialized, and dynamic rural economy has developed. This has been achieved through a combination of constraints and inducements characteristic of a corporatist system. The relationship is one of mutual dependence, with the local state holding the winning hand: the local state coopts enterprises by the allocation of scarce resources and in return, the enterprises adhere to local corporate interests and turn over substantial portions of their revenue to the local governments. The degree of dependence and the amount turned over to the local government vary according to who holds the property rights over the enterprises. The local state holds firm control over collectively owned enterprises, which it does not have over privately owned enterprises. Nonetheless, even the private sector has been mobilized and coopted into the large corporatist structure through the use of constraints and inducements. This has been facilitated by the preexisting Maoist infrastructure, but the system has been adapted by the local governments to an emerging market economy.

Pooling Risks and Capital

One key indicator of the corporate nature of rural industrial development is the degree to which funds and risks are pooled within the local community that holds ownership rights, i.e., either the township or village. Profits from collectively owned enterprises are extracted to pay for expenditures and reinvestment of other local firms or even other sectors of the economy, such as agriculture. But what has allowed rural enterprises to flourish is that Chinese local governments not only extract substantial revenues from their most productive enterprises, but also intervene to facilitate the development of these enterprises. Unlike the rent-seeking situations that one finds in some developing countries, the relationship in China between local governments and their enterprises is not a zero-sum game.

Revenues flow from the enterprises to the local government, above and beyond standard tax assessments, but more importantly, there is also a substantial flow of funds and support services *from the local government to the enterprises*. Pooling capital is a constraint or an inducement of the corporatist system, depending on whether the enterprise receives or gives. The growth of the enterprise from which funds are taken is hampered in the short run, but if the unit of concern is the growth of the village or township over the medium run, this type of extraction does not necessarily have a negative impact on the development of rural enterprises within the community. The question is how these extracted funds are used. The extraction of profits from enterprises can be an important mechanism that allows local governments to facilitate corporate growth within the community as a whole. As the holders of the rights over income flows, local governments can decide, much like a corporation, how to use the profits from its various enterprises and how to redistribute income. Mutual dependence rather than predation may be more apt in describing the relationship. This relationship explains why large extractions of revenue have not negatively affected growth, as the literature on rent-seeking shows is occurring in other developing countries (see e.g., Krueger 1974).

Also like a large corporation, villages and townships grant loans to poor enterprises and new enterprises are started from the profits of the more prosperous enterprises.[11] Profits may also be used to subsidize and bear necessary corporate overhead. Funds may be given to industries that are not particularly efficient or profitable because they provide jobs for the village's surplus labor force, or because the enterprise carries prestige and thus gives "face" to the village. Local authorities may require enterprises with substantial profits to pay *ad hoc* surcharges, often termed "loans" or "rent paid in advance."[12] Such extractions may not necessarily increase local revenues, but they do further the larger corporate good.

Similarly, the debts of a village or township are the responsibility of the collective. Interviews reveal that in a number of localities, when a collective enterprise fails and defaults on its loans, the debt is paid off by the other enterprises regardless of the specifics of the contracting system. Theoretically, the debt is the responsibility of the guarantor of the loan, but because most loans are guaranteed by the township economic commission[13] or by the village government, the debt burden is divided among the remaining enterprises owned by the collective. In one township in 1987, four enterprises folded, leaving a debt of 120,000 *yuan*. The township economic commission had funds to repay 60,000 *yuan* to the bank; but the remainder of the debt was divided among the other enterprises.[14] These enterprises had to pay, however grudgingly, because their own future depended on the goodwill of the local authorities who controlled credit and investment opportunities.

This collective financing and debt repayment system softens the "budget constraint" of township and village enterprises, but it may also be a reason why these rural enterprises have been able to grow with limited funding. Each new enterprise does not have to raise all the funds it needs for its start-up operations—it can borrow funds from sister enterprises within the local corporate community. The fiscal health of an enterprise depends not only on its own internal sources of wealth and the credit that it can mobilize, but also on the financial resources of the corporate state of which it is a part. This corporate financing may be a way of sidestepping the need for outside financing. This strategy is all the more feasible because many of the village and township enterprises start out on a relatively small scale.

III. Cooperation between County, Township, and Village Governments

Townships and villages own many of the most important rural enterprises, and they are the entrepreneurs whose efforts ultimately will determine whether a township or village does well. However, the success of township and village enterprises is not entirely due to the efforts of those who hold the property rights to these enterprises. The successful industrial growth in China required entrepreneurship by township and village governments *and* the intervention of county-level governments. While each of the three lowest levels of local government may be considered independent economic entities with separate interests, the rapid growth of the rural economy has *not* been the product of independent actions by officials at only one level of local government; it is the result of an interrelated effort by all three levels based on mutual need and dependence. In this sense, the corporate community encompasses the county.[15]

The lower levels now have access to inputs for economic activity, but it is unlikely that either villages or townships have *sufficient* access to all of the key inputs needed for the *rapid* economic development that has taken place in China during the period of reform. The rapid development of rural industry has been a two-stage process. Township and villages, as entrepreneurs, must facilitate and oversee development within their own level of administration to the best of their abilities. But because of their administrative and economic relationship to the higher levels, they can go beyond their administrative bounds to the county, and if necessary, to prefecture or province, for assistance. Each township and village has its own resources and strives to be self-sufficient, but each can appeal to the next higher level for positive intervention.

There are conflicts of interest and differing agendas operating at the different levels of local government, but there also exists a commonality of interests that prompts higher levels of government to use their bureaucratic position to assist enterprises not only within their administrative level but those below them as well. This recourse to upper-level support has been essential for successful local development. The end result has been a coordinated effort that requires input from all three levels of local government.

The County's Role

A. Doak Barnett noted almost thirty years ago that the county is the "most important administrative unit in rural China now, as in the past . . . Most counties have tended to be relatively stable administrative units, because more often than not they have constituted natural centers of transportation, communications, industry, and commerce. Traditionally, the county seat has served not only as an administrative headquarters but also as the economic and social center of a fairly well-defined region" (Barnett 1967, p. 117). This description remains apt today in many respects, with the exception that the county has now taken on a much more active role in fostering local economic development in response to the fiscal pressures and opportunities offered by the reforms.

The county government oversees, guides, and promotes the direction of growth in the county, including that of its townships and villages. Concretely, in practice this means arranging for the necessary inputs and bureaucratic services that allow local enterprises to prosper. County officials describe their own role as that of coordinating (*xietiao*). *The county facilitates development at all three levels.* All lower levels appeal to the county for assistance if problems cannot be resolved locally with existing resources. However, *the degree of county involvement in a township or village enterprise depends on the project, its technical sophistication and costs, abilities of township or village officials, and most importantly, on the importance of the project or enterprise to the overall well-being of the county.*

The county can take on this facilitator role because its officials are likely to have the broadest knowledge of developments outside their county and to have the widest network of personal and professional relationships. County officials go on fact-finding missions, such as to the more developed areas of Jiangsu to study advanced models of development, and even abroad. They are the ones with whom foreign investors meet and they guide foreign investors to particular sites within the county.

The county continues to use planning to guide development within the county, including its townships and villages. It still issues targets, plans, and budgets and employs an extensive reporting system that is similar to that used in the Maoist period. These reports monitor how well the county's plans and targets are being implemented. All township enterprises send reports to the township economic commission which then submits reports to the county, along with reports from other sections of the township government. It is at the village level where the required preparation of reports is attenuated. Although townships are the administrative superiors of the villages, they seem to have lost control over the latter, especially the highly industrialized, wealthy ones. But unlike the planning of the Maoist period, the plans that are issued are not mandatory, nor do ideas for development always stem from the county.

While planning still plays a part, counties now rely more on inducements and contrasts similar to that found in the East Asian NICs to realize their development strategies. This is done through their ability to allocate material resources and bureaucratic services selectively. The county, in this respect, is distinct from both township and village. The county has the largest amount of goods that it can preferentially allocate. However, with the increasing availability of production materials on the open market, the county's effectiveness in using material supply as an inducement is likely to wane and certainly will vary significantly from county to county.

Some counties continue to guide the allocation of materials because their own resources have expanded with the growth of markets. For example, in 1980 a county material supply bureau consisted of only two subsidiary companies, and employed a total of 131 people. By 1990 it had expanded its operations to employ 249 people in ten trading companies which handled total sales of close to 100 million *yuan*. It now has an impressive array of supplies to offer, obtained from a variety of sources, including trade with the former Soviet Union in a border area of Heilongjiang Province. In addition, various other county agencies have set up service and supply companies, such as the material supply companies set up by the township enterprise management bureaus. Counties can also usually, in an indirect manner, affect market supplies because the largest periodic markets and the material exchange centers are at the county seat.

Bureaucratic Support

In addition to providing production materials, county governments also promote certain enterprises by providing bureaucratic services. These include help in securing licenses, certifications and prizes for products, and tax breaks. Some of these inputs are procedures to start up businesses. Others provide economic advantages, such as tax breaks and loan deferrals. Again, support is not uniform. Local officials selectively reserve their energy for key enterprises and projects.

This source of county power is independent of the growth of markets. This is a major distinction between the county and the lower levels of government. The township may have a role in initiating bureaucratic procedures, but the county must give final approval. For example, the county licensing process through the industrial commercial management bureau determines who may operate a business. The village level has no powers to grant such a license; the township can help in the process, but the license is given by the county. Similarly, product certification and registration is usually dependent on county-level agencies, most importantly the rural enterprise management bureau. Production certification and grading are not essential to operate a business, but it certainly helps to promote one's business if the products receive recognition. In addition, larger loans, tax breaks, agency loans, as well export-related issues are controlled by the county. For example, the office of the science and technology commission at the township level propagates technology, but it has no money to help enterprises. The contacts between the enterprises and the county commission are directly for financial assistance.[16]

County agencies critical to rural enterprises, such as the commission on science and technology and the rural enterprise management bureau, spend large amounts of time and energy to represent local industries at higher-level key agencies to acquire technology, materials, funding, and so on. Officials from these county agencies may personally accompany factory managers to the higher-level bureaus. The daily routine of cadres at the county-level rural enterprise management bureau is filled with trips to the prefecture, even to Beijing, on behalf of specific enterprises. Local governments in China see it as part of their *duty* to lobby on behalf of their enterprises.

In addition to routine services, China's local state corporatist system is distinguished by its ability to mobilize not just one, but all agencies and bureaus within the local government to nurture selected township and village enterprises and provide services well outside their administrative domain. For example, the county tax bureau not only collects taxes and gives tax breaks, but it also helps enterprises train accountants and find scarce technical personnel, a pressing problem facing rural industry. Agencies use their connections to influence other agencies, for example banks, to bend the rules in favor of a particular enterprise. The tax bureau may provide one of the most important advantages an enterprise may receive, i.e., a tax break, but it may also allow an enterprise to repay the bank loan before taxes are assessed, in order to win the bank's support for the loan.

In addition to providing routine and extraordinary service to selected enterprises, counties—through their various bureaucratic agencies, such as the tax bureau, the finance bureau, and the science and technology commission—have funds that they may directly loan to favored enterprises. Although banks are still the major sources of credit, local government bureaus may unilaterally provide no- or low-interest loans to help certain industries. Although these amounts are not large, they can be significant, particularly if a factory needs circulation funds to purchase raw materials. These sources of support and funding are critical when the upper levels of government try to rein in growth by cutting credit, as was done in 1988–89.

Local officials may also indirectly promote local industry by licensing semi-private credit institutions. Counties have set up special credit institutions for private entrepreneurs, and financial service centers have been established at the township level. These institutions have only limited funds, but they too provide a crucial alternative in periods of tight credit to bypass regulations aimed at constraining local growth.

Investment and Credit

Perhaps the most effective lever that county governments have in shaping local development is through investment and credit decisions. The county officials and their representatives at the township-level credit cooperatives control investments and credit by exerting their influence over the operation of the limited credit sources available in the rural areas. How dependent any enterprise is on the county or the township varies according to the amount of the loan required, and to the funds possessed by the village or township itself. Increasingly, however, with larger capital outlays needed to purchase technology, credit is a key factor in the way development is being shaped, not only by the local state, but by higher levels as well.

In the rural areas, the major bank at the county level serving peasants and rural enterprises is the Agricultural Bank (*nongye yinhang*).[17] At the township level are branches of the Agricultural Bank, known as a business office (*yingye suo*), and the credit cooperatives (*xinyongshe*). Officially these are two separate organizations, but in practice their funds are linked. Enterprises prefer to receive loans from the branch of the Agricultural Bank because its funds are state funds which are received and loaned at lower interest rates. The credit cooperative funds are from local savings and carry higher interest rates. Only the larger villages have substations of the credit cooperative or the Agricultural Bank. The graduated approval system that sets limits on the size of loans that different levels of the banking system and government can approve further ensures that the county has an input into the investment process. For example, the county Agricultural Bank must approve all loans above 10,000 *yuan*; the townships have authority to approve loans under 10,000 *yuan* (these amounts are set locally). This means that most loans for rural enterprises have to be approved by the county.

Local government control was further enhanced by a State Council requirement that all enterprise loans had to have guarantors to insure repayment. This order came approximately at the same time that rural enterprises began to develop. Prior to this requirement, the enterprises would repay as much as possible whenever possible. The bank would try to get back whatever they could and the county branch of the Agricultural Bank would make up for the additional amounts. Some loans went unpaid.

In addition, counties have taken additional measures to ensure preferential allocation of limited funds to enhance economic development. Beginning from the mid-1980s, county officials rate enterprises annually to determine the fixed capital credit as well as the financial services available for each enterprise at the local bank or savings cooperative. This system identifies those enterprises deemed important by the local government. Enterprises with a rating (*haiding e*) are accorded the quickest approval for loans within their prescribed credit limit; automatic approval is guaranteed from the township savings and loan cooperative or the local branch of the Agricultural Bank, without county approval.[18]

This is a selective system; not all enterprises receive such a rating. Enterprises that are found to be in deficit (*kuisun*) do not receive a rating. The degree of services and amount of credit are tied to the ranking received. The differences may be minimal, but in times of tight credit, they are significant. For example, those that have a first class rating receive almost the same benefits as the special first class enterprises, but the special first class enterprises have priority. Moreover, there is no need to obtain a guarantor with a special first class rating; if the Agricultural Bank has the funds, these enterprises are the first to receive loans at lower interest rates, rather than a more expensive loan from the credit cooperative;[19] it would also receive first priority for fixed capital loans.

Relations within the Larger Corporate Community

The degree of dependence and cooperation between levels of government is no longer determined by strict bureaucratic hierarchy, nor is assistance given equally or to all. The degree to which townships and villages comply with the county has become increasingly shaped by the balance of resources between the county and the townships and villages. After a decade of reform and an increasing concentration of resources at the bottom levels of the bureaucratic hierarchy, there are an increasing number of alternatives by which the lower levels can bypass the bureaucratic hierarchy for the supply of material goods. Township- and village-level governments may now enjoy new powers based on their economic accomplishments. Villages that have successfully developed village-level enterprises have independent funds to pursue the development of economic enterprises, without having to depend on financial assistance from the upper levels. They can also independently provide various welfare and other social services for their members. Successful villages boast that they do not need to seek outside loans to fund development. In fact, one village secretary boasted that the township had come to him for loans!

The dependence of the lower levels of government on higher levels for material production inputs is no longer determined only by bureaucratic rank, rather it is determined by the scarcity of the inputs, the quantity of goods needed, the technological sophistication of the machinery required, and the price people are willing to pay for them. Only where there are no alternative sources, or when sophisticated technology or scarce resources are needed, is it necessary to go up the bureaucratic hierarchy. The exception is bureaucratic inputs and services located at the county. While villages at the bottom of the bureaucratic ladder may in practice have more material resources than the township, and while each level now has increasing resources and alternative channels of material supplies, control over one type of resource still does not necessarily translate into control over another type of resource. The political economy and distribution of resources is such that certain types of power are still very much tied to the local state bureaucracy.

The cooperation between these levels of government stems partly from bureaucratic routine, but what makes local state corporatism work is that each level benefits from rural industrialization. The benefits for townships and villages to develop their own village or township enterprises are fairly obvious, but the rationale is less obvious as to why township officials would want to develop village enterprises, or why county officials would want to develop either township or village enterprises. The reasons center on revenue, but the type of revenue that each level receives from township and village enterprises differs.

Township and county government have the right to retain a portion of the taxes generated within their administrative boundaries; villages do not. Villages cannot keep any of the national or local taxes that these enterprises pay. Instead, they benefit from their village-owned enterprises through the collection of contract fees from those who rent or lease enterprises from the collective, or from the revenues retained within the enterprises after taxes are paid. As was indicated above, with decollectivization, alternative sources of income have become crucial determinants of the operating funds of village government and cadre power.

Townships, on the other hand, receive a management fee from each of its township-owned enterprises as well as the contract (rental) fee, access to any of the after-tax revenues, and a portion of the tax revenues paid by its own enterprises and those paid by village enterprises within its domain. The county, unlike either the township or village, is not entitled to any of the non-tax revenues. It benefits primarily through the collection of tax revenues, with a small portion of the management fees collected by the township. The revenue sharing system that was put into effect in the early 1980s determines what taxes are shared and in what proportions (for further details see Oi 1992 and Oi forthcoming).

A further point that must be understood is that the county need not promote township or village enterprises at the expense of county-level enterprises. County governments provide essential help to township and village enterprises, and at the same time, they also try to maximize their own county-owned enterprises.

This is not necessarily an either/or proposition. As shown above, much of the assistance counties give to enterprises relies on the ability of the county officials to mobilize bureaucratic resources they control as part of their administrative position.

Tensions and conflicts certainly arise over the use of limited resources, and different counties no doubt provide different levels of support to their township and village enterprises. But overall, promoting rural enterprises is a development strategy that allows counties to expand their revenue base beyond their own limited county enterprises with relatively little investment. Township and village enterprises bring in additional tax revenues with relatively little *fiscal* input from the county itself.

IV. Corporatist Control and Development

Communes have been disbanded, peasants now farm as households, property has been contracted to individuals, but the collective remains an important force in significant parts of China's countryside. Somewhat ironically, those areas that have progressed the farthest from the Maoist agricultural past seem to have the strongest sense of the collective community. Where there is the greatest degree of rural industrialization—usually collectively owned industry—local governments and cadres exert the strongest influence in the operation of the local economy. In such areas, local governments are *economic* actors who actively oversee local economic development. The collective nature of these township and village economies have allowed local firms to maximize their growth potential beyond what one would expect of independent firms of comparable size.

How long the collective will continue to be important is uncertain. Local state corporatism emerged in China's transitional economy. As such, we should expect changes and perhaps even its eventual demise. The private sector has been growing at a rapid rate since the late 1980s. But the emergence of a private sector in itself does not mean the end of local state corporatism. On the contrary, areas whose development was previously based almost exclusively on collectively owned enterprises are now beginning to encourage actively the development of private enterprise. The economic success of the local corporate state is advanced through the preferential allocation of constraints and inducements to local enterprises. This can be done for private as well as collectively owned firms. Neither the growth of the market nor the rise of a private sector is an adequate indicator of the existence of an activist developmental state, as the case of Japan and the other East Asian NICs has shown. What will determine whether local state corporatism will persist is the flow of benefits and services between local governments and local enterprises.

Notes

1. In particular, the share-holding system may provide a more entrepreneurial and independent role for those who run and own major shares of the factory. Initial findings on this system can be found in Vermeer 1996.

2. In Chinese the term "state-owned" is *guoyou*, which means owned by the nation or the entire state. What most think of as "state owned" (*quanmin suoyou*) are firms found in large cities and at the county level. These firms are the core of the centrally planned economy, their inputs and products were and to some degree still may be allocated under the plan; they traditionally have produced for the plan, although increasingly they may also produce for the market.

3. This includes production as subcontractors to large "state-owned" firms.

4. An alternative explanation for the success of collectively owned enterprises is presented in Weitzman and Xu 1994. The authors argue that rural industry has been successful because of the cooperative nature of Chinese society. This formulation leaves unexamined the institutional basis from which such cooperativeness might stem. They also seem to assume that all members receive benefits because they hold shares in the collective.

5. This does not rule out official corruption, but that too is different from privatization.

6. For a description of the variations in contracting, see Oi 1990.

7. Vermeer's study suggests this is changing in areas that have instituted the share-holding system (Vermeer 1996). Before any firm conclusions can be drawn, one needs to know more details of the actual property rights arrangements.

8. Christine Wong makes a similar point (Wong 1988).

9. It is in these regards that the share-holding system may bring major changes (see Vermeer 1996).

10. Local plans may or may not be mandated by upper-level quotas. Provinces send plans to the prefectures, which send them to the counties, which then send them to the townships. For example, the county still sets annual procurement quotas for agricultural goods, such as grain and cotton, and allocates the agricultural tax to the townships. Each of the specialized banks is given growth quotas for deposits by the prefectural banks. Both of these are mandated by centrally set targets. In addition, localities, from the province downwards, also set annual industrial production and fiscal targets which are not necessarily dictated by upper-level directives.

11. As might be expected, this direct redistribution is limited to collectively owned township and village enterprises. The private sector might benefit from redistribution by official loans, but it is unlikely that local governments would pay the debts of the private sector.

12. China Interview 72388.

13. A township economic commission is the bureaucratic agency at the township level responsible for township and village enterprises.

14. China Interview 17788.

15. The term "local" encompasses all levels of government from the province to the village. One can argue that all of these levels of government are involved in developing their local economies. Those at the higher levels—the provinces and the prefectures—create a conducive environment for rural enterprises, encouraging development and providing assistance. But those that have played a key role in the rapid growth of rural industry are the bottom three, i.e. county, township, and village.

16. China Interview 71888.

17. The structure of the Agricultural Bank remains strikingly similar to that during the commune period, as described by Barnett, except that the branches of the People's Bank are now township branches of the Agricultural Bank. Barnett 1967, pp. 293–4.

18. China Interview 22688.

19. These pre-approved loans can come from either the credit cooperative or the Agricultural Bank. In 1991, the rural enterprise circulating fund (*liudong zijin*) loan interest rate was 13.82 percent; the interest on a loan from the Agricultural Bank to rural

enterprises was 8.64 percent. The rates vary depending on the duration of the loan. For agricultural loans the rate was 11.23 percent from the credit cooperative, but only 8.1 percent from the Agricultural Bank. China Interview 8991.

References

Barnett, Doak. 1967. *Cadres, Bureaucracy, and Political Power in Communist China.* New York: Columbia University Press.

Gershenkron, Alexander. 1962. *Economic Backwardness in Historical Perspective.* Cambridge: Harvard University Press.

Krueger, Anne. 1974. "The Political Economy of the Rent-Seeking Society." *American Economic Review*, vol. 64, pp. 291–303.

Liu, Yaling. 1992. "Reform from Below: The Private Economy and Local Politics in Rural Industrialization of Wenzhou." *China Quarterly*, June, no. 130, pp. 293–316.

McMillan, John, and Naughton, Barry. 1992. "How to Reform a Planned Economy: Lessons from China." *Oxford Review of Economic Policy*, vol. 8, Spring, pp. 130–143.

Nee, Victor. 1989. "A Theory of Market Transition: From Redistribution to Markets in State Socialism." *American Sociological Review*, no. 54, pp. 663–681.

Oi, Jean. 1990. "The Fate of the Collective after the Commune." In Deborah Davis and Ezra Vogel, eds., *Chinese Society on the Eve of Tiananmen*, pp. 15–36. Cambridge: Council on East Asian Studies, Harvard University.

———. 1992. "Fiscal Reform and the Economic Foundations of Local State Corporatism." *World Politics*, vol. 45, no. 1 (October), pp. 99–126.

———. 1994."Cadre Networks, Information Diffusion, and Market Production in Coastal China." Paper prepared for the World Bank Project on "Explaining Growth: Chinese Coastal Provinces and Mexican Maquiladoras."

———. forthcoming. *Rural China Takes Off: Incentives for Industrialization.* Berkeley: University of California Press.

Pei, Minxin. 1994. *From Reform to Revolution: The Demise of Communism in China and the Soviet Union.* Cambridge: Harvard University Press.

Vermeer, Eduard B. 1996. "Experiments with Rural Shareholding Cooperatives: The Case of Zhoucun District, Shandong Province." *China Information*, vol. 10, nos. 3/4 (Winter 1995/Spring 1996), pp. 75–107.

Walder, Andrew. 1996. "Markets and Inequality in Transitional Economies: Toward a Testable Theory." *American Journal of Sociology*, vol. 101, pp. 1060-73.

Weitzman, Martin, and Xu Chenggang. 1994. "Chinese Township Enterprises As Vaguely Defined Cooperatives." *Journal of Comparative Economics*, vol. 18, April, pp. 121-45.

Wong, Christine. 1988. "Interpreting Rural Industrial Growth in the Post-Mao Period." *Modern China*, vol. 14, no. 1, pp. 3–30.

5

Township-Village Enterprises, Local Governments, and Rural Communities

The Chinese Village as a Firm During Economic Transition

Pei Xiaolin

Over the past sixteen years, the total output of the township-village enterprises (TVEs) in China has grown at an average rate of 30 percent per annum. In 1994, TVEs produced 47 percent of the nation's total industrial product and provided employment to 120 million people (*People's Daily*, overseas edition, 2 March 1995); *China Township Enterprises Daily*, 27 September 1994). The TVE sector has been the major driving force of both the Chinese reform and the high growth of GNP (Weitzman and Xu 1994, p. 123). This has evoked intensive study and debate on China's TVEs in international publications (e.g., Oi 1992, 1995; Weitzman and Xu 1994; Chang and Wang 1994). In my view, the heart of the debate is the basic paradox raised by Weitzman and Xu: According to almost any version of mainstream property rights theory, TVEs, as vaguely defined cooperatives, should operate relatively badly. But in practice, TVEs are enormously successful. Why do theory and practice seem so diametrically opposed in this important area? (Weitzman and Xu 1994, p. 136).

As the features of ownership and performance of TVEs and the role of local governments in them have been well documented by empirical studies (e.g., Lin 1987; Nee 1992; and particularly Byrd and Lin 1990), the study of TVEs is now entering a more theoretical stage, as manifested by the studies of Weitzman and Xu, Oi, Chang and Wang. Researchers have come to different conclusions by different approaches, which implies that the choice of approach is crucial. The debate on TVEs is to a great extent a result of these different approaches. The question, then, is: Which approach can best unravel the nature of TVEs?

At first sight, Weitzman and Xu's approach seems to be very promising. Their argument begins with the assertion that "[t]he key missing element [in traditional property rights theory] is the ability of a group to solve potential conflicts internally, without explicit rules, laws, rights, procedures and so forth." This argument exposes a major weakness of traditional property rights theory and touches on the key to TVEs' success. In contrast to Oi as well as Chang and Wang, Weitzman and Xu try to explain the TVEs' success by pointing to an internal factor.

However, on closer scrutiny, their approach turns out to be overhasty. Having discussed the possibility that a group can solve potential conflicts internally, they immediately extend this possibility to a society, and take it "as a more or less given function of culture," the so-called "cooperative culture" (Weitzman and Xu 1994, pp. 136–143). They then proceed to use this concept to explain the different models of economic transition in China and Eastern European countries, instead of focusing on the internal features of TVE organization. First, they do not identify the type of group. Not every type of group is able to solve potential conflicts internally without explicit property rights. Second, Weitzman and Xu do not reveal those cooperative elements of the group which in my opinion are the most important in the case of Chinese TVEs. Third, the ability of a group is not the same as the ability of a society. I would argue that the success of TVEs is mainly the result of specific elements of a village or rural community, and not of general cultural factors.

Oi does not study TVEs directly, but rather places them within her framework of local state corporatism: "[t]he corporatism that I refer to here pertains to local governments, specifically to counties, townships, and villages. As Collier and Collier stress [Collier and Collier 1979, pp. 967–986] corporatism refers not to the unit that does the organizing and aggregating, but to a form of state-society relations where narrow interests within society are organized and integrated so as to achieve higher order goals—namely, stability and economic growth for the state and society as a whole"(Oi 1995, p. 4). While Oi uses the state-society dichotomy as her basic framework to analyze the relationship between local governments and TVEs, I would argue that it is precisely this dichotomy which should be questioned.

One could wonder why only governments at the county, township and village levels play a determinant role in the success of TVEs, and governments at the provincial and prefectural levels do not, although these can also be regarded as local governments. In this chapter, I aim to show that there are certain specific features in township and village governments which result in specific relationships between these governments and TVEs. This, in my opinion, explains why these local governments differ from governments of prefectures and provinces, and perhaps also from local governments of other developing countries. My thesis is that the reason for the success of TVEs lies precisely herein.

The first difference between township and village governments and governments above the township level is that most officials of the former type of government are at the same time members of collective organizations in the townships and villages, simply because they are local residents of the village or the township (Pei 1994, pp. 187–189; Rozelle and Boisvert 1994, p. 30). As such, they are also owners of TVEs.[1] This dual role of government official and organization member explains why the so-called "government intervention" in townships and villages is not purely government intervention, but rather a form of business administration within an economic organization.

The second difference is that township/village officials have considerably more horizontal personal connections (e.g., kinship and friendship relations) and sympathy with local citizens than officials above the township level. As Feuchtwang has pointed out, "As a political scientist, Oi focused attention upon hierarchical relations rather than horizontal relations of personal connexion and sympathy . . . Horizontal relations of personal connexion are far more important than vertical, hierarchical relations for the great majority of households [in rural China]" (Feuchtwang 1995, pp. 12–16).

In Oi's sharp state-society dichotomy, the above two important relations between township/village officials and TVEs are not manifested, so that the basic question why China's cooperative TVEs perform so well is not answered. Although Oi's framework is the state-society relationship, in her analyses she actually only focuses on the role of local governments, without dealing with the role of local citizens and members of TVEs. The internal mechanism that is responsible for the TVEs' success, however, is rooted in the latter and not in the former. Without the participation of local citizens and members of TVEs, the local governments alone would be unable to make the TVEs a success.

The explanation offered by Chang and Wang of the nature of TVEs does not focus on TVEs themselves or local governments, but on the so-called "center's design." "The ownership structure of TVEs is not the result of free contracting among private agents as in a market economy. It is, instead, a product of an environment in which an authoritarian government with monopolistic political power plays a dominant role in economic life" (Chang and Wang 1994, p. 450). If this conclusion were correct, China's pre-reform economic results would have been much better than its post-reform performance, and there would have been no need for reform. In actual fact, the success of China's economic reform is a result of the decentralization of the center's political power (e.g., Nee 1989; Qian and Xu 1993a, 1993b). Moreover, it is common knowledge that the success of an enterprise cannot be generated by an external factor, in this case central design. As Weitzman and Xu noted, even "Deng Xiaoping admitted in 1987 that the amazing growth of the township and village enterprises was the greatest achievement of the reform and was completely unexpected" (Weitzman and Xu 1994, p. 123). According to my own experience in the 1980s when I worked in the State Planning Commission of China as a policymaker, the central government always criticized TVEs and tried to stop them from competing with the state industry for raw materials and markets.

In contrast to the above researchers, I would argue that the success of TVEs is not determined by local governments and not even by the TVEs themselves, but rather by the organizational features of China's rural communities. Furthermore, the features of local governments themselves are rooted in these features. China's TVEs are built on the basis of township-village organizations, and they cannot act independently of township and village control. It is therefore necessary to analyze the features of the township-village organization in order to reveal the mechanism underlying the success of TVEs.

Four important points should first be clarified. First, in order to narrow the focus of the discussion, this paper seeks to study the Chinese village organization. Because the difference between township and village is only in degree and not in kind, it will not be necessary to undertake a separate analysis of the features of the township organization in order to make my point. Second, the type of village discussed here is an administrative, collective and natural village[2] and mainly refers to villages in southeast China, a recently industrialized rapid growth area. Third, the village enterprise I refer to in this chapter is not a private enterprise, but one collectively owned by all villagers. Fourth, the period analyzed here is limited to the 1980s, when I worked in the State Planning Commission of China as a policymaker and investigated about 100 TVEs. To answer the question why, without privatization, the Chinese reform could be so successful at the start, one must take the pre-reform period into consideration. The situation of the 1990s is rather different, as private enterprises have become more numerous.

My analysis of the features of the Chinese village will be based on three key points. First, the management of common property in a village group or a rural community is quite different from a situation where the boundaries of the common property are unclear. Before economic reform, cooperative elements or interspecific resources, such as low information cost, kinship ties, trust and cooperative spirit were shared by all villagers. This point relates to my argument with Weitzman and Xu. Second, the linkage between the village official and the state is gradually being dissolved during reform, with the official returning to his own village organization, although this process is not yet completed. This point relates to my argument with Oi as well as Chang and Wang. Third, the original interspecific resources of villagers and the identity of the government official as the village leader are institutionalized as specific contractual relations in China's specific reform circumstances, and the Chinese village behaves as a firm-type organization during the economic transition. We will now turn to a discussion of these three key points.

The Conditions for Management of Common Property in a Village Group

Weitzman and Xu regard TVEs as vaguely defined cooperatives, with three particular features. First, the typical TVE has no owner in the sense of traditional property rights theory. Nominally, TVEs are collectively owned enterprises, i.e., all the community members are nominal owners. In a typical case, these collective owners do not have clearly defined shares. Second, there is no residual claimant in the traditional sense. Third, in a typical case, the TVE assets are non-sellable, non-transferable, and non-heritable both for the residents and for the executive owner. According to traditional property rights theory, TVEs should operate relatively badly and the only solution would be privatization. But in fact, TVEs, without privatization or well-defined ownership, operate as efficiently as private firms. This is the basic paradox raised by Weitzman and Xu (1994, pp. 131–136).

According to the above features, TVE assets can be regarded as common property in a township or a village. As Wade points out, "[E]xclusive possession (freehold) is one extreme on a continuum of property rights. No property, as in ocean fisheries or the atmosphere, is the other extreme. In between lies common property, where the rights to exploit a resource are held by persons in common with others" (Wade 1987, p. 96). Thus, Weitzman and Xu's basic paradox can be transformed into a question of management of common property: Can collective action be an alternative to privatization in a village group? Wade has given a positive answer to this question, showing that the theories of collective action and common property are not always appropriately applied to village circumstances (Wade 1987, 1988). He has addressed the problems inherent in the three popular collective action theories, i.e., the prisoners' dilemma model, Hardin's "tragedy of the commons," and Olson's logic of collective action. These theories argue that common property is bound to be over-exploited by free-riding. Wade, however, has pointed out that firstly, if the prisoners' dilemma game is repeatedly played, the logic of non-cooperation changes, and the chance of cooperation increases. As this situation obviously applies to the TVE case, and Weitzman and Xu correctly emphasize it (1994, p. 137), we will not discuss it further.

Secondly, Wade points out, "Hardin, like many others who argue that common property resources are bound to be depleted without effective state regulation, fails to make the distinction between situations of no property and situations of common property. He begins his argument by assuming 'a pasture open to all.' The case is quite different where a joint ownership unit exists, and access is open only within the bounds of this unit. Here the chances of getting compliance with rules of restrained access are much better. Yet Hardin and others, by ignoring the distinction, inappropriately generalize their results for no property to cover common property as well. Peasant cases of successful common-pool resource management all involve common property rather than no property" (Wade 1987, p. 101). This is a crucial point of difference between Wade and many others.

Weitzman and Xu also fail, at least theoretically, to make the distinction between situations of no property and situations of common property when they say that "[f]or the typical TVE there is no owner in the spirit of traditional property rights theory." They describe the cooperative factor as intangible and attribute it to culture, extending it to the whole society. "The Folk Theorem states that the outcome of a repeated non-cooperative game played among suffi-ciently patient players may look as if it is the outcome of some cooperative process or some legally binding agreement to play cooperatively, or it may not. It all depends upon an intangible expectational factor that might legitimately be identified with the history or culture of the group of players" (Weitzman and Xu 1994, p. 137). However, if the bounds of the village are identified, it can be shown that the cooperative factor does not depend on culture but on specific factors within the bounds of the village. They are not "intangible" at all.

Thirdly, within the bounds of the village, the prisoners' dilemma model and its variants assume that each participant does not possess information about the other's choice. In this case, this does not apply. As Wade puts it, "Here, monitor-ing the condition of the commons, and of cheating, is frequently fairly easy" (Wade 1987, p. 100). Furthermore, "the villagers generally do have some control over the structure of the situation in which they find themselves. Insofar as this is true, rational choice-making is different in village resource use from what is rational in anomic situations like the Prisoners' Dilemma parable. In villages, rational individuals can (subject to other conditions to be discussed) voluntarily comply with rules of restrained access" (Wade 1987, p. 99). Moreover, the rules are generated by the village itself. As Wade points out, "the successful cases of locally devised systems indicate that it is not necessary for regulation of the commons to be imposed from the outside" (p. 103), such as the central govern-ment, as suggested by Chang and Wang.

Fourthly, Wade writes, "just as the Prisoners' Dilemma says nothing about how the calculations are affected by different absolute values of the payoff, so Hardin's parable does not distinguish between commons where the resource is vital for the individual's survival, and those where it is not. It is more likely that Hardin's relentless logic will operate where the resource is not vital than where it is. Where survival is at stake, the rational individual will exercise restraint at some point" (pp. 100–101, citing Kimber 1983). Thus, when survival is at stake, cooperation is more likely than non-cooperation. In the Chinese case, the dense population in the village and the geographic immobility create precisely such a situation.[3] The population density determines that agriculture is insufficient for survival: "[i]ndeed, survival in the densely populated North China plain required supplementing the meager fruit of the harvest with sideline, commercial, or industrial incomes associated with the market or the city" (Friedman, Pickowicz and Selden 1991, p. 280. Note that population density is much greater in South China than in North China). The geographic immobility of villagers determines that the shift of labor from agriculture to industry can only take place within the bounds of the village. This is the case everywhere in China. Together with the fact that industrialization makes joint action necessary, these factors have stimu-lated cooperation and the development of TVEs. "The role of prices [interest rates] in TVP [township, village, and private enterprise][4] capital allocation mech-anisms is limited. In the case of household capital, interest rates on enterprise and community-bound issues can be distorted upward or downward by community governments. Moreover, when the main benefit of providing capital is getting a job in a labor-surplus environment, the interest rate does not mean much, and in fact often no interest payment is involved . . . If an enterprise shuts down, outstanding debts become the responsibility of its community government owner and are usually transferred to another enterprise under the same government" (Byrd 1990, pp. 202–203).[5] Thus, the struggle for survival in rural communities is conducive to cooperation.

Fifthly, Wade argues that the central factor explaining the presence or absence of cooperative action in village groups is the net collective benefit of that action, not selective inducements and punishments as suggested by Olson's logic of collective action (Wade 1987, p. 102).[6] This is proven both by Byrd's empirical study quoted earlier and my own investigations. It is also confirmed by Weitzman and Xu's study, although they fail to explain the phenomenon: "There is no residual claimant in the traditional sense. The typical resident waits passively to receive or to enjoy the benefits, of which the major part is not in monetary form but in the form of communal social investment, which is shared by everyone in the community . . . two econometric studies find that the wages of TVEs are lower than their marginal labor productivities, lower than wages of state enterprises, and are not correlated with the profitability of the TVEs" (Weitzman and Xu 1994, p. 133). In practice, this is true, but the method of comparison and evaluation used by Weitzman and Xu is open to question.

According to the investigation of about 100 TVEs which I conducted in the 1980s, many TVEs, in order to compete with state industry, sold their products at such a low price that no profit was made. When I asked them why, they said, "If we wouldn't do so especially at the beginning, our enterprises would be unable to survive and production could not continue. But if we do, at least many laborers can get jobs and wages in industrial production, and their wages will at least be higher than what they could earn in the agricultural production in our communities." This rationale was a product of the real situation, in which there was a big gap between rural and town incomes, and especially from the comparison of the net collective benefits between past agriculture and present industry within the rural community. I regard this as the competitive advantage of TVEs *vis-à-vis* the state sector. Weitzman and Xu argue differently since they separate TVEs from the community organization, fail to recognize that employment is most important in the community, and do not compare the community's present with its past.

Finally, Wade offers us a long list of conditions for collective action in village groups, such as conditions of the resources, technology, user group, noticeability, relationship between resources and user group, and relationship between users and the state (1987, pp. 104–105). Due to space limitations, they cannot be dealt with here, but it should be emphasized that all these conditions are tangible, and there is no reason to suppose any "intangible expectational factor" as suggested in Weitzman and Xu's culture-centered approach. The central idea is that "the greater the overlap between the location of the common-pool resources and the residence of the users, the greater the chances of success" (Wade 1987, p. 194) in cooperation, which is quite different from the situation in which the boundaries of the common-pool resources are unclear. I would add that the more vertical integration there is of common property in technology, such as TVE assets (which are different from the common water, grazing and trees in, for example, South Indian villages), the greater the chances of success are in cooperation between villagers.

Wade draws the important conclusion that collective action is likely to be much cheaper, in terms of state resources, than privatization or state regulation. Going against Weitzman and Xu's cultural explanation, this explains the difference in the models of economic transition in China, the former USSR, and Eastern Europe (Pei 1994; Pei and Gunnarsson, forthcoming).

Cooperative Elements in a Collective Village Group

Generally speaking, the Chinese village is a collective organization, since the village land and assets of village enterprises are collectively owned by all the villagers. Village enterprises are an organic part of the village organization, and I agree with Weitzman and Xu who regard the TVE as a vaguely defined cooperative. This gives rise to the following questions: Can cooperative elements exist among villagers in a collective organization? If so, then what are these elements, and where do they come from? Weitzman and Xu do not raise these questions, as they do not study the features of the Chinese village and simply attribute villagers' cooperation to "Chinese culture."

Both Draheim and Bonus have pointed out that cooperative elements existed in 19th-century German villages and that they played an important role in early industrialization (Draheim 1952; Bonus 1986). They found that the village, as a social group, had certain specific features, and that these features played a key role in the forming of early rural cooperatives. Draheim and Bonus have formulated the influential concept of the *dual nature of cooperatives*: the rural cooperative is *both* a social group *and* a business enterprise. Although the Chinese village is not a pure cooperative organization, it is undoubtedly a social group with a long history. As such, it has the same group features that Draheim and Bonus have defined for 19th century Germany. As the main group features of rural cooperatives they list *low information cost, trust, cooperative spirit*, and *"centripetal"* force. All these features can also be found in the Chinese village. They will be discussed here in turn.

Cooperation among people is based on knowing, understanding and trusting one another. Therefore, information that enables one to select a reliable contract partner and evaluate people's performance is extremely important. In cities or an industrialized society, the cost of this information is very high, while it can be very low in the village. As members of a social group, they know one another very well with regard to family background, strengths, weaknesses, etc. As a result, villagers can set up a long-term contract very quickly and at low cost.

In a social group, trust can easily grow at comparatively low cost. As Bonus explains:

> To trust somebody means to understand that his own set of inner rules will bar him from taking advantage of weak positions; and the same holds for the relationship toward a social group. Such a set of inner rules governing an individual or a social group evolved over time and manifested themselves in repeated prior conduct. Trust therefore grows out of experiences one has had with a person or group. The intimate personal knowledge that members of early cooperative associations shared about each other thus had another important advantage, besides constituting a high-value information pool. The members knew the individual history and the family background of their fellow members in great detail. They knew what to expect from each other; and as long as they would meet frequently, social control was easy. Under such circumstances, the formation of "trust capital" was very much facilitated (Bonus 1986, p. 183).

There is no doubt that this kind of low information cost and trust existed in the Chinese village group both before and after economic reform. According to Byrd and Lin, "Most TVP workers probably work considerably harder and for longer hours than their counterparts in state enterprises. Labor relations in TVPs seem surprisingly good, particularly considering the hard work, long hours, difficult working conditions, and relatively low wages. Possibly this is because TVP employees are first-generation industrial workers accustomed to the rigors of farm life" (Byrd and Lin 1990, p. 275). During my own investigations, I found that this description of work attitudes and relations is correct, although the explanation offered by Byrd and Lin is at most only half true. There were considerably fewer managers in TVEs than in the state sector, and they were mainly engaged in marketing. Nevertheless, the workers, without supervision in the workshop, worked very hard and efficiently. I was surprised and impressed by this because it was so different from my working experience in a Chinese state factory. When I asked a young director of a village enterprise why there was no supervision, he said: "We have grown up together and I knew who in my village worked hard and who didn't before I selected workers. Therefore I trust my workers and they will not let me down."

Furthermore, in a rural cooperative group, economic and psychological factors are closely interrelated. According to Bonus, "[a]s a social group, the cooperative was characterized by a collective mind manifesting itself as an '*esprit de corps*' 'atmosphere,' or 'climate.' The well-known *Genossenschaftsgeist* (cooperative spirit), then, was nothing but the *esprit de corps* characteristic of cooperative associations. It was this spirit alone that would form a coherent social group.

Each true cooperative, therefore, would have to appeal not just to rational think-ing, but also to feelings" (Bonus 1986, pp. 171–172). Thus, the cooperative spirit can be viewed as the "atmosphere" of a social group. In the Chinese village, this atmosphere was already there before reform, and the cooperative spirit directly arose from this atmosphere after reform. "There is thus evidence of considerable willingness to help with their firm's financing ... Only 27 percent of sample workers say that the best use of factory profits is direct distribution to workers; 65 percent favor substantial reinvestment of profits in the firm. This response is probably related to the low mobility of labor and the consequent importance of firms in the future income streams of workers and their families. In response to a hypothetical question, 65 percent indicate they would accept a 50 percent pay cut and remain to help their firm through difficulties rather than actively look for another job ... Sample workers consider their income levels to be average or slightly above the levels in their communities ... This suggests that pay tends to be set largely with reference to the income levels prevailing in the community of which the firm is a part" (Gelb 1990, pp. 286–287).

There is another factor which is even more important, i.e., the family or kinship ties in the Chinese village. The power of local authorities is the combined power of local officials and kinship authorities.[7] According to Byrd and Lin and Johnson, this factor has played a key role in village cooperation since reform (Byrd and Lin 1990, p. 6; Johnson 1991). "A dominant and distinctive feature of villages throughout the Pearl River delta is that they are lineage villages. Chinese lineages are property-holding corporations that socially integrate groups of households whose male heads trace their descent to an apical ancestor. They may be simple, small, and of only shallow genealogical depth, occupying a hamlet or a village fragment. They can also be large and complex, have a history of many tens of generations, and have a multisettlement character ... Kinship connec-tions and local loyalties have become a central part of local development initia-tives ... The corporate kinship structures of the delta are the buffers that allow a highly flexible response to the dramatic possibilities of the reform period."[8]

But if low information cost, kinship ties, trust and cooperative spirit poten-tially existed in the Chinese village group before the economic reform, why did they not work at that time? There were two related reasons. One was that the village could not enjoy the net benefit of collective action as it was captured by the state. The other was that local authorities had no power to ensure that the local communities enjoyed these benefits. These problems were solved by the decentralization of both benefits and power at the beginning of China's eco-nomic reform.

According to Bonus, although the combination of low information cost, trust and cooperative spirit can stimulate collective organization, it is also necessary that there are *benefits of collective organization*. In other words, people must have the guarantee that engaging in collective action will pay off. This generates a "centripetal" force so that the cooperative spirit can begin to take effect (Bonus

1986, pp. 172–173), a situation present in China since the reforms.[9] But when the benefits of collective organization cannot be protected or are directly captured by the central government's political power, there will be a "centrifugal" force affecting the efficacy of low information cost, trust and cooperative spirit, a situation which prevailed during the pre-reform period.

Thus, the decentralization of political power, or the increase of the power of local authorities, is a condition necessary to ensure that collective benefits remain in the rural community. As Wade states, "the less the state can, or wishes to, undermine locally-based authorities, and the less the state can enforce private property rights effectively, the better the chances of success [in collective action]" (Wade 1987, p. 104). At present, the township and village governments can play such an important role in ensuring that collective benefits remain in the rural communities because power was decentralized at the start of reform. This is an important factor. Another factor is that the collective organizations of township and village have not been changed since reform. If they had been privatized, the local governments would not have been able to assume the important role they are playing now. As Byrd and Lin have found, "[w]hen the bulk of the TVP labor force is in TVCEs (as in Wuxi), community governments can control wages effectively. If there is a substantial number of private enterprises (as in Nanhai), community governments cannot set TVCE wages below market-clearing levels because their employees would move to the private sector *en masse*" (Byrd and Lin 1990, p. 278. TVCE is the authors' abbreviation for "township and village community enterprise" *(xiangcun qiye))*.

As both Wade and Bonus emphasize, the major factor explaining the presence or absence of cooperative action in village groups is the net collective benefit of that action. In the Chinese case, the presence of cooperative action and the net collective benefit of village groups and TVEs is the result of decentralization, not a product of the center's monopolistic political power as suggested by Chang and Wang.

The Independence of Village Leaders from the State

To understand the independence of village leaders from the state, it is necessary to appreciate that the Chinese village is an organization which integrates government administration and economic management (Luo 1990, p. 166–168). This is determined by two factors. One is that the village is the grass-roots administrative unit in rural China. The other is that the village is a collective organization, as its land and industrial or other commercial enterprises are collectively owned by all the villagers. Since the reform, these two basic features have remained the same.

The village head is the pivot in this organizational structure. He has a dual role, since he is both the director of the village organization and the administrator of the village *(cunzhang)*. This is often the case in rural China and is called "unified leadership" or a system of one-man leadership.[10] Thus, "many leaders of grass-roots units work as government officials and simultaneously represent the owners of community enterprises" (Luo 1990, p. 169). "It is certainly difficult to identify whether a person acts as a representative of the state or pursues his or her own interests, or indeed the collective interest. Or all at the same time" (Christiansen 1995, pp. 1–2). It all depends on the situation.

The integration of administrative unit and collective organization of the village designed by the central government during the 1950s was a consistent part of the planning system and the heavy industry-oriented strategy. Due to the combination of these two roles (*cunzhang* and economic manager) in one person (Luo 1990, p. 169), the state could directly command and control the collective organization through the administrative hierarchy, with the village leader acting as the pivot between the hierarchy and the collective organization. The purpose of the state was to force the collective to sell "cheap" and buy "dear" in order to achieve a high rate of saving and investment[11] for the development of heavy industry. The state used punishments and inducements to make the leader fulfill the state plan, mainly the three fixed quotas for production, purchase and marketing of grain. If the leader could not fulfill the set objectives, he was removed from office and lost the related benefits. If he could, he was promoted to a higher position, say, township (previously, commune) leader. This was the general picture before reform, but the principle still works in the post-reform period.

Rozelle and Boisvert have made an econometric quantification of Chinese village leaders' multiple objectives, namely promotion, status, job security, independence from officials at higher levels, personal profits and commitment to the village. What they found was that "[g]rain yields and technological progress in agriculture were the two elements most closely associated with status, promotion, and job security . . . 72 percent of the respondents agreed that most promotions led to positions in the agricultural system . . . When his village became a 'model of good agricultural management' which adopted the most advanced technology, promotion into a township position was shortly forthcoming" (Rozelle and Boisvert 1994, pp. 28–30). There are a number of reasons for this. The grain price is still mainly controlled by the state; the agricultural sector is still the least profitable; and higher grain yields and increased investment in the most advanced technology mean a larger contribution to the state at the expense of the village organization (ibid., pp. 37, 41).

Since in pre-reform rural China, agriculture was the leading sector, the village leader, as the pivot between the hierarchy and the village organization, made a rational choice by strengthening his links with the state and weakening his ties with the villagers, in spite of the fact that he was also a member of the village. Through him, the interests of the collective village were subordinated to those of the state. However, now that rural industry has become the leading sector, especially in post-reform southeast China, the logic has changed entirely.

The independence of village leaders from officials at higher levels is the result of the decentralization of the power and finance systems as well as the rapid development of industry in the village. "China's highly centralized public finance system dates back to 1950 . . . Except for some local taxes and a few small income items that could be retained by local government to offset certain expenditures, all income was concentrated in the hands of the central government. Similarly, all outlays (except local supplementary expenditures) were included in the state budget . . . it was not until 1980 that China began to break away from overcentralization and excessively strict control and to offer more financial autonomy to local governments and state enterprises" (Song and Du 1990, p. 342).

One important reason for the fiscal reform was the huge state budget deficit at that time, and the center, not being able to solve this problem, had to decentralize the fiscal burden. A tax responsibility system was set up, and revenue and expenditure were simultaneously decentralized. The reform was a bottom-up revenue-sharing system in which governments at each level only submitted a portion (e.g., 30 percent) of their revenues to the next, higher level and could retain all of the remainder (Song and Du 1990, p. 342). This made localities at every level independent fiscal entities which had a relatively well-defined property right to use the surplus and assume the responsibility for local expenditures. The unprecedented power and right of the village leader to ensure that the benefits would be enjoyed by the village no doubt encouraged him to promote economic development and generate more profits. The question was how to proceed in the changing circumstances.

"The two great resources over which village administrations have powers are, of course, land and industrial or other commercial enterprises" (Feuchtwang 1995, p. 8) and village leaders achieve their goals by selecting the levels of important agricultural and industrial decision variables. Interestingly, "village leaders benefit less from village agricultural enterprises than from industrial activity. The implication of the differences between the coefficients of the agricultural and industrial variables is important in understanding observed behavior of village leaders. When village leaders face decisions involving resource allocation between industrial activities and agricultural enterprises . . . they are likely to favor the industrial activity" (Rozelle and Boisvert 1994, p. 40). There are several reasons for this. Beside the non-technical factors mentioned above, there is also the fact that Chinese agriculture is facing a situation in which the law of diminishing returns operates. Also important is that the household responsibility system made the household the unit of production and accounting in agriculture. The village leader's managerial functions in agriculture and its related benefits were reduced (Song and Du 1990, pp. 346–347). Moreover, while returns on investments in the newly developed rural industry are rapidly increasing, the price of industrial goods produced by TVEs is now almost totally determined by the market. This means that the chances of promotion for the village leader have decreased since the reform. Finally, s/he now enjoys opportunities for achieving goals which are more attractive than promotion which did not exist before reform.

The most important change is that three goals of the village leader, i.e., raising his personal income, independence from the township, and concern for the villagers, can now be simultaneously achieved by developing village industries. His own interests are no longer opposed to but congruent with those of the villagers. "70 percent of the respondents were willing to admit that rural industry is also the vehicle through which they could raise personal incomes . . . When asked to provide observations about their peers in other villages, local leaders consistently mentioned the extent to which other village leaders were profiting from industrial enterprises . . . 77 percent of village leaders surveyed agreed that independence is an important goal attained primarily through either higher levels of industrial profits or industrial assets . . . If village profits from industry were to go up 10 percent then village leader utility would increase by nearly 4 percent. It is interesting that the capital variable has an elasticity about twice the magnitude of profits. Perhaps this indicates that capital and profits both have the same effect on cadre utility, for example, through increased independence from the township or increased personal income" (Rozelle and Boisvert 1994, pp. 28–41). With higher levels of industrial profits and more industrial assets, some village leaders can even reverse their original relations with higher officials in some aspects. "Successful villages boast that they do not need to [depend on financial assistance from the upper levels]. In fact, one village secretary boasted that the township had come to him for loans!" (Oi 1995, p. 51).

"Every village leader in the sample is a local resident. Hence, as it is for most village headmen or local leaders in any developing country, close kinship and friendship ties within the village make local welfare an important goal. In Chinese villages, there are rights, responsibilities, and standards of fairness that villagers expect from their leaders. They demand that all in the village have equal income earning opportunities. Moreover, discontent grows quickly when the development efforts of a village slow relative to other villages in the area. Farmers frequently compare their own standards of living to those in other villages. Off-farm employment opportunities can be thought of as a measure of the village leader's ability to increase the welfare of the village. In 42 percent of the responses, village leaders indicated that off-farm job opportunities are in highest demand by farmers . . . The remaining variable, non-farm employment, also has a relatively small elasticity. Thus, increasing the possibilities for individuals in some village households to move off the farm into other employment categories does have a positive, albeit small, utility-increasing effect on village leaders" (Rozelle and Boisvert 1994, pp. 30–40). The reason for this is that the main source of benefits for the leader has shifted from his relation with the state to the industrial development in his own village. As he cannot develop the industry individually, he has to cooperate with his fellow villagers. This would suggest that his linkage with the state hierarchy is weakened and his linkage with his own organization strengthened. His original identity as a member of the village is restored and he begins to further the collective benefits of his own village. The collective is thus gradually moving away from state control. Although the leader still needs his identity as a government official, its function is different from the pre-reform period. In the next section, it will be shown that after reform, the integration of government administration and economic management designed by the central government for the state's benefit is being used by the village leader for the benefit of the village.

Not only has the forced linkage between the village and the state been broken, the same trend goes for the township— although the process has not yet been completed (see e.g., Nee 1989, 1992). The township is also a collective organization where government administration and economic management are integrated, and it differs from the village only in degree and not in kind. It is this trend which explains the dynamics of China's TVEs. The thesis of local state corporatism does not penetrate to this level, looking only at the surface of things.[12] Moreover, our findings show that Chang and Wang's description of "an environment in which an authoritarian government with monopolistic political power plays a dominant role in economic life" does not apply to the actual trend in China.

Transaction-Specific Resources, Quasi-Rents, and the Forming of Village Coalitions

The definition of "the firm" has been far from consistent among economists, and some even believe it is a waste of time to define it at all (Picot 1984, p. 53). This is going too far. Debates on how to define the firm have greatly developed economic theory. R.H. Coase's "The Nature of the Firm" (1937) is a good example, although "his primary distinction between transactions made within a firm and transactions made in the marketplace may often be too simplistic . . . It may be more useful to . . . consider the firm as a particular kind or set of interrelated contracts" (Klein, Crawford and Alchian 1978, p. 326). On the basis of this idea, Alchian has outlined a general economic theory of contract in his paper, "Specificity, Specialization, and Coalitions," on which this section is based (Alchian 1984).

One important point should be clarified immediately. While the collective village is of course not a typical capitalist firm, it is undoubtedly an economic organization which may behave as a firm, according to Alchian's definition of the firm (see below), in a special situation. "Whether or not that definition [of the firm] is accepted, the important question is what kind of contractual relations are institutionalized or used in what circumstances" (Alchian 1984, p. 39). We will focus on the kind of contractual relations in the village organization that are institutionalized in the transition environment.

> In forming a coalition, some members will make investments the value of which elsewhere will be less than the value in the coalition (and also less than its costs). If its value in the coalition is higher than elsewhere, it is defined to be specific to the coalition. Some of the resources have values independent of the coalition. They will be able to earn just as much elsewhere. They are

nonspecific to this coalition. If the coalition fails, they lose nothing ... An input with "specificity" is one whose value depends on—i.e., "is specific to"— the behavior of some other particular resource. The return on the investment cost that is non-salvageable if the other resource to which it is specifically dependent disappears is called the specific quasi-rent (Alchian 1984, p. 287).

The low information cost, kinship ties, trust and cooperative spirit of the collective are transaction-specific resources of the Chinese village coalition. Their values are higher in the coalition than elsewhere, and may even be zero elsewhere. If anyone leaves the village, he cannot obtain the quasi-rent of these specific resources.[13] "What counts is the loss one experiences in the event one must leave the coalition—i.e., not be able to transact with the coalition" (Alchian 1984, p. 38). "The general picture is consistent with the hypothesis that the TVP sector follows a communal model and that in some cases the firm itself is a considerable part of the community. It also confirms the propositions that workers perceive a strong link between pay and profits and that many view their relationship with their firms as long term rather than transient. This is no doubt because of the limited mobility of labor. In this sense TVP workers have *de facto* equity in their firms even if they do not formally own shares. Many, it seems, would consider a degree of formal shareholding in their firms as well" (Gelb 1990, p. 287).

However, the realization of specific quasi-rent is also determined by factors related to the village coalition and external factors. As there were no market relations and networks in China at the beginning of economic reform, the only, or most credible, institution to establish an exchange between different organizations was the network of government administration. Organizations outside this network had higher business risks. For example, private enterprises or even pure cooperatives found it very difficult to obtain bank loans and persuade others of their credibility. If they wanted to break contracts, they could disband the cooperative or simply "disappear." This was especially true at the beginning of the reforms. In contrast, village officials were much more credible and successful than pure cooperatives when doing business on behalf of the village. In the first place, they were members of China's administrative hierarchy, and banks, providers of raw materials and the commercial network were, at the start of the reform, all in the state sector or under state control. The village officials had long-standing relations with these departments and enterprises even before reform. In the second place, the administrative identity of village officials, the fixed location of the village, and its assets all constituted mortgages or guarantees for the village in doing business (Pei 1994, pp. 187–188).

Thus, the administrative identity of village officials became a central transaction-specific resource of the village. As mentioned above, the village officials can be regarded as having dual identities; they are both members of China's administrative hierarchy and members of their own villages. As it is very difficult for someone to be a village official in another village, the value of his administrative identity can only be realized in his own village. Furthermore, the value of this central transaction-specific resource depends on other particular resources of the village, such as low information costs, kinship ties, trust and cooperative spirit. They are specific to each other, and the officials and other members of the village are interdependent. Without the administrative identity of village officials, the low information costs, kinship ties, trust and cooperative spirit of the social group were insufficient to obtain a return. We may thus define the specific quasi-rent of the administrative identity of village officials as the return on the collective village as compared with the return on an organization without such an identity.[14] A village coalition can form naturally when its return is higher than without such cooperation.

The quasi-rent of the administrative identity of village officials is a specific rent during a transitional period in history. Before economic reform, this identity was used by the state to capture the benefits of the village. If in the future, the conditions on which this identity depends were to disappear, this specific quasi-rent will also disappear, and the collective village may evolve towards other forms. But at the present time, this identity is still a central-specific resource for the formation of the village coalition and its business activities. This organization is a hybrid model in which market and hierarchical elements are blended, in response to the economic transition from planning to market. The evolutionary feature of the Chinese reform, which is different from the developments in Eastern Europe and the former USSR, is determined by this hybrid model (for this argument, see Pei 1994; Pei and Gunnarsson, forthcoming).

As shown by the experience of China's economic reform, the model is capable of linking the different economic systems, whereby the market elements can gradually overcome the state-planned elements. As we have pointed out, the market elements do not arise from external factors, but from factors within the collective village.

Opportunism, Protective Arrangements and Internalizing Quasi-Rents

As several writers have pointed out, "[t]he specific quasi-rent is expropriable if the owner (or administrator) of the 'specializing' resource can control its own effects on values of the resources specific to it (Klein, Crawford and Alchian 1984, p. 37). Thus, "[a]nticipation of expropriability of quasi-rent will motivate pre-investment protective contractual arrangements. The owner of a resource whose value is alterable or affected by specific other people will have an interest in controlling or restricting their acts. If arrangements are made between the several resource owners to restrict or control the future actions, the several are said to be a coalition" (Alchian 1984, p. 37). In this section, we will take a closer look at the position of the village official, problems of opportunism, protective arrangements, and the internalization of quasi-rents.

The Village Official

As the possessor of the specific resource of his administrative identity, every village official has the means to become an opportunist, and there are many examples. On the other hand, in a village group, protection is also easy to arrange. First, China's village officials, unlike officials above the village level who are appointed by higher authorities, are elected by village members and affirmed by higher authorities.[15] One cannot monopolize this position in the village indefinitely. Moreover, when a village official conducts business for the collective village, he acts in the capacity of both village official and deputy of the villagers. In this sense, the transaction-specific resource belongs to all the villagers, not to a specific person.

Second, because of the low information costs of the social group and the geographic immobility of village officials, the cost of selecting personnel and evaluating performance is very low. Third, the value of the administrative identity depends on other particular resources of the village group. Unlike the pre-reform period, the official cannot extract personal benefits from this specific resource on a continued basis, since this would lead to the loss of his reputation and the benefits connected with it. Thus, it is in the official's own long-term interests not to jeopardize his reputation. The benefits of village officials must be realized through profit maximizing of the village coalition.[16]

There is another fundamental difference between village officials and officials above the village level. While the latter receive salaries from the Chinese state, the income of the former is derived from the village and therefore more closely related to the productive conditions of the villages (Pei 1994, pp. 187–188). The internalization of quasi-rents in the village takes place through the double identity of village officials as *cadre-entrepreneurs* (Nee 1992, p. 1). The mechanism of internalizing quasi-rents in the village works via the double identity of village officials. The specific quasi-rents can be made through the official's administrative identity, and his/her identity as village member will encourage him/her to try to internalize the quasi-rents in the village coalition. Or, we may say that the entrepreneurial function of the official originates from his or her double identity.

I encountered a vivid example of this when I went to a village in Jiangsu Province in 1984 to investigate the development of rural industry. Since I worked in a powerful agency, the State Planning Commission of China, the village official invited me, as he often did with people from important departments and enterprises, to a very good dinner. After that I went to a workshop of the village alone, and had an interesting dialogue with a young worker:

> "Don't you get angry with the official when you work so hard here and he, often using the money of your village, eats and drinks with other people?"
> "No."
> "Why not?"
> "The more he eats and drinks with important people the more he can negotiate, and the more I can get from the income distribution."

According to Alchian, "[t]he people who direct and manage a coalition are those who own the resources specific to the coalition or they are responsible to them. Owners of those resources have the most of their coalition value to lose by failure of the coalition. They have a greater incentive to manage or be responsible for selecting and monitoring the management of the coalition" (Alchian 1984, pp. 42–43).

Thus, three factors determine the position of village officials as directors or managers of village organizations. First, they "own" or are responsible for the central transaction-specific resources of village organizations. As members of the administrative hierarchy, they have more outside relations, information and knowledge of the government's policies than ordinary villagers. These resources are key factors to village business. Second, since the village land and enterprises are collectively owned by all villagers, and the leader of a village is elected by all village members, he bears more responsibility than others for the management of village assets. Third, the village is an organization which integrates government administration and economic management. The village leader is both elected by villagers and affirmed by the government at a higher level. According to the principle of management, there should be only one authority in the village organization, and since the village leader is both administrator and manager, he is just this authority.

Generally speaking, the so-called "government intervention" in the village is not government intervention, but rather business management. Real government intervention is an external force exercised on an economic organization. The village leader, as he is both member and head of the organization, is not an outsider to the organization. Under the specific conditions of the transition period, the leader uses his identity as village official to benefit the business of his own organization.

The Administrative Border of the Village As a Natural Protection Against Outside Opportunists

The discussion in this section relates to Wade's conditions for collective action discussed earlier. The internalization of quasi-rents is made easy in the village by the village border which can be used against outside opportunists. It even functioned before the economic reforms. The failure of the communes and the Great Leap Forward in 1958 was to a great extent due to the breaking down of this protective border. When it was rebuilt, the situation improved.[17] Thus, prior to the reform, there was a big difference between distribution in the rural sector and that in the state sector. While in the latter, distribution was egalitarian, there could be considerable differences in income between two bordering villages, in spite of the fact that egalitarianism prevailed within each village.

The shifting of labor from the agricultural to the non-agricultural sector can immediately increase the level of income and benefits in the village. However, due to differences in natural resources, technology, capital and development levels among different villages, the speed of the shift is not the same. As income gaps among different villages and areas are rapidly increasing since the reforms, outside opportunists can easily acquire higher incomes simply by moving from a poor village to a rich one. The geographic immobility of rural labor and the administrative border of the village are protective arrangements against such opportunists.[18] Since the reforms, there has been a popular saying in the Chinese countryside: The water containing fertilizer is not allowed to flow into the land of outsiders *(fei shui bu liu wai ren tian)*! The villagers have been trying to internalize benefits and quasi-rents in their own village. Since the reform, there has been intensive competition in industrial development among China's massive collective villages.

The village border can also protect and internalize the high value of outside technicians. During the period of industrial establishment, the collective village had to obtain technical advice from engineers and technicians who, at the time, worked in the state sector and lived in cities. Because their contribution to the village is generally greater than what they get in return, they are always very welcome. In 1982, I went to a successful village near Shanghai to investigate why its goods were so competitive. The village official explained:

> "There was a very qualified technician who worked in a state factory in Shanghai but was badly treated by the factory. When I heard this, I offered him a much higher salary and the best house in my village. Then he began to work here and the quality of the goods has rapidly improved."
> "Can I talk to him?"
> "Sorry, no."
> "Why?"
> "Generally we do not like outsiders to contact him."

Protective Arrangements Against Inside Opportunists

Since inside opportunism also presents a real danger to the village coalition, protective arrangements must be made as soon as the coalition is set up (Bonus 1986, p. 327). Because of the low information cost in a village group, inside opportunists are easily found. They were also easily found in the pre-reform period, but protective arrangements were impossible in the collectivist set-up of those days.

China's agricultural reform was immediately successful thanks to the household responsibility system (HRS) which provided protection against opportunists. The HRS is based on a contract between the village and the household. Households are entitled to keep whatever surplus output remains after paying a farm tax to the state and contributing to the accumulation and public welfare fund of the village. Furthermore, households can sell their products on the market. According to Bonus, private farming is effective and collective farming is futile because in the latter, the directions issued by headquarters are usually wrong, while the former benefits from the farmer's own personal experience and knowledge, and his more correct evaluation of the circumstances (Bonus 1986, pp. 185–186). This is perhaps only half true. The futility of collective farming in China was more due to the farmer's own opportunism encouraged by the pre-reform organizational set-up. The HRS is an organizational arrangement which can solve both the problem of inside opportunism and that of wrong directions from the center.

The protective arrangements in village industrial production are: 1. vertical integration; 2. villagers competing for jobs in industry; and 3. cooperative spirit. Industrial production is considerably more vertically integrated than agricultural production. "Vertical integration is examined as a means of economizing on the costs of avoiding risks of appropriation of quasi-rents in specialized assets by opportunistic individuals ... However, vertical integration does not completely avoid contracting problems" (Klein *et al.* 1978, p. 299). These problems are solved by the intensive competition for jobs in village factories. Job opportunities there are limited, while incomes are higher than in agriculture. Therefore, those who work in a factory will try to retain their jobs by working harder. As a result of the low information cost, the costs of selecting personnel and evaluating performance are also very low. Moreover, when there is intensive competition among villages to get rich, and the benefits of village cooperation are greater than the benefits of independent operation, the cooperative spirit can prevail over the "centrifugal" forces.[19] "The set of inner rules governing the policies of a cooperative association to prevent opportunism is called the cooperative spirit— something that was essential to Draheim's 1952 thesis. When Draheim stressed the crucial role of the cooperative's 'dual nature' (being a social group and a business enterprise at the same time), it was because it is the social group that must develop and keep alive the cooperative spirit in order to avoid opportunism" (Bonus 1986, pp. 188–189).

When the protective arrangements are in place, agriculture and industry can play complementary roles. For example, when workers are dissatisfied, lose their jobs, or when a factory as a whole goes bankrupt, workers can still make a living from agriculture, since every household has a plot of land to use. When the income gap between agriculture and industry becomes larger, the profits of industry can be used to fill the gap or to buy agricultural machinery. These profits are managed mainly by village officials (Pei 1994, pp. 188–189).

Conclusion: The Village As a Firm During Economic Transition

As Alchian states, the firm can be defined in terms of two features: the detectability of input performance and the expropriability of quasi-rents of interspecific resources: "[a] firm is a coalition of interspecific resources owned in common, and some generalized inputs, whose owners are paid, because of difficulty of output measurability according to some criteria other than directly measured marginal productivity, and the coalition is intended to increase the wealth of the owners of the inputs by producing salable products" (Alchian 1984, p. 39).

The Chinese village is such a coalition. The administrative identity of the village leader, the kinship ties, the low information cost, trust and cooperative spirit of the village group are all interspecific resources. There are also other resources which can be regarded as such, e.g., the special knowledge derived from long-term learning-by-doing and the special local product. Only the local people know the special features and the technological process involved in making the product, and a specific quasi-rent can be derived from it. Many villages get rich by producing increasing quantities of their special local products which have been famous for many years, but there are also many opportunists who imitate such products. The quasi-rents of all the above interspecific resources are expropriable, and when this happens, the specialized investments are non-salvageable. Therefore, there must be pre-investment protective arrangements. The contractual relations which are institutionalized by the village coalition in respect to these interspecific resources could therefore be defined as a firm.

The resources are not always interspecific, or are only interdependent during a specific period of time. For example, some village enterprises have now become very successful, their products have become very competitive and well known, and the Chinese market economy has been gradually developing. With these changes, the successful enterprises find it easier than before to obtain bank loans and inspire trust in marketing and negotiation activities, and their dependence on the administrative identities of village officials is beginning to decrease. This suggests that a maximum of specific quasi-rents of interspecific resources exists only during a specific period. If a coalition seizes the opportunity at the right time, it can make the most of the temporary potential benefit; if it does not, it stands to lose out.

As we have seen, the nature of TVEs and the real function of township-village governments are rooted in the features of the Chinese township-village organization. The management of common property in a village group or rural community is quite different from the situation in which the boundaries of the common property are unclear. Collective action can, subject to the specific conditions described in this chapter, be an alternative to privatization in a village group during a specific period. The major factor explaining the presence or absence of cooperation in the Chinese village or "the vaguely defined cooperative" is the net collective benefit of that action. Before reform, this benefit was captured by the Chinese state and cooperation was absent, although there were interspecific resources which made the forming of a corporate coalition a potential option. It is the independence of the village leader from the state, together with rapid industrialization in the village, that have made this potential option a reality.

The Chinese village after reform is a hybrid organizational model that encompasses elements of both market and hierarchical governance. This model can link the planned and market economies and make the transition smooth and evolutionary. The village organization behaving as a firm easily resulted from a coalition of the interspecific resources owned in common by all villagers at the start of reform. Opportunism can be avoided by protective arrangements, and massive quasi-rents of specific investments (or the collective benefits) can be internalized during economic transition. The links with the state hierarchy may even be used by the village group to stimulate the internalization of quasi-rents and benefits in the prevailing special circumstances.

Acknowledgments:

The author would like to thank Eduard B. Vermeer, Christer Gunnarsson, Woei Lien Chong, Lennart Schön, Rolf Ohlsson, Laixiang Sun, Anne Jerneck, Somboon Siriprachai, Jaya Reddy and participants in the "International Conference on Chinese Rural Collectives and Voluntary Organizations: Between State Organization and Private Interest," Leiden, The Netherlands, 9–13 January 1995, for helpful discussions and comments. The paper on which this chapter is based has also been published in *The Economics of Transition*, vol. 4, no. 1, 1996, a journal published by Oxford University Press for the European Bank for Reconstruction and Development.

Notes

1. "[A]ll the residents in the township or village that establishes the TVE own the firm collectively" (Weitzman and Xu 1994, pp. 127–128).
2. Feuchtwang (1995) has surveyed, beginning from the Song dynasty, the historical change and types of Chinese villages, such as natural place, administrative place, collective place, collective and natural place. The type I study here is the most common in China nowadays, a type standardized by the Chinese Communist regime.
3. Three factors have led to the geographic immobility of rural labor and population. First, China's basic condition of relatively little arable land combined with abundant labor supply. Second, the rapid growth of the population which has further aggravated the basic conditions since 1949. Third, the heavy industry-oriented pattern of industrialization from 1949 to 1978 and the government-imposed household registration system (*hukou* system) which impedes migration. The third factor made rural-to-urban mobility of labor impossible. Mobility of rural labor between villages was not a real option since labor supply exceeded labor demand in nearly every village (see Byrd and Lin 1990, p. 4).
4. Byrd and Lin use the abbreviation TVP for this set of rural non-state enterprises *(xiangzhen qiye)*, including production team enterprises. See Byrd and Lin 1990, p. xi. The scope of this study is broader than mine.
5. Byrd here refers to the fact that when there is a lack of capital to set up TVEs, the policy of community governments is often to give priority in getting jobs in TVEs to households who can provide capital.
6. It is not suggested that selective inducements and punishments do not play a role, only that they are not the central motivating factors.
7. There is much literature on the expansion of local officials' power after reform. For example, Johnson (1991) presents a very interesting account of how the Communist government disrupted the traditional kinship structure before reform, and how this structure has revived since reform, playing a key role in local development.

8. The feature observed by Johnson in the Pearl River delta is in fact present in most parts of rural China. See Johnson 1991, pp. 109–131.

9. In 1994, 75 percent of rural total output value of society was produced by TVEs; 65 percent of annual increase of rural household per capita income was generated by TVEs (*People's Daily* (overseas edition), 4 April 1995).

10. The system of one-man leadership can reach an extreme when someone is simultaneously Party secretary, *cunzhang*, and director of the collective organization. This situation prevailed during the Cultural Revolution, when it was called "strengthening centralized Party leadership." The Party secretary is usually the most powerful person in the Chinese village. In order to narrow the focus of the discussion, this chapter seeks only to analyze the integration of government administration and economic management in the village organization.

11. "[O]ne of the purposes of collectivization was to facilitate the imposition of a high rate of involuntary saving on agriculture, either through increasing taxes and/or through manipulating price relations between agricultural and non-agricultural goods in such a way that the farming sector was forced to sell 'cheap' and buy 'dear'. These price manipulations enabled the state trading companies to earn large monopoly profits, which were then paid into the government budget and became a source for financing investment and other government expenditures" (Eckstein 1977, p. 51).

12. Oi emphasizes the identity of a government official without paying attention to his identity as village member and the changing trend between the two identities. Moreover, since independence from the state is a very sensitive topic and often cannot be talked about openly in China, a difference must be made between the rural leader's actions and his words.

13. The geographic immobility of rural labor is a general but not absolute condition, particularly since the reform. However, only few villagers with special skills are able to leave the village temporarily. Interestingly, most of the successful persons who come back to their villages after having made enough money become the leaders of industrialization in their own villages (see *People's Daily* (overseas edition), 25 November 1994, 13; and 14 February 1995). The reason is perhaps that the villagers' skills are not specific to the coalition, so that they will be able to earn just as much or even more elsewhere. If the coalition fails, nothing is lost. This is why those who are able to do so leave the village. The reason they come back is not only that they have earned enough money elsewhere, but also because they do not want to lose the specific quasi-rent. The value of their money, if combined with transaction-specific resources (low information cost, the kinship tie, trust and the cooperative spirit), will be higher in their village group than elsewhere.

14. In rural China, many private enterprises or relatively pure cooperatives, in order to obtain help from local governments and reduce business risks, prefer the designation of "collective enterprises." As they must pay local governments for such a designation, this payment may be regarded as the specific quasi-rent of the administrative identity.

15. This is particularly true since the reforms. "The village bureaucracy consists of the village committee *(cunmin weiyuanhui)* chaired by the village head *(cunzhang)*. Because the members of this committee are directly elected by members of the village, this body has received some attention as an important step in the democratization of village politics" (Oi 1995, p. 37).

16. "Compression within communities means that the incomes of leading community members (government leaders and enterprise directors) depend at least to some extent on the average income levels in the community" (Byrd and Gelb 1990, p. 364).

17. "The smaller and more clearly defined the boundaries of the common-pool resources the greater the chances of success" (Wade 1987, p. 104).

18. "[V]illage leaders could provide little substantive information about the industrial

activity of neighboring villages" (Rozelle and Boisvert 1994, p. 30).

19. "If . . . the benefits of independent operation ('centrifugal' forces) increase, then the members will either leave the cooperative, or reduce their demand from it" (Bonus 1986, p. 173).

References

Alchian, A.A. 1984. "Specificity, Specialization, and Coalitions." *Journal of Institutional and Theoretical Economics*, no. 140, pp. 34–49.

Bonus, H. 1986. "The Cooperative Association As a Business Enterprise." *Journal of Institutional and Theoretical Economics*, no. 142, pp. 310–339.

Byrd, W.A. 1990. "Entrepreneurship, Capital, and Ownership." In W.A. Byrd and Lin Qingsong, eds., *China's Rural Industry: Structure, Development, and Reform*, pp. 189–217. Oxford: Oxford University Press.

Byrd, W.A., and Alan Gelb. 1990. "Why Industrialize? The Incentives for Rural Community Governments." In W.A. Byrd and Lin Qingsong, eds., 1990.

Byrd, W.A., and Lin Qingsong, eds., 1990. *China's Rural Industry: Structure, Development, and Reform*. Oxford: Oxford University Press.

Chang, C., and Y. Wang. 1994. "The Nature of the Township-Village Enterprise." *Journal of Comparative Economics*, no. 19, pp. 434–452.

Christiansen, Flemming. 1995. "State Intervention, Migration and the Development of Agricultural Resources: The Collective as Mediator?" Paper presented at the International Conference on "Chinese Rural Collectives and Voluntary Organizations: Between State Organization and Private Interest," 9–12 January, Leiden University, The Netherlands.

Coase, R.H., 1937. "The Nature of the Firm." In Oliver E. Williamson and Sidney G. Winter, eds., *The Nature of the Firm: Origin, Evolution, and Development*. New York: Oxford University Press, 1991.

Collier, Ruth Berins, and David Collier. 1979. "Inducements and Constraints: Disaggregating 'Corporatism'." *American Political Science Review*, no. 73, pp. 967–986.

Draheim, G. 1952. *Die Genossenschaft als Unternehmungstyp*. Göttingen: (2nd ed. 1955).

Eckstein, Alexander. 1977. *China's Economic Revolution*. Cambridge: Cambridge University Press.

Feuchtwang, Stephan. 1995. "What Is a Village, Between State Organization and Private Interest?" Paper presented at the International Conference on "Chinese Rural Collectives and Voluntary Organizations: Between State Organization and Private Interest," 9–12 January, Leiden University, The Netherlands.

Friedman, E.; Pickowicz, P.G.; and Selden, M. 1991. *Chinese Village, Socialist State*. New Haven and London: Yale University Press.

Gelb, A. 1990. "TVP Workers' Incomes, Incentives, and Attitudes." In W.A. Byrd and Lin Qingsong, eds., 1990.

Grossman, S. J., and O. D. Hart. 1986. "The Costs and Benefits of Ownership: A Theory of Vertical and Lateral Integration." *Journal of Political Economy*, vol. 94, no. 4, pp. 691-719.

Johnson, G.E. 1991. "Family Strategies and Economic Transformation in Rural China: Some Evidence from the Pearl River Delta." In D. Davis and S. Harrell, eds., *Chinese Families in the Post-Mao Era*, pp. 103–136. Berkeley: University of California Press.

Kimber, R. 1983. "The Tragedy of the Commons Reappraised." Mimeoscript, Department of Politics, University of Keele.

Klein, B.; Crawford, R.G.; and Alchian, A.A. 1984. "Vertical Integration, Appropriable Rents, and the Competitive Contracting Process." *Journal of Law and Economics*, no. 21, pp. 297–326.

Lin Qingsong. 1987. "The Reports of the China United Investigation Team on TVE." In Institute of Economics, CASS (Chinese Academy of Social Sciences), eds., *Zhongguo xiangzhen qiye de jingji fazhan yu tizhi* (The Economic Development and Economic Institution of China's TVEs). Beijing: China Economics Press.

Luo, Xiaopeng. 1990. "Ownership and Status Stratification." In W.A. Byrd and Lin Qingsong, eds., 1990.

Nee, Victor. 1989. "A Theory of Market Transition: From Redistribution to Markets in State Socialism." *American Sociological Review*, no. 54, pp. 663–681.

————. 1992. "Organizational Dynamics of Market Transition: Hybrid Forms, Property Rights, and Mixed Economy in China." *Administrative Science Quarterly*, vol. 37, no. 1, pp. 1–27.

Oi, Jean. 1992. "Fiscal Reform and the Economic Foundations of Local State Corporatism in China." *World Politics*, no. 45, pp. 99–126.

————. 1995. "Local State Corporatism: The Organization of Rapid Economic Growth." Paper presented at the International Conference on "Chinese Rural Collectives and Voluntary Organizations: Between State Organization and Private Interest," 9–12 January, Leiden University, The Netherlands.

Pei, Xiaolin. 1994. "Rural Population, Institutions and China's Economic Transformation." *The European Journal of Development Research*, vol. 6, no. 1, pp. 175–196.

———— and Christer Gunnarsson. "Agrarian Structures, Property Rights and Transition to Market Economy in China and the Former Soviet Union." In Jacques Hersh and Johannes Dragsbaek Schmidt, eds., *East Europe: Between Western Europe and East Asia—From Big Bang to Governed Markets*. International Political Economic Series. London: Macmillan, forthcoming.

Picot, Arnold. 1984. "Comment to 'Specificity, Specialization, and Coalitions'." *Journal of Institutional and Theoretical Economics*, no. 140, pp. 50–53.

Qian, Y., and C. Xu. 1993a. "The M-form Hierarchy and China's Economic Reform." *European Economic Review*, no. 37, pp. 541–548.

————. 1993b. "Commitment, Financial Constraints, and Innovation: Market Socialism Reconsidered." In P.K. Bardhan and J.E. Roemer, eds., *Market Socialism: The Current Debate*, pp. 175–189. New York: Oxford University Press.

Rozelle, S., and R.N. Boisvert. 1994. "Quantifying Chinese Village Leaders' Multiple Objectives." *Journal of Comparative Economics*, no. 18, pp. 25–45.

Song, Lina, and Du He. 1990. "The Role of Township Governments in Rural Industrialization." In W.A. Byrd and Lin Qingsong, eds., 1990.

Wade, Robert. 1987. "The Management of Common Property Resources: Collective Action As an Alternative to Privatisation or State Regulation." *Cambridge Journal of Economics*, no. 11, pp. 95–106.

————. 1988. *Village Republics: Economic Conditions for Collective Action in South India*. Cambridge: Cambridge University Press, 1988.

Weitzman, M., and C. Xu. 1994. "Chinese Township-Village Enterprises As Vaguely Defined Cooperatives." *Journal of Comparative Economics*, no. 18, pp. 121–145.

6

Decollectivization and Functional Change in Irrigation Management in China

Eduard B. Vermeer

The experience of local water conservancy management over the past decade is of considerable significance in the evaluation of government performance and farmers' responses to a situation of rapid political and economic change. About half of China's farmland is under some form of irrigation, and it provides more than two-thirds of China's output of grain and cotton. Water conservancy and irrigation had been a major, if not the most important, motive for collectivization and the formation of larger management units in agriculture during the 1950s. Water conservancy accounted for the major share of state budgetary investments in agriculture. The people's communes and production brigades assigned a big proportion of their organized labor force, both on a regular basis and as corvée labor during winter and spring, to the construction and maintenance of water conservancy and irrigation facilities (Vermeer 1977).

There may have been ulterior political motives behind the sudden drop in state investments and attention to water conservancy construction in 1979–1980. In 1979, the policies of promoting rapid agricultural mechanization came under strong attack. Recently, an author has argued that "since the Dazhai clique envisaged agricultural mechanization as the key to modernizing China's agriculture and to preserving Mao's legacy of the collective economy, the reformers had first to reduce the importance of mechanization in order to weaken the power of Hua Guofeng and the Dazhai clique as well as to generate a persuasive rationale for a highly decentralized, commercialized and individual system of agricultural production" (Jae p. 289). Even if Jae has overstated the reformist agricultural policy goals at that time, and one might interpret the 1979 statements down-playing agricultural mechanization more simply as a rationalization of the government's failure to achieve the highly publicized target of "basic mechanization by 1980," the shift towards liberalization and reduced political involvement in agriculture was quite clear. Water conservation and irrigation being the most mechanized of all agricultural activities were particularly affected by this political trend.

In Chinese reports, the 1970s have been described as the Golden Age of water conservancy and irrigation. There were many positive factors responsible for the construction of facilities, their maintenance and management, and distribution of irrigation water: unified planning and execution of projects; existence of large users' units (people's communes and production brigades); excess of rural labor which could be mobilized at will; a growing body of managerial and technical personnel at the county and village levels; low prices of pump fuels and electricity; and political priority for agricultural production. In most cases, decisions to build new facilities were based less on cost/benefit considerations than on the local political efforts to increase grain output. Financial yardsticks were introduced only in the early 1980s, but even so, high hidden or overt price subsidies (notably for electricity fees of high-lift pumping stations) continued to obscure real costs. As local governments did not have to bear the costs of such subsidies, they did little to curb their expansive investment behavior.[1]

The negative effects of decollectivization on irrigation management were manifold and obvious. In the early 1980s, farmland was split up among numerous small users. Crops were no longer sown over large stretches of land, but diversified and scattered over many tiny plots. Gauging the water use of so many individual farmers was impossible. Farmers did not organize repairs because of lack of capital, know-how, organization, or insufficient insight in the vital importance of irrigation facilities. Instead, farmers started to drill their own wells, construct their own ponds, or divert water from existing surface-flow systems on their own initiative. Thus, overall control over water resources was seriously reduced. Many areas reported a virtual breakdown of large parts of their irrigation systems.[2] Farmers had grown accustomed to the free use of irrigation water and other public facilities under the communal system. It took time to change their attitude. Peasant sentiments towards the use of irrigation water found expression in statements such as "water comes from the sky," "we have too much water here already," "flood control projects are for the common good," and other arguments to justify their unwillingness to pay for water use and maintenance of conservancy projects (Wang Shouqiang 1986).

Worried by the breakdown in rural organization, the Chinese government concluded in 1982 that the management system of farmland water conservation needed strengthening. All but the individually owned facilities should be managed by state or collective governments, and the latter should contract the management of facilities out to specialized teams or offices, groups or individual farmers. Contracts could cover the complete management and operation of irrigation systems, and provide for financial responsibility (*ZGNYNJ 1982*, pp. 408–9). Contracts could also be seasonal and for limited operations only, e.g. for the distribution of irrigation water, or maintenance. A Japanese scholar concluded that the government was "forced to take measures to prevent a complete break-down of the water conservancy management system. ... The collapse of the people's communes also meant the collapse of the organizations for managing water conservancy" (Kojima 1988, pp. 718–9). However, such a conclusion is unjustified for three reasons. The word "collapse" over-dramatizes the changes in local administrative control at that time; it was not only government but rather local Party and village leaders who took remedial action, and control over irrigation districts was maintained by local government organizations. In reality, in 1983–1984 the main economic functions of the people's communes and production brigades were transferred to so-called regional cooperative economic organizations. These functions included management of collective land and other natural resources, collective assets and companies; planning of investments; organization of agricultural capital construction; and protection against natural disasters. National and local governments continued to carry out some major tasks at the macro and microlevel: the setting of prices of electricity; financing of medium- and large-scale projects; levying of water fees; planning, construction and maintenance of projects; allocation of water use; and settlement of disputes. Moreover, they did not abandon their role in the mobilization and direction of corvée labor, the popularization of techniques and provision of services.

The contracts concluded between farm households and *xiang* governments in those years established a new basis for mutual obligations. There was no uniformity. Some governments maintained the centralized management of all irrigation facilities, while others sold off all equipment and privatized or abandoned collective services. Separation of administrative and economic functions of the rural governments (*xiang* and *cun*), a declared policy goal, was often in name only. Survey data showed that the extent of privatization of facilities and services differed greatly between regions and villages. The differences could be explained only partly by different levels of development. Apparently, whatever directives from the Communist Party or government there may have been, they were unable by themselves to stem the tide of deregulation and privatization. The formal and informal local village leaders' view of the future economic organization of their village played a decisive role.

This article begins with a quantitative survey of the development of water conservancy projects, irrigation facilities, equipment and irrigated area since 1980, and discusses their relation with output of food grain and the farmland area stricken by droughts and floods. It will be shown that after decollectivization and rising costs had depressed farmland irrigation, decisive government action produced a turn-around in 1986 and sustained growth since then. Next, it considers continuities and changes in the internal organization of China's large irrigation districts in the 1970s and 1980s, and their decision-making processes. It will be argued that in as far as they were able to become financially self-supporting, their independence from government and Communist Party has increased. Intermediate-level managerial and technical cadres, together with more or less organized individual water users themselves, became dominant in some districts.

The next section discusses the resurrection by government of peasant corvée labor. This was an age-old tradition which had been continued and expanded by the people's communes, although it had rapidly eroded during the early years of rural reform. It proved to be a crucial element in producing the 1986 turn-around. The question is, why old-fashioned campaign-style politics were more effective here than in most other areas of government concern.

One of the greatest changes in rural collective ownership and management occurred with irrigation pumps and wells. In section five, share-holding cooperatives and individual ownership are shown to have become popular forms, but recentralization has also occurred. Neither form has been able to stop the uncontrolled over-drawing of ground water, a long-standing practice which in the author's view might effectively be reduced by more adequate pricing of water and electricity.

In the section on the provision of irrigation services, the author will show how decollectivization was followed by a serious decline in services. After 1986, many were reorganized in different forms. Common characteristics were professionalization, specialization and staff reduction. Some services cut through former administrative divisions, and most became more commercial. Here again, a substantial recovery occurred in the late 1980s. Three forms of water conservancy services may be distinguished: state-operated, mixed state-collective and mixed collective-private. Many suffer from serious difficulties of personnel and finance.

Finally, our analysis of the financial basis of water conservancy stations and irrigation systems will show the inadequacy of the system of water fees and funding. Most organizations ran into considerable difficulties since decollectivization, because government and water users paid too little, and too late. In spite of the provisions of the new water law of 1985, for political and bureaucratic reasons provinces and districts did not increase irrigation water fees to levels which would cover most of the costs of supply. Although their reasons have not been spelled out publicly, the author ventures to suggest that the political reasons were closely linked with the government's ideas of rural control and protection of the farmers' short-term economic interests.

These and other questions raised in this article will hopefully provide some useful insights into the nature of China's rural political system. In each section, our main questions concern the government's response to the problems caused by the sudden decollectivization of China's rural villages. Our exploration of the changing relations between state organizations, village organizations and the water-using farmers is a very incomplete and preliminary one, because of the limitations of our data and the complexity and regional diversity of water conservancy and irrigation systems. The changes in management of local service units, and the tendency towards commercialization, privatization, and independent decision-making by farmers appear to be part of the general trend of China's rural development since the 1980s. However, by its very nature, water conservancy and irrigation require a great deal of central planning, coordination and regulation of individual behavior. There is continuous tension between the necessary control from above and day-to-day decision-making by water-using farmers. Both are needed for an optimal utilization of water, and cannot be effective if they do not support intermediate organizations for the direction of investments, maintenance and water distribution. The changes in the intermediate organizations during the reform period have a logic of their own, but also reflect changed concepts of the function of government and the changed position and demands of the individual farmer.

Quantitative Developments during 1980–1992:
Decline, Countermeasures, and Turn-around

After decollectivization and the introduction of the household responsibility system in rural areas in the early 1980s, water conservancy and irrigation started on a negative course. Facilities and equipment were neglected and sometimes even destroyed or plundered. Investments in infrastructure and expenditures on collective services were sharply reduced. Communal labor organization virtually ceased to exist. Corvée labor, which was traditionally organized by the county government and villages partly to complement state projects during the slack season, was much reduced. In part, the dramatic decrease in rural labor input was due to the much reduced scale of state-planned water conservancy project construction, to about one-quarter of what it used to be before 1980 (see Table 6.1). The greatest decrease[3] occurred in the year 1980, at a time when political relaxation had set in although the collectives were still in place. Nevertheless, the major reason for the decline was decollectivization itself. Before 1980, peasants were mobilized by cadres of rural collectives—who might gain political credit by reporting a high turnout—and paid no wages other than "work points." As peasants regained their independence and returned to their own plots of land or other gainful occupations, corvée and collective labor sank to heretofore unknown lows and became almost taboo in the early 1980s.[4]

The favorable weather conditions and increasing grain yields of the first half of the 1980s (from 321 million tons in 1980 to a record of 407 million tons in 1984) help explain why the government's and farmers' propensity to invest in construction and maintenance of irrigation facilities was reduced. In most areas of China, irrigation is only supplementary, and less needed if rainfall is good. Of course, the professional cadres of the water conservancy bureaus knew better. All through the 1980s, the Ministry of Water Conservation and the professional cadres at local levels voiced their concerns about decreasing investments[5] and the continuing deterioration of water conservancy and irrigation facilities since decollectivization. It is hard to ascertain as to how far this deterioration was real; in any case, it was perceived as such by many. Of course, it may have been in the

Table 6.1

**Water Conservancy Project Construction and Corvée Labor
Output, 1976–1991: Amounts of Earth, Stone and Concrete** (annual averages)

Years	State-planned construction			Corvée labor, county-level and below (earth/stone) (billions of cu. m.)
	Earth	Stone	Concrete	
	(millions of cu. m.)			
1976–1980	1,389	166	6.8	n.d.
1981–1986	232	21	2.4	1.7–1.9
1987	310	26	2.8	3
1988	293	23	3.0	4
1989	317	29	3.3	4.2
1990	332	27	4.4	5
1991	401	31	5.1	5.6
1992	6.3			

Sources: Zhongguo shuili nianjian 1990, p. 659; *1991,* p. 702; *1992,* pp. 681–3; *Zhongguo nongye nianjian 1983,* p. 163; *1987,* p. 18; *1991,* pp. 21, 130; *1992,* p. 21; *1993,* p. 117.

interest of cadres to stress the decline. Most likely, during the 1980s farmers became more vociferous in pressing their (increasing) demands for reliable sources of irrigation water. Once grain harvests went down again in 1985 and food grain ran short in 1986, these concerns were translated into political action. The CCP Central Committee decided in 1986 that the construction of water conservancy projects by village labor should be revived and expanded, and that government itself should also increase its investments. This set the tone for the return of irrigation to the government priority list during the next few years.

A leading article on water conservancy problems under rural reform noted the need for fundamental changes at that time. In 1987, one-third of China's farmland had been stricken by drought or floods. Grain output did not rise. More than 40 percent of the reservoirs were defective and dangerous. Dikes were in need of repair. One-quarter of the equipment was too old. The equipment in more than half of all wells had to be replaced soon. In the past decade, investments had declined drastically. Farmers had contracted for farmland, but were not given the responsibility for maintaining the ditches. It was felt that government policies should be redirected towards promoting active farmers' involvement in irrigation and drainage (Zhou Zhiping 1989). In response to such criticisms and the objective need to increase grain output, the government increased its investments again, either directly or through the Agricultural Development Fund.[6]

As a result of these and other efforts, between 1986 and 1992 the number of irrigation and drainage stations rose from 456,000 to 494,000, and their installed

Table 6.2

Irrigation and Drainage Facilities in China, 1980–1992 (Selected Years)

Year	Irr./dr. stations ('000)	Capacity (GW)	Machine wells ('000)	Capacity (GW)	Irrig. area (million *mu*)
1980	524	18.0	2,089/2,599*	20.7	673
1983	475	19.1	2,118/2,672*	22.8	670/728
1986	456	19.2	2,114/2,364*	22.8	663/718
1989	465	20.0	2,442/2,633*	25.9	674/725
1990	474	20.1	2,565/2,731*	26.6	711/726
1992	494	22.2	n.d. /2,946*	27.3	729/n.d.

Sources: Zhongguo nongye nianjian 1981, 1984, 1987, 1990, 1993; Zhongguo shuili nianjian 1990, 1991.

*The second set of figures, from the Ministry of Agriculture, includes wells which lack equipment or have run dry because of lowered ground water tables. Possibly because of the exclusion of one of those two categories (each of which was about 10 percent of the total), the Ministry of Water Conservation has published somewhat lower figures, viz. 2,291,000 and 2,413,000, for 1980 and 1983. For 1986, one source gave a high figure of 2,674,000 for all wells, implying no change from 1983 (*Zhongguo shuili* 1987, no. 7, p. 28). The official figures used by James Nickum in 1988 show a sudden (and unlikely) jump from 2,095,000 outfitted wells in 1982 to 2,410,000 in 1983 (quoted by Bruce Stone 1988, pp. 772–3).

N.B. It seems that from 1990, the State Statistical Bureau (from whom the agricultural yearbooks took their figures) started using a different set of figures for the effective irrigated area, moving closer to the (second) set of figures used by the Ministry of Water Conservation. Both sets represent the farmland area which *could* be irrigated with existing facilities *under normal conditions*, and are considerably higher than the figures for *actual* irrigated farmland area, which of course is related to weather conditions. For instance in 1990, the actual irrigated area was 621 million *mu* or almost 20 percent lower than the effective irrigated area. In all cases, irrigated areas designated as forest, fruit orchards, tea and mulberry plantations and grassland are excluded.

capacity by 15 percent; similarly, the number and installed capacity of mechanized wells rose by 20–25 percent (see Table 6.2). Partly as a result, the irrigated area began to increase slowly again. Foodgrain yields mounted to well over 400 million tons, an increase which should be attributed in part to improvements in irrigation water supply, and continued to rise (see Table 6.3).

Official data on the changes in provincial irrigated acreages during this period are shown in Table 6.4 on page 144. Some observations can be made. The modest decline of the area designated as "effective irrigated area" between 1980 and 1986 was spread very unevenly over China. Anhui,[7] Sichuan and Henan saw a net decline of more than five million *mu* each, and Guangdong of almost three million *mu*. In most other provinces, the decline was less than 5 percent. Hunan and, to a lesser extent, Jiangxi registered significant increases; percentage-wise, Guizhou also registered a large increase.

Table 6.3

Effectively Irrigated Acreage in China's Provinces, 1980, 1986, and 1992

	(100,000 *mu*)			% change over 1980	
	1980	1986	1992	1986	1992
China total	6,733	6,633	7,420	−2	+10
Heilongjiang	101	108	174	+7	+73
Liaoning	114	110	171	−4	+50
Jilin	110	108	137	−2	+25
Inner Mongolia	166	151	255	−9	+54
Ningxia	35	37	49	+6	+40
Gansu	128	124	142	−3	+11
Xinjiang	392	406	423	+4	+8
Qinghai/Tibet	46	43	55	−7	+19
Guizhou	69	80	86	+17	+23
Yunnan	137	145	166	+6	+22
Guangdong/ Hainan	316	287	364	−9	+15
Guangxi	215	203	227	−6	+6
Fujian	132	137	142	+4	+8
Jiangsu	512	531	578	+4	+13
Zhejiang	229	224	220	−2	−4
Anhui	366	314	415	−14	+13
Jiangxi	250	272	278	+9	+11
Hunan	362	416	402	+15	+11
Hubei	352	338	354	−4	+1
Beijing/Tianjin/ Shanghai	160	151	147	−5	−8
Henan	530	482	567	−9	+9
Hebei	543	533	585	−2	+7
Shandong	661	682	689	+3	+4
Shanxi	167	158	175	−5	+5
Shaanxi	187	187	195	−/+	+4
Sichuan	453	409	426	−10	−6

Sources: Area figures taken from *Zhongguo nongye nianjian 1981, 1987, 1993.*

Six years later, China had expanded its irrigated area to about 10 percent above the 1980 level. Strikingly successful were the northern border provinces of Heilongjiang and Inner Mongolia. The South and Southwest (Yunnan, Guizhou, Guangdong) have also witnessed considerable net expansion. In most areas there was room for agricultural intensification, and the government anti-poverty pro-

Table 6.4

China's Grain Output and Farmland Area Stricken by Floods and Droughts, 1980–1993 (million tons; million *mu*)

Year	Grain output (million tons)	Stricken area (million *mu*)	Affected by floods	Affected by droughts
1980	321	263	75	187
1983	387	200	86	114
1985	379	290	134	156
1986	392	305	84	221
1989	408	318	89	229
1990	446	201	84	117
1991	435	378	219	158
1992	443	322	67	255
1993	456	260	130	130

Sources: Zhongguo shuili nianjian 1992, pp. 645–6; *Zhongguo nongye nianjian 1993*, pp. 448–9; *Zhongguo tongji zhaiyao 1994*, p. 70.

N.B. These are official figures for "seriously affected areas" *chengzai*, that is, areas suffering a loss of more than 30 percent of normal output because of floods or drought; additionally, 15 to 20 percent is stricken by other disasters such as pests, hail and frosts.

gram provided much-needed investment funds for the purchase of equipment. In the Yangzi basin, most provinces have added a little over 10 percent since 1980, but there has not been much change in Zhejiang and Hubei. Sichuan is exceptional; two-thirds of the 10 percent drop in Sichuan was registered in the year 1985; part of this may have been a belated adjustment of a too high figure for 1980. Its growth since 1986 has been very modest. The three municipalities noted a steady decrease, which may be attributed to their shortage of water resources, increased household and industrial water demand and the loss of farmland to other uses, all of which are nationwide phenomena.

In spite of increased pumping capacities, the severity of floods and waterlogging has increased. During the 1980s, about 80 to 90 million *mu* of farmland suffered severely from flooding every year (somewhat less than that in 1981 and 1987 and considerably more in 1985). In the 1970s, the affected areas were less than half that amount (1977 excepted). The floods of 1991 were the most serious since the founding of the PRC; again, 1993 and 1995 witnessed major floods. For many years, the Ministry of Water Conservation and high-level water conservancy cadres had voiced serious concerns about the increasing danger of floods, but their warnings went unheeded. Apparently, the Chinese government (as so many others) found itself incapable of giving sufficient priority to the long-term interest of flood control, which, other than irrigation, does not yield any immediate benefit but only reduces the chance of serious losses of life and property. The great annual variations in the severity of flood and drought disaster show the limited capacity of irrigation and drainage facilities: on average, one-fifth of China's farmland is seriously stricken by floods or droughts.

Authors in China have suggested a direct relation between the sluggish performance of foodgrain production during 1985–1988 and the neglect of irrigation facilities during the early 1980s. Similarly, they have linked the higher levels of foodgrain output reached during the 1990s with increased attention to and investments in irrigation projects since 1987. Both relations seem self-evident at first sight. However, no such relation was apparent in the 1970s, when the extraordinarily great attention to water conservation did not result in significantly higher output. Moreover, if we reduce annual fluctuations in grain output during the 1980s by using moving three-year averages, it appears that there was a fairly steady annual increase of about 3 percent. This steady rise belies the impact of the supposed neglect of irrigation facilities during the early 1980s. Apparently, the decrease of availability of irrigation water in some areas did not necessarily reduce overall output. This leads us to the conclusion that at that time, in a significant number of areas the use of irrigation water was uneconomical, because crops received excessive amounts of irrigation water. The available evidence suggests that many facilities were either over-extended or overlapping, and competed, at considerable cost, for the same scarce water sources.

Thus, there are sufficient reasons to consider the early 1980s more positively as a period of rationalization of water supply, and reduction of mostly idle and therefore costly facilities. Nevertheless, the reductions may have been uneven and painful, and were poorly understood. Local officials, farmers and technicians all complained about local deterioration of their water supply facilities.

Organization of Large Irrigation Districts

Large and medium-sized irrigation districts are responsible for almost one-half of China's irrigated area.[8] The structure of their management dates back to the 1950s or 1930s, or even earlier. Considering their great resilience, the question which interests us most is how these organizations were affected by, and had to adapt to, the political and economic liberalization of rural China since 1980. The external changes can be classified under four different headings: decollectivization, the waning of Communist Party control, reduction of state involvement in rural affairs, and an increasingly market-like environment.

As a starting point, we may consider the organization of the Shaoshan Irrigation District in Hunan at the end of the Cultural Revolution period. The publication of its experiences in a three-volume set of books in 1978 supported the rise of Hua Guofeng to power (Hua had been responsible for its construction in 1966). This 60,000-hectare project resorted under the Xiangtan prefectural government.[9] It had a Congress of Irrigation District Representatives, comprising about 110 people, composed of various segments: (1) representatives of counties, districts, people's communes and production brigades in the beneficiary area, who had been selected by their respective units; (2) leading CCP cadres from the same; and (3) responsible personnel from the Provincial Water Conservancy and Electric Power Bureau, the hydro-power station and the Shaoshan Irrigation Project Management Office. Their annual meeting lasted from five to seven days. The representatives listened to the annual report of the Management Committee, summed up experiences, applauded the achievements and brought forward remaining problems. They discussed the improvement of management and examined and approved the annual plans for repairs and expansion. Over the past few years they had approved management rules, water fee rules, afforestation rules, and the 1976–1980 construction plan.

Under the formal authority of this Congress were an Irrigation District Management Committee, and a hierarchy of management committees at county level and ten main canal sections (according to the administrative borders of the people's communes). Each of the latter had three or four state employees, and one or two cadres paid for by their collective. At the branch canal level and below, management was mainly handled by the collectives. For each ditch system, a Ditch System Management Committee was set up. For the branch canal irrigation areas which crossed the borders of a commune, management stations were set up under the next higher administrative authority, with three to five personnel. Out of a total of 6,192 management personnel (that is, as many as one employee for every ten hectares!), only 184 were state employees, who received fixed salaries. The others received work points from their respective collectives (*Shaoshan* 1979 pp. 3–6).

The organizational structure described above was similar to those of other state-managed irrigation districts established throughout China in the 1950s. The Congress of Irrigation District Representatives was not meant to represent the end-users of irrigation water. Instead, it was a platform which brought together leading government and CCP cadres, representatives of rural collectives, and water conservancy technicians. Most were actively involved in the management of the irrigation district they were called upon to discuss. Nevertheless, both in a formal and in an informal way, this assembly could break through the existing bureaucratic channels of communication and lines of command. Of course, it provided the authorities with an opportunity to hand down general policies and explain their annual plans. At the same time, it constituted a check on top-down planning and management practices, as it functioned as a platform for voicing grassroots-level concerns and demands. Internally, it helped establish an *esprit de corps*. Externally, it constituted a strong organized lobby for the irrigation district's interests with the provincial and local authorities.

Half a dozen years later, the irrigation districts were still in place, but their organization had changed. A 1983 article by a Shaanxi provincial official stressed the newly created diversity of management forms. The districts derived their income from water fees and diversified operations. Salary levels and duties were decided by the government, but units and individuals could receive bonuses for good performance or overfulfilment of their contracted tasks, according to the technical and economic indices for irrigation district and pumping station management adopted by the Ministry of Water Conservation. The few which were profitable and paid annual dues to the government, such as the Luohui Canal District,[10] were able to operate with some independence. Some less profitable ones, such as the Jinghui and Baojixia districts, tried to balance their budget over the years. They established a responsibility system for their employees, and a third level of management and accounting, that of the local station. The latter became responsible for the execution of contracted tasks within their head gate. However, most large irrigation districts ran at a considerable loss and depended on local government subsidies. Thus, their management had little room for manoeuvre (He Zhengyuan 1983).

In 1985, the Ministry of Water Conservation suggested that greater financial independence on the basis of higher water fees and multipurpose operations should become the pillars of reform. Irrigation district management should gradually develop towards "entreprization and socialization." The irrigation district chief should be empowered to determine the administrative set-up, staffing, distribution of bonuses, etc. The employees should diversify their operations in order to increase income. On the one hand, the Ministry suggested that "the role of the irrigation district congress should be brought into full play. In principle, the representatives of the irrigation district should be elected by the beneficiary households," but on the other hand, it indicated that the leading cadres, the employees of the irrigation district, technicians and basic-level management personnel should be represented as well.[11] It allowed a trial system whereby the representatives of the beneficiary households chose a board of directors which in turn should solicit and hire the irrigation district head. In this way, state management was to be transformed gradually into collective management of the beneficiary households (Ministry 1985). This official document reflected the optimistic mood of the 1984–1985 reform period. None of the institutional suggestions were realized in subsequent years; apparently, the political and economic basis for such a devolution of power into cooperative or even private hands remained too weak—and may have become even weaker as democratization was arrested and the profitability of crop growing declined.

Large irrigation districts had management stations for each of the branch canals, and below that, for each head gate (which typically controls areas between 300 and 700 hectares). This three-layered management held three types of meetings: a spring conference to decide on water distribution and use; brief meetings to decide on operational problems during the irrigation season; and a summing-up meeting at the end of the season. It made sure that gates were opened only according to plan, that water use was recorded, that after gates had been closed the results of irrigation were summed up, and that all records and documents were filed. Lower units had to keep records of their water intake, the irrigated area, the periods of use of the canals, allocated water quantities, and the efficiency of irrigation (*ZGNYNJ 1985*, p. 372).

The 1980s saw a definite trend towards technical specialization. Professional societies must have played an important role in this process at the higher levels, but there is little information about their activities.[12] The composition of the Irrigation District Congresses changed along the lines of the 1985 document. Most of the political organizers had gone. There were no more representatives of the CCP, communes or production brigades. Irrigation management and water conservancy project construction was not a profitable business and not likely to become one. Those cadres who jumped the bandwagon of economic reform and privatization of government business could not find attractive opportunities for technological modernization, entrepreneurship, high profits, travel and kickbacks in this sector. Thus, the sector was left largely to its own devices—and thereby lost much of its previous political influence.

We have seen above that at the end of the 1980s, the central government, worried by sluggish growth in food grain production, tried to reassert its traditional authority in commanding the local governments' and CCP's attention to water conservancy work. It sent out directives that more financial and labor resources should be mobilized. However, this hardly affected irrigation management, which became further decentralized.

Within the congresses, the intermediate-level managerial and technical cadres dominated in numbers over both the leading state cadres and the water users. However, the latter commanded much more respect than before, because they were the ones who contributed to the system and particularly to its lower levels through their payments of water fees. The influence of the provincial and county cadres was likely to have been strongest in those irrigation districts which needed large subsidies. Though the CCP was no longer represented as an institution, it continued to exert considerable influence in the irrigation districts through its national propaganda, political dominance in government bureaus and local members. The CCP constantly reminded government cadres of their duty to protect the farmers' interests and alleviate their burdens. Also, it tended to support the rights of poorer communities to water. Because of their changed composition and the scarcity of external funding, the irrigation district congresses were inclined to focus on the internal organization and management of water distribution and maintenance of facilities. Taking their cue from the various new responsibility systems of the early 1980s, they devised numerous regulations to promote a more efficient use of their personnel and facilities.

Subsequent developments showed that the new formal arrangements and detailed incentive systems did not guarantee good results. An analysis of the deterioration of an irrigation system in Sanyuan[13] shows both external and internal causes. First, there were upstream problems. The total water intake of the Jinghui Canal system had halved to 200 million cubic metres, and water supply was down to only about 20 cubic metres per second. Half of the reservoir capacity in the county had been lost because of siltation. Second, there were problems with management. Because of uncontrolled pumping, the underground water level

had sunk by four to eight metres and the quality of soil and water had deteriorated. There were feuds about water use between villages. Third, there were
financial problems. Water fees covered less than half of the costs of irrigation
water supply, and the irrigation district management had no means to repair or
renew equipment and facilities. During the 1980s, investments had declined by
two-thirds to a mere 800,000 *yuan* per year. It was quite clear that the irrigation
district lacked control over its most pressing problems. Similar examples of weakening management and worsening conditions have been reported elsewhere.[14]

A recent article notes that in Shandong, only one-third of its thirty-three large
and medium-sized irrigation districts enjoy basic independence in their authority
over water distribution (opening and closing water gates, adjustment of water
volumes, etc.) and finances (receipt of water fees and managing their use). Most
have to follow the instructions of the local governments in these matters as well
as in repairs and surveillance of the canals. Their conflicting demands and instructions throw the irrigation system into confusion. Water is wasted terribly,
projects and facilities deteriorate and people evade payment of water fees. The
author of the article suggests that management should receive stronger support
from local party and government organizations, but at the same time he warns
against too much interference and control by their leading departments. He holds
that a democratization of decision-making and management would bring a solution, and that this might best be done through the establishment of Congresses
of Irrigation District Representatives, which should "arrange the annual work
plan, listen to and decide on the management committee's work reports, approve the methods of collection and management of water fees and project
management rules etc., choose members of the management committee, and
decide on some major problems in the irrigation district." Moreover, staffing
levels, which had fallen to less than half the official standards (of three to five
employees for every 10,000 *mu*) should be raised again. Every village *cun*
should set up an irrigation management group of three to five people for the
provision of services (Geng Min 1993). There is nothing new in this description
of the role of irrigation district congresses. Apparently, they have not been
functioning in most districts. Notably absent is the authority to decide about the
tariffs of water fees, which still is a prerogative of provincial government. As
long as irrigation districts are financially dependent on the provincial and local
governments, it seems unduly optimistic to believe that their management could
be freed from outside interference.

One method of improving efficiency in large systems is the decentralization
of duties and responsibilities to lower units. In connection with this, perfor-
mance-based remuneration systems have been devised for units and individual
employees. The People's Irrigation District in Shanxi, which later became a
national model unit, introduced a total performance standard based on eight
indices composed of a total of 49 variables in 1988. In 1992, these were adjusted
to four elements with several indicators each: irrigation management (including

water transport, irrigation quota, serviced area, times of irrigation); financial management (advance fee collection, percentage of realized receipts, completeness of accounts, shortages); project management (safe transport of water, clearance of silt and reconstruction, completion of works, project quality); and finally promotion of "spiritual civilization" (ideological quality, records of diligence and absence of negative behavior, managerial creativity, management of additional income-generating activities such as forestry, orchards etc.) (Bi Jinfeng 1992). Most standards of performance were quantitative rather than qualitative.[15] While such remuneration systems may be useful reminders of the goals of the organization, and provide more objective performance standards for personnel, they add considerably to the administrative load of the organization, and tend to become routinized and merely symbolic. Moreover, reductions of staff, declining real wages and other exogenous factors may put any kind of remuneration system in jeopardy.

The other route taken by this and other irrigation districts was privatization of some of the smaller parts of the water distribution system and mechanized wells. It was noted that the abolition of the collectives had created a huge gap between the district management and the many small water users, causing a general neglect and breakdown of facilities. Poor management was considered to be the major factor.[16] In 1985, a remedy was sought whereby the maintenance of irrigation canals was contracted out to lower units, and subsequently, all branch canals, head gates and field ditches to individual farmers or groups of farmers. The farmers involved received a management fee of .1 to .2 cents per cubic metre of irrigation water. Enormous savings were reported to have resulted from these changes: one-quarter of the irrigation water was saved and 60 percent of the labor; the completion rate of projects was raised from 75 percent to over 90 percent (Fan Shengde 1992). However, part of the improvements should also be attributed to the introduction of modern monitoring equipment, such as automatic gauges and remote measuring devices (*Zhongguo shuili* 1992, no. 11, p. 34). In the (rather exceptional) case of auctioning small reservoirs, their management might be most attractive because of the rights to live in the reservoir buildings, raise fish and grow crops on the hilly sides of the reservoirs. Such contracts might be very profitable.[17] The changes in ownership and management of machine-pump wells are discussed separately below.

Before their abolition in 1984, the rural collectives had started to conclude all kinds of contracts for the construction, operation and maintenance of water conservancy facilities. Those with fairly many irrigation facilities established specialized teams responsible for their management. Wells, ponds and other small projects were contracted out to teams, individuals or groups of farm households. Fish rearing, tree plantations and other sideline activities were contracted out to employees, and so were specific management tasks, e.g. management of small hydro-power stations. The collectives also concluded contracts for seasonal maintenance of facilities with the county government. Specialized technical teams, such as for sprinkler irrigation, sprang into existence, offering their services to interested collectives. The main advantages of these systems were greater control over costs, and more cost awareness at various levels; a reduced need for state subsidies; greater attention for additional income sources; greater personal and group responsibilities. The result was higher output and better protection of facilities against the prevalent tendency of neglect and destruction (He Zhengyuan 1983).

Under the collective system of the 1970s, several overlapping, non-antagonistic hierarchies were in evidence in large irrigation systems. State organizations under the water conservancy bureaus took major decisions about water supply. Together with officials of the Agricultural Bureau they were responsible for the allocation and distribution of water to the collectives. They determined quantities of water, periods of supply, water prices, expenditure on maintenance and investment in large and medium-sized facilities. Thus, outside agents determined most of the basic conditions of water supply. For surface water, this situation has continued till today. Nevertheless, there has been a change in the superior status of state organizations versus water users. Their relation has come to be based more on contracts, and they are more service-oriented. A greater part of investments and maintenance costs have been explicitly contributed by the users. Government organizations have been underfinanced for many years now and their employees have lost their advantage in salaries and their political and socioeconomic status has become more modest. In contrast, the economic status of the farmers who are water users has been enhanced. They have gained part of the power which used to be vested in intermediary administrative and political organizations. Some more power has accrued to the local water conservancy stations, where the state employees are a minority now. Most employees are village technicians and managers. Though formally under the leadership of the county water conservancy bureau, their personnel has become more and more dependent on the financial support of the local farmers.

The abolition of the collective system led to a number of inequalities among the farmers in irrigation communities. Rules were no longer set by the government authorities alone. Villages decided on their own water utilization rights and forms of management. Compliance with rules varied. In the absence of outside agencies, systems must be controlled by the interested parties themselves. Those farmers who were willing and able to invest in irrigation machinery captured a larger and more assured share of underground and surface water. Those who formed groups could, in principle, dictate the conditions of commercial supply of water, though the village government still might exert price control.

Through the continued subsidies of both electricity and water, governments at all levels still yield considerable influence—such subsidies have become part of its legitimacy, with the government seeing to it that the farmers' burden does not increase. This may be the major reason why subsidy systems have been so persistent, in China as elsewhere. Whether such subsidies really contribute to more equity is questionable. In most cases (notable exceptions being poor villages in arid areas which are serviced by high-lift pumping stations, and new irrigation projects in farmland reclamation areas), subsidized water supply means that the largest water users, farmers with high-yield irrigated farmland or large plantations, farmers raising fish, cattle or pigs, and farmers engaged in other highly-productive agricultural activities do not have to pay the full cost of production. Where rich farmers have captured control over village government, inequalities and inequities are likely to increase.

However, the social and political pressures arising from the egalitarian tradition of the village are very much in evidence. The weakness of individual ownership rights and government political orientation towards maintaining equity work in diametrically opposite directions. Most irrigation communities, large or small, continue to be bound by the common interests of all users, and by the representation of those interests with the higher authorities. These common needs explain the permanence of the irrigation district systems and their collective or "socialized" services.

The Mobilization of Labor

As we have seen above (Table 6.1), after the introduction of the household responsibility system in rural China, the peasants' contribution of corvée labor to water conservancy construction fell dramatically. Different systems were in use. Under the centralized systems, the county government planned a number of projects and assigned labor days to lower administrative levels. Usually, substitution by other laborers was permitted, either hired by the peasant himself or recruited by the village and paid the local wage. The number of work days might be calculated from the amount of work to be done and converted into cash. Beneficiary villages or groups of farmers might have to pay an agricultural construction fee, in order to pay for the labor of those villages and groups of laborers which did not benefit. Such fees were decided by the *xiang* government. In some cases, the obligation to provide corvée labor for water conservancy projects had been included in development projects for which farmers had concluded contracts (at auctions or in direct negotiations) with the village government (Wu Haian 1986).

The 1986 Document No. 1 of the CCP Central Committee demanded that "villages should establish the necessary labor accumulation system, improve methods of mutual cooperation and joint undertakings of farmland capital construction." The actual amounts should be decided by the provinces and municipalities. It was expressly forbidden to transfer labor to other localities without adequate compensation. Over- or underperformance should be compensated over the years. Based on the assumption that one-half of all farmers would contribute fifteen days per year, a commentator expected that this would produce 150 million x 15 = 2,250 million labor days, at two *yuan* per day, 4.5 billion *yuan* of labor investment per year (*Zhongguo shuili* 1986, no. 9, pp. 12–13).

Referring to this CCP decision, in October 1988 the Ministry of Water Conservancy formally demanded that on average, ten to twenty labor days per rural laborer should be invested. This excluded work in large and medium-scale state projects, anti-flood work, and work within one's own contracted farmland (*ZGSLNJ 1990*, p. 41). Following the 1986 Document, provincial and local governments adopted preliminary regulations. These included an indication of the number of days, the price of substitution (which by that time had increased to 3 to 4 *yuan* per day), the obligation to keep records at the village *cun* level, and sanctions against village governments which did not comply: the government could withhold its financial support for the annual water conservancy investment plan (*Xinfengxian* 1990, pp. 192–3).

There was great variation in local rules. Some localities had stipulated that this type of labor should be used for maintenance and repairs of water conservancy projects managed by the county or rural governments; other localities stipulated that it should be used for construction of new projects. In some, all laborers, including shopkeepers etc., had to participate, but in other localities only farmers were called upon. In some areas, the people claimed that because labor, farmland resources and the benefits of irrigation were not equally distributed among households, so the obligation to contribute corvée labor should not be the same for all. In some rich areas, the farmers themselves had to hire the required labor from elsewhere, but other places (such as Jiangsu) had ruled that the labor obligation could simply be bought off with money (according to precise rules; the rates varied according to rural wage levels and tended to increase over time) and the funds went into the *xiang* budget (Zhang Fang 1994). The degree of compliance varied. Some governments gave inducements in the form of cheap grain, oil, fertilizer, etc. In other places, "the Party Secretary just commanded the peasants to go build a sea dike, and when asked whether the peasants had a direct interest or would be compensated, he answered: 'That is something for later. When the Old Secretary calls for action, the peasants don't have a word to say.' " (Li Wenzhi 1989, p. 82)

The year 1989 showed that campaign-style politics still played some role in China. On October 15, the State Council decided that labor input in water conservancy construction should be greatly increased, arguing that in spite of the increased labor investment in the 1986–1988 period, the deterioration of facilities had not been arrested. A big three-to-five-year effort was needed. Some areas might go beyond the required ten to twenty days per laborer (*Zhongguo shuili* 1989, no. 11, pp. 3–4). Tian Jiyun explained that all provinces should exert themselves. "Some provinces mobilize rural laborers for an average of more than twenty days per year, but other provinces only three to five days per year; some provinces have increased capital investments in many aspects, but others still have not regained the 1980 investment level. Within each province and county, great differences occur between counties and villages. We hope that after the State Council decision there will be one movement. ... However, one should proceed from each area's actual conditions, and not demand uniformity" (*ZGSLNJ 1990*, p. 32). Evidently, the leadership recognized the fact that the tradition of and need for water conservancy labor was much stronger in some areas than in other areas. Moreover, while some areas had included corvée obligations in the contracts under the household responsibility system, other areas had not. Nevertheless, provinces started competitions for the "Heilong Cup," the "Great Yu Cup," the "King Yu Cup" (in Heilongjiang, Liaoning and Shanxi, respectively). Political priority was reinforced with extra state investments, and it was demanded of the localities to produce a much higher labor turnout than in the past decade. This was not blind expansion of construction such as during the Great Leap Forward. Emphasis was on "repairs, restoration, completion or transformation" (*ZGNYNJ 1990*, pp. 21, 126).

It was tempting to push for more. The next year, State Councillor Song Ping demanded that the amount of labor accumulation, which had been 10.5 days per laborer in 1989, should be raised. "The rule is 10 to 20. Hunan just said that they used 20 labor days. And that may not be the maximum. In a poor Shandong county it was much more. We do not demand too much, if we ask that it reaches 21 days like in Hunan. We must lead it, organize it. . . ." (*ZGSLNJ 1991*, pp. 27–8). His demand reflected the thoughts of some local Party officials, who had advocated recentralization of water control, particularly for the aspects of planning, organization of labor, adoption of modern techniques and services. In 1991, a Shanxi official even proposed that the farmers spend thirty to forty days of obligatory labor in water conservancy construction (Wang Wenxue 1991).

One Sichuan county may serve as an example of the form which this campaign could take at the local level. The first step was recognition by the political leadership of the weak links in water conservancy, such as dilapidated reservoirs, low anti-flood standards, high seepage losses in canals, siltation of ponds, etc. This was followed by the setting up dozens of "leading groups" for specific targets, enforcement by the county, district and *xiang* heads of an individual responsibility system, and the setting up water conservancy construction offices. Meetings were convened at all levels, where the government policies and measures were introduced, and rewards of 200 *yuan* were announced for the top five performers. Models which were set were studied by almost a thousand cadres. Four county meetings were convened to study specific problems. Secondly, extra capital was raised for construction: to that end, the county and lower governments pledged to provide subsidies, e.g., for each kilometre of canal built, the county and district gave 3,000 *yuan* each, the *xiang* gave another 6,000 *yuan*; yet the major part had to be paid from capital raised by the village *cun* and beneficiary farmers. Thirdly, labor investments were redirected. Three types could be distinguished: "accumulation labor," "labor under unified use," and corvée labor. Each agricultural unit calculated how much work was to be done in water conservation, allocated this burden on the basis of labor force or land contracts, and submitted its plan to the village assembly *shehuiyuan dahui* for discussion and approval. Three times a year, inspections were carried out by the authorities.

The higher labor input was consolidated in 1992. Pains were taken to explain that free labor in water conservancy capital construction did not add to the peasants' burden, a major policy concern in that year, but served their own interests. A Jiangsu official wrote that water conservancy work helped maintain rural stability. "Because of the 1991 floods, our province of Jiangsu suffered more than 20 billion *yuan* in terms of economic losses. . . . Urban and industrial losses greatly surpass rural and agricultural losses, and may affect social stability. So we cannot relax; in order to guarantee social stability we must make a good job of constructing anti-flood projects" (Dai Yukai 1994). The demand placed on China's peasantry is to contribute free labor not only for its own good, but also to protect industrial and urban China.

The question why China's corvée labor could be revived in this modern age of reform is not easy to answer. Of course, the perceived need for infrastructural projects and their maintenance is a prerequisite. Its effectiveness and widespread acceptance may be due to the still existent tradition of service to government, the strength of its local organization which is structured by a combination of county and village government, the otherwise low direct taxation of farmers, and considerable seasonal unemployment. Moreover, some flexibility has been built in. Socio-economic differentiation in China's rural areas has enabled the richer farmers to shift their burden to poorer laborers, who are willing to work in their place for some additional income. Apart from all these factors, the most fundamental reason lies with the continued *hukou* (household registration) system, which ties most farmers to the soil of their village.

Changes in Ownership and Management of Pumps and Other Assets: Shareholding Cooperatives and Other Forms

After decollectivization, many small water conservancy facilities were contracted out to farmers, or put up for auction. Most contracts concerned the ownership or operation of mechanized wells. Under such contracts, farmers paid an agreed sum every year to the irrigation district or village government. They collected water fees to cover their expenses. The village government or irrigation district set the periods of water supply, guaranteed the supply of fuel or electricity, set standards for the water fee, and saw to it that the wells remained operable (*Zhongguo shuili* 1989, no. 1, p. 31).

During the early 1980s, very few farmers owned pumping equipment, wells or other water conservancy facilities. The existing collectively owned facilities were still in good order. The individual parcels of farmland were too small, and farmers lacked the necessary funds for investment. However, in many areas these conditions changed in subsequent years. State and collective investments in water conservancy decreased and so did the quality and quantity of irrigation services. Entrepreneurial farmers amalgamated their land. Large plantations were created on the slopes of hills. Some farmers became rich and had money to invest in expansion and technological improvement. Large farmers and fruit growers began to construct private wells. Around 1990, shallow wells could be built at a cost of about 5,000 *yuan*, which was within the reach of many farmers or partnerships of farmers. Thus, in many cases the collective neglect of irrigation equipment led to its privatization. An alternative was recentralization of control.

Under the household responsibility system, many villages had allocated some fields to "well households" or "well chiefs" who had contracted for the operation and maintenance of mechanized wells. Subsequently, some of these fields had been repossessed, and the wells had been transferred to the responsibility of the water conservancy stations, but without compensation. In 1991, a Henan county forbade this practice and ordered the allocated fields to be reinstated. Moreover, it bought back over one thousand pumps from their individual owners, improved the service networks, and entrusted all its mechanized wells to the management of "well chiefs." These received two cents per kWh as floating wage (Han Peixun 1992). Such repossession of neglected wells had not been uncommon, and often they produced better results under new contracts.[18]

Privatization and private construction of wells became more and more popular, braving the objections by many local cadres. For instance, the number of irrigation and drainage pumps owned by farmers in Shandong doubled to 1.2 million between 1985 and 1990; at the same time, those owned by collectives decreased by 20 percent to only 320,000.[19] On the basis of the 1988 Water Law, farmers were required to submit applications to the village administration. They were inspected by the *xiang* water management station and submitted for approval to the county water conservancy bureau. Usually, the new well itself remained collective property, but the machinery and its management were private. The advantages were that private investments helped to speed up the replacement of old and worn-out equipment; in earlier years, farmers often had refused to pay for the renewal of collective assets. Moreover, they ran the supply of irrigation water on a commercial basis, by charging real costs of irrigation water to other users. They took better care of the equipment than the collective had done before. While recognizing such advantages of privatization, many rural cadres objected on ideological grounds (Yang Jianbin 1992).

The objections raised by local cadres were of a dual nature. Many feared the loss of political power. But there was also genuine concern over loss of control over water use. Most buyers decided themselves about the type and capacity of their pump. The county water conservancy bureaus were ill-equipped to assess the effect of new wells on existing facilities in other villages, and might give in too easily to individual requests. Consequently, in many places too many facilities have been created, which in turn has brought on increased costs. Sometimes there are as many pumps for one well as there are farmers, each having his own (Ma Chengxin 1993).

A third alternative to privatization or recentralization was the establishment of share-holding cooperatives. Under this system, introduced in the late 1980s, the original water conservancy facilities remained collective property, but the recently and newly built or purchased ones were acquired by shareholders and became joint collective-private property. Share-holder committees decided about maintenance, repairs and fees. Some practised the "four fixed and one contract," that is, recruitment of employees was determined by the number of water conservancy facilities; the number of years equipment could be used was determined by its quality; the fees for maintenance and repairs were determined by depreciation rates; and irrigation water fee standards were based on all three factors. The contract was put out to tender and awarded to the highest bidder, and contained penalty and bonus clauses.

One such cooperative made the purchase of shares more attractive and nurtured a cooperative spirit by having its shareholders pay only half the water fee of non-shareholders. Shares were transferable, but could not be cashed in. Individual dividends could be freely disposed of, but the collective dividend of the village had to be reinvested. Possibly foreseeing the dissatisfaction of non-shareholders, it was stipulated that if they damaged facilities, they would be fined two or three times in excess of the costs of repair; in the case of shareholders, such damages would simply be deducted from the value of their shares. The result of the new system was not only that extra capital was obtained for investment, but also much better care was taken of the facilities (*Henan shuiliting* 1994). Recent articles have described three forms of shareholding cooperatives in the Dezhou Region in Shandong, where 50,000 farmers bought 20 million *yuan* worth of shares in 9,000 wells, 20 water pumping stations, 200 fish ponds and other facilities. The authors noted many advantages, but pointed out that the legal basis of such cooperatives was ill-defined and might become a source of friction with government or non-participating villagers.[20] Shareholding systems seem useful indeed for making a new start, but how well they will function depends on their ability to maintain their independence versus village government (the general rule is that village government should control 60 percent), the availability of water and reasonably-priced electricity, and maintenance of equipment. There is the danger of local dissatisfaction and suspicion of collusion if a village government appears to have sold off its assets too cheaply. A just assessment is very difficult.[21]

Some observers see an advantage in the relative freedom from interference by government and village cadres, which such cooperatives enjoy once the "democratic management" by the board of directors of the shareholders cooperative has been instituted (Chen Xueren 1994). The shareholding cooperatives are said to contribute to a greater sense of responsibility for water management among the shareholders; annual repairs and the collection of fees are less problematic. Also, it becomes easier to derive additional income from fishery and other sidelines (Guangxi Yulinshi 1994). Recently, Chinese authors have stressed the advantages of privatization and commercialization.[22] They are said to reflect the farmers' preference to own not just the equipment, but the water source itself (Dong Junhai 1994). However, it is to be feared that uncontrolled privatization and collective drilling of wells will contribute to a further over-exploitation of ground water resources, which has already reached alarming proportions in some areas.

The Provision of Irrigation Services

In the early 1980s, county governments established water conservancy service stations in order to fill the growing vacuum between government and water users. Their organizational position varied. Some were based on existing stations belonging to the irrigation districts, their territories corresponding either to watersheds, canal sections or administrative divisions. Others were newly established by village governments. Some functioned as specialized service centers for a wide area; smaller stations might be privately run by collectives or entrepreneurs, while the larger ones might be run by the Water Conservancy Bureau and control the entire county. Often, rearrangements broke with administrative divisions and control, stressed professional and technical leadership, and established common organizations of state employees, *xiang* technicians and private entrepreneurs. Some of their managers were even democratically elected (Song Lusheng 1984). The government ordered that the district and *xiang* water conservancy stations, with their more than a hundred thousand state-employed staff, should become service centers, with independent budgets (*ZGNYNJ 1985* p. 302). Contractual arrangements with individual farmers were expected to produce better services at lower costs.[23] However, many districts and villages were unable to continue the cheap and labor-intensive provision of services which had been common in the collective period.

Surveys of deterioration of rural services produced alarming results. The percentage of villages providing collective irrigation services declined from 64 percent in 1980 to 56 percent in 1984 and 44 percent in 1987. In the eastern areas of China, the percentages remained almost the same (at 86, 88 and 85 percent for the respective above-mentioned years). In the central parts they declined by one-quarter (from 77 to 61 percent to 57 percent, respectively), and in the western parts by almost one-half (from 28 percent both in 1980 and in 1984 to 15 percent in 1987). Even though the decline was less than other rural services, 20 percent of the farmers who wanted unified irrigation service were unable to obtain it.[24]

Since the late 1980s irrigation and drainage services have made a substantial recovery. Official surveys show an increase by one-third between 1986 and 1990. However, in the western parts of China there was no recovery whatsoever.[25] Collective or village cooperative service organizations were responsible for 52 percent of the irrigated area (in the eastern parts of China for only 39 percent, in the western parts for 79 percent, in central China for 62 percent). Other forms of service organizations took care of 19 percent of the irrigated area.

Farmers took care of 30 percent (38, 21 and 15 percent, respectively, in east, middle and west of China). Reasons for the regional difference were partly technical (in the east, more of the irrigation operates by gravity flow, while in the middle and west, pump irrigation is more important), and partly linked with the scarcity of water (which makes conflicts about water use more likely, and constitutes a greater need for the collective to mediate). No relation was found between the economic strength of a collective and its forms of irrigation services, and the survey concluded that the presence of village-run irrigation services reflected the service consciousness of village cadres.[26] The trend of a restoration and extension of irrigation services, together with a shift from collective to private services, has continued since then.[27]

We may now distinguish three types of water conservancy service organizations in rural China:

1) about 18,000 specialized technical service organizations, with 370,000 employees. They are mostly state-owned: county water conservancy technical service centers and designing units, experimental stations, and medium-sized water conservancy project management units;

2) about 29,000 management and coordinative organizations, with 500,000 employees (120,000 of whom are state employees). These organizations are mainly district and *xiang* water conservancy stations set up by the county. Their main functions are support for water conservancy construction; popularization of techniques; and intermediate-level management of farmland irrigation. They suffer from problems of lack of facilities and equipment (one-third of the stations do not have an office), and deficient funding for activities and wages;

3) village and private organizations with several million employees: service teams, drought prevention teams, dike guards, water distributors, etc. Their income is derived from village enterprise subsidies and water fees.

Problems shared by all levels are the low level of education, the lack of measuring devices and other equipment, and low salaries. Many are part-timers. The education level of one-half is lower secondary school or less. Most are young and lack experience (Gu Binjie 1990; Yang Xiaoxin and Gu Binjie 1992).

Yet the demands made on personnel are becoming heavier. For instance, new techniques of water savings require better sampling techniques, and sprinkler irrigation requires higher technical skills.[28] The tendency is for service stations to have greater responsibility in the design and execution of small projects (Zhang Gang 1990). The stations needed graduates from water conservancy schools. However, because stations were fully-staffed already, and also because many graduates did not want to go to the country, these graduates could not be employed. Several countermeasures were suggested: recruitment of students from the villages; establishment of water conservancy cadres' schools with three-year programmes; short-term training programmes for employees; etc. (Zhou Fengduan 1990). The personnel situation seems to be worsening. Often, wages are not paid in time, because farmers refuse to pay water fees in full, or village governments keep most of the receipts. Many employees lack professional knowledge and training, and some do not care any more about their performance.

Finance and Water Fees

According to the Water Fee Law adopted in 1985—the year of price reforms—the water fees for grain crops should be based on costs of water supply, and be slightly higher for commercial crops.[29] In the 1970s, most areas which were managed by people's communes had not levied water fees at all, and wages and investments had come directly from the collective. Since 1980, most provinces had begun to raise their standards, but with few exceptions,[30] fees were still much too low. This reflected the tradition of free or subsidized provision of public and collective goods. Nevertheless, between 1978 and 1983 total income of the 14,000 state-owned water conservancy project management units had increased from only 300 million *yuan* to one billion *yuan*. Of those sums, 100 and 400 million *yuan*, respectively, came from diversified undertakings such as fishery and fruit growing (*ZGNYNJ 1985*, pp. 432–3).

The law stipulated that costs of water supply included operating costs (wages, fuel, management, etc.), maintenance, depreciation of assets (except those created by the peasants themselves through "accumulation labor"), large-scale repairs, and other expenses. Depreciation was based on a fixed percentage of the historical price, and became unrealistic because of inflation. By 1992, actual replacement costs were more than twice as high as officially calculated costs. Typically, water fees were (and are) based on the irrigated area and the number of irrigations. If there were gauges, water volume charges might also be used. With pumping stations, the running time of machinery might be taken into account (mainly the cost of electricity or diesel oil consumed). More sophisticated systems used a combination of variables.[31]

It goes without saying that once various government and collective subsidies were reduced, irrigation water fees inevitably went up. Nevertheless, they did not even come close to covering supply costs, especially in the case of high-lift pumping stations. A 1989 survey of Shanxi showed that irrigation water supply costs averaged between 5 and 20 cents per cubic metre, but that prices were still between 3 and 6 cents. In large stations, costs were triple the water fee. Some of those costs reflected inflation or increased electricity prices and were beyond the control of local units. However, other sources of cost increases were poor water management, high seepage losses, theft of water, wilfully onerous labor obligations imposed by local cadres, and corruption. Stations were overstaffed, and their employees were idle during much of the year (Liang Rutao 1989).

At the National Water Fee Conference held in 1989, it was noted that with regard to agriculture, water fees were much too low. They amounted to only 8 percent of production costs. The provinces of Sichuan, Guangxi and Fujian received praise for stopping allocations of water to units which did not levy fees according to the rules. The first two had expressed their water fees in agricultural products, so that price changes resulted in corresponding adjustments. Water fees had increased from 220 million *yuan* in 1980 to 647 million *yuan* in 1985 and 801 million *yuan* in 1987. However, by then water fees still covered only 40 percent of water supply costs.[32] Moreover, only two-thirds of the fees were actually paid up. Fees did not sufficiently reflect differences in region, period and water quality (*ZGSLNJ 1990*, pp. 76–82; Xiao Jian 1991).

In 1991, it was estimated that at least 3.6 billion *yuan* in water fees should be levied each year, which was twice the amount actually collected. There were hardly any sanctions against non-payers. "Although the State Council has stipulated that the authorities may stop the supply of water, this is always difficult to put into practice, particularly in agriculture. Who dares to stop irrigation water at the height of the season?" Moreover, there were no legal rules about the level of fines for non-payers (Hu Yongfa 1993).

Most provinces were very reluctant to raise the water fees. An author cited four reasons why receipts were so low. Cadres feared that the farmers' financial burden would increase. Fees were collected from an area smaller than that actually irrigated. Sometimes, water fee receipts were diverted to other purposes. Finally, it was difficult to introduce fees based on volumes of water supplied because high water use was often due to defective facilities. However, the most important reason of all was public policy, which set prices at much too low levels (Li Lishan 1993; Cai Rudang 1994; Jia Ziyu 1993).

From local investigations in Hubei, it appeared that only one-third of the water fee payments actually reached the water conservancy units, and two-thirds remained at the *xiang/zhen* government level. Village governments had tagged on all kinds of extra expenses: hosting guests, dinners, presents to visiting officials, etc. Some irrigation districts managed to strike back. For instance, the People's Irrigation District in Shanxi decided that farmers should no longer pay their water fees through their village government, but directly to the Irrigation District Bureau. Under this new system, water users and the district authorities "directly faced each other." To that end, the old administrative divisions were abolished and new divisions created on the basis of ditch systems and natural divides (Liu Huizhong 1992).

There is no shortage of suggestions for remedies. For example, it has been suggested that depreciation rates of facilities and equipment be based on a reevaluation of the value of assets, which should include previous peasant labor. They should be raised to 4 percent, and repair fees to 2.5 percent. Greater effort should be made in the popularization of successful practices such as linking water prices to grain and advance payment. In water-deficient areas, new industries should be charged the marginal costs of increased water supply instead of average historical costs. Water fees should be adjusted every three to five years (Zhu Weidong 1992). However, in times of inflation as the past few years, any monetary tariff will be outdated by the time government has actually established it. As long as a formal decision by the central or provincial government is needed to set new prices for water, and the government refuses to allow for automatic index-linked price increases, fees will lag behind costs. The most practical solution is to set fees expressed in food grain or other agricultural crops.

One may wonder why for the past decade, provincial governments and irrigation districts have not tried to raise water fees to the level prescribed by the 1985 Water Fee Law. It seems to be another example of the weakness of the Chinese legal system. Apparently, without the full cooperation of the Communist Party, local governments and local communities, some laws are bound to be ineffective. Although there may be sanctions against non-compliance, enforcement in the face of opposition is very difficult. In the case of water fees, there seems to have been a communality of interests of local government, Party and water users to keep prices down. For the CCP members, water conservation is one of the few traditions of collective village action which they still cherish. For local government cadres, caring for low-cost water conservation and irrigation is a source of legitimacy of their rule. One is reminded of the county magistrates of imperial times, who prided themselves in reducing local taxes. Farmers who are water users have been accustomed to low-priced water for a long time, and are bound to reject any increase of the costs of inputs, especially if they have no say over its economic use and costs cannot be sufficiently passed on.

Of course, there is nothing wrong with a system of subsidized provision of services. However, such subsidies have been much too low, because of the defective Chinese system of cost calculation, decreasing state budgets and belated adjustments of water fees. As a result, during most of the 1980s China has allowed its irrigation systems to deteriorate. Moreover, the financial dependence of all those working in the irrigation system and their users has constituted a psychological barrier against efficiency increases and a more economic use of China's scarce water resources, and it continues to be so. If, for reasons of efficiency and equity, the government should want water-using communities to manage water resources themselves (within the framework of the law) and be genuinely self-sufficient, this cannot be achieved without financial independence. Though improvements were made in the late 1980s and early 1990s, in the past few years inflation and a lack of skilled personnel have undermined again the capacity for independence.

Conclusion

Decollectivization led to a rather serious decline of state- and collective-owned water conservancy facilities, particularly in western China. Investments, maintenance and labor organization were reduced or discontinued. The effects of the decline were not immediately apparent, for a number of reasons. There is an inherent time lag between investment and benefit. In many areas, water supply facilities had been built in excess of normally available water volumes. 1983 and 1984 were blessed with excellent weather conditions, and harvests were bountiful. The optimistic mood of 1985 produced a water fee law and irrigation management directives which were based on the idea that the farmland water conservancy sector could become virtually independent and be responsible for its own budget and services. However, this assessment proved to be wrong. The main causes were the lack of willingness of farmers to pay for irrigation water, and the financial and organizational difficulties of maintaining rural services.

The CCP and Chinese government reacted rather quickly to the decline in irrigation water supply. From 1987 onward, they gave greater support in a number of ways. One method was affirmation of state authority. County water conservancy bureaus reasserted their control over water conservancy stations, and, sanctioned by the CCP and State Council decisions, local governments strengthened their command over peasant corvée labor. The central government and the CCP decided that a revival of corvée labor was necessary in order to be able to maintain infrastructural facilities. In general, the government has sought to protect the long-term interests of Chinese water users mainly through the law and other institutional arrangements, such as inalienable state or collective property rights of water resources and water distribution facilities. Moreover, it continued to subsidize irrigation water use through low prices for electricity and water. These legal and economic measures stood in the way of more efficient water use, and were a disincentive for investments. There may have been conscious and subconscious political reasons for maintenance of such dependency on government: the Chinese government's support for the peasantry is part of its legitimacy, and it considers water to be a most vital resource which should remain under state control.

Other economic measures such as diversification of forms of investment and management of facilities have had a positive impact. They ultimately led to privatization of facilities and their management in many of the more developed parts of east and central China. There were and are obvious limits to the economic and managerial independence of irrigation districts: most depend on large-scale state-owned facilities for their water supply. Moreover, the successful application of any management method was restricted by the continued tradition of dependency on state subsidies. Thus, though irrigation management has changed since decollectivization, as this study shows, it has not changed as much as one would expect in view of the enormous change in the size of landholdings. This indicates a continuing strength of collective property rights in most rural areas of China, and that in irrigation, some form of cooperative or collective ownership and management may be indispensable for agricultural operations.

On the other hand, long-standing collective traditions, both of the people's communes and of the pre-revolutionary period have broken down in the past decade, and could not be rebuilt. Construction of facilities, their maintenance, and distribution of irrigation water are three separate activities which all used to be managed by people's communes or a combination of government and commune organizations. Since the 1980s, these activities have been split up along functional lines and organized by different organizations. Such functional specialization has produced considerable savings in costs and labor. The financial strength of local communities seems to be an important determinant of the form of organization of irrigation. Poor communities are more likely to depend on government organizations or abandon any form of irrigation services; richer communities tend to contract such services out to village collective structures or leave irrigation to private initiatives of individual farmers.

The falling underground water levels in the North China Plain and the floods of 1991 have shown in a painful way that state control over the allocation of surface water is no guarantee whatsoever against floods or droughts, shortage or excess of facilities, or economic use of water. In a situation of declining state budgets at all levels, a virtual absence of means to enforce central rules, and a shortage of qualified personnel, the Chinese government is only beginning to accept that most of its functions might better be devolved to local communities. At the county level, it seems that such insights have progressed much further.

The role of government in irrigation in China has not been spelled out clearly, and still varies according to local traditions and local government initiative. The 1985 Water Law was not very specific, and moreover, has not been applied properly. It is obvious that the Chinese farmers and villages need technical guidance *and* proper economic incentives *and* credible enforcement of the law, in order to achieve a more economical exploitation of surface and underground water. Although the tendency for the state to pull away from the rural economy has been less strong in water conservancy and irrigation than in most other sectors, village governments and farmers are now supposed to take over the responsibility for irrigation water themselves, but the forces of tradition are still strong. The economic and legal conditions set by the central government make it very difficult or even impossible to rationalize the use of water. A better definition of the role of village government (both *xiang* and administrative village) is urgently needed, and national regulations should be formulated which define the ways in which various water users can articulate their interests. Obviously, such regulations should reflect differences in size and type of irrigation projects, which call for different forms of ownership and management.

Our study shows that most of the changes in irrigation management were copies of the general political and economic reform measures taken by the Chinese government. Decollectivization in the early 1980s, the price reform of 1985, the factory director responsibility system of 1986, the contracting out of collective or government activities in the late 1980s, the interdiction of village government exactions in 1992—all these essentially political measures had little or no connection with irrigation, yet were immediately applied to the irrigation sector.

Not surprisingly, results were not entirely satisfactory. It shows that politics in China is still conducted in an overall campaign-style manner, rather than being geared to the specific needs of each separate economic sector, and also, that further decentralization and functional specialization of political and administrative powers are called for.

Notes

1. To give one example: the average construction costs of large and medium-sized irrigation projects built in central Shaanxi during the 1970s were between 20 and 60 *yuan* per *mu* of irrigated farmland. However, Chang'an county had built a reservoir project irrigating 1,300 hectares which had cost 196 *yuan* per *mu*. With an internal rate of return of 5.6 percent, it fell short even by the very lenient 1984 IRR standard of 6 to 7 percent used by the Ministry of Water Conservancy and Electric Power, and by the 6 percent charged by the Agricultural Bank for long-term investment loans. I have described the 1980 shift in irrigation development policy for this province at some length. The rising prices of electricity and low profitability became arguments for the central government (or rather, the Ministry of Finance) to withhold approval from high-lift projects. Yet the province mostly got its way (Vermeer 1988, pp. 216–219; Jia Shenghua 1989). During the 1970s, many high-lift water pumping stations had been constructed at a high cost, of 350 *yuan* and more per *mu*; because of electricity price increases, their operation became more and more costly, and in the mid-1980s many were no longer in use (Tian Deyang 1988).

2. For instance, in 1986 a Shandong county complained that more than 60 percent of its ditches had been destroyed, attributing this, apart from decollectivization itself, to the lack of leadership; an 80 percent decrease in investments; favorable weather conditions; a neglect of the water conservancy responsibility system; and lack of control over wilful destruction and theft (Shandongsheng 1986). In the Jinzhong Region in Shanxi, more than half of all water conservancy projects had increasingly fallen into disrepair, partly due to deliberate destruction or theft (*Zhongguo shuili* 1988, no. 10, p. 25).

3. Labor input in construction work fell from 2 billion cubic metres of earth, 163 million cubic metres of stone and 7.5 million cubic metres of concrete in 1979 to only 0.6 billion, 54 million and 5 million, respectively, in 1980.

4. Corvée labor is distinct from what is called "accumulation labor" *(jilei laodong)*. In principle, the latter excludes the regular "corvée labor" which farmers are traditionally obliged to provide for the maintenance of river dikes and other large state-owned facilities.

5. During 1976–1980, the Chinese government spent 5.7 percent of its annual budget on water conservation, but during the next five years only 3.4 percent, and from 1985 till 1989 only 2.4 percent (*ZGSLNJ 1991*, p. 710). The share of water conservation in budgetary investments for the agricultural sector declined from about one-half to one-third and to even less in 1989.

6. From 1988 through 1993, 59 percent of the 8.2 billion *yuan* allocated by the central government under the Agricultural Development Fund was invested in water conservancy projects (*Zhongguo shuili* 1994, no. 7, pp. 17–18).

7. The Anhui figures show a particularly large decline, followed by an equally extraordinary recovery. Between 1980 and 1986, the area irrigated by mechanized wells in North Anhui decreased by 75 percent. There were several causes. After the 1979 floods, government attention and irrigation machinery were diverted to drainage. Under the household responsibility system, management of water conservancy slackened; facilities were destroyed or allowed to deteriorate and fall into disrepair. From 1986 onwards, after

the provincial government had decided to revitalize water conservation, a partial recovery occurred, and the number of wells and size of irrigated area went up to about one-half of the 1980 figures (Wang Yongle and Ding Biran 1994). If this is correct, most of the irrigated area increase must have been from surface water sources.

8. In 1985 there were 5,281 such districts, each irrigating more than 10,000 *mu*. Together, they irrigated 2,080,000 hectares or 43 percent of the national total (*Zhongguo shuili baike quanshu* 1990, vol. IV, p. 2463).

9. "At the time its management structure was decided, he had given directives several times that all Party organizations in the irrigation district area should grasp management work" (*Shaoshan* 1979, p. 3). For its power generation, it resorted directly under the Provincial Power Bureau.

10. Its profitability may have been due to its excellent recent performance: it doubled its effectively irrigated area to 50,000 hectares, reduced the irrigation volumes by one-third to 40 to 50 cubic meters per *mu*, and raised effective irrigation water utilization rates from .35 to .60 (*ZGNYNJ 1985*, p. 303).

11. The continued representation of professionals has been overlooked by Manoharan 1990 (p. 182).

12. In the early 1980s, professional societies of water conservancy engineers and technicians were established in many counties and all higher levels. As non-state organizations, their leaders were democratically elected by the members. Main activities were discussion sessions when sudden problems needed to be solved urgently, investigation, training (including that of new members), popularization of techniques, exchange of experiences, etc. (see e.g., *Xinfengxian shuilizhi* 1990, pp. 167–170).

13. Sanyuan is a county at the lower end of the Jinghui Canal District with a long-standing tradition of irrigation. By 1990, one-third of its 3,300 mechanized wells were no longer working. Only half of its 223 water pumping stations functioned well. More than one-half of the 32 million *yuan* of water conservancy assets at the *xiang* and village level had either been stolen or destroyed. As a result, 7,000 hectares of farmland could no longer be irrigated. Around 1990, the county government tried to remedy this situation by planning the construction of a new reservoir, wells, sluices and other facilities, and field improvements, but this plan had to be paid for and managed by the villages and farmers of the irrigation district (Liu Shuji 1991).

14. According to a recent article, in Hubei the previous concern for water conservancy disappeared as a result of reforms of the rural management system. The irrigation district representatives' congresses weakened, and labor accumulation for water conservancy projects was reduced, particularly in those irrigation districts which transcended administrative borders. As a result, facilities deteriorated or were destroyed. Water feuds became more prominent, and the irrigated area decreased (Cai 1994).

15. See, for instance, the 1987 introduction of greater job responsibility and reward systems for the personnel at the district and *xiang* levels of irrigation management in Sichuan. It was stipulated that in repair work, 90 percent or more of the planned labor days and 90 percent or more of the planned financial receipts should be realized, and that disputes should be solved. As for the distribution network, 95 percent or more of all destruction cases and more than 90 percent of fish thefts should be solved. The dikes should be protected from being trampled by cattle, and planted with crops. Annual repairs of the canals, irrigation and storage of water should be up to standard. Flood warnings should be given in time. As for the collection of water fees, the newly raised tariffs should be collected, and from more than 90 percent of the effective irrigated area (Du Bing 1987).

16. According to a 1985 survey conducted in Henan Province, the deterioration of small water conservancy and irrigation facilities was caused by changes in hydrological

conditions (10–15 percent), run-down equipment and facilities (30 percent), and poor management (50–55 percent) (*Henan nianjian 1986*, p. 271).

17. In Xintai municipality in Shandong Province, a villager named Wang paid 5000 *yuan* per year for a contract for the operation of a small reservoir. In 1990 and 1991, he invested 16,000 *yuan* of capital and 15,000 labor days, raised the reservoir dam by half a metre in order to increase its capacity, built a stone spillway, constructed three fish ponds, a sluice, reclaimed three hectares of wasteland, planted a thousand fruit trees, sowed three hectares of peanuts and bred a hundred thousand fish. His resulting annual income was more than 30,000 *yuan*, enough to cover the project management expenses, pay his dues, and reap a nice profit. In general, such contracts contained a precise description of the facility and the land that was part of it, subsidies to which the contractor was entitled for the construction of new buildings, and the annual amount to be paid to the authorities. This amount was based on the sum of expenses for major repairs, depreciation, water resource management costs, and the contract fee. The latter varied between 10 and 30 percent of the expected annual turnover. There were clauses about the contract duration (usually 10 to 30 years), its termination, and mutual obligations and sanctions (Qu Changyou 1992).

18. In the Limin irrigation district in Shanxi, all of its 43 pumping stations and over 80 percent of its over 100 mechanized wells were bought back by the irrigation district from the villages or individuals in 1986, in order to undertake their complete overhaul. Contracts were concluded; those villages which did not want to transfer ownership were obliged to undertake repairs as well. One of the reasons why their equipment had been allowed to deteriorate was that irrigation water fees had been much lower for natural flow irrigation water, viz. 1 cent per cubic metre as against 4 cents for pumping station water and 6 cents for mechanized well water. Thus, during 1980–1987 the utilization rate was 79 percent for the former but only 19 and 14 percent, respectively, for the last-mentioned. After these changes, these utilization rates jumped by almost 150 percent (Huang Baochuan *et al.* 1993).

19. There were twice as many diesel pumps as electrical pumps, the main reason being the shortage of rural electricity supply. The average size of pumps went down slightly, from 8.1 kW to 7.5 kW, farmers opting for small, light, and easy-to-move pumps, suitable for individual household use. Some governments gave subsidies; e.g., in 1989, Jiehei municipality decided to subsidize each purchase of a pump with 200 *yuan* (Ma Chengxin 1993).

20. "Remaining problems are: (1) their nature is still that of a gentleman's agreement, without sufficient legal basis; (2) benefits are shared, but how losses are shared is not regulated; the function of the Leading Committee is not clear; it is a "profit distribution committee" rather than anything else, largely made up of village cadres, that is, with administrative functions; sometimes, the village government disregards the cooperative and its rules, and continues to consider its water conservancy facilities as collective property" (Wen Zhizhong 1994; Xu Guodong 1994).

21. The assessment of the value of water conservancy assets and the determination of ownership rights are difficult operations. Most of the irrigation network has been created by the local farmers many years ago, under the collective systems of the Great Leap Forward or the Cultural Revolution periods. Part of the materials, especially equipment, may have been provided by the county government. Till today, neither government nor the Party have established any principles for such an assessment, or indicated how it should be organized and who is responsible. The conflicting interests are obvious: county government, *xiang* and administrative village government, the natural village, and those individuals or organizations which made a sizable contribution in the form of capital, materials or labor all may press claims. On the other hand, ownership implies the respon-

sibility for maintenance; thus, when costs seem to outweigh benefits, there is little enthusiasm for setting up share-holding systems. In a recently studied example, assessment was done by a small group of people composed of technical personnel of the county water conservancy bureau, managers, cadres and farmers, but how this group was composed and which level of government had the authority to revise or approve the group's findings remains unclear.

22. Xiajin county in Shandong received national recognition as a model of progress because of its commercialization of well management since 1987. The county had organized more than 30 well drilling teams which offered water surveying and drilling services to interested farmers. The county provided the necessary materials (about 150–300 *yuan* per well) free of charge, and the *xiang* government supplied 25 litres of low-priced diesel oil. Small groups of farmers, usually three to ten persons, paid for the drilling work and equipment, and received shares on the basis of the capital they had put up or their farmland size. These farmer-stockholders of the so-called "share wells" had priority in using water from the well. They could transfer or sell this right to others. Also, the shareholders as a group could decide to sell irrigation water, and share its profits. When changes occurred in population or acreage, shareholders might decide, after joint deliberations, to accept new shares or divest their shares and receive their money back (taking account of depreciation of equipment). Over a five-year period, 5,000 wells were drilled in this way, more than double the existing number. Maintenance and utilization were considerably better than before (Zhang Lianjun 1992).

23. For example, a township in Zhanjiang municipality operated its water conservancy services on a new basis in 1984. The maintenance of existing facilities was entrusted to specialized groups with a fixed number of laborers (102 in all), who contracted for repairs of sections of the irrigation system and for water distribution. Each person took care of 10 to 17 hectares. The personnel of the local water conservancy station worked half-time on maintenance and half-time on water distribution; those who did not show up were fined (by 2 to 5 kg of grain per day). The station concluded contracts with individual farmers for the maintenance of sections, specifying the amount (to a maximum of 27 cubic metres of earth) and quality of work for which they were to be paid. In some cases, the station specified only the total amount of work to be done and left it to the village government to arrange the actual work. By using strict criteria in the selection of personnel (and firing those who did not perform well), fixing remuneration at an adequate level (about 2.5 kg of grain per *mu*), providing rain coats, boots, and promising bonuses on the basis of work assessment by the water conservancy station, both the quality and quantity of work were strongly improved. The average cost of work done went down from five *yuan* per cubic metre of earth to less than one *yuan* (Zhanjiang shiwei 1990).

24. According to an official investigation of regional cooperative organizations among 1,200 villages throughout China conducted by the Ministry of Agriculture (Nongyebu 1989).

25. This is confirmed by another survey, which showed a decline of irrigation services in mountain villages between 1984 and 1990 (Nongyebu 1992).

26. Official investigation of regional cooperative organizations in 5,389 villages throughout China conducted by the Ministry of Agriculture. See Nongyebu 1991.

27. See Nongyebu 1993.

28. According to Mei Fangquan, director of the CAAS Economic and Technical Development Institute (*Nongye jingji wenti* 1989, no. 9, p. 20), "in the future, services will be more specialized and more highly qualified . . . Comprehensive water-saving techniques are required: piped irrigation saves about 30 percent, and has been applied to over 20 million *mu* already, and will be expanded to 80 million *mu*, which saves 16 billion cubic metres. Sprinkler irrigation is now used on 10 million *mu*, saving 30–50 percent,

and will be expanded to 40 million *mu*, saving 8–13 billion cu. m. Surface flooding systems may be converted to networks of ditches, saving 20 percent; if expanded to 100 million *mu*, saving 12 billion cu. m. Anti-seepage channel projects and field ditch improvement may raise irrigation efficiency by 10 percentage points, saving 16.5 billion cu. m. Water-saving rice cultivation techniques and dry rice cultivation in the north may save additional water." See also Li Suying 1994.

    29. For details, see Manoharan 1990.

    30. For instance, Bazhong county in Sichuan charged 50 to 80 cents per irrigated *mu* plus 10 cents per cubic metre of water; for industries, 5 to 10 cents; and for rural industries, 5 percent of their income from processing. These fees were adequate (*ZGNYNJ 1985*, pp. 301–3).

    31. E.g., in the famous Pishihang irrigation project in Anhui, water fees were raised to a more satisfactory level in 1990. Between 1984 and 1989 water fees had doubled. Even so, they averaged only about 6.5 percent of the total grain production costs (material inputs only; this was about as much as the cost of pesticides and only one-eighth of the cost of fertilizer). A calculation by the authorities showed the actual costs of irrigation to be three times as high as the 1989 receipts from water fees. In order to cover these costs as fully as possible, a new tariff was instituted. It was made up of two elements: a basic fee of 3.4 kg of rice per *mu*, irrespective of water use, and a fee of 3 kg of rice per 100 cubic metre of water supplied (Zhang Linong 1991).

    32. The water conservancy departments are unable to recover part of their losses in irrigation with income from hydroelectricity, because the prices which small hydro-electric power stations receive for electricity supplied to the grid are too low. A survey of 87 such stations in South China showed that most received 5 or 6 cents per kWh; in some provinces, notably Guangdong and Zhejiang, receipts were 7 to 10 cents per kWh (*Nongtian shuili yu xiaoshuidian* 1993, no. 2, pp. 43–47).

References

Bi Jinfeng, "Luoshi baxiang jishu jingji zhibiao, gaohao chengbao zirenzhi" (Realize the Eight Technical and Economic Targets, Implement the Contract Responsibility System Well). *Zhongguo shuili* 1992, no. 11, pp. 29–30.

Cai Rudang, "Guanqu liangxing yunxing guanli jizhide tansuo" (Exploration into a Beneficial Management Mechanism in Irrigation Districts). *Nongtian shuili yu xiaoshuidian* 1994, no. 5, pp. 5–7.

Changshu shuili zhi Editorial Committee, eds., *Changshu shuili zhi* (Record of Water Conservancy in Changshu). Beijing: Shuili dianli Pub., 1990.

Chen Guanghua, "Sichuansheng Guang'anxian shuili jianshe qingkuang diaocha." (Investigation into the conditions of water management in Guang'an county, Sichuan province). *Nongtian shuili yu xiaoshuidian* 1993, no. 1, pp. 21–23.

Chen Xueren, Qiang Kaipeng, "Gufen hezuo zhi zhiru nongcun shuili houde chengxiao, yingxiang yu qushi" (Effectiveness, Influence, and Tendencies of the Share-Holding Cooperative System after Its Introduction in Rural Water Conservation). *Zhongguo shuili* 1994, no. 7, pp. 18–19, 23.

Dai Yukai, Wang Ming, "Zonglun 1994–niandu dongchun nongtian shuili jiben jianshe" (A General Discussion of Farmland Water Conservancy Capital Construction in the Winter and Spring of 1994). *Jiangsu shuili keji* 1994, no. 3, pp. 19–21, 49.

Dong Junhai, Zhang Yinglin, "Guangzongxian nongmin rugu daqing shi ge hao banfa" (Taking Shares for Drilling Wells is a Good Method of the Farmers in Guangzong County). *Zhongguo shuili* 1994, no. 1, p. 18.

Du Bing, "Quxiang lingdao ganbude shuili guanli zirenzhi" (The Responsibility System in Water Conservancy Management for Leading District and Village Cadres). *Zhongguo shuili* 1987, no. 4, pp. 36–37.

Fan Shengde, Gao Lujun, "Tuixing zhiqu touqu nongqu zhuanren chengbao" (Promote Contracting by Special People of the Branch-, Head-, and Farm Ditches). *Zhongguo shuili* 1992, no. 11, p. 33.

Geng Min, "Tan guanqu guanli tizhi gaige" (About Structural Reform of Irrigation District Management). *Zhi huai* 1993, no. 6, pp. 19–21.

Gu Binjie, "Quxiang shuilizhan xiankuang he wenti" (The Present Situation and Problems of District and Village Water Conservancy Stations). *Zhongguo shuili* 1990, no. 12, pp. 31–32.

Guangxi Yulinshi shuili dianli ju (Water Conservancy and Electric Power Bureau, Yulin Municipality, Guangxi), ed., "Yulinshi shuili touru shixing 'gufenzhi' " (Yulin Municipality Implements the "Share System" in Water Conservancy Investments). *Zhongguo shuili* 1994, no. 1, pp. 16–17.

Guowuyuan guanyu dali fazhan nongtian shuili jiben jianshede jueding (State Council Decision Regarding the Energetic Strengthening of Capital Construction in Farmland Water Conservancy). *Zhongguo shuili* 1989, no. 11, pp. 3–4.

Han Peixun, Tian Zihong, "Kanzhunlede jiu yao jianchixiaqu" (What Has Been Approved Should Continue to Be Maintained). *Zhongguo shuili* 1992, no. 6, p. 36.

He Zhengyuan, "Establish and Perfect the Water Conservancy Management Responsibility System, Bring into Full Play the Benefits of Existing Projects." JPRS translation from *Zhongguo Shuili* 1983, no. 2, pp. 19–22.

Hebei Bureau of Geology and Mineral Resources and China University of Geosciences, Wuhan, *The Evaluation of Environmental Degradation Caused by Overextraction of Ground Water in the Hebei Plain (P.R. China) and the Development of Strategies for the Prevention of Future Deterioration.* Project Proposal Executive Summary, November 1993.

Henan shuiliting (Henan Water Conservancy Bureau), "Dongzhanggancun tuixing shuili gufen hezuozhi" (Dongzhanggan Village Promotes the Share-Holding Cooperative System in Water Conservancy). *Zhongguo shuili* 1994, no. 3, p. 12.

Hu Yongfa, "Shui faguizhong jingji shouduande yingyong yu sikao" (The Use of Economic Procedures in the Water Laws and Regulations and Some Reflections). *Zhi huai* 1993, no. 8, pp. 9–10.

Huang Baochuan *et al.*, "Guanqu shui ziyuan tongyi guanli duicede yanjiu" (An Investigation into Unified Management Measures in Regard to Irrigation District Water Resources). *Nongtian shuili yu xiaoshuidian* 1993, no. 7, pp. 18–20.

Jae Ho Chung, "The Politics of Agricultural Mechanization in the Post-Mao Era, 1977–87." *The China Quarterly* 1993, no. 134, pp. 264–290.

Jia Shenghua, "Xiaogu shuiku guangai gongcheng jingji xiaoyi fenxi" (An Analysis of the Economic Benefit of the Xiaogu Reservoir Irrigation Project). *Nongye jishu jingji* 1989, no. 1, pp. 40–43.

Jia Ziyu *et al.*, "Shuiguan danwei shixing 'yi shou de zhi, caiwu baogan' de guanli banfa" (The Management Method of "Cover Expenditure with Receipts, Be Responsible for Your Own Finance" implemented by Water Management Units). *Nongtian shuili yu xiaoshuidian* 1993, no. 3, pp. 1–4.

Kojima Reeitsu, "Agricultural Organization: New Forms, New Contradictions." *The China Quarterly* 1988, no. 116 (1988), pp. 706–735.

Li Lishan, Shao Yuanliang, "Guanyu shuili gongcheng shuifei wentide yanjiu baogao." (Report on research into the problems of water fees for water conservancy). *Shuili jingji* 1993, no. 2, pp. 26–29.

Li Sansheng, "Shandongsheng shuifei gaige qingkuang diaocha" (An Investigation of Water Fee Reform in Shandong Province). *Shuili jingji* 1993, no. 5, pp. 12–13, 6.

Li Suying, "Jieshuixing jishu dui nongye shuiziyuande tidai" (Water Saving Techniques as a Substitute for Agricultural Water Resources). *Nongye jishu jingji* 1994, no. 3, pp. 30–34.

Li Wenzhi, "Nongcun shuili laodong jilei zhidu yao fuhe shangpin jingji yuanze" (The "Labor Accumulation" System in Rural Water Conservancy Must Be in Accordance with the Principles of the Commodity Economy). *Shuili jingji* 1989, no. 2, pp. 4–6.

Li Yusen, "Pailao bengzhan zai kangzaizhong xiaoyi ji cunzai wenti yu duice" (The Benefits of Drainage Pump Stations in Combating Calamities and Remaining Problems and Remedies). *Nongtian shuili yu xiaoshuidian* 1994, no. 6, pp. 33–37.

Liang Rutao, Shuai Ziming, "Dazhongxing yangshuizhande kunjing yu chulu" (Problems and Solutions of Large and Medium-Scale Water Pumping Stations). *Zhongguo shuili* 1989, no. 10, pp. 29–31.

Lin Jiangtan, "Nongmin ziyuan lianhe ban shuili" (Peasants Want to Manage Water Conservancy Themselves in a Joint Effort). *Zhongguo shuili* 1986, no. 12, p. 14.

Liu Huizhong, Du Guosheng, "Guanqu yu yonghu zhijie jianmian" (The Irrigation District and the Customers Face Each Other Directly). *Zhongguo shuili* 1992, no. 11, p. 32.

Liu Shuji et al., " 'Baicaixin' de youlü he chulu" (Concerns and Solutions in Regard to the "Heart of the Cabbage"). *Zhongguo shuili* 1991, no. 2, pp. 19–20.

Ma Chengxin, "Shandongsheng 'qi wu' baiguan jixie fazhan qingkuang jianxi" (A Simple Analysis of the Development of Irrigation and Drainage Machinery in Shandong during the Seventh Five-Year Plan). *Nongtian shuili yu xiaoshuidian* 1993, no. 2, pp. 24–25.

Manoharan, Thiagarajan, "Irrigation Management at the Collective Sector Level." In J. Delman et al., eds., *Remaking Peasant China.* Aarhus: Aarhus University Press, 1990, pp. 177–203.

Ministry of Water Conservancy and Electric Power, "Opinions on the Reform of the Business Management Structure of State-Operated Irrigation Districts." *Nongtian shuili yu xiaoshuidian* 1985, no. 5, pp. 2–4, as translated in JPRS CAG-86–001, pp. 27–33.

Nickum, James E., (ed.), *Water Management Organization in the People's Republic of China.* New York: M.E. Sharpe, 1981.

Nongyebu. (Ministry of Agriculture), "Zhongguo nongcun diyuxing hezuo zuzhide shizheng miaoshu" (A Positive Description of the Regional Cooperation Forms in China's Villages). *Zhongguo nongcun jingji* 1989, no. 1, pp. 5–16.

———. (Ministry of Agriculture), "1990: Zhongguo nongcun tudi chengbao zhidu ji hezuo zuzhi yuanxing kaocha" (1990: An Investigation of the Land Contract System in Rural China and the Functioning of Cooperative Organizations). *Nongye jingji wenti* 1991, no. 9, pp. 44–47.

———. (Ministry of Agriculture), "Dui 274–ge nongzhuang jiti wei nonghu tigong shengchan fuwu qingkuangde diaocha" (Survey of the Situation in Collective Supply of Production Services to Farmers in 274 Farm Villages). *Zhongguo nongcun jingji* 1992, no. 3, pp. 23–27, 48.

———. Nongyebu nongcun hezuo jingji yanjiu ketizu (Ministry of Agriculture, Research Group for Rural Cooperative Economy), "Zhongguo nongcun tudi chengbao jingying zhidu ji hezuo zuzhi yunxing kaocha" (An Investigation of the Land Contract System in Rural China and the Functioning of Cooperative Organizations). *Nongye jingji wenti* 1993, no. 11, pp. 45–53.

Qu Changyou, Wei Shujie, "Xiaoxing shuili gongcheng chengbao guanli fangfade yanjiu yu yingyong" (Research into and Applications of Methods of Contracted Management of Small-scale Water Conservation Projects." *Zhongguo shuili* 1992, no. 8, pp. 16–18, 20.

Shandongsheng Rongchengxian zhengfu bangongshi (Rongcheng County Government Office, Shandong Province), "Guanyu nongtian shuili sheshide diaocha" (An Investigation of Farmland Water Conservancy Facilities). *Zhongguo nongcun jingji* 1986, no. 12, pp. 35–37.

Shaoshan guanqu (Shaoshan Irrigation District), Vol. 3: *Yunxing guanli* (Active Management). Changsha: Hunan shuili dianli Pub., 1979.

Song Lusheng, "Nongtian shuili, shuitu baochi fuwu zhongxinde xingshi he tedian" (Forms and Characteristics of Service Centers for Farmland Irrigation and Water and Soil Conservation). *Nongye jingji wenti* 1984, no. 1, pp. 44–46, 13.

Stone, Bruce, "Developments in Agricultural Technology." *The China Quarterly* 1988, no. 116, pp. 767–822.

Su Qingjun, "Yonghao laodong jilei gong, shengchan tiaojian dei gaishan" (In Order to Make Good Use of the Labor Involved in Labor Accumulation, Production Conditions Must Be Improved). *Zhongguo shuili* 1991, no. 1, p. 16.

Sun Shanlong, "Weinan nonghu ban shuilide 5–zhong leixing" (Five Types of Water Conservancy Undertaken by the Farmers of Weinan). *Zhongguo shuili* 1994, no. 1, p. 19.

Tian Deyang, "Zunyixian shuilunpeng zhandi jianshe he guanli" (The Establishment of Turbine Pumping Stations in Zunyi County and Their Management). *Zhongguo shuili* 1988, no. 8, pp. 18–20.

Vermeer, Eduard B. *Water Conservancy and Irrigation in China*. The Hague: Leiden University Press, 1977.

———. *Economic Development in Provincial China: The Central Shaanxi since 1930*. Cambridge: Cambridge University Press, 1988.

——— ed. 1992. *From Peasant to Entrepreneur: Growth and Change in Rural China*. Wageningen (the Netherlands): Pudoc, 1992.

Wang Mengqun et al., "Dui guoyou zichan jinxing quanmian qingli" (Execution of Complete Clearance of State-Owned Assets). *Zhongguo shuili* 1994, no. 5, pp. 8–10.

Wang Shouqiang, "Jiangsu shuili gaige zai tansuozhong qianjin" (The Reform of Water Conservancy in Jiangsu Is Advancing While Explorations Are in Progress). *Zhongguo shuili* 1986, no. 1, pp. 14–16, 24.

Wang Wenxue, "Shenhua nongcun gaige shi daguimo kaizhan nongtian shuili jianshede dongli" (Deepening Rural Reform is a Motivating Force in the Large-Scale Development of Farmland Water Conservancy Construction). *Zhongguo shuili* 1991, no. 4, pp. 10–11.

Wang Yongle, Ding Biran, "Jiaqiang guanli, wajue qianli, tigao xiaoyi" (Strengthen Management, Exploit Hidden Potential, Raise Effective Benefit). *Nongtian shuili yu xiaoshuidian* 1994, no. 6, pp. 22–26.

Wen Zhizhong, "Shuili gufen hezuozhi chuyi" (A Preliminary View on the Share-Holding Cooperative System in Water Conservancy). *Shuili jingji* 1994, no. 8, pp. 26–28.

Wu Haian, "Anhuaxian caiyong duozhong laodong jilei xingshi xingban nongtian shuili" (Anhua County Uses Many Forms of Labor Accumulation in Undertaking Farmland Water Conservancy). *Zhongguo shuili* 1986, no. 11, p. 9.

Wu Linxin, Ding Shoumin, "Jidian baiguan guanli tizhide gaige yijian" (Ideas on Reform of the Management System in Mechanical and Electrical Drainage and Irrigation). *Zhongguo nongcun jingji* 1986, no. 3, pp. 38–41.

Xiao Fu, Xin Li, "Jiaqiang shuifei lianzheng, jianshe wending guangai yongshui shichang" (Strengthen the Policy of Low Water Fees, Establish a Stable Market for the Use of Irrigation Water). *Zhongguo shuili* 1991, no. 1, p. 17.

Xiao Jian, "Shuiguan danwei qiye gaige mianlinde nandian jiqi duice chutan" (The Difficulties Facing Enterprise Reform of Water Management Units and a Preliminary Exploration of Remedies). *Zhongguo shuili* 1991, no. 2, pp. 12–14.

Xinfengxian shuilizhi Editorial Group, eds., *Xinfengxian shuili zhi* (Record of Water Conservancy in Xinfeng County). Xinfeng County Water Conservancy Bureau, 1990.

Xu Guodong, "Qianyi shuili gufen hezuozhi wenti" (Some Superficial Ideas on the Problems of Share-Holding Cooperatives in Water Conservancy). *Shuili jingji* 1994, no. 8, pp. 29–33.

Yang Jianbin, "Lun nonghu xingban shuili shiyede jiji zuoyong ji yindao fanglüe" (About the Positive Function of Execution of Water Conservancy Projects by Farmers and Guidance Strategies). *Zhongguo shuili* 1992, no. 8, pp. 14–15.

Yang Xiaoxin, Gu Binjie, "Woguo nongcun shuili fuwu tixide xiankuang ji fazhan qianjing" (Present Situation and Prospects of Development of the Rural Water Conservancy Service System in Our Country). *Zhongguo shuili* 1992, no. 2, pp. 4–7.

Zhanjiang shiwei zhengce yanjiushi (Policy Research Office of the Zhanjiang Municipal Committee), "Fahui xianyou shuili sheshide xiaoneng guanjian zaiyu gaige shuiguan tizhi" (The Key to Bringing the Present Capacity of Water Conservancy Facilities into Full Play Lies in the Reform of the Water Management System). *Zhongguo shuili* 1990, no. 8, pp. 14–15.

Zhang Fang et al., "Jiangsusheng jianli duoyuanhua shuili touzi tizhide 7–zhong xingshi" (Jiangsu Province Establishes Seven Forms of Diversified Water Conservancy Investment). *Zhongguo shuili* 1994, no. 4, pp. 17–18.

Zhang Gang, "Jiaqiang jiceng shuili fuwu tixi" (Strengthen the Base-Level Water Conservancy Service System). *Zhongguo shuili* 1990, no. 5, pp. 26–27.

Zhang Lianjun et al., "Da 'gufenjing,' mai shangpinshui" (Drill 'Share-Wells,' Sell Commercial Water). *Zhongguo shuili* 1992, no. 12, pp. 10–11.

Zhang Linong, "Guangai gongcheng shuili jingji liangxing xunhuande yanjiu" (Research into the Beneficial Cycle of the Economy of Water Conservation in Irrigation Projects). *Zhongguo shuili* 1991, no. 12, pp. 31–32.

Zhang Yue, "Woguo nongtian shuili jiben jianshede fazhan qianjing he duice" (Prospects for the Development of Capital Construction in Farmland Water Conservancy in Our Country and Measures). *Nongtian shuili yu xiaoshuidian* 1991, no. 12.

ZGNYNJ. Zhongguo nongye nianjian 1980– (China Agricultural Yearbook). Beijing: Nongye Pub., 1981–.

ZGSLNJ. Zhongguo shuili nianjian 1990, 1991, 1992 (China Water Conservancy Yearbook). Beijing: Shuili dianli Pub., 1991, etc.

Zhongguo shuili baike quanshu (Encyclopedia of Water Conservancy in China), 4 vols. Beijing: Shuili dianli Pub., 1990.

Zhou Fengduan, "Xiangzhen shuilizhan jishu rencai buzu wenti jidai jiejue" (The Problem of Insufficient Technical Personnel in the District and Town Water Conservancy Stations Urgently Awaits Solution). *Zhongguo shuili* 1990, no. 6, pp. 30–31.

Zhou Zhiping, "Nongcun gaige shinian zhongde shuili wenti" (Problems of Water Conservancy during a Decade of Rural Reform). *Zhongguo nongcun jingji* 1989, no. 5, pp. 30–34.

Zhu Weidong et al., "Dui shenhua shuijia gaigede yijian" (Views on Deepening the Reform of Water Prices). *Zhongguo shuili* 1992, no. 8, pp. 19–20.

Zou Shili, "Yu kunjingzhong qibu" (Moving Forward Out of a Difficult Situation). *Zhongguo shuili* 1988, no. 8, pp. 16–17.

7

Institutions, Households, and Groundwater in an Inner Mongolian Oasis

John Morton and Robin Grimble

This chapter describes the changing role of institutions and households in an irrigated oasis settlement in western Inner Mongolia, with particular reference to the most crucial resource, water from an underground source or aquifer. After a sketch of the recent history of the scheme in the Yao Ba district, and the adoption within it of the household production responsibility system, the fate of two levels of organization under this system is discussed. While the former commune has adopted the reduced role of a district administration, the production brigades have remained strong, corporate and property-owning bodies. Evidence for this is given in an account of the day-to-day management of the irrigation system. Other, higher-level bodies specifically responsible for water have found great difficulties in formulating and enforcing a policy which addresses the problems of depletion and degradation of the aquifer.

The Yao Ba Scheme: Location and Origins

Yao Ba[1] is the name given both to a district (formerly a commune) in western Inner Mongolia, and to the irrigated agricultural scheme on which the great majority of the district's people are settled, and which is responsible for the production of most of the district's income.

Yao Ba is located in the Left Banner of Alashan League,[2] Inner Mongolia, at 105°40'E, 38°50'N, about two hours drive from Yinchuan, capital of the neighboring Ningxia Hui Autonomous Region (see map). It is situated in the corridor between the Helan mountains and the sandy Tenggeri desert, at an altitude of about 1200m. The climate of the area is typical of the Asian steppes, characterized by cold winters, high winds and low rainfall. Annual rainfall in the area is only about 250 mm/yr, which falls in the summer months from July to October.

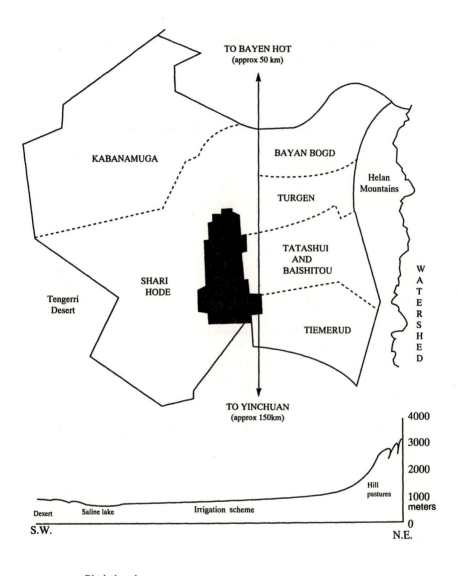

TO BAYEN HOT
(approx 50 km)

KABANAMUGA

BAYAN BOGD

Helan
Mountains

TURGEN

TATASHUI
AND
BAISHITOU

SHARI
HODE

Tengerri
Desert

W
A
T
E
R
S
H
E
D

TIEMERUD

TO YINCHUAN
(approx 150km)

4000

3000

2000

Hill
pastures

1000
meters

Desert   Saline lake   Irrigation scheme

0

S.W.

N.E.

—————— District boundary

- - - - - - - - Gatcha boundary

N.B. Hechu Borega gacha owns no pasture land and Gange owns pasture only in
neighbouring Xiangendalahai district.

Map 7.1 **Yao Ba district, gacha grazing areas and topographic
cross-section.**

The scheme currently includes about 44,000 mu (29 km²) of irrigated land and has a population of over 7000 people.[3]

Before the scheme was established, the area was composed mainly of desert scrub, used mainly by livestock, benefitting from a good growth of shrubs after the summer rains, but not distinguished as a particularly fertile grazing area. There were small areas of rainfed agriculture towards the mountains, and a few shallow wells in the desert for cultivation of fodder to supplement natural grazing.

Immigration of Han Chinese into the area has been a long and gradual process, unlike in other parts of Inner Mongolia. One village leader, a Han, proudly mentioned that he had five generations of ancestors buried in Yao Ba, and other informants talked of a similarly long Han presence in the area, and of widespread intermarriage, past and present. Han (and possibly some Hui) immigrants were coming from Gansu and Ningxia, provinces with greater pressure on natural resources than Inner Mongolia. These pressures were combined later with military insecurity and the threat of conscription during the Warlord and Civil War periods. The Han immigrants seem to have adopted a very similar agro-pastoral lifestyle to their Mongolian neighbors.

During the mid-1960s, work was started on preparations for the irrigated scheme, which was to draw water from an aquifer at a depth of between 15m and 60m below the surface. The villagers of Turgen in the foothills were moved 5 km or so into the desert, to an area in the northeast of the present scheme that was named Dong Fang Hong ("The East Is Red"). These villagers were organized as a production brigade to prepare the land, and construct channels and bunds.

Other villages, also organized as production brigades, were engaged at that time in more ordinary agro-pastoral production. Share Hode Brigade comprised three villages, each organized as a production team, extending from the western edge of the current scheme into the desert. In the late sixties, the First and Second Teams were raising livestock, while the Third Team was cultivating fodder around shallow, donkey-driven wells. Food for the brigade members was imported into the area through a government grain station. It seems that the Third Team was mainly Han in composition, while the First and Second Teams had a higher proportion of Mongols.[4]

The scheme officially became operational with the sinking of the first electric production boreholes in 1972, and there was large-scale resettlement of farming families around 1974. These families, almost entirely Han, came from the same over-populated areas of Gansu (in particular Minqin County) and Ningxia that had been supplying a smaller stream of immigrants for generations. It was suggested that some settlers were brought from much further afield, such as Shandong Province, but this was not confirmed. It has also been suggested that a small number of the settlers were "intellectuals" forced into the countryside by the Cultural Revolution—one such farmer was met by the authors. In any case, the current population of the district is about 81 percent Han and only 16 percent Mongolian. The Mongolian population is largely composed of herding families with a tenuous connection to the scheme.

The scheme grew, both in terms of people and in numbers of boreholes, throughout the 1970s. By 1975, 198 boreholes had been sunk, and by 1984, 279. Generally boreholes were laid out on a grid pattern, with each serving an area of around 450m by 450m. The boreholes were being sunk at increasing depths, starting at less than 50m and increasing to over 110m.

Administratively the scheme included nine production brigades of Yao Ba Commune, and three state farms directly managed by the Banner Bureau of Agriculture and Animal Husbandry. Seven of the nine brigades corresponded to villages, or groups of villages, that already existed in the surrounding area. These brigades combined, in varying degrees, farming on the scheme with production of livestock on the open range. Relocation of people from the herding villages to scheme land was by no means total. The brigades, which occupied discrete areas of the scheme, continued to administer the original village sites and the range-land that went with them.

Of these seven brigades, Kabanamuga, the only brigade to have a Mongolian majority, was assigned very little irrigated land. Shari Hode, already mentioned, had and has a significant Mongolian population as well as some Han who have tended to work in livestock production, so land was assigned only for the agri-cultural team. For the other five brigades based on existing villages, agricultural settlement on the scheme was the norm, and only a few families remained as specialist herders.

Of the two new brigades, Hechu Borega was entirely composed of new set-tlers and controlled no rangeland, while Xianggandelahai was made up of fami-lies settled on the scheme from the commune of that name to the south. It was administered by that commune (later district) until quite recently and still main-tains rangeland there.

The main initial objective of the Yao Ba scheme, and thus of the production brigades, was to produce fodder. As the ground is frozen and unproductive for several months each winter, the production of large amounts of storable fodder is a necessity for increasing livestock production. The production of fodder on the Yao Ba scheme contributed to livestock production by the brigades themselves, but also by other herders in the wider regional economy. At the same time, the door was not closed to production of grain for human consumption; at a meeting in 1970 it was decided that maize and sorghum would be permitted as fodder crops with possible dual-use, as grain for either livestock or human consumption, and cut green solely for livestock. Also in 1970, permission to grow some wheat was granted.

The three state farms had specialized roles within this scheme of things. The largest, the Seed Production Farm, was established in 1973 to produce seed of fodder crop varieties for use on the scheme and elsewhere. Originally on the southeast of the scheme, it expanded in 1982 to take in another area in the northwest, and now accounts for about one quarter of the irrigated area. The

Animal Production Farm is a specialist unit rearing pigs and poultry under fairly intensive conditions, and has diversified more recently into rearing silver fox for fur. The Sand Protection Team, considered a "state farm," is in fact a unit that services the whole scheme by planting and maintaining trees as windbreaks.

Decollectivization

Since 1982 Yao Ba has been subject to the same trends of decollectivization and liberalization which have affected the whole of rural China, frequently summed up under the heading of the household production responsibility system. Land and livestock have been distributed among farming households, which have been given progressively more responsibility to decide their own cropping patterns. Under this process the production brigades have lost much, but by no means all of their role as organizers of production. They are now known as *gachas*, the Mongolian for village, though many include more than one settlement, with either a new village on the scheme and an old village outside, or several villages on the scheme.

Land

Between 1982 and 1988, the production brigades began to divide their lands and livestock among their member households under the new household production responsibility system. It appears that the leadership of each production brigade had considerable influence over the timing of such decisions. The richest brigade, Turgen, was the last to implement the policy.

In the case of most production brigades, land was divided equally between all members of the brigade. The land was first of all divided into three categories according to fertility, and every individual brigade member (adult and child) was allotted an equal amount of each category. This rule contributed to the major fragmentation of holdings found today, with households farming an average of four, and up to ten, non-contiguous parcels. It is possible to consolidate holdings by land-swaps within the same fertility category, but this right has not been much exercised, and there have been no exchanges across fertility categories.

The initial allocation varied with the brigade, within the range of 4 to 6 *mu* per individual, and was in some cases affected by the simultaneous distribution of livestock. In Kabanamuga, the brigade most dominated by animal production on desert rangeland, herding families were given a share in the brigade's livestock and no scheme land, and in Shari Hode brigade, also on the desert edge, herding families were given land at 2 *mu* per person compared to 4 *mu* for farming families. Two other brigades followed similar policies.

Today land remains the property of the *gacha*. Land is individually held and ownership is resumed by the *gacha* in cases of death or permanent out-migration. Land is granted by the *gacha* when women join the *gacha* on marriage, and

Table 7.1

Average Land Holdings on State Farms and Gachas

	Land per household	Land per capita (*mu*)
Gachas[5]	17.7	4.8
Seed Production Farm	28.8	8.3

when children are born within the limits of the population policy, though such allocations may not be made for some time due to lack of land to re-allocate. On other occasions a *gacha* may find it has surplus land and allocate extra to each holder for this reason alone. Land granted in the name of children is not affected by the death of senior household members, so there can be some continuity of holdings over generations. Comments by Banner leaders and others suggested that land-grants were made for 15 years: the first 15-year period has not elapsed and therefore potential problems with the continuity of the system have not yet been tested. However, the 15-year limit was not raised as a problem by any farmers. Land cannot be sold but there is some rental market. One *gacha*, Shari Hode, rents out land off the scheme, to the chemical works operated by the Banner.

In 1984, land on the "Seed Production Farm" was distributed to workers on a basis of equal shares of around 15 *mu* for working members of the farm, but land grants have subsequently been made in the names of newborn children. There is a similar degree of fragmentation of holdings. As liberalization has continued on both the state farm and the *gachas*, the most important difference between them actually affecting farmers is that per household and per capita land holding is considerably higher than in the *gachas* (see Table 7.1).

This fact, and the somewhat more comprehensive social and health services provided on the state farm, compensate for the slightly greater control of marketing and higher rates of taxation on the state farm. Farmers on both categories of land saw the overall quality of life as roughly equivalent.

Livestock

Livestock had been collectively owned by the production brigades, we can assume since at least 1968 (see Longworth and Williamson 1994). The decollectivization of livestock and grazing land in Inner Mongolia took a variety of forms: a shift through a leasing system to the outright sale of stock, with or without the distribution of pasture land (Longworth and Williamson 1994). In Yao Ba, the distribution of stockownership from brigades to households took place in 1983, at the same time as the distribution of lands. Households paid the brigades/*gachas* a small sum in return for ownership rights over the animals. Grazing land remains the collective property of the *gacha*, as do water points other than those immediately near homesteads (which belong to the households). Summer pastures in the Helan mountains remain the property of the Forest Department, which assigns grazing licenses for a fee. *Gachas* assign the use of grazing lands to particular households, but on a flexible basis, with only informal boundaries between household territories. Grazing and water resources can be used by members of other *gachas*, depending more on good relations between individual households than on official relations between *gachas*. Conflict between *gachas* over grazing rights may be on the increase, but an equally important issue, in the eyes of officials, are the incursions of people from neighboring provinces gathering desert plants for food and medicinal purposes.

Distribution of livestock was organized by each brigade on a per capita basis, but distinguishing between herders and farmers. Herders, who had received smaller allocations of irrigated land, or none at all, received in the region of seven animals per household member. For non-herders initial allocations of livestock were small: a non-herding family in Shari Hode had been given only one sheep and one ox.

Current livestock holdings are a function of the original *gacha* endowment in livestock and rangeland, combined with the luck, management skills and other resources of the household (such as the shelter and cultivated fodder necessary to avoid mortality among livestock during the harsh winters). As such they are necessarily inequitable. Farmers on the state farm (which controls no grazing land), and a few in the *gachas*, keep no stock. Average holdings in the non-herding *gachas* are probably very low, only a few pigs or sheep. Among herding families, average holdings are rising, with the wealthiest herding families keeping up to 200–300 smallstock, plus camels. During the limited period of research it was not possible to discover to what extent this inequality in pastoral holdings was an important issue in inter-household relations or local politics.

The herds of farm households are mostly herded in the foothills and desert in summer by specialist herders, often members of herding households, for a small fee per head. In winter the animals are stall-fed; farmers arrange to grow sufficient fodder for their animals' needs and only market fodder crops if there is a surplus. Animals in Hechu Borega *gacha*, which has no rangeland, are fed on cultivated fodder (plus household waste and standing crop residues) all year round.

Reliable statistics on livestock numbers were hard to obtain, but it is generally agreed that livestock numbers are rising. Official sources link this to the degradation of pastures, characterized by reduced density and size of plants, and government has attempted to introduce a pasture policy summed up in the slogan "Livestock Numbers Must Depend on Pasture." Farmers and herders are less likely to see degradation of pastures as a problem, and such a policy appears unenforceable. The movement of people into the area, and the availability of cultivated forage from the scheme, are almost certain to have increased livestock numbers. According to farmer interviews, decollectivization has increased overall livestock numbers as standards of husbandry have risen and mortality rates have fallen. When animals were owned by the brigades, they were badly looked after and suffered high mortality, especially at lambing. Stallfeeding is encouraged by government and increasingly practiced, but only around 2000 animals are kept in compounds all year round.

Cropping Decisions

During the 1980s farmers were gaining more individual rights over land, but were still strongly subject to production decisions made by the commune or the state farm, and the obligation to market crops through official channels. Simultaneously, the scheme experienced a drift from its original purpose of growing fodder to one of growing wheat, which rose sharply around 1983 and represented about 70 percent of cultivated area in the *gachas* by the early 1990s. The state farm was made responsible for balancing its own budget in 1984, and virtually abandoned its former purpose of forage seed production to shift into wheat (it also owns a coal mine and a small hotel in a nearby town). Wheat had to be sold to the Grain Station, which was seen as a strategic grain reserve for the Banner and part of the reserve for Inner Mongolia as a whole.

Since 1992 the process of decollectivization has been taken further. Farmers in the *gachas* and on the state farm, which increasingly resembles the *gachas* in respects most important to farmers, are now able to take their own cropping decisions. In the *gachas* there is still in theory a quota, of 70kg per *mu*, for grain (wheat) to be produced and sold through the Grain Station, but under current conditions farmers generally grow wheat greatly in excess of this, so that the quota is not perceived as an issue. Farmers take cropping decisions based principally on their own subsistence needs, anticipated market prices and soil quality (which varies across the scheme).

With the exception of the small grain quota, *gacha* farmers are now able to sell their crops wherever they wish. Wheat is sold privately to Yinchuan, which although situated in a major rice-growing area, represents a major market for wheat. Yinchuan-based merchants travel to Yao Ba from harvest onwards, and for farmers prepared to wait a few months offer significant price advantages. The Grain Station continues to present some advantages as a purchaser, particularly for smaller farmers: sales can be used immediately to repay operating loans, through the credit co-operatives. Nevertheless, its overall share is falling, and it appears that this will affect its ability to act as a strategic reserve, but that the implications of the change have not been fully absorbed.

The effects of this deregulation on cropping patterns are still unclear for lack of data. Wheat remains by far the most popular crop, but has recently declined in popularity, partly because of diseases, to around 57 percent of cultivated area in 1995. If there were a further decline, for reasons of disease or of falling prices, the question of the grain quota might become more salient. In 1994 there was some interest in growing barley, for the brewery in Yinchuan, but this proved unprofitable, and has not been sustained.

Maize, and to a lesser degree sorghum and millet, which are all mainly produced for animal consumption, direct or as processed products, account for most of the rest of the cultivated area. Specialist fodder crops such as lucerne are still grown in small quantities. One cash crop that is starting to be grown is fennel, for which there is a market in Yinchuan, and for which merchants may be providing seed.

The state farm continues to act as the marketing channel for its farmers, certainly as regards wheat, but its own sales are made on the open market, primarily to Yinchuan, and the prices it offers to farmers reflect free-market prices. It also acts as a channel for marketing sorghum to the Left Banner Distillery.

The District and the *Gacha*

The years since 1982 have seen the transformation of the commune and production brigades from collective institutions for organizing production to something more like tiers of local government with essentially non-economic functions. However, this transformation has been partial and uneven, and has affected the commune far more than the brigades. It has also been complicated by the continuing ability of Chinese government institutions at all levels to operate economic enterprises outside their geographical areas and their supposed "core" functions.

The district (Mongolian *sumu*), as the commune is now known, is an important level of government for the day-to-day administration of the Yao Ba area, the provision of basic services, the collection of taxes, and the co-ordination of activities of other agencies such as the sectoral bureaux of the Banner government. In 1994–95 it increased its responsibility for agricultural services, but lost its already residual authority over development of water resources.

The district lacks any significant authority over various enclave economic enterprises on its territory, and their workforces. Chief among these are the three state farms, which account for 22 percent of the population of the district, but there are also agro-industrial enterprises (notably a concentrates factory) run by the Banner Bureau of Agriculture and Animal Husbandry, "small collective farms" run by a bewildering variety of Banner and other government institutions (including several schools and the army) and a sodium sulphate works outside the scheme but within the district, run by the Banner. The leader and government of the district thus have authority essentially over the leaders and people of the *gachas*, which amounts to about 60 percent of the population, and about 50 percent of the irrigated land.

The district government collects an agricultural tax and a special tax on "economic crops" (oilseeds, vegetables, etc.) assessed in advance on planted areas, but is dependent on the Banner for the bulk of its budget. There was a ¥970,000 net flow from Banner to district government in 1993, an amount which increased in 1994. This excludes the resources, notably subsidies for new boreholes, which bypass the district by flowing direct from Banner to *gacha*, and Banner investments in productive enterprise within Yao Ba.

While the *gachas* have lost their role in organizing agricultural production (which was in any case that of channelling production decisions made at a higher level), they are still the most important land-holding units. They have granted to their constituent households the right to use agricultural land on a revocable basis, and still own and control rangeland. *Gacha* land is "collective land" in terms of the Chinese constitution, and cannot be expropriated by state bodies or transferred to other *gachas*. *Gachas* may own other important assets—accumulated savings in bank accounts and productive enterprises such as brick kilns and small coal mines in the Helan mountains. These enterprises are the inalienable properties of the *gacha*, managed by the *gacha* leadership with wage labor from the *gacha* or elsewhere, for the benefit of the *gacha* members. Their possession or otherwise contributes to the significant inequalities between *gachas*. The *gachas* are also important units of grassroots local government.

Each *gacha* has at least one full-time leader (Turgen has two) and a part-time committee, elected by the *gacha* members. The *gacha's* financial resources can consist of accumulated savings, income from productive activities, and a regular levy on members. For Turgen, undoubtedly one of the wealthier *gachas*, savings stood at around ¥200,000, industrial income at ¥100,000/year and regular contributions from members at ¥30,000/year.[6] From these resources a *gacha* is expected to support childless elderly people (who are established in special houses) and other especially needy people; to contribute jointly with the district in paying teachers and running education services; to make productive investments in the livestock economy (boreholes and dips); to organize cultural activities and sport; and to pay its own administrative expenses. The *gacha* is also responsible for resolving disputes among its members, enforcing population policy, and carrying out any other tasks delegated to it by the district government.

The *gachas* play a major role in managing, and in some cases investing in, irrigation. This will be discussed below, after a description of the water extraction system and the threat of salinization it faces.

Groundwater and Its Management: Farmers and *Gachas*

There are around 260 boreholes, powered by electricity, currently used in Yao Ba, all but a handful for agricultural use. The great majority were sunk in the 1970s as from 1980, the Banner implemented strict restrictions on the sinking of new boreholes. These were temporarily relaxed in 1986–87, when a plan to convey water to Yao Ba from the Yellow River was mooted, which would have reduced pressure on groundwater. In 1988, restrictions were reimposed and no new boreholes have since been sunk, though some that have failed and been abandoned have been replaced.

Owing to the fragmentation of land holdings, a farming household may utilize a number of boreholes: farmers interviewed in Hechu Borega, Shari Hode and the Seed Production Farm each used four boreholes, those in Turgen only one or two. The number of farmers using a borehole varies considerably, and can be as low as 10 or more than 20.

Farmers are responsible for irrigating their own fields. The different parcels of land served by a borehole are irrigated according to a fixed rota, starting with those nearest the borehole and moving across and down the channel system. In some areas the sequence, at least of major blocks of land, is reversed in alternate years, but with this exception, the sequences have not changed since they were laid down at the time of land distribution.

Water is distributed from a borehole to farmers' fields through a system of channels. Primary channels leaving boreholes are lined with concrete. Each field is bounded by shallow bunds to contain water. To direct water flow, channels are blocked and bunds opened, as appropriate. When the time to irrigate a parcel comes, the farmer opens and closes his channel as necessary, and enters an electricity meter reading in the logbook at the pumphouse. He then has the right to keep the water flowing for as long as he wants, but in practice stops when water levels reach a depth of between 15 and over 20 cm. Obviously farmers use their experience in these matters, and levels differ according to soils and other factors. Some farmers mentioned that their fields were not level and they would irrigate until the highest lying ground was covered with water. The depth of irrigation was not seen to vary between the major crops.

When a parcel has been fully irrigated the farmer notes the meter reading at the pumphouse, and the flow of water is transferred to his neighbor. He will then have to wait between 10 and 20 days before he can irrigate the parcel again, although in that time he will irrigate other parcels elsewhere in the sequence.

There were considerable variations in farmer responses but, on average, wheat crops were found to receive five or more irrigations per season, maize and sorghum four, and sesame, millet and fennel three. These differences are in part a result of the fact crops other than wheat are planted later in the season, and therefore can be expected to benefit from summer rainfall, whereas wheat is harvested in mid-summer. Because of the variation in frequency of application, however, the volume of water applied per crop per season can vary considerably. Discussion with farmers and government officers suggests, for example, that the water applied to wheat over a season varies between 400 and 1000 m^3 per *mu*. The limited control by individual farmers over irrigation volumes and sequencing, however, limits opportunities for experimenting with different irrigation regimes.

There is a peak period during which boreholes are pumping continuously for 24 hours a day, described in most areas as mid-April to mid-July. This peak period, however, varies according to the density and capacity of the boreholes, and on the Seed Production Farm this was said to last from March to September. Although some boreholes observed during our first visit (in late May) were not continuously pumping, it must be concluded that many farmers face a period when the interval between successive irrigations of a parcel is perceived to be too long. One farmer explicitly mentioned that irrigating his wheat the desired five times was impossible; the wheat was already ripe for harvesting by the time of the last irrigation (whereas for a better crop yield he would like to have left a clear 15 days between the last irrigation and harvesting).

Water can be characterized as scarce in the formal sense that farmers would use more if more were available (as evidenced by boreholes working at full capacity). On the other hand, this scarcity is not critical: farmers are not constrained from producing a decent crop, particularly as they have a range of crops with differing water requirements to choose from. Changes between 1994 and 1995 connected with the rise of electricity prices (see below) suggest that significant reductions in water-use could be made with little reduction in yields.

Water use is not presently a major source of conflict among farmers. Farmers' rights to water under the rota system are so clearly defined that there is little scope for conflict over water use. Farmers generally denied that there were any such conflicts.[7] Obviously more prolonged research might uncover more of farmers' views of water supply and water distribution, and farmers' strategies for manipulating them. It is still likely that the great majority of farmers are taking their turns in the rota and ensuring the functioning of the system, even in the absence of explicit mechanisms to enforce co-operation. It should be noted that this is happening despite the new economic importance of individual households, and despite the fact that the majority of *gachas*, composed of recent migrants, are very far indeed from what Feuchtwang would call a "natural village" (see his contribution to this volume). However, if the current depletion and degradation of groundwater continues, a continuing absence of conflict cannot be guaranteed.

Within the last six or seven years, the heavy development of groundwater resources has depressed the water table, led to inflows of saline water, and increased the cost of pumping. One solution to the salinity problem has been the widespread adoption of winter irrigation to flush salts from the soil, another has been the large-scale importation of sand from the desert edge. Salinization has become a major concern to the authorities, who enlisted the assistance of the Comprehensive Institute of Geotechnical Investigation and Surveying (CIGIS) from Beijing to investigate its causes and likely future development. While the situation is known to farmers, and likely to get worse in the next few years, the problem is still largely one of water being in excess of national standards for salinity, rather than salinity being a major constraint on production as perceived by farmers. There are exceptions to this in a number of boreholes in the southwest of the scheme.

Borehole 176, in Hechu Borega *gacha*, is one such example. This borehole has been pumping extremely saline water since 1991. When the problem developed the farmers notified the *gacha* leader, who in turn notified the Water Bureau of the Banner Government, which had a sample tested in Yinchuan.

About 25 farmers use this borehole, each of whom also have access to another three boreholes, not necessarily the same three.[8] They seem to have been unable to agree on financing a new borehole, but, steered by the *gacha* leader, have found another "solution" to the salinity problem, by which they have ceased to grow wheat on land watered by the salty borehole. Crops are most susceptible to salty water at germination, and some crops, such as sunflower and watermelon, are less susceptible than others, particularly wheat. For this reason, on most of the affected land (226 *mu* out of 250 *mu*) they have learned to plant sunflower for preference, or maize or sorghum. These crops can be started on water pumped from borehole 175, slightly uphill and to the east, and will then tolerate irrigation with salty water once established. Four *mu* of barley and 20 *mu* of wheat were planted in 1994 on land previously irrigated by borehole 176, which will receive all their water from 175. As the users of 175 are largely the same people as the users of 176, or at least their relatives and neighbors, there has been no dispute, despite the extra demand placed on the water produced from borehole 175. Some informants generalized this to state that such arrangements would be possible within *gachas*, but not across *gacha* boundaries.

Farmers are aware that two years of wheat (or barley) followed by a year of maize and sorghum would be a good rotation pattern. Relatively small holdings, and the popularity of wheat as a known and easily marketable crop probably means that this is seldom observed in practice. Permanently discontinuing wheat cultivation on land watered by 176, about a quarter of each farmer's holding, has therefore been one more factor militating against proper rotation of crops. The switch to sunflower has been acceptable in the short-term to the farmers of Borehole 176 (as evidenced perhaps by their lack of enthusiasm to sink a new borehole). If more boreholes start to run as salty as 176, this sort of solution will become increasingly inadequate to sustain farmers' livelihoods.

Routine maintenance and minor repairs of the pumps are undertaken by a pump mechanic. The mechanic, who is also a farming member of the *gacha*, is elected by the members of the *gacha* (rather than by users of a particular borehole) and may manage a number of boreholes, at least as many as four. Systems of remuneration differ: farmers in Hechu Borega pay ¥1/*mu*/year/borehole directly to the mechanic as salary, in Shari Hode farmers pay ¥3.5/*mu*/year for the salaries of a mechanic, a book-keeper, and as a contribution to repairs. These amounts are distinct from other charges paid by farmers, directly or indirectly, for water (see below).

The duties of the mechanic are maintenance and minor repair. Some have formal training, in many cases undergone in the early 1970s when the Banner Electricity and Water Bureaux were combined. The mechanics collaborate with the Water Bureau as necessary, for example when the Bureau needs to take a water sample, but they are *gacha* employees and not responsible to the Bureau. In some cases, the mechanics are primarily responsible for mobilizing communal labor for channel maintenance, while in others this role is performed by the *gacha* leader. Mechanics appear to resolve the few disputes over water that do arise.

Maintenance and repair of channels is organized by the mechanic or by the *gacha*, mobilizing the labor of households using each borehole. In one case, a farmer mentioned a quota set by the *gacha* of 1.4 labor-days per *mu* per year to be given to the tasks, but actual labor appears to be given more on a need basis: households had given between zero and 30 labor-days to channel maintenance in the last year. Households unable to donate labor can pay a cash fee instead.

More substantial investment, especially the sinking of replacement boreholes and the purchase of new pumps, is managed by the *gacha* authorities. In recent years, the Water Bureau has required that farmers and/or *gachas* pay around half of the cost of sinking a new borehole, and the entire cost of a pump. Costs of sinking boreholes vary with depth, and it seems that the proportion met by the Water Bureau is also somewhat variable. It seems that the intent is now to pass on total investment costs to the *gacha* but this is still negotiable and has not yet been enforced.[9]

Depending on the amount needed, a *gacha* can pay for investments and major repairs in a variety of ways, determined by the wealth of the *gacha* and its farmers, and its organizational strength. In Hechu Borega, all such funds would have to be raised on a one-off basis directly from the farmers who would benefit. The *gacha* has a limited capacity to initiate and enforce such a policy: farmers have been unable to agree to contribute the ¥1000 or so per household for a replacement borehole for 176, which would probably be a reasonable medium-term solution.[10] In Shari Hode, the *gacha* levy on farm area, which also pays for the mechanic's salary, is sufficient to purchase new pumps, three having been installed last year. More substantial investments would be funded from a one-off levy on farmers, collected by the mechanic. In the Seed Production Farm (not of course a *gacha*) the Farm would pay for replacement boreholes from its own account, but farmers would be charged for pump repairs and new pumps. In Turgen *gacha*, which accumulated substantial reserves during the collective period, and has an income from industrial activities, the *gacha* has funded all expenditure on repair and investment from its own funds. The *gacha* has also spent its funds on the lining of channels with concrete, an activity normally the responsibility of the Water Bureau, but scarcely carried out by them in the last few years.

Water Charges and Water Policy

The nature of the hydrogeological problem affecting Yao Ba is still under technical investigation. It is likely that there is no significant recharge of the Yao Ba aquifer, which poses a question of trade-offs between whether water should be used now or retained for use in the future. In addition, there is the growing problem of salinity, for which a range of technical solutions (casing of boreholes above certain depths, pumping only at certain times of the year) are under investigation.

As water, particularly good quality water, becomes scarce, there is a need to improve the efficiency of water use. While the authorities have addressed overall water extraction through imposing a ban on new boreholes, they have not been able to equip themselves with the instruments to reduce extraction at the borehole level and enforce more efficient water-use. Water charges, which could act as an incentive to efficient water-use, are set too low to do so and, it appears, do not even cover the costs of administering and maintaining the system. The reasons for this state of affairs are found in the complex relations between local, regional and national policy.

The Water Utilization and Conservancy Bureau is the organ of the Banner Government responsible for administering and developing the water resources of the Banner. Its functions, as stated by its leader, are:

a) to implement government policy by formulating and enforcing regulations in the light of local conditions;
b) to investigate water resources (including a limited responsibility for hydrogeological work);
c) to construct, manage and maintain water systems, and to carry out disaster prevention and relief (in the case of floods and droughts).

While the Bureau has responsibility for groundwater utilization throughout the Banner, its efforts are concentrated on the Banner's five major irrigation systems. Of these, Yao Ba is the largest in area and in water use, although it may in the future be overtaken by Luanjing, a very large scheme to be irrigated from the Yellow River, currently under construction. Only one other major scheme, Charhatan, relies on underground water supplies.

The Bureau is represented in Yao Ba by a Water Management Station. The Station reports jointly to the Bureau in Bayanhot and Yao Ba District. It was reported in 1995 that this Station was about to close. The Station's functions, as summarized by its leader, were:

a) installation and management of boreholes and channels;
b) implementing water policies and water laws from higher echelons of government;
c) monitoring of groundwater levels and quality.

In addition, the Station owned and managed a large flour mill, a not unusual example of government bodies supporting themselves by taking on completely novel functions.

The Water Bureau has been concerned for many years about non-sustainable use or over-exploitation of the aquifer. Limiting discharges from individual boreholes is not institutionally practical: the Bureau lacks resources,[11] and probably the support from above to enforce such an unpopular policy. A policy of actively taking boreholes out of production and/or decreasing the irrigated area would also be extremely unpopular, and therefore difficult to administer. The Bureau's main water management strategy has been one of limiting any expansion in irrigated area and sinking of additional boreholes. While some officials have talked about a planned area for the scheme of over twice the current irrigated areas (to 100,000 *mu* from 43,000 *mu*), this is regarded as completely impossible; the Water Bureau now clearly states that there is insufficient water for such expansion, and would be happy if the irrigated area in fact declined to a more sustainable level (which could only be determined with further hydrogeological study). There does not appear to be any serious lobby for scheme expansion; Banner and League politicians now have other possibilities for large-scale irrigation at Luan Jing to consider.

Between 1980 and 1986, there were severe restrictions on the sinking of new boreholes. While the regulation was apparently strictly enforced for private farmers, it was at times circumvented by other government bodies. Apparently in 1982, the Bureau encouraged the Seed Production Farm to relocate 100 families from the south to the north of the scheme, on the understanding that the irrigated area would be correspondingly reduced in the south; an understanding that was not adhered to.

After a relaxation in 1986–87, a policy of no new boreholes has been more universally enforced. Since that time, only 28 replacement boreholes have been installed, and only three since 1993. In 1993 the policy was formalized and strengthened by the introduction of a system of water licenses, which must be renewed each year and can be revoked or lapse through non-use.

The Water Bureau is in principle responsible for the collection of various charges on water-use, both for cost recovery and as a disincentive to over-use. However, in practice its powers to determine the nature and level of such charges are severely restricted by laws and policies, sometimes conflicting, that emanate from higher echelons of government. At present, water charges are nominal. It would appear that both in Yao Ba and the Banner as a whole, charges collected by the Water Bureau are completely insufficient to cover its own operating budget, and costs are only covered through subsidies from other Banner income.[12]

The water-related charge which is most felt by farmers is in fact neither imposed nor collected by the Water Bureau, but is the charge for electricity consumed in pumping water from the aquifer. This charge is made by the Electricity Bureau of the Banner. The charge to farmers is calculated from the logbooks at pumping stations. For most farmers the bill is charged in advance in January, and rebates based on actual use are made at the end of the year.

In 1994, the Electricity Bureau ended its element of subsidy to farmers. We were assured that current electricity charges now represent the full economic cost for electricity, although it is not completely clear to what extent they include investment costs and overheads, as well as operating costs. In any case, charges have risen steeply from a 1991 level of ¥0.088 per kilowatt-hour to ¥0.207 per kilowatt-hour in 1994. For farmers this means, according to figures provided by the district administration, a cost of ¥90 per *mu* of wheat, representing 27 percent of the total costs of wheat. Charges per *mu* for other crops which require less irrigation, such as maize and sorghum, are lower. Electricity consumption figures, and thus charges, are more sensitive to variations in pumping depth, which means that there is great variation in the costs of irrigation across different parts of the scheme.

While the increase in electricity prices was coincidental rather than the result of a policy to reduce water use, it is beginning to have that effect. This charge was mentioned explicitly by nearly all farmers as their biggest financial outlay and perceived problem. Interviews in 1995 clearly suggested that farmers were already reacting to rising electricity charges by reducing the number of irrigations, and that in general this was not causing significant reduction in yields.

Besides electricity charges, two different charging systems for water itself have been imposed in recent years: the water fee and the water resource charge. The water fee has been imposed in the Left Banner since 1989. The Autonomous Region and Banner governments delayed somewhat in implementing this policy, which had been promulgated by the central government in 1985. An Autonomous Region document sets forth the rationale for a water fee: to pay for new investment, repair and maintenance of channels, operating costs and repairs to boreholes. The Water Bureau set the level at ¥2/*mu* for grain crops, and has since been unable to raise it (see below). The rate for "economic crops" (vegetables, oilseeds, etc.) is between ¥3.5 and ¥5/*mu*. In most cases this represents only some 1 percent of total expenditure on the crop. The Water Station in Yao Ba collected this fee from farmers, and in principle it went to the installation of water-saving technologies, but was insufficient even for the salaries of the Water Station employees.

In 1992 a new charge, the water resource charge (WRC) was introduced, to be based as far as possible on actual water use by individual farming households (as measured by electricity consumption). This charge was to be levied alongside and not to replace the existing water fee. The Water Bureau of the Banner drafted substantial modifications of regulations published by the Autonomous Region Government.[13] While the basic charge of about ¥10/*mu* was not particularly high, charges for water-use over designated quotas rose steeply.

In fact the policy was declared too late in the year for the Water Bureau to be able to track and act upon farmers' total water consumption, as farmers had already used an indeterminate amount of water. In the event, therefore, no farmers were charged with exceeding the specified quotas.[14]

In 1993, the central leadership in Beijing announced a policy of "Reducing the Burden on the Farmers."[15] Such a national policy, announced in vague terms and with an uncertain legal status, in practice outweighs the laws and regulations laid down by regional and local governments. As a result, the collection of the WRC has been suspended, and other charges on farmers have been frozen, such as the water fee. This last is the case despite the rationale for it given by the Autonomous Region Government, which is evidently applicable to Yao Ba.

Despite the coincidental effect of rises in electricity prices, the leadership of the Water Bureau in the Banner are clearly concerned at their inability to raise revenue and to influence farmer water-use by volumetric charging or even by raising charges per unit area. A report submitted to the Banner government recommending the continuance of the WRC or similar charges was not accepted, as such a policy question was felt to be in the sphere of the Autonomous Region Government.

The consequences of the policy are locally to transfer the cost of water management and operation from the user (the farmer) to the Bureau (and ultimately taxpayers elsewhere in China). As next to no charges are made for water itself, as opposed to the cost of its provision, this has the effect of encouraging the non-sustainable use of water now, and running down supplies, at the expense of retaining supplies for future use. As central government subsidies to peripheral areas such as Inner Mongolia are declining (Cannon 1989), this also ultimately weakens the capacity of the Water Bureau to monitor the situation and to invest in the development of water saving technologies.

Investigations in the area have demonstrated the need and opportunity to introduce more direct water saving technologies. The Water Bureau presents itself as having a major responsibility for this. In practice this has been largely limited to the lining of channels with concrete, and this activity was mainly carried out in the late 1970s, with no new work in recent years. A few years ago, a plan to install buried concrete pipes was discussed and tested in a small area, but this was never followed up due to the Bureau's budgetary constraints. The Agricultural Technology Popularization Station of the Agriculture and Animal Husbandry Bureau has had some success in introducing agricultural technologies that reduce water needs, such as the use of plastic sheeting to reduce evaporation. Transparent sheeting is now quite widely used by farmers, particularly for "economic crops."

The effect of the "Reducing the Burden" policy raises a number of questions it has not been possible to answer in our research. In particular, there are the questions of how much this sort of pressure from above reinforces and depends upon political pressure from below—pressure from farmers upon local officials not to raise charges, and of what forms such pressure from below can and does take in contemporary rural China. There is also a question of how electricity charges have been able to rise while water charges have not, the answer to which may relate to deep-lying perceptions of water in Chinese society.

Conclusion

Since 1982, Yao Ba has seen a massive shift towards the economic independence of households, a shift that was still continuing with the end of centralized cropping decisions and the liberalization of marketing in 1992. This shift, however, has not diminished the importance of what used to be known as production brigades and are now known as *gachas*. The *gachas* continue to be strong corporate bodies and retain not only the ultimate ownership of land, but also (in some cases) accumulated financial savings and non-agricultural productive assets. This situation has the potential for allowing serious inequalities between *gachas*, and there is some evidence that this is actually occurring. On the other hand, there is no evidence of serious strains to solidarity within *gachas*.

Gachas play a substantial role in the day-to-day management of the irrigation system, especially through the employment of pump mechanics, and have considerable autonomy in how they finance this role. At least one *gacha* has been involved in the short-term management of the salinity problem. *Gachas* also have a potential role in investment in irrigation, a role which in practice varies with their differing levels of wealth. The fragmentation of farmers' holdings between boreholes has probably encouraged the development of *gacha*-wide rather than more local management and maintenance. The process appears to have been encouraged by the historical circumstances by which the *gachas* (unlike the commune) emerged from the collectivist period with their assets intact.

What the *gachas* cannot do is limit the amount of water used, although it is likely that reduction will become necessary in the face of depletion and increasing salinity. Groundwater is in an important sense a common property resource, and subject to the tendency of overexploitation that, it has been argued, is intrinsic to common property. This general argument on common property has, quite rightly, been attacked as a gross oversimplification of many real-life common property systems, but usefully describes the situation of Yao Ba, post-liberalization. There are three important aspects of this situation.

Firstly, the reserves of groundwater, and their rate of depletion or replenishment, are quite literally invisible to the ultimate users. Secondly, liberalization has provided the environment which enables and encourages farmers to maximize crop production, in part through the use of more water. In the absence of volumetric charging there is no incentive to economize on water use, and introduce water saving technologies.[16]

Thirdly, no overarching institution exists that can effectively govern the exploitation of groundwater. The *gachas* cannot do so because they each only govern a fraction of the total community of users. The District might have been in a position to do so, but it has neither the mandate nor incentives to manage water abstraction or allocation, and its minimal involvement appears to be declining further.

At present, higher-level institutions such as the Banner Water Bureau can limit further expansion of the scheme, but have practical difficulties controlling extraction from existing boreholes. The amount of water abstracted is determined by the design of the scheme and density of the borehole layout, which does not significantly set a limit to the volume of water which can be abstracted. The system of operation leaves farmers free to take as much water as they deem necessary without sanction (subject to a rota system which ensures equity). In the absence of volumetric charging for the water itself, there are no incentives to reduce waste and encourage water-use efficiency. The introduction of fully-costed electricity has only to a certain extent provided these price signals.

Behind this absence of a policy are two underlying factors. Firstly, the Water Bureau lacks the technology and resources to monitor and control water-use. The general reduction in the flow of subsidies from the central government to peripheral areas is significant here. Secondly, increasing charges to affect indirectly water consumption, and still more so directly reducing consumption, would be unpopular with farmers, and, following the "Reduce the Burden" policy, officials in Yao Ba have no authority to impose measures against the short-term interests of farmers, even when there are sound long-term reasons for doing so. The Banner Water Bureau is currently impotent to cover its own running costs from water charges, let alone to institute such a regime.

We should not leave the impression, however, that with a different political or institutional system the problem of groundwater depletion and degradation would disappear. Studies in progress by one of the authors of water depletion and degradation under a variety of different institutional set-ups around the world suggest that such environmental problems are global. The situation is certainly not significantly worse in China than elsewhere.[17] Such problems are inevitable where the demand for water is growing fast but water supplies are inelastic or at least subject to rapidly increasing costs.

Indeed, comparison with the situation in other parts of Asia (e.g., India), where more or less open access to groundwater resources is possible, and where competition is rising through the advent of new technologies (allowing deeper and/or cheaper boreholes) and rapidly increasing and uncontrolled demand, suggests that the Chinese problem is less serious and potentially more controllable. At least in Yao Ba, new boreholes are not being constructed and abstraction is not taking place with unhindered competitive zeal. Moreover, the existence of the Water Bureau and similar overarching authorities could at least potentially provide the means for efficient and sustainable water-use.

Acknowledgments:

This paper is based on a visit to Yao Ba by the authors in May-June 1994, on an ODA (UK) funded project with the British Geological Survey to provide technical assistance to the Comprehensive Institute of Geotechnical Investigation and Surveying, Beijing. A further visit was made by Robin Grimble in September 1995 under the NRI/BGS Groundwater Resource Degradation Project, funded by the Economic and Social Research Council of the UK. He was accompanied by Don Brown, whose contribution to data-gathering and analysis is gratefully acknowledged. Additional funds were made available by ODA for the preparation of this paper and John Morton's attendance at the "International Conference on Chinese Rural Collectives and Voluntary Organizations," Sinological Institute, Leiden University, January 1995.

The authors would like to thank their colleagues from BGS and CIGIS for practical assistance, including the provision of interpreters in the field. They would also like to thank the officials of Alashan League and Alashan Left Banner, and the leaders and people of Yao Ba District. Views expressed in the paper are the responsibility of the authors alone.

Notes

1. The Mongolian name Barunbieli is also increasingly used.
2. A "Banner" in Inner Mongolia and certain other Mongolian-speaking areas corresponds to a "county" elsewhere in China, and a "League" to a "prefecture."
3. Even different official population figures are at variance and both 7,734 and 7,218 people were cited. Over 90 percent of the district population reside on the scheme.
4. See Huang (1982) for a similar situation on the Ordos Plateau of Inner Mongolia.
5. Aggregate of five *gachas* where all members were given equal shares of irrigated land.
6. Members were taxed at ¥7/*mu* of cultivated land, and ¥0.5 per head, per year.
7. One of the eight farmers interviewed mentioned disputes over mistaken entries in the logbook, one mentioned that farmers do not always observe the sequence. In both cases, the pump mechanic was the person who resolved the disputes.
8. We were told that all 36 households of Shunfaho each used all 9 of its boreholes, but we subsequently learned this was an exaggeration.
9. "If gacha leaders have good relations with the Bureau," as one official put it, the Bureau will make a substantial contribution.
10. As credit would be available from the Co-operative Credit Union, the problem is absolute willingness to pay, rather than cash-flow.
11. There is no equipment for directly monitoring water flows: they could be monitored by proxy through electricity consumption, but with boreholes pumping from different depths this is not straightforward.
12. The Banner government itself is highly subsidized by the Autonomous Region, and the Autonomous Region government by the center.
13. The charge was determined as follows. Farmers were not to be charged for the first 300m^3/*mu* (a condition specific to the Banner) and above that were to be charged at ¥0.02/m^3 up to a "quota." The quota was set for Yao Ba at 500, 550 or 600m^3/*mu* depending on the sandiness of the soil. Above the quota Autonomous Region regulations against over-use were to apply: if over-use was within 30 percent of the quota it was to be charged at twice the standard rate, if between 30 percent and 60 percent of the quota at four times the standard rate, and if over 60 percent at six times the standard rate. In principle, there was a possibility that Yao Ba could have been exempted altogether from the water resource charge, through a clause in the Autonomous Region regulations exempting areas where "groundwater development is planned and encouraged by the regional institutions responsible for water." That this did not happen could be deemed to show either that the regional government recognized the need for water-pricing in view of the limited water resources in Yao Ba, or that Yao Ba, essentially an initiative of Alashan League, has never been accorded much importance in Hohhot.
14. As farmers' water use was recorded through the proxy of electricity consumption by the Electricity Bureau, this bespeaks either poor record-keeping or poor interdepartmental cooperation.
15. See Lu (1995).
16. It is difficult completely to substantiate this argument, as it is difficult to track total water use on the scheme, especially for the earlier periods. Total water use has certainly increased markedly since 1989, relative to the period 1982–89. How a heavily collectivized system would have dealt with the current problem is of course impossible to say.
17. Although there are particular problems associated with the "drive to modernize"

the arid areas of northern and western China, which is associated with the geographical expansion of Han into minority areas (see Cannon 1989).

Bibliography

Cannon, T. 1989. "National Minorities and the Internal Frontier." In D.S.G. Goodman, ed., *China's Regional Development*. London: Routledge.

Huang Zhaohua. 1982. "A Pastoral Commune on the Ordos Plateau—The Sumitu Commune." Pastoral Development Network Paper 14b. London: Overseas Development Institute.

Longworth, J.W., and Williamson, G.J. 1994. *China's Pastoral Region: Sheep and Wool, Minority Nationalities, Rangeland Degradation and Sustainable Development*. Wallingford: CAB International.

Lu Xiaobo. 1995. "From Redistributive to Regulatory: The Rationalization of the State in Rural China." Paper presented at the International Conference on Chinese Rural Collectives and Voluntary Organizations, Leiden University, January.

8

Ownership and Control in Chinese Rangeland Management Since Mao

A Case Study of the Free-Rider Problem in Pastoral Areas in Ningxia

Peter Ho

> *"I don't think our village-head can solve the problem of our*
> *grasslands. As a matter of fact, I don't think the grasslands*
> *can be regulated at all. If I graze my sheep on somebody*
> *else's land today, and tomorrow, and the day after tomorrow . . .*
> *who is there to stop me? Fines would not help,*
> *for I would break the rules day after day."*

—A Ningxia farmer

The opinion expressed by the Chinese farmer quoted above is not motivated by unwillingness to take care of the grazing lands of his village, but rather by despair that has gradually turned into indifference. His indifference is the result of the decades-long inability of the central and local governments to find a solution to the problem of grassland degradation, ever since the pastoral areas in China were nationalized and brought under collective rule in 1956.

During the period of the People's Communes, the grasslands were state property. Although the rangelands were collectively used by farmers organized in so-called production teams, the property rights were not vested in the direct users themselves, but in a higher administrative level, the commune. With the introduction of the rural reforms in the early 1980s, China broke with its collectivist past and made a beginning with the arduous transition from a centrally planned economy to a free market economy. The communes were disbanded and communal land was distributed to family farming units. The communes were replaced by a family-based contract system, the

Household Contract Responsibility System (HCRS), that offered farmers more managerial freedom by linking rewards directly to production and efficiency. Farm households could lease a certain plot of land, initially only for five years, but later for periods up to twenty or twenty-five years, while land use rights could also be subcontracted or inherited.

The first period of rural reforms was marked by success as the grain production increased enormously and a bumper grain harvest of over 400 million tons was achieved in 1984. These initial successes legitimized the trend in rural politics towards the fragmentation and individualization of agriculture. In the same spirit of euphoria, and with widespread support from peasants who welcomed the increased economic freedom, a certain degree of privatization in other agricultural sectors, such as forestry and animal husbandry, was effected. The HCRS was extended to include grazing areas, and in 1985, the Rangeland Law was promulgated, which stipulated that rangeland may be contracted to a collective or an individual for livestock farming. The Rangeland Law also aims to deal with the effects of grassland degradation, mainly by focusing on the effects of farming activities. It prohibits farming and any other activities that are harmful for the rangelands, while simultaneously empowering local governments "to stop anyone from farming a rangeland in violation of the provisions of the present law, to order the person to restore the destroyed vegetation, and to pay a fine if serious damage has been done to the rangeland."

At present, however, the Rangeland Law is void in certain regions of China, and the contract system for grasslands has woefully failed. The latter has even aggravated the degradation of grazing areas, as the new economic freedom for livestock farmers stimulates them to increase production at the cost of the grassland for short-term profits, rather than to adopt sustainable farming.

This chapter examines the actual consequences of the HCRS for animal husbandry in the Ningxia Autonomous Region. It argues that the failure of the Rangeland Law stems from the rash transfer of the HCRS from agriculture to the livestock sector without taking the specific requirements of the latter into account. In order to draw attention to the full historical scope of the problem of grassland degradation in Ningxia, an analysis will be made of the shifts in rangeland management and the pattern of grassland usage there over three periods:

1) the period before 1956 when grassland was owned privately, but collectively used;
2) the period 1956–1978, when grassland was both used and owned collectively. Livestock basically belonged to the collective, although during some periods, it could also be owned privately on a small scale, depending on the political wind;
3) the period 1978–present, in which the state has attempted to implement a hybrid form of a state and private property regime by contracting grassland to individual farmers—who again obtained ownership rights of their

livestock—while simultaneously leaving the property rights of grassland with the collective.

It will be argued that the cause of the present alleged "tragedy of the commons" in Ningxia is a result of the establishment of collectivist institutions under Mao, which delegitimatized existing customary right structures over the regulation of grassland usage. The commune was organized in such a way that it failed to create the necessary socio-economic and regulatory conditions that would allow individual users to pursue their own well-being without destroying the livelihood of future generations. Moreover, this failure occurred at a crucial time when the grasslands were becoming scarce due to expanding livestock and loss of arable land as a result of political campaigns. This external change could not be adequately counterbalanced within the institutional structure of rangeland management during the time of the communes. Instead, a pattern of resource use developed which bore all the traits of an open-access regime, thus leading to the squandering of pastureland. In the same way, the present attempt of privatization and parcelling of rangeland fails to provide the users with the essential guarantee that cooperation and abiding by the rules is actually the best option, both for themselves and the natural resource on which they depend. Since the use of grasslands has in this respect remained unaltered since the collectivist period, the problem of free-riding still remains unsolved.

Degradation of the Grasslands in Ningxia

The Ningxia Hui Autonomous Region shares borders with Shaanxi Province in the east, Inner Mongolia in the north and west, and Gansu Province in the south. Total land surface is 66,400 km^2 and total population 4.24 million people, of which 1.37 million (32 percent) belong to the Islamic Hui minority. Instead of being administered as a province, Ningxia was carved out as an Autonomous Region for the Hui in 1958 (see also NHZGB 1986).

This chapter is based on research done by the author in 1994 on the present institutional and non-institutional regulation of grazing in the Ningxia Hui Autonomous Region (see Map).

Fieldwork was carried out in the spring of 1994 in two ecologically different regions: the semi-arid desert and steppe area of Yanchi County in the middle eastern part, a region dominated by animal husbandry; and Guyuan County in the mountainous (about 1600 meters above sea level) and highly erosive Loess Plateau in the south, a region where a mixed farming operation of agriculture and animal husbandry prevails. Guyuan County is the poorer of the two counties, and has been officially designated by the Ministry of Agriculture as a "low-income region."[1] It has inadequate access to drinking water, a poorly developed infrastructure, while the rate of illiteracy is about 36 percent (60 percent of which are women). The population of

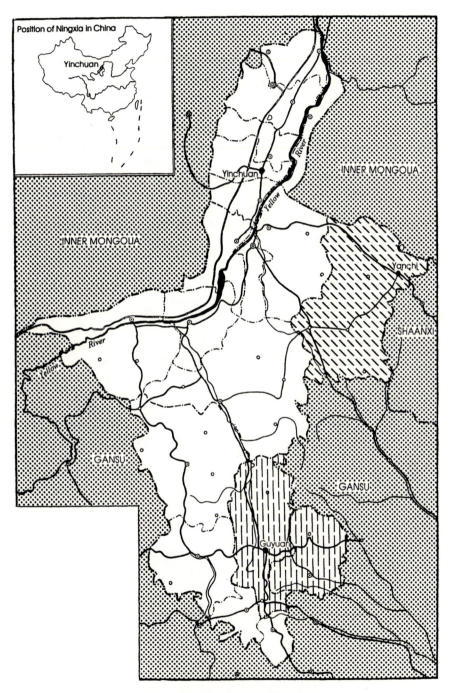

Position of Ningxia in China

Yinchuan

INNER MONGOLIA

Yinchuan

Yellow River

INNER MONGOLIA

Yanchi

SHAANXI

Yellow River

GANSU

GANSU

Guyuan

Map 8.1 **Map of Ningxia**

Guyuan County consists for the greater part of the Islamic Hui (approximately 80 percent).

Ningxia once belonged to a region which was called "the land of grass." The whole landscape was lush and magnificent until its reclamation by agricultural settlers. Reports from Sven Hedin's dangerous expeditions in search of the hidden treasures of the Silk Route in the 1920s, and other reports published in the 1930s, make it clear that the Ningxia rangelands have badly deteriorated (Hu, Hannaway and Youngberg 1992).

The region boasts a total grassland area of 3.0 million ha, which is 45.2 percent of the total land surface of the Autonomous Region. Of this, 2.3 million ha (or 96 percent of the grasslands of northern Ningxia) has been reported to be affected to some degree by desertification or soil erosion, while 2,341 km^2 rangeland was classified under severe desertification.[2] Desertification occurs mainly in the northern and central part, causing serious problems as the drifting sands damage agricultural and grazing lands and affect communication lines between the cities and villages.

Bielfeldt and Steinbach have listed the following causes for degradation of the steppe ecosystem in Ningxia (Shen and Steinbach 1993):

1) Population pressure. The density of the human population has increased to 75 persons per km^2 of arable land, which is more than ten times the upper limit, for arid zones, of 7 persons, as proposed by the United Nations (see Liu and Huang 1993, p. 59);

2) Overgrazing. The density of livestock is by far the highest among all pastoral regions in Northern China (80.8 animals per km^2, Liaoning Province coming second with 41.8 and Gansu third with 38.0 animals per km^2)[3];

3) Reclamation of unsuitable lands. As a consequence of the population pressure, new lands are reclaimed for cultivation that are unsuitable for agriculture;

4) Excessive irrigation with groundwater. This leads to a quickly receding groundwater level;

5) Digging of medicinal plants, particularly the liquorice root (*Glycyrrhiza uralensis*) and black moss (*Nostoc flagelliforme*), which produces deep holes in the rangelands that easily erode;

6) The use of shrubs as firewood. When the shrubs are dug out, the soil becomes loosened and subject to erosion.

Bromley writes that natural resource destruction in developing countries is often falsely blamed on population growth, while the root of the problem, in many instances, was the delegitimatization of customary and traditional property rights due to the establishment of colonial rights. After decolonization, local-level systems of authority and control over management of natural resources continued to be destroyed by national governments that were in most cases incapable (or too corrupt) to prevent the degradation of natural resources (see Bromley 1991).

Something similar applies to the pastoral areas in China. In 1956, the so-called Higher Agricultural Producers' Cooperatives (HAPCs), the predecessor of the People's Communes, were established. From then on, all grassland that was formerly owned by landlords or small communities yet commonly managed, was nationalized and managed by the state through the collective. The collectivization of agriculture led to the destruction of the pre-1956 customary right structures. In the following, the grazing regulations and the pattern of resource use before collectivization will be explained.

Vast and Abundant: The Period Before 1956

The use and ownership of rangelands in Ningxia is quite different from other pastoral regions of China. According to historical records, animal husbandry already developed in what is presently Guyuan County. The area was first inhabited by nomads belonging to ethnic minorities. Already in the period 179 B.C.-143 B.C., during the Han dynasty, the Chinese imperial government established horse ranches for military purposes, which continued to exist till the early days of the Chinese Republic.[4] Yanchi County, on the other hand, was populated much later by Mongolian herdsmen, in the last centuries of the Qing dynasty (1644–1911) (see YXBWB 1983, p. 39). However, all forms of traditional pastoral nomadism vanished in Ningxia by the turn of the 19th century. The reasons for this will be listed below.

The majority of the present population of Ningxia consists of immigrants who moved to this region either during the second half of the Qing dynasty, or the early years of the Republic.[5] The Muslim Hui minority, of which a large concentration can be found in the south of Ningxia, were driven to this desolate region during military campaigns against them by the Qing government.[6] A certain proportion of the Han Chinese farmers comprised landless peasants or refugees who were settled in remote areas specially designated by the Nationalist government for land reclamation in the 1920s and 1930s.[7] Others had fled because of famine (e.g. in 1899 a great famine ravaged present Gansu Province) and opened up land on their own accord. During this period, Ningxia was frequently the seat of war, and life was turbulent for its inhabitants till the end of the 1930s, when the Kuomintang was driven out of Ningxia and the Shaan-Gan-Ning border region established by the Chinese Communist Party.[8]

The landless farmers and war refugees (Han, Hui and other ethnic minorities alike) who immigrated to Ningxia and opened up virgin land, or land that had been abandoned by others, were traditionally not livestock farmers, and not used to the practice of transhumance on the grasslands. Instead, they led a settled life on farms and set up a mixed farming operation of agriculture and animal husbandry. As the grasslands were then still vast and abundant and the population scarce, the institutional structure for guiding resource use which these migrants introduced in Ningxia—essentially different from pastoral nomadism—fitted well into the ecological environment. It was only after the Communist Revolution in 1949 that certain traits of this pattern of resource use proved to be one of the determinants in the destruction of the rangelands, as its authority system had been delegitimatized by the establishment of the People's Communes.[9]

From the last century of the Qing dynasty[10] till the establishment of the rural cooperatives in 1956, the rangelands were in general owned by landlords,[11] or small communities, yet commonly used by the livestock farmers. During the period that Ningxia partly belonged to the Shaan-Gan-Ning border region (1936–1949), an initial land reform was carried out, and certain parts of the grasslands were taken from the landlords and redistributed to individual farmers.[12] After the Communist Revolution in 1949, a second land reform movement (1950–1952) was carried out in which all agricultural and grazing land was distributed to the farmers. However, in regard to grassland management, there were no essential policy differences between the Communist Party and the Kuomintang in the period 1911–1956, as the property rights for grasslands remained vested in individual users,[13] lineages, or the village community as a whole. During Republican times, the authority for delegating the rights to graze on a certain plot rested in principle with the village elders, the heads of the clans, the individual owner of the grassland and, in those exceptional cases when pastoralists from outside the county were involved, the ward head (or *bao* head).

Unlike regions where pastoral nomadism was practiced, there was no detailed regulated system of grazing (such as rotational, seasonal or deferred grazing) in place in Ningxia,[14] probably due to the historical reasons of immigration mentioned above. In principle, the people of one village were all free to make use of the rangelands, while between different neighboring villages, a tradition of overlapped grazing (*chuanmu*) existed (NHZN 1964, p. 125). Grazing on a certain plot of grassland occurred after mutual agreement was reached between the groups of users (of various villages) involved. If people from outside the village wanted to pasture their flocks on village land, permission had to be asked from the head of the *bao*. The head of the *bao* was also responsible for the resolution of conflicts over the use of rangeland or wells. At the time, this arrangement was the best solution for a relatively abundant resource base that varied highly in productivity due to erratic rainfall, and that benefited more from flexible boundaries than from fixed ones.

Now and then, temporary nomads (who were normally settled farmers) from neighboring counties would come with flocks as large as a thousand sheep to graze on village-owned land. Although this was common practice during times of drought, it did not constitute any problem as such. Only in case of reclamation of wasteland, recompensation had to be paid to the owner (personal communication

1994). During Republican times, all land reclamation in Ningxia—whether in areas designated for landless farmers of the province itself, Mongol tribes, the military, or immigrated peasants—had to be approved and administered by a so-called office for land reclamation, to be established in each of these four specially designated areas (i.e. for landless farmers, Mongol tribes, military and immigrated peasants).[15]

When elderly farmers in Guyuan and Yanchi were asked about the period before the establishment of the collectives, they unanimously responded that the grasslands were so abundant and vast that they simply did not need any additional regulations, such as deferred or rotational grazing, for its utilization (personal communication 1994). The absence of these forms of grazing implies that, unlike resources in the modern economy, the rangelands in Ningxia could formerly renew themselves continually. Furthermore, the needs that the grasslands had to satisfy were not yet determined by the demand for goods and services of a growth-oriented national or international market, but rather constantly adjusted and limited within the local social system itself (*The Ecologist* 1992).

However, since the foundation of the People's Republic, the grazing areas gradually decreased, as much grassland was reclaimed and turned into agricultural land. In the period 1949–1956 alone, an area of over 5,300 km² grassland was opened up, equalling the total area of wasteland in Ningxia designated for land reclamation by the Bureau for Land Administration in Republican times.[16] There was, however, no change in actual rangeland management.

After the land reform movement had been completed in 1952, the Chinese government set itself the task of collectivizing agriculture. This process passed through several—sometimes overlapping—stages. The first stage (1950–55) was the establishment of the Mutual Aid Teams (MAT), which were based on the traditional peasant custom of mutual help in farming activities. Individual ownership of land and the other major means of production remained unchanged, while households that had joined a MAT continued to receive the produce from their own farm.

Then, from 1952 till 1956, the Lower Agricultural Producers' Cooperatives (LAPCs) were set up. These cooperatives pooled land, labor and capital in units of 20 to 25 farm households. In principle, everyone was free to become a member of these cooperatives, while the income which workers received was based on the amount of land, capital and labor they contributed. Neither the MAT or LAPC period had any direct consequences for rangeland management.[17] It was only the establishment of the HAPCs in 1956 and the People's Communes in 1958, in addition to the increase in livestock and the political campaigns during the Cultural Revolution in the 1960s and 1970s, that would prove to be calamitous for the grazing areas in Ningxia.

The Defeat of Collectivism: 1956–1978

In 1956, when the HAPCs were initiated, all rangeland was nationalized. All livestock was brought under collective ownership as well, although a small private sector was retained, which implied that farmers could raise some poultry, hogs, sheep and goats for their own use. Private plots (with a maximum of 5 percent of the arable area) were also allowed.

In order to expand the decision-making unit of the HAPCs to the township level, a radical reorganization of agriculture was executed by the Central Government. Over 740,000 HAPCs were merged into approximately 23,000 People's Communes, with an average of 5,440 households per commune (Chen and Buckwell 1991, p. 36). The excessive size of the communes, the lack of producer incentives and the total abolition of the private sector caused serious problems in the agricultural sector. Problems inherent to the character of the communes in combination with severe natural disasters during 1959–61 caused a nationwide famine. As a result, the Central Committee of the CCP reversed its decision, and ordered a reorganization of the communes.

In 1961, the system of "three-level ownerships with the team as the basic unit" was established. From then on, every peasant household belonged to a production team (the present "natural village" with 100–150 persons), which was headed by a team leader selected by the Party; several production teams together formed a production brigade (the present administrative village, with 200–400 households); and a number of production brigades made up a commune (the present township), comprising approximately 15,000 members, depending on the region. The commune often consisted of a small market town with its surrounding villages.

Under the People's Communes, the property rights of rangeland were vested in the commune, while ownership of livestock was directed to the production brigade. The production team owned farm implements, and was responsible for the actual livestock production. Within the production team, a pasture group was formed charged with the herding of the flock. Unlike the early days of the communes, private initiative was once more encouraged through a production responsibility system that allowed individual farm households to contract livestock. Each team member was rewarded with work points for the amount of labor done, the production of livestock, and investments he had made for the means of production (fodder, construction of corrals, etc.). The work points were calculated in cash value to cover the expenses of rations, such as grain, vegetables and oil, while surplus in cash value was paid in money.[18]

The Section for Animal Husbandry set up in 1952 was responsible for the management and protection of rangeland. Throughout Ningxia, the so-called County Grassland Management Stations founded under the Section for Animal Husbandry in 1958 were directly responsible for rangeland management and protection. Disbanded in 1967, they were re-established in 1978. Within the commune itself, there was no authority for the management and protection of rangeland, other than a veterinary station. In 1959, the Section for Animal Husbandry was merged with other departments into the Department for Agriculture, Forestry, Water Conservancy and Animal Husbandry. One year later, this institution was renamed the Department for Agriculture and Animal Husbandry, a name it held till 1984, when a department solely for animal husbandry was again established, i.e. the Bureau of Animal Husbandry. Veterinary tasks were left to separate institutions in each commune, such as the County Veterinary Stations and the Veterinary Stations. Their tasks were strictly limited to prevention and treatment of livestock disease.

Later on, it will be shown that the institutional structure of the People's Communes as described above lay at the root of the failure of rangeland management in Ningxia, in spite of the attempts at sustainable livestock production undertaken in the early 1960s. The period 1956–1978 can be subdivided into two shorter periods, i.e., 1956–1966 and 1966–1978.

Lull Before the Storm: 1956–1966

From 1956 till 1966, rangeland management was not much affected by political campaigns, and animal husbandry experienced stable development. Ever since the establishment of the communes in 1958, the Ningxia government furthered the simultaneous development of animal husbandry and agriculture, with emphasis on the former. The political preference for raising livestock production led to a rapid increase in ruminants over this period. The downward trend in the number of sheep and goats that started in 1954 stopped in 1958 (a decline of 15.2 percent, from 2,059,200 ruminants in 1954 to 1,745,700 in 1958) after which followed a steady growth.

From 1958 till 1965, the total number of sheep and goats for Ningxia as a whole increased by 91.5 percent, reaching a historical record of 3,343,500 animals, which is virtually a quadrupling of the number of ruminants in 1949 (see also Figure 8.1).[19] In addition, there was a continued rise in population from 1,200,000 people in 1949 to 2,270,000 people in 1965 (up 89.2 percent), with a slight decrease between 1960 and 1962 of 14,000 people (or 6.6 percent).[20] Figure 8.2 on page 207 shows the growth of the population of Ningxia over the period 1949–1989. As a result of these factors, grassland became scarce, and the need arose for more regulation concerning its utilization.[21]

In the early 1960s, the Ningxia government promulgated the "Order on the Protection of Grazing Lands." Many institutions in the region, such as the Section for Animal Husbandry and the Department for Agriculture, were much concerned with the protection of pastures and attempted to develop a sustainable use of the grazing areas. Small-scale attempts were undertaken in counties dominated by animal husbandry towards a clearer delimitation of grassland by fencing, which should have paved the way for a possible common property regime arrangement.

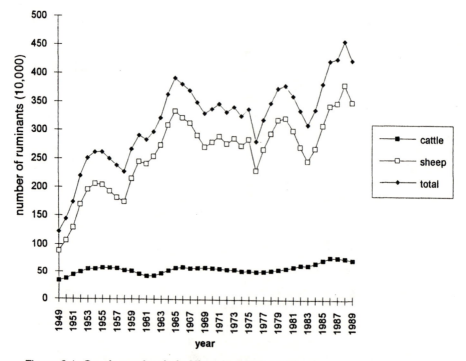

Figure 8.1 **Grazing animals in Ningxia, 1949–1989**

The idea was that neighboring communes or production brigades would form special organizations for rangeland management, in charge of common management, use and protection of grazing areas. Simultaneously, techniques such as deferred and rotational grazing were introduced, and land reclamation and the digging of medicinal herbs strictly regulated, or in most cases even prohibited.[22]

In Yanchi County, for example, much research was done on rotational and seasonal grazing as applied by nomads in Inner Mongolia, and the possibilities of disseminating these practices in Yanchi itself. Pastoral nomadism in China was traditionally based on the extensive use of pastures, which implied not only seasonal migrations from one grazing area to another, but also fairly rapid movement over each pasture area. All year round, nomadic pastoralists wandered through different types of grasslands classified according to the various seasons, thus ensuring that their pastures would not be overused (see Hu *et al.* 1992).

In general, the summer grazing lands were located in the mountains and shady slopes of higher elevations, where the climate is much cooler and forage and water in ample supply. The distance between the summer and winter grazing lands could add up to 100 km (as in Xinjiang). The summer grazing period was mostly from mid-May to mid-August. Autumn grazing was practiced on the middle elevations of the mountains or highlands from late August to November.

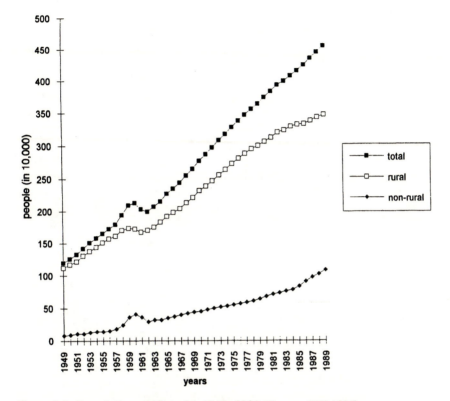

Figure 8.2 **Population of Ningxia, 1949–1989** (*Source*: GTZ 1990)

Autumn grazing land is also used for spring grazing in years when the supply of the grazing lands is limited. The winter grazing land is similar to the spring grazing land, located in the lowlands, basins, valleys and sand dune areas where the weather is warmer than at higher altitudes. The forage plants that grow during this season are tall and are able to penetrate the snow cover. The period for winter grazing is generally from November to March (see Hu *et al.* 1992). The major constraint in this sort of nomadic pastoralism lies in the available area of winter and spring grazing lands, since this is the season of gestation and birth for the grazing animals, and sufficient forage supply is crucial to avoid massive starvation (see Hu *et al.* 1992).

In Ningxia, it was and is still believed that rotational grazing as practiced by nomadic pastoralists can only be applied by clear demarcation of the natural resource into plots. It was for this reason that the grasslands in Yanchi County were fenced in on an experimental basis after assessment of the carrying capacity of the different plots. The fencing took place, however, on a very modest scale. In 1956, only 4.5 percent of all natural grassland in the county had been fenced in, and by 1963, scholars were still urgently pleading for an expansion of the

1956 experiments.[23] At the beginning of the Cultural Revolution in 1966, the area of fenced-in grassland had risen to 18 percent of all natural grassland, yet by 1976 it had again decreased to a meager 4.2 percent.[24]

Other measures included the sinking of new wells to spread the pressure of grazing more evenly, as grazing was concentrated around watering places and the paths leading to them. Furthermore, man-made forage areas were established to solve the problem of available fodder during winter and spring. These capital investments were made in order to augment the productivity of pastureland, while the attempts to build up a common property regime tried to unite the users in grassland management groups that had to be formed by the commune or the production brigade. Both plans ended in failure, for a number of reasons.

The first reason was connected with the property rights structure within the communes. The attempts to effect "collective maintenance, collective management and collective usage" by the production team (and the possible grassland management groups) conflicted with the existing property rights structure. In principle, the direct users of the natural resource (the members of the production team) were generally not the owners of the grassland, as this was the commune. Thus, the term "collective" did not refer to merely one institutional level, but three: the production team, the production brigade and the commune. The ownership of the grassland was vested in the commune, the ownership of livestock in the brigade, while the team was only charged with the herding of the flock. With this institutional setting, the direct users had no interest in a sustainable use of the pastures, as they did not perceive it as being their own.

I do not mean to argue that simply giving the property rights to the team (or grassland management groups) and the brigade would have solved the problem. For this would assume that establishing and enforcing regulations of grassland management can be done without any transaction costs in bargaining, as long as property rights are clearly vested in one party. My point is merely that in the case of the commune, property rights were vested in an administrative level too abstract and too high for the direct users to feel a sense of responsibility towards the grassland.

The second reason was that there was no set of entitlements and rights within the communal system, other than those of possession. In the commune, there were no operational rules determining who could participate under which conditions, what the privileges and obligations of the participants were, and how they were to be rewarded, or penalized if they transgressed the rules. There were no rules concerning boundaries, membership, allocation, input or penalties.

As described previously, since Republican times, Yanchi County (and Ningxia as a whole) has a tradition of overlapped grazing, which is a system of regulation of extensive grazing irrespective of administrative boundaries and suited to the local conditions under a given population density, provided that a change in the size of the group of users is appropriately dealt with. Throughout the period of the communes, this manner of grassland usage continued to prevail all over Ningxia. The attempts to fence in rangeland do not only collide with the tradition of overlapped grazing, but are also unsuited to a natural resource with highly variable productivity, such as the grasslands in China's semi-arid Northwest. As will be pointed out later, grasslands that are characterized by unstable productivity over time benefit more from flexible arrangements than from rigid ones. It should therefore be no surprise that the experiments for dividing the rangeland into delimited plots have failed.

Moreover, one would expect that the establishment of the administrative boundaries of the communes and production brigades would have impeded the practice of overlapped grazing. In practice, the custom of overlapped grazing was tolerated throughout the collectivist period.[25] This fact seems to run counter to experiences in some other localities. For example, in Mongolia and Inner-Mongolia a decrease in herder mobility has been ascertained,[26] suggesting an undermining of customary grazing arrangements as a result of state intervention. If we suppose that stricter administrative boundaries were one of the factors affecting herder mobility in Ningxia, the question remains what its relative importance is. Even if the Chinese government would have opted for rigid boundary rules for rangelands (which it did not) their enforcement might have proved extremely difficult and costly, as the communes and herders' collectives lacked the means and inclination for such a task.

Regarding the membership rules, it can be stated that in essence everyone was automatically a member of a commune, and designated to a certain production team. There was no restriction on the number of sheep, nor were participants excluded from the team because pastures would otherwise be threatened with overgrazing.

The rules of allocation (how the resource base is used in response to the productivity of the resource, as well as the number of users) and input (the contributions which users have to make to the natural resource) were mainly concentrated on animal production and not on the productivity of the resource in relation to the demand placed on it. In some cases, capital investments were made to increase the productivity of the pastures, but as there were no rules for allocation or the boundaries of the natural resource, the grasslands continued to be squandered, and these capital investments in the end proved in vain. This was inevitable, as especially the most essential set of rules, namely those concerning penalties, could not be enforced under the People's Communes.

A system of penalty rules must be related to an authority that is charged with its enforcement. At the time, the enforcement of penalty rules was left to an institution external to the commune, namely the Grassland Management Stations under the Section of Animal Husbandry.[27] The property regime under the communes was not one of common property but a state property regime, supervised by state institutions such as the Section of Animal Husbandry. Unfortunately, these institutions lacked financial means and were seriously understaffed (e.g. the Grassland Management Stations of Yanchi County had a total of seven persons to manage an area of 3,170 km^2 in the period from 1958 till 1967) (see YXBWB 1983, p. 42). It is striking that from the beginning of the Great Leap till the end of the Cultural Revolution, the management of rangeland was supervised by institutions that had multiple tasks of which animal husbandry was merely one.

The institutions charged with rangeland management were also subject to the political wind, which was reflected in the frequent reorganizations, mergers with other institutions, and even disbandment. The Grassland Management Stations, which were specifically charged with the daily enforcement of regulations for grazing and grassland protection, were completely abolished in the period from 1967 till 1978.

In addition, the actual responsibility for the management and protection of the grassland was left to the same external institutions. Also, within the brigade and the team, there were no formal structures that could have taken on that role. The only organization that could have done so, the Poor and Lower-Middle Peasant Association, did not function, as there were no grass-roots elections of its representatives, so that the incumbents simply retained their title. Moreover, they played only a minor role in consultations about village affairs (Mearns 1996, p. 304). Croll states that external information was scarce in the commune, as the entire flow of information had to pass through the village cadres, which put them in a privileged position vis-à-vis the peasants (Croll 1994, pp. 123–124).

The situation in the commune was not conducive for the horizontal flow of information between users needed for consultations over the use of a natural resource under a common property regime arrangement, or for village discussions over the regulation of grazing. In a common property regime, it is essential that within the direct group of users, structures—over which *common* agreement has been reached—are present that allow negotiations over the offtake of the resource in relation to the demand. Furthermore, specific authority structures for the enforcement of the various regulations of grazing should have been present at a level that allowed for sufficient social control. In other words, the authority for the enforcement of herding rules should have been vested in the production team, and not in the commune or brigade.

As already stated, the custom of overlapped grazing in Republican times continued to persist throughout the period of the communes. The only essential difference was that the former rights structures within the village concerning the use and management of the rangelands had been replaced by the institutional structure of the communes. Moreover, the communes could not be but ineffective in the management and protection of grassland, due to the organizational set-up as described above. Therefore, serious doubt can be expressed about the viability of overlapped grazing during the collectivist period. First of all, the available area of grassland per ruminant had dramatically decreased as a result of a rise in livestock. Secondly, traditional rights structures had been undermined due to government intervention and thus could no longer provide a solid basis for autonomous collective action among herders. A similar phenomenon has been reported in Mongolia by Robin Mearns. He writes:

> The expanded realm of government during the era of collectivised production may have constituted a significant threat to effective governance in the management of natural resources (Mearns 1996, p. 304).

It is clear that the property regime in Ningxia following the establishment of the People's Communes was one of open access or nobody's land, and would ultimately lead to the squandering of the grazing areas. Prospects for improvement in grassland management were further hampered by the political instability of the Cultural Revolution, a period of serious destruction of China's grasslands.

The Consequences of the "Grain First" Policy: 1966–1978

During the Cultural Revolution, the so-called "Grain First" policy was formulated. It was a reaction to the greatest famine of human history with a death toll of an estimated 30 million people (see Smil 1987, pp. 216–217). This famine was the result of the disastrous Great Leap Forward of 1958, which had led to an enormous grain shortage. As a result, the Chinese government became preoccupied with attaining the highest rate of local self-sufficiency in cereal production possible.

This emphasis on grain production for human consumption led to large-scale reclamation of vast areas of wasteland, forests, and rangelands that were ecologically unsuitable for agriculture. In regard to animal husbandry, politics solely focused on increasing the number of ruminants, rather than on their productivity and quality. The Grassland Management Stations and Veterinary Stations in the communes were all disbanded. Moreover, the piece-rate system, as well as the household sideline activities, were all branded as "capitalist tails" and abolished, thus taking away the peasants' incentives for livestock production.

The consequences of policies such as "grain is the line in agriculture" and "planting crops in the middle of lakes and on the top of mountains" were serious degradation of pastureland, increased desertification, and decreased forage production, while many grazing animals died from starvation. As a result of the "Grain First" policy, more than 30 percent of the livestock died in Yanchi County (one of Ningxia's main livestock regions) over the period 1966–1976 (see Zhang Guangzu 1986, p. 156). The number of grazing animals for Ningxia as a whole showed a decrease of 28.5 percent over the same period, or a decline from 3,223,700 ruminants in 1966 to 2,306,700 in 1976 (see GTZ 1990, p. 897; and Figure 8.1).

It is most likely that Ningxia suffered losses of arable land as a consequence of the agricultural policies of the Cultural Revolution. However, the official statistics of Ningxia seem to contradict this conclusion (see Figure 8.3), while

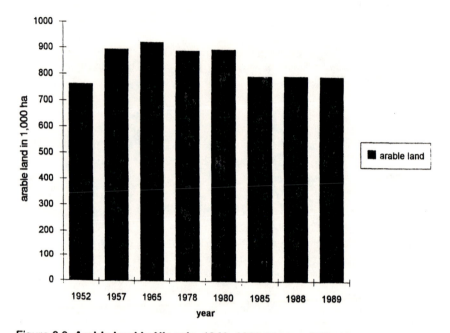

Figure 8.3 **Arable land in Ningxia, 1949–1989** (*Source:* GTZ 1990)

data on the extent of pastureland affected in the Autonomous Region as a whole are entirely missing. Nevertheless, one can get an idea of the impact of the "Grain First" policy from the increase in desertified area in Yanchi County (over 170,000 ha, or 40 percent of the total area of rangeland in the county) between 1962 and 1976 (see Zhang Guangzu 1986, p. 156). A serious decrease in productivity of the grazing lands has also been reported in the neighboring provinces. In Inner Mongolia, the decrease was 40 percent–60 percent, and in Xinjiang 50 percent, over the period from 1965 till 1975 (see Hu *et al.* 1992, p. 76).

Chan *et al.* and Croll have rightly remarked that the political struggle campaigns, apart from great physical damage, have also had profound psychological and social consequences for those living in the communess,[28] and that the latter were in essence not used for the aims they claimed to further, but for the manipulation of patron-client relations within and outside the village. Instead of establishing a sense of social unity within the villages, the subsequent waves of political campaigns provided the breeding ground for conflict, social division, repression and manipulation, thus weakening the peer-group social pressures so essential in a common property arrangement. Farmers grew tired of Maoist visions of a new moral order that were based on dedication, altruism and, cooperation.[29]

The abolition of the piece-rate system took away the production incentives of farmers, leading to an overall atmosphere of accepted free-riding at the cost of

production. After all, everyone was taken care of by the commune anyway.[30]
Croll writes:

> [I]ndividuals in China frequently felt themselves divorced from collective performance, which ultimately threatened the existence of the very collective structures—the team, brigades and communes themselves (Croll 1994, p. 13).

As for the grazing areas, the Chinese government began to look for new ways of managing them, more than ever inclining to privatization as a result of the failure of collective grassland management under the communes. However, due to the disastrous policies, the total area of grassland had been diminished dramatically, leaving scarcely any room for political manoeuvre, and making the need for a sustainable utilization and successful management of the rangelands as urgent as ever.

Eating From the Big Rice Pot: 1978–Present

As already stated, during the early 1980s, privatization and decentralization were regarded as the magic solutions for agriculture, as a result of the initial successes of rural reforms. After the abolition of the communes, an attempt was made to apply the same principles of the HCRS used for contracting agricultural land, to grazing lands. The government sought to shift the use of and responsibility for the grasslands to individual farmers. Article 4 of the Rangeland Law promulgated in 1985 stipulated:

> [A]ll rangeland within the country is state property . . . except the rangeland which is owned by a collective . . . All rangeland . . . assigned to a collective for long-term use may be leased under a contract to a collective or an individual (ZCX 1985, p. 2).

In order to implement the HCRS for the grazing areas, the plan was to classify grassland into good, average, and poor lands, and to distribute it equally among all households, also taking the productivity of the plot into account. For example, in Henan Province, pastureland was distributed according to the number of people within each household, ranging from 0.06 ha per person in a lowland village to 0.75 ha per person in the highlands (Croll 1994, p. 43).

In Ningxia, this proved to be a rather arduous task, as the area of grassland is more extensive than in Henan (1.3 ha of usable land per person in 1985; see Liu and Huang 1993, p. 59), and not only used as a forage area, but also for a mobile manner of grazing. Nevertheless, Ningxia did make attempts to distribute grassland to individual households. Only in one instance did the county government choose complete nationalization of the rangeland, by the establishment of the Provincial Yunwu Mountain Nature Reserve in Guyuan County. Within the boundaries of the nature reserve (2,330 ha or 0.6 percent of the total area of natural grassland in Guyuan County), grazing is forbidden, but farmers are allowed to gather forage there during fixed periods.

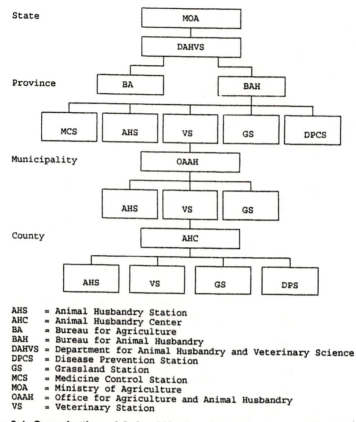

AHS	=	Animal Husbandry Station
AHC	=	Animal Husbandry Center
BA	=	Bureau for Agriculture
BAH	=	Bureau for Animal Husbandry
DAHVS	=	Department for Animal Husbandry and Veterinary Science
DPCS	=	Disease Prevention Station
GS	=	Grassland Station
MCS	=	Medicine Control Station
MOA	=	Ministry of Agriculture
OAAH	=	Office for Agriculture and Animal Husbandry
VS	=	Veterinary Station

Figure 8.4 **Organization of Animal Husbandry Institutions in Ningxia**

In Ningxia, the Provincial Bureau of Animal Husbandry (PBAH) is responsible for the overall supervision of rangeland management. Here, as in all provinces or regions where livestock production forms an important part of the rural economy, the PBAH is equal in status to the Provincial Bureau of Agriculture (PBA). At the central level, the PBAH is administered directly by the Bureau of Animal Husbandry and Veterinary Science (BAHVS), which forms part of the Ministry of Agriculture. The BAHVS consists of sixteen different divisions and two offices, of which a few relevant ones have been depicted in Figure 8.4.

The PBAH has branches at the municipal/prefectural and county levels. At each level there are special stations responsible for various tasks such as animal disease prevention, improvement of domestic animals, and rangeland improvement. Every station is charged with the extension of the specific knowledge within their range of work. One of these is the Grassland Management Station, which is responsible for the management and protection of rangelands under its jurisdiction (see Figure 8.4).

In order to enforce the Rangeland Law, a special police force was set up, the grassland police, which belongs to the so-called economic police force. The grassland police can impose fines, but is not allowed to arrest or confine people, or to carry any weapons. The police force of the Yunwu Mountain Provincial Nature Reserve, however, has a status equal to that of the ordinary police. The grassland police is stationed at the County Grassland Management Stations (with the exception of the Provincial Grassland Management Station at the Yunwu Mountain Nature Reserve), which as an institution is responsible for the management and protection of the rangeland under its jurisdiction, as well as for the extension of improved forage seed varieties and veterinary services. The County Grassland Management Stations share the latter task with the County Veterinary Stations.

In principle, all rangeland in Ningxia has been contracted to individual users. For instance, it is stated that in Guyuan County in 1992, 64.3 percent of total rangeland area had been contracted to individual farmers, joint households, or collectives (see Chen and Song 1993, p. 414). The tenant was from then on bound by the regulations stipulated in the Rangeland Law, and could thus, in theory, be held responsible for any damage done to the grassland he had leased:

> The rangeland vegetation shall be conserved. Farming of the rangeland and other activities which damage it are strictly forbidden (Article 10 of the Rangeland Law).

In reality, the whole idea of contracting rangeland to individual households or collectives has become a complete failure in Ningxia. During an interview, the vice-director of the Provincial Bureau of Animal Husbandry stated:

> The household contract responsibility system is just something on paper, the actual delimitation of land has failed. Therefore the situation in the grasslands in Ningxia is now one of "eating from the big rice pot." You see, nobody feels responsible for the rangelands anymore (Personal communication 1994).

The failure of the HCRS in relation to grazing areas has seriously undermined the effectiveness of the Rangeland Law, as its premise—the leasing of grassland to collectives, households, or joint households—has proven to be unfeasible. Without tenants who can be held responsible for the use of the resource leased, the Bureau of Animal Husbandry and the Grassland Management Stations are faced with the insurmountable task of supervising a vast area of "nobody's" pastureland.

The management of nationalized pastureland has also run into problems. The nature reserve in Guyuan County has come under a great deal of pressure, as most farmers in the region still venture with their flocks into the protected area. Strikingly, a majority of the farmers interviewed mentioned the establishment of the Yunwu Mountains Nature Reserve as the main tangible difference in rangeland management between collectivist times and the present, and not the promulgation of the Rangeland Law as such, the content of which few were actually acquainted with. According to the farmers, the nature reserve has taken up so much of their former village grassland that it has become very hard to find pasture for their livestock. Transgressions of the Rangeland Law are frequent, said one of the grassland police officers, although no exact figures on the extent of transgressions are available.

The Rangeland Law stipulates that if there are disputes over the right of ownership, or right of use of rangeland, the parties involved may appeal to the Bureau for Animal Husbandry of the local government at the county level and above. Moreover, the Bureau of Animal Husbandry has the authority to make binding judgments and order the payment of compensations. One may also file a suit at a local court. However, in reality, conflicts are rarely brought to court. If farmers have transgressed the law, the grassland police in most cases do not impose any fine, or only mete out a symbolic penalty. A grassland police officer stated:

> We try to teach the farmers that they should abide by the Rangeland Law out of their own interests. Only in the case of serious offences, or when a farmer is not willing to correct his behavior after repeated warnings, will we impose a fine.

Whether a farmer is fined and how much also depends on the nature of the relationship between him and the police officer involved. If his *guanxi* (personal connections) are good, then the farmer will merely be told off, after which he is released.

Another issue mentioned by the head of the County Grassland Management Station in Yanchi is the fact that many disputes within or even between villages are underreported. Conflicts over the use of grassland are mostly resolved by the villagers themselves, or by the village head, or in some cases even left to linger on for years out of fear of retaliation by the other party. The underreporting of disputes is perceived as a problem by the Bureau of Animal Husbandry, which views it as a sign of the failure of national law. However, in the light of an eventual common property arrangement, it should be seen much more positively. Further research is needed on customary (or Islamic) rights structures, and the role these could potentially play within a common property regime.

At present, the situation as regards the grazing areas in Ningxia is one of open access, in spite of the presence of formal user rights, liability rights, inalienability rights, and the formal institutions needed to enforce those regulations. Apart from the increase in soil erosion and desertification, there are many other symptoms of the failure in rangeland management.

Lingering conflicts about wells and the paths used for herding have often been reported in Guyuan County (in the south of Ningxia). These conflicts are often related to the illegal conversion of grassland into agricultural land. In the eyes of grain farmers in the region, grassland is nobody's land, and not an essential resource for their own livelihood. The ensuing conflicts between grain and livestock farmers[31] are seldom reported to the grassland police, and can in some exceptional cases go on for years. For example, in one of the villages visited, a farmer had reclaimed grassland around a well, thus preventing the herdsmen from watering their flocks. The dispute had been going on for three years before it came to the attention of the grassland police.

Another problem that has even caused peasants' demonstrations in the county capital in 1993 and 1943[32] is the on-going digging of liquorice root in Yanchi County. The problem also bears signs of ethnic conflict, as the blame is mainly put on poor Muslim Hui farmers from neighboring counties.[33]

Several factors have contributed to the failure of the Rangeland Law and the HCRS, ranging from political and economic to institutional factors. These will be discussed in detail below.

The Failure of the Rangeland Law

When considering the political factors, the question which comes to mind concerns the actual motives for the proclamation of the Rangeland Law. It does not in itself contain regulations that pertain to a limitation of livestock on a given plot of grazing land, nor does it provide a solid basis for the users of pastureland to take on responsibility for the management of the natural resource. Was the preservation of rangeland then really its political aim, or was it merely a symbolic law? Moreover, did the political aim and the motives of the policy makers who supported it remain unaltered from the time the law was drafted till its present implementation?

In a country such as China where politics are extremely opaque, questions like these will remain difficult to answer. Illustrating the Obligatory Tree Planting Campaign as merely symbolic because it was propelled by political considerations rather than ecological, Ross can assuredly state in his article that "Chinese politicians are familiar with the use of symbolic politics to disguise one's true intentions and to divide one's critics" (Ross 1987, p. 251).

However, according to a report of the CSCPRC, Li Yutang, chief of the Bureau of Animal Husbandry and Veterinary Science under the Ministry of Agriculture, has stated that the Rangeland Law could not be strictly enforced because of the following reasons:

1) it would affect the livelihood of those farmers who had opened up new land under the stimulation of the government;
2) it would require the approval of the Central Government, which would not be well received by local authorities;
3) it would not help to solve the basic problem of grassland degradation by overgrazing.

Therefore, the Ministry of Agriculture gradually aims to implement a policy in four phases:

1) allocation of livestock to individual farm households;
2) allocation of grazing lands to individual users;
3) assessing of carrying capacities for each allocated plot of land by local authorities;
4) implementation of a system of incentives and sanctions to make the grassland users abide by the formally established carrying capacities (CSCPRC 1992, pp. 32–33).

If the policy line for rangeland management indeed follows the gradual four-phase scheme as described above, phase two would be in progress at present, while phase three and four are still awaiting execution. Apart from the question about whether the distribution of land and animals to individual users can or should be carried out separately from an assessment of carrying capacities and the implementation of a wider regulatory system, it can already be stated that the second phase seems to have stagnated in quite a number of regions in China.

In contrast to what Li Yutang has stated, nothing has changed in the actual practice of rangeland management and utilization since the proclamation of the Rangeland Law in 1985. In other words, overgrazing has persisted as the problem of open access, or what in Chinese is called "eating from the big rice pot," has not been solved. There are several factors that may be at the root of this fiasco.

The first factor is that the HCRS, which was viewed as the key to success in the reform in agriculture and imposed nationally without considering the local variations (White 1993), was simply transferred to animal husbandry, with scant regard for the specific technical and physical properties of a natural resource like rangeland.

Another factor can be found in the nature of the resource itself. Livestock grazing areas have variable boundaries. When rainfall is sufficient, restricted wandering will suffice, but under the conditions of low and unpredictable rainfall and deteriorating fodder resources, a considerably wider movement over the range is necessary to satisfy forage requirements (Van de Laar 1990). As stated before, Ningxia has a tradition of overlapped grazing, which was inevitable due to erratic rainfall and the limited area of grassland. Under such circumstances, livestock farmers cannot be expected to abide by fixed boundaries.

During the 1950s and 1960s, when attempts were made to introduce deferred grazing by fencing in plots of rangeland, a frequent problem was the rivalry between villages. If a certain plot had been closed for grazing by a certain village, others simply continued to allow their flocks to graze on it. "If deferred grazing is ever to succeed, we have to do it in a coordinated way. All neighboring villages have to close a plot of rangeland at the same time, and also resume grazing at the same time," the head of the County Bureau of Animal Husbandry in Yanchi said. If the properties of the rangeland in Ningxia are not taken into consideration, any policy towards privatization will certainly fail.

Another, equally important factor, is the property rights structure under the

HCRS. The latter is aimed to hold individuals and groups responsible for their own economic performance, while simultaneously holding on to what in essence is still a planned economy. Between central reformists and conservatives, there was disagreement as to the role of the market; freeing the markets meant the expansion of markets in labor, finance and land. The reformers deemed the establishment of private ownership over land essential to increase investment by the peasants themselves, which implied establishing a *de facto* land market. The conservative faction on the other hand, tried—in particular during the early 1990s, when the reforms had run into problems—to strengthen those state institutions that had been undermined by the rural reforms, in order to re-establish certain principles of central planning.[34]

The contract system, being in essence a political compromise between reformers and conservatives, is ambiguous. For the management of the grasslands in Ningxia, the compromise formula has proved to be inadequate. A basic condition to avert the squandering of a natural resource has always been the establishment of clear property rights over it. At present, the type of property regime of rangeland in Ningxia bears many similarities to the regime prevalent during Mao's rule. Indeed, the property regime under the contract system is basically still a state property regime. Property rights are now vested in the village collective, while rangeland management and protection, as well as enforcement of regulations of grazing, are charged to the Bureau of Animal Husbandry and the County Grassland Management Stations.

The village collective and the Bureau of Animal Husbandry, as representatives of the state, are by definition external to the direct users of the grasslands. The question is how users of grassland—be they individual households or joint households—can have any interest in long-term investments in the maintenance of grasslands without clearly vested property rights in organizations they can regard as their own. The problem is aggravated by the fact that the newly gained economic freedom for farmers through the contract system does not particularly stimulate long-term perspectives, but rather encourages farmers to strive for short-term profits by maximizing their production. Livestock farmers will increase their flock in order to maximize profit, while policies to curb flock size have had no significant effect so far.

Shue speaks about a "thickening of the state" in the Chinese countryside, as a result of the rapidly changing social, economic and political situation caused by the post-1978 economic reforms:

> As society becomes more differentiated and complex, local state organizations are challenged to do the same. Many have begun to introduce greater differentiation into their own procedures and services. The structural sameness and the near uniformity of interests, of responsibilities and of wealth that were characteristics of the old commune-brigade-team organization are now past (Shue 1990).

However, for those institutions in Ningxia that are responsible for managing the grasslands it can be asserted that they are hardly equipped to handle their new task in a decollectivized economy as they are still too "thin" in their organization and services. Moreover, as White points out, there is an inevitable direct tension between a streamlining of the bureaucracy for a changing socio-economic environment on the one hand, and raising levels of functional specialization and technical expertise of local cadres on the other (White 1993). The Bureau of Animal Husbandry, for example, hardly provides any extension services[35] to farmers, while veterinary services only include the inoculation of livestock. The grassland police headed by the Bureau of Animal Husbandry is seriously understaffed, and is incapable of patrolling the vast areas under their jurisdiction. As for the village collective represented by the village leader, his power has clearly weakened following the disbandment of the brigades and teams (White 1993), and he seems unable to play a significant role in the management of rangelands. Property rights have not been given to individual households or collectives, out of fear of large-scale illegal land reclamation.

The third main factor is economic. The villages in the mountainous region and the desert and steppe region in Ningxia are characterized by few income-generating activities, absence of village amenities and enterprises, poor ecological conditions, endemic diseases, inadequate infrastructure, shortage in water supply, and underdeveloped structure of voluntary collective marketing cooperatives (Shen and Steinbach, 1993; and NHZGB, 1986). Pang Jian writes that although most of the agricultural land resources in Ningxia are dominated by animal husbandry, the livestock sector lags behind the agricultural sector, which is aggravated by the low procurement prices of meat products of state supply and marketing cooperatives as a result of the "urban bias" (Pang Jian 1993).

Due to the above-mentioned economic conditions, productivity in animal husbandry is low. It is therefore likely that the local government will favor industry (including rural industry) over agriculture and animal husbandry, in view of its quicker and greater economic returns. Local governments have also been supported in these efforts by the central government in order to develop the industrial sector (White 1993). As a result of all this, the management and protection of pastoral areas rank low on the political agenda of the local government. Nationwide, the total investment for range development since 1956 has only been 4.6 million *yuan*, or 0.3 *yuan* per ha per year. As financial support for the livestock sector remains inadequate, losses continue to be high. Presently, approximately two million grazing animals are lost every year, in particular during winter and early spring (CSCPRC 1992, pp. 48–49).

The last factor is the sociological context in which law enforcement in China takes place. The vice-director of the Provincial Bureau of Animal Husbandry stated that the representative of the Chinese state at the village level—the village head (or "team leader" as he is often still referred to)—is often caught between the interests of the state and those of his fellow villagers. The village head himself is a part of the village community in which he lives and not replaced over time like the county and township officials. In order to retain a socially acceptable position in the village community he cannot afford to be too stringent in the implementation of national policy measures, and as a result chooses to mitigate certain policies.

As Lieberthal and Oksenberg write, "what on paper appears to be a unified, hierarchical chain of command turns out in reality to be divided, segmented, and stratified. Indeed, the fragmentation of authority is a core dimension of the Chinese system."[36] In addition to the formal bureaucratic structure there is also a whole system of personal ties and networks (*guanxi*) that is often branded as corruption. The concept of *guanxi* is essential in Chinese politics. For example, over the last decade, village heads have effectively caused the policy to impose a quota on the number of sheep per farmer to fail. Amongst other reasons for this failure, many interviewed cadres also listed *guanxi*. Actual numbers of livestock are often falsified for the purpose of tax evasion, with the knowledge of the village leader.

Additional Policy Measures

Apart from the Rangeland Law and the HCRS for grassland, there are four other policy lines in Ningxia which will also be briefly mentioned here. One is the "three high, one quick" policy (*sangao, yikuai*) implemented since 1978, which aims at "a high total increase, high-quality, high commercial rate and quick returns." Ten month old lambs have the most favorable ratio between total meat weight and forage needed, while older sheep need more forage in proportion to the amount of meat they yield. By increasing the total number of young lambs and slaughtering them before they are one year old, quick returns are attained, while the grazing pressure on grasslands is simultaneously reduced.[37] However, the policy seems to have run into problems where extension is concerned.

The second policy is that of using transmigration as a means to reduce the population pressure in the poverty-stricken area of south Ningxia. The former "Suspended Village Project" (*diaozhuang*) and the new "1236 Project" have been designed for this purpose. The Suspended Village Project, which was executed from 1983 till 1992, was aimed at the transmigration and resettlement of farmers from the poor southern counties to counties in the middle part of Ningxia, where irrigated land is available. The term "suspended village" used to denote the simple dwellings that were formerly built by farmers near land that was far away from their farm. It was only temporarily used during the planting and harvesting seasons. At present, the term "suspended village" refers to villages constructed by the government for the resettlement of migrants from the poor hilly areas. In the resettlement areas, not only farm houses have been built, but also irrigation facilities. Approximately 200,000 people have since been moved (Wang and Niu 1993, pp. 441–447).

This project will be followed up by the prestigious 1236 Project, which will be implemented in 1996. It derives its name from its objectives:

1) to solve the poverty problem of one million people;
2) to open up 2 million *mu* of land, which will be irrigated with water from the Yellow River (1 ha=15 *mu*);
3) to invest 3 billion *yuan*;
4) the project will last for six years (1995–2001).

A total of 746,000 people will be moved from the south to middle and north Ningxia (see also Bureau for Water Conservancy 1994). As the project has not even entered its initial stage, it is still too early to evaluate its impact.

The third policy measure is the most interesting of the four. Since March 1994, the county government has been advocating a policy of auctioning off user rights (*paimai zhengce*) of delimited plots of wasteland to individual farmers,[38] a campaign which has been frequently aired on television. Only the user rights are leased, while the property rights are still vested in the village collective (village committee). The land may be used for animal husbandry and forestry, while agriculture is strictly prohibited. This policy, which has been announced as a "great change in the management of natural resources," is actually a variation of the HCRS, and will face the same problems in its implementation and execution. Whatever political considerations may have motivated it, the policy of "auctioning off the four wastelands to farmers" does not have any practical value, and purely shows the weakness of the provincial government in tackling the problem of rangeland management.

Last but not least, in accordance with the Rangeland Law, new and more detailed rules and regulations on rangeland management were promulgated by the Ningxia government in December 1994. These rules and regulations add new specifications to the Rangeland Law in the following ways:

1) for the use of state-owned grassland a user's fee will be levied in the future;
2) the digging of liquorice root is being restricted through a system of licenses and set annual harvest quotas;
3) authorities at the municipal, county and township levels are required to set up a supervisory system for rangeland management under the new rules;
4) the authorities at the municipal, county and township levels have also been made responsible for assessing carrying capacities for various plots of grassland, and the enforcement of these limits;
5) a detailed system of fines as per offence has been established.[39]

Although these rules and regulations are much more detailed than the Rangeland Law, they do not seem to offer an approach to rangeland management that is distinctly different from that advocated by the Rangeland Law itself. It remains to be seen how the Ningxia government will achieve the assessment and enforcement of stocking rates, while simultaneously dividing responsibility for management and utilization rights between local authorities and pastoralists.

Further research is needed to determine the exact political background of these new policies and the new rules and regulations on rangeland management, as well as their feasibility within a different property regime setting.

Privatization: Not a Panacea

Ever since the decision of the Communist Party that "the little private parcels of land of commune members, the rural workshops and the village markets are necessary complements of the socialist economy," the Bureau of Animal Husbandry and the village collective are caught in a double bind situation. On the one hand, there is an obvious tendency in politics towards privatization—and in an exceptional case nationalization—of the grasslands, because of the failure of grassland management under collectivist structures.

On the other hand, in view of the physical and technical aspects of the resource, serious doubts can be formulated against privatization, in favor of a common property arrangement. Even more so when one realizes that the reason for opting for privatization stems from an erroneous analysis of past experience. It is not that the grasslands degraded as a result of a common property regime under the People's Communes, but because of the fact that the Chinese government failed to recognize that the sort of common property regime they tried to implement was nothing else but "eating from the big rice pot."

All too often, a natural resource regulated by a common property regime is confounded with an open-access resource, and said to lead automatically to its destruction. At this point it becomes necessary to define the term "property." We will adhere to Bromley's definition: "Property is not an object such as land, but rather is a right to a benefit stream that is only as secure as the duty of all others to respect the conditions that protect that stream." Moreover, Bromley reminds us that "there is no such thing as a common property resource; there are only resources controlled and managed as common property, or as state property, or as private property"(Bromley 1991, p. 2).

Common property resource management implies private property for a group—as opposed to those who are excluded from the resource in use and decision making—while all group members have rights as well as duties regarding the resource (Bromley 1991, p. 2). And it is exactly these rights and duties that the communes failed to guard and to enforce, as a result of a political fear to vest property rights clearly in either individual users or a group of users. The dissolution of the communes in the early 1980s has brought no solution to this problem, and in spite of efforts to set up an alternative rangeland management, the grasslands continue to degrade as the situation of open access persists.

In order to turn the grasslands away from a situation of open access, the Chinese Central Government only adheres to the prevailing notion of collective action. However, as Wade notes: "If a group of people are placed in a situation where they could mutually benefit if all adopted a rule of restrained use of a common pool resource, they will not do so in the absence of an external enforcer of agreements" (Wade 1987, pp. 95–106). Prompted by a similar distrust of common property arrangements, the county government in Ningxia remains determined to tackle the present free-rider problem among livestock farmers by privatization of the resource.

However, establishing a private property system is a very costly affair. First of all, administrative costs will soar in setting up a cadastre, whereby all the individual plots are demarcated and verified with a clear title. In addition, there are the costs of keeping record of changes in land holdings, as well as the official costs associated with the actions of the private owners. There are also material costs, because fencing of pastures is often needed to separate the plots and enable differentiation between the different types of land use and users.[40] Furthermore, one should not forget the costs necessary for the enforcement of regulations, which are most likely the highest of all.

This is not to say that a common property regime does not involve costs. Transaction costs for bargaining are often high, because meetings among village members are needed to settle various issues such as who can participate in the use of the resource, how conflicts over usage are resolved, and so forth. But all in all, it can be reasonably stated that the costs of privatization are far higher than those of setting up a common property regime.

Furthermore, the natural environment in Ningxia is such that it creates uncertainty about the income streams from this resource. The application of labor and capital per unit land is low, as well as the economic returns. This is generally the case for grasslands in China, where due to insufficient and variable rainfall (and to low temperatures for the pastures at higher altitudes, such as in Qinghai and Tibet) productivity is far below that of other pastoral areas in the world. The average carrying capacity for China's pastures is merely 0.8 sheep per ha, as compared to 30 in the former USSR, nearly 50 in the U.S., and over 110 in New Zealand (Smil 1993, p. 65). In sum, this means that the benefits of a private property regime are not all that obvious in the Chinese grassland situation, as privatization is only feasible if it leads to returns of livestock production that are higher than the administrative costs for privatization.

Moreover, a private property arrangement also has the disadvantage that the strategy to appropriate from the resource is less flexible than a common property regime. This is important when the natural environment is highly erratic. Under the more rigid arrangements of a private property regime, it is much more difficult for the various users to collaborate in order to overcome the effects of natural disasters.[41]

Finally, an important argument against privatization in Ningxia would be the fact that the Rangeland Law cannot be enforced externally by the grassland police. One of the local cadres said: "The grassland is too vast, and the police force too small in order to make the law effective. No, instead of a rangeland management enforced by the grassland police, we need to organize the farmers to manage the grasslands by themselves, to enforce rules of grazing by themselves"(Personal communication 1994).

Considering the fear of the local and central governments of large-scale illegal land reclamation under private property arrangements, there is much to say for a common property regime, whereby flock owners are organized into flock owners' associations that are responsible for the management of the grazing areas. This would most certainly alleviate the tasks of the grassland police and the Bureau of Animal Husbandry, as rules concerning boundaries, membership, input, allocation and penalties would then be determined and enforced by the flock owners' associations themselves. The various institutions could then devote themselves to the tasks for which they were originally established, such as veterinary services and agricultural extension.

Taking all these considerations into account, it can be concluded that the most viable option for regulating grazing in Ningxia is by means of common property resource management. For a successful management of a natural resource and its preservation for future generations, the following points are important for the organization of its users:

— the criteria for participation in a property regime;
— the type of access to which part of the natural resource, based on criteria commonly agreed on (e.g. membership);
— the manner in which decisions will be made for appropriating from or providing for a resource base;
— the manner of conflict resolution and nature of penalty for transgressors, within the ensuing patterns of resource use.[42]

In the case for China on the whole, and Ningxia in particular, establishing a common property regime for rangeland management will not be an easy task, as it will mean going against the national tendency towards privatization.

Summary and Conclusion

In both Chinese and foreign academic and development aid circles, the reasons for degradation of pastoral areas by soil erosion and desertification in China are often too easily sought in technical and demographic factors, while the institutional environment is neglected. Policy recommendations and project targets are usually phrased in terms such as: "propagation of deferred and rotational grazing," "assessing the carrying capacity of grasslands," "sinking wells in order to spread grazing pressure," "reducing the stocking rates," "establishment of fodder depots," "closing of critical areas (such as catchment areas of major rivers)," "strengthening of extension services," and so forth.

However, such measures will have little effect if they are not embedded in an institutional framework that will provide the incentives for collective action by the users of the resource base, by minimizing the risk of free-riding. The destruction of grasslands in the Ningxia Hui Autonomous Region cannot solely be blamed on population growth, reclamation of unsuitable lands or overgrazing. Rather, the problem is that the Chinese government over the decades has been unable to create the conditions under which livestock owners could cooperate to protect the natural resource on which they depend against degradation. This political inability in the management of natural resources is not a recent problem that has occurred with the recent economic reforms. Of course, the major transition from a centrally planned economy to a market economy in China has led to a great deal of confusion and ambiguity in rangeland management, but the problem itself can be traced back to long before the reforms.

The reasons for the decay of the pastoral areas in China show similarities to other developing countries. The degradation of the grass- and forestlands in most developing countries can be traced back to the destruction of the customary rights systems that were in place before they were wiped out by colonial and later by national rights systems. After decolonization, national governments took over the role of the former colonial government, and local control over natural resources continued to be systematically undermined. As in other developing countries, grasslands in China were all nationalized, thus delegitimatizing the local customary rights systems over the usage of grassland. As the central and local governments failed to provide an environment for the users of grasslands in which mutual cooperation would become their most preferred option, a situation of open access arose.

The factors that caused free-riding to be the prevailing attitude of the users can in essence be divided into two different denominators:

1) the property right structure under the People's Communes and the village collectives in post-Mao China;
2) their system of rules regarding boundaries, membership, allocation, input, and penalties.

In 1956, the management of rangeland entered a new era as individual ownership of the grasslands—common during Republican times—was replaced by collective ownership. In principle, collective ownership can be a good solution for sustainable use of grazing areas, but under the condition that ownership rights are well defined. Under the communes this was not the case, as ownership rights were divided over three administrative levels: the commune, the production brigade and the production team. The actual property rights of the rangelands were vested in the commune, which was a level too remote and abstract for the direct users to feel a sense of social responsibility for the protection of the resource base. The ownership of livestock was in the hands of the production brigade, while the production team—equal to the present natural village—was only left with the task of herding the flock.

As regards the rules other than ownership during the commune era, they were either non-existent or proved to be impossible to enforce. As we have seen, membership rules and boundary rules did not exist, while the rules for allocation and input merely concerned the livestock production and not the resource base. The implementation of penalty rules to prevent the squandering of the rangeland, as well as the later's daily management, were directed to local state institutions—the County Bureau of Animal Husbandry and the Grassland Management Stations—that were external to the direct group of users.

After the disbandment of the communes and the initiation of the rural reforms in the late 1970s, the central government tried to privatize the grasslands by means of the HCRS. It is doubtful that the HCRS is applicable to rangelands.[43] The reason that it was expanded from agriculture to the livestock sector is probably that it had become the political norm for the reform strategy. It was applied to the livestock sector without consideration for local variations and the specific traits of the natural resource on which livestock production relies.

Furthermore, the Household Contract System in itself is ambiguous. It was introduced because the government shrank back from completely decentralizing the power it had wielded in the centrally planned economy—in the form of collective property rights—to individual farmers. Although the rights of usufruct and the ownership rights of livestock were passed on to individual farm households, the ownership rights of grassland as well as the responsibility of enforcing the regulations on grazing as stipulated in the Rangeland Law were entrusted to external institutions. The Bureau of Animal Husbandry and the village collective, headed by the village head, however, failed in their new tasks of providing farmers with incentives for a coordinated use of rangeland in a completely changed and much more complex socio-economic environment. As a result, a pattern of resource use emerged which was similar to that of the commune era. The institutional structure of rangeland management also showed similarities to that of the communes: a two-level resource management whereby rights of usufruct are vested in individual households, but property rights remain with an external organization which is responsible for the enforcement of grazing regulations.

As the contracting of delimited plots of grassland to individual users failed, the only distinct point of difference with the communes also faded away. The proclamation of the Rangeland Law in 1985, and the establishment of the grassland police, did not lead to real improvement, as the areas under control of the grassland police are simply too vast for effective law enforcement. Except for the fact that livestock could now be owned by the farm households themselves, the situation became in principle similar to that under the communes, when there was no rangeland management at all, but only a situation of tolerated open access.

Although the establishment of a common property regime can be recommended for Ningxia for the reasons explained in this study, one has to remember that it is also not a panacea, and does involve risks of failure. Transaction costs will be high, and the number of livestock and users of rangeland will still have to be curbed. Nonetheless, under a common property arrangement, restricting the number of ruminants and users has a greater chance of success than under a state or private property regime: a common property regime draws on support from a broader layer of society, as it makes use of more democratic procedures of consultation over resource use within the users' group itself. Still, the fact which should not be overlooked is that a common property regime has to be embedded in a larger framework of political and economic measures. Among other things, it means that alternative employment has to be found for livestock farmers who have to give up their herd, by stimulating the development of rural enterprises.

Only by embedding a common property regime in a larger institutional framework can one hope to reverse the legacy of the free-rider problem that originated in a collectivist past, and work towards a sustainable use of China's pastoral areas. It is this heavy responsibility that weighs on the Chinese government for the coming decades. The question remains whether it will be able to deal with this task.

We urgently need to fill the gap in our understanding of the political background of rangeland degradation in China. How high is rangeland protection actually rated on the political agenda of the central and local governments? Have the real limits of development already been reached in regions such as Ningxia, or have statistics been manipulated for political purposes? Some scholars have even challenged the view widely held by most Chinese and Western researchers that increases in stocking rates, and thus overgrazing, are the major causes of grassland degradation in China. They have suggested that China's herds could fluctuate around a "normal" capacity that the rangelands in China have sustained in the past and could also sustain in the future.[44]

All in all, we can assuredly state that the management of rangelands in China cannot be solved by technical measures alone. In fact, the whole concept of carrying capacity itself is essentially flawed within the Chinese context, as the sustainability of grasslands hinges very much on the political issue of accountability and its enforcement. For China and for many other countries where forests, wetlands and grasslands are degrading at an alarming speed, the questions that we need to ask are: Who is accountable? And how is accountability enforced with regard to the physical properties of the resource, as well as the wider socio-economic context? If the government will not solve the problems of accountability and enforcement, the free-rider problem will persist, as will the squandering of natural resources.

Acknowledgement:

For the lengthy process of putting this article together, I would like to express my heartfelt thanks to Ward Vermeer, as well as to the participants of the Conference on Chinese Rural Collectives and Voluntary Organizations held in Leiden, The Netherlands, January 1995, who have provided me with their constructive comments and vivid ideas. I would in particular like to thank Margaret McKean, George Brown and Han van Dijk. Last but not least, I am extremely grateful to Ji Kunqi of the Ningxia Science and Technology Commission and Gao Guiying, my inseparable counterpart, for their help during my fieldwork.

Notes

Abbreviations used in notes:

HAPC = Higher Agricultural Producers' Cooperative
CCP = Chinese Communist Party
CSCPRC = Committee on Scholarly Communication with the People's Republic of China
LAPC = Lower Agricultural Producers' Cooperative
GDDB = Guyuan diqu difangzhi bangongshi
GTZ = Guojia tongjiju zonghesi
GDG = Guyuan diqu gongchandang
GXBWB = Guyuan xianzhi bianzuan weiyuanhui bangongshi
HCRS = Household Contract Responsibility System
MAT = Mutual Aid Team
NHZT = Ningxia Huizu zizhiqu tongjiju
NHZN = Ningxia Huizu zizhiqu nongyeting
NHZGB = Ningxia Huizu zizhiqu gaikuang bianxiezu
YXBWB = Yanchi xianzhi bianzuan weiyuanhui bangongshi
ZCX = Zhongguo caoyuan xuehui
ZKNNZK = Zhongguo kexueyuan Neimeng Ningxia zonghe kaochadui

1. In 1993, the limit was set at a net rural per capita income of 133 *yuan* per year. The national average net income per year at the time was 602 *yuan*.
2. See *Ningxia tongji nianjian* (Ningxia Statistical Yearbook) 1990; Liu Yingxin and Huang Zhaohua 1993.
3. See CSCPRC 1992, p. 28. Liu and Huang have stated that in Ningxia, the upper limit of 1 livestock unit per 5 ha in arid zones as stipulated by the United States has been exceeded by 36 percent: see Liu and Huang 1993, p. 59. Vaclav Smil has even mentioned a much lower actual carrying capacity for China, only 0.8 sheep per ha: see Vaclav Smil 1993, p. 65.
4. See Chen Tongming and Song Guogui 1993, p. 405; Guyuanxian wenwu gongzuozhan 1981, p. 5; and Wang Yuesheng 1987, p. 14.
5. As a result of subsequent wars, the administrative system disintegrated. For this reason, exact figures of the migration to Ningxia during this period, which was connected to war and war-related famines, can only be estimated.
6. Small communities of "Hui Hui," as the Hui Muslims were called, used to live in the Yellow River basin in the 12th century A.D. (Yuan dynasty, 1276–1368). It was after several Muslim rebellions in the Northwest (1648–1650, Gansu; 1781–1784, Shaanxi; 1862–1871, uprising of the New Sect in Gansu under Ma Hualong) that the Hui of Ningxia and the neighboring provinces were driven away from their original dwellings to remote and poor places such as the hilly areas of Guyuan County on the Loess Plateau. See Lai Cunli 1992, p. 94; and Raphael Israeli 1980, pp. 105, 133, 169.
7. See map in Ningxiasheng dizhengju 1942, p. 3. In Republican times, present Ningxia belonged (for Guyuan till 1935 and for Yanchi till 1936) to the area that was designated by the Ningxia Bureau for Land Administration as "people's land to be reclaimed by landless farmers from the province itself and adjoining provinces." The part of Ningxia, however, which is now Inner Mongolia, was for the establishment of military colonies, or designated for land reclamation by Mongol tribes and war refugees. This involved the greater part of what was then Ningxia.
8. The Republican Gazetteer of Guyuan County writes that ever since the earthquake in 1919, Ningxia was dominated by bandits, and torn by war. It was only by the end of the

1930s that the situation became more peaceful. See Zhang Xianzhu 1991, p. 9; and Wu Zhongli and Liu Qinbin 1993, pp. 344–352.

9. David Bromley also mentions the danger of migrants introducing forms of institutional resource use which are unsuitable to the ecological environment. See Bromley 1991, p. 133.

10. Although within the framework of this research project, no literature from the pre-1800 period has been studied, there is strong evidence that even before 1800, pastoral nomadism was not a regular practice in Ningxia.

11. The regions investigated (Guyuan and Yanchi counties) did not belong to the grazing territories that were formally enfeoffed to Mongol princes (*jasagh*) during the Qing dynasty.

12. See Zhang Bo 1989, pp. 381–386; and Liu and Huang 1993, p. 139.

13. See GXBWB 1981, p. 28; YXBWB 1983, p. 43; and Yang Hongchun 1964, p. 125.

14. GXBWB 1981, p. 28; GDDB 1987, p. 36; Zhang Guangzu 1986, p. 155; YXBWB 1983, p. 39.

15. See Ningxia dizhengju 1942, p. 4. At the time of writing, no material has yet been found about the actual functioning of these institutions.

16. Guo Sijia and Xin Zhongzhi 1993, p. 3; and Ningxiasheng dizhengju 1942, p. 3.

17. For more details on rural institutions during the period 1949–1956, see also Chen and Buckwell 1991, pp. 33–41.

18. See Chan, Madsen, and Unger 1992; Croll 1994; Oi 1992; YXBWB 1983; Chen and Buckwell 1991.

19. See also GTZ 1990, p. 897. The article only refers to sheep and goats when the word "ruminant" or "grazing animal" is used, because in Ningxia, cattle are mainly used as draft animals and not reared as grazing animals. Furthermore, the trends in the number of grazing animals are mainly determined by the number of sheep and goats, not cattle.

20. See GTZ 1990, p. 885. The statistics compiled by the Ningxia Statistical Bureau in the 1960s differ somewhat from those mentioned in the article, namely an increase from 1,112,552 people in 1949 to 1,921,985 people in 1965 (72.8 percent increase), while there was a slight decrease of about 40,000 people from 1960 till 1961. See also NHZT 1966, pp. 2–3.

21. At the same time, a change occurred in the perception of scarcity of the grasslands, which has been confirmed both by interviews with elderly farmers and the literature. See also NHZN 1964, p. 127; and ZKNNZK 1963a, pp. 6–7.

22. See Lei Zhizhong *et al.* 1964; YXBWB 1983; ZKNNZK 1963a; ZKNNZK 1963b; NHZN 1964; and Yang Hongchun 1964.

23. Lei Zhizhong *et al.* 1963; and YXBWB 1983.

24. YXBWB 1983, p. 54; and Zhang Guangzu 1986, p. 163.

25. The continuity of traditional land tenure arrangements during collectivist times has also been noted in Mongolia. See Robin Mearns 1993, pp. 73–103; and Robin Mearns 1996, pp. 283–325. I am much indebted to Robin Mearns for sending me the final version of his article on collective action and common grazing in Mongolia (forthcoming in the *Journal for Development Studies*).

26. The effect of administrative boundaries on herder mobility in China and Mongolia during collectivist times is by no means clear. In their case-study of the Hurqige production brigade, Li, Ma and Simpson contend that long-distance nomadic movement changed into short-distance nomadic movement within the brigade boundaries in Inner Mongolia in the 1960s and 1970s. However, the authors do not mention the rigidity with which brigades guarded their boundaries against herders from outside. See Li Ou *et al.* 1993, pp. 63–72. Both Mearns and Potkanski state that in Mongolia during this period, public policies geared towards raising the living standard of pastoralists (winter shelter construc-

tion, provision of animal fodder and transport etc.) particularly reduced herder mobility. See Mearns 1993, p. 98; and Potkanski 1993, pp. 123–35. As Mearns stated in a later article, he does not exclude the possibility that decreased herder mobility is the result of the extension of "administrative control over territories the boundaries of which bore little relation to the actual patterns of mobility of local herders." See Mearns 1996, p. 304.

27. In 1958, these had been separated from the Veterinary Stations, with which they used to form one single institution.

28. This is not to say that the intensity and impact of the struggle campaigns were similar for every region in China. It seems that some villages hardly experienced anything of political campaigns such as the "Big Clean Up" or the "Cleansing of the Class Ranks." See also Chan *et al.* 1992, note on p. 167.

29. Chan *et al.* 1992, pp. 249–250, 265; and Croll 1994, pp. 12–13.

30. See also Chan *et al.* 1992, p. 256; and YXBWB 1983.

31. Note that in Guyuan County, livestock farmers seldom depend on livestock production alone for their livelihood, but often engage in a mixed farming operation of agriculture and animal husbandry.

32. Personal communication 1995. See also Sun Minghe 1993.

33. For works on the relation between the Han and Hui, see Gladney 1991; Israeli 1980; and Mackerras 1994.

34. For more details on the political background of the rural reforms, see White 1993.

35. This does not only pertain to technical extension, but also to political and social extension. Farmers in Ningxia are in general utterly unaware of policies that directly concern them, such as the proclamation of the Rangeland Law, and the leasing of wasteland in 1994.

36. For more details of the authority structure in China, see Lieberthal and Oksenberg 1988; and White 1993, for the relation between the central and local government.

37. For more details on this policy see also Shen and Steinbach 1993.

38. The main difference between this policy and the Household Contract Responsibility System is that the highest bidder can now buy the rights to lease a plot of wasteland, much the same way as in an auction. The wasteland does not comprise any nature reserves, grasslands or forests. See GDG 1994.

39. See Ningxia Huizu zizhiqu renmin daibiao dahui changwu weiyuanhui 1994, p. 3.

40. For more details see also Van de Laar 1990; and Bromley 1991.

41. Bromley has written extensively about the relationship between economic marginality and its implications for the type of property regime. See Bromley 1991.

42. For more details on the variables and conditions for the emergence of an organized group of individuals who withdraw resource-units from a common property regime, see Ostrom 1992; and Oakerson 1992.

43. Longworth and Williamson have found that in Inner Mongolia, much of the rangeland (in some counties even up to 70 percent of contract grazing land) is still grazed in common despite attempts of the state to allocate separate plots of pasture to individual households. See Longworth and Williamson 1993, pp. 99 and 171. In contrast, after the start of the economic reforms in 1980, the government of Mongolia seems to have purposefully chosen a common property arrangement for rangelands. Unlike arable and hay land, pastures are excluded from private ownership. On this, Mearns writes: "[Pasture land] will remain in state hands as 'common' land under the jurisdiction of the relevant local authorities at provincial and district levels. In practice, it falls under the effective control of local herding groups as *de facto* common property." Mearns 1996, p. 294.

44. See also CSCPRC 1992, pp. 34–35. For a good summary of the critique on conventional rangeland management on the basis of stocking rates see Behnke, Scoones and Kerven 1993.

References

Behnke, Roy H.; Scoones, Ian; Kerven, Carol, *Range Ecology at Disequilibrium: New Models of Natural Variability and Pastoral Adaptation in African Savannas*. London: Overseas Development Institute, 1993.

Bromley, David W., *Environment and Economy: Property Rights and Public Policy*. Oxford: Blackwell, 1991.

———— ed., *Making the Commons Work: Theory, Practice and Policy*. San Francisco: Institute for Contemporary Studies Press, 1992.

Bureau for Water Conservancy, *Daliushu Ningxia guanqu diyiqi fupin gongcheng yuke-xingxing yanjiu baogao* (Feasibility Study for the First Phase of the Poverty Allevia-tion Project in the Irrigated Area of Daliushu, Ningxia). Yinchuan, Internal Report, 1994.

Chan, Anita; Madsen, Richard; and Unger, Jonathan, *Chen Village under Mao and Deng*. Berkeley: University of California Press, 1992.

Chen Liang Yu and Buckwell, Alan, *Chinese Grain Economy and Policy*. Wallingford: CAB International, 1991.

Chen Tongming and Song Guogui, *Guyuan xianzhi* (Local Gazetteer of Guyuan County). Yinchuan: Ningxia renmin chubanshe, 1993.

Croll, Elisabeth, *From Heaven to Earth: Images and Experiences of Development in China*. London: Routledge, 1994.

CSCPRC. Committee on Scholarly Communication with the People's Republic of China, *Grasslands and Grassland Sciences in Northern China*. Washington D.C.: National Academy Press, 1992.

The Ecologist. (anon.), "The Commons: Where the Community has Authority." In *The Ecologist*, vol. 22, no. 4, July/August, 1992, pp. 122–147.

Gladney, Dru, *Muslim Chinese: Ethnic Nationalism in the People's Republic*. Harvard East Asian Monographs, No. 149. Cambridge: Council on East Asian Studies, 1991.

GDDB. Guyuan diqu difangzhi bangongshi, ed., *Guyuan diqu shizhi ziliao* (Historical Gazet-teer of Guyuan Region), vol. II. Guyuan: Guyuan diqu difangzhi bangongshi, 1987.

GDG. Guyuan diqu gongchandang, ed., *Guanyu paimai "sihuangdi" shiyongquan ruogan zhengce guiding* (Some Policy Regulations Concerning the Rights of Use of "Four Leased Wastelands"). Documents of the Guyuan Communist Party, No. 20, 1994.

GTZ. Guojia tongjiju zonghesi, ed., *Quanguo ge sheng, zizhiqu, zhixiashi lishi tongji ziliao huibian* (Compilation of National Historical Statistics of all Provinces, Autono-mous Regions, and Cities Directly under the Central Government). Beijing: Zhongguo tongji chubanshe, 1990.

Guo Sijia and Xin Zhongzhi, *Ningxia caodi shahua yu duice* (Desertification of Grasslands of Ningxia and Countermeasures). Ningxia xumuju, August 1993. Paper presented at the International Conference on Rational Utilization of Arid Lands, Yinchuan, 1993.

Guyuanxian wenwu gongzuozhan, ed., *Guyuan xianzhi* (Local Gazetteer of Guyuan County). Guyuan: Guyuanxian wenwu gongzuozhan, 1981. Reprint of *Guyuan xianzhi*, vol. V, 1935.

GXBWB. Guyuan xianzhi bianzuan weiyuanhui bangongshi, ed., *Guyuan xianzhi xumuzhi* (Local Gazetteer of Guyuan: Gazetteer of Animal Husbandry). Guyuan, 1981.

Hu, Peter Shing Tsung; Hannaway, David B.; Youngberg, H.W., *Forage Resources of China*. Wageningen: PUDOC, 1992.

Israeli, Raphael, *Muslims in China: A Study in Cultural Confrontation*. Scandinavian Institute of Asian Studies, Monograph Series, No. 29. Richmond, Surrey: Curzon Press, 1980.

Lai Cunli, *Zhongguo Huizu shehui jingji* (The Economy and Society of the Chinese Hui). Yinchuan: Ningxia renmin chubanshe, 1992.

Lei Zhizhong; Guo Gang; Yang Hongchun; Mo Dayan, "Ningxia Huizu zizhiqu Yanchixian caoyuan diqu mumin liyong caodi fangfa de diaocha yanjiu" (Research of Methods of Grassland Utilization by Pastoralists in Grazing Areas in the Ningxia Hui Autonomous Region). In *Ningxia Huizu zizhiqu 1963 caoyuan yanjiu baogao xuanbian* (A Selection of Grassland Research Reports of Ningxia Hui Autonomous Region). Internal Document, Ningxia Huizu zizhiqu nongyeting xumuju, 1964.

Li Ou; Ma Rong; Simpson, James R., "Changes in the Nomadic Pattern and Its Impact on the Inner Mongolian Steppe Grasslands Ecosystem." In: *Nomadic Peoples*, no. 33, 1993, pp. 63–72.

Lieberthal, Kenneth, and Oksenberg, Michel, *Policy Making in China: Leaders, Structures and Processes*. Princeton: Princeton University Press, 1988.

Liu Yingxin and Huang Zhaohua, "Desertification and Revegetation of Dunes and Rangelands in Ningxia." In Shen Changjiang and Jörg Steinbach, eds., 1993.

Longworth, John W., and Williamson, Gregory J., *China's Pastoral Region: Sheep and Wool, Minority Nationalities, Rangeland Degradation and Sustainable Development*. Wallingford: CAB International, 1993.

Ma Hongda, *Ningxiasheng zheng yaoshu* (General Outline of the Administration of Ningxia Province). Yinchuan, 1934.

Mackerras, Colin, *China's Minorities: Integration and Modernization in the Twentieth Century*. Hong Kong: Oxford University Press, 1994.

McKean, Margaret, "Management of Traditional Common Lands in Japan." In: *Common Property Resource Management*. Proceedings of a Conference prepared by the Panel on Common Property Resource Management, Board on Science and Technology for International Development, Office of International Affairs, National Research Council. Washington D.C.: National Academy Press, 1986.

Mearns, Robin, 1993. "Territoriality and Land Tenure among Mongolian Pastoralists: Variation, Continuity and Change." In: *Nomadic Peoples*, no. 33, pp. 73–103.

———, 1996. "Community, Collective Action and Common Grazing: The Case of Post-Socialist Mongolia." In: *The Journal for Development Studies*, vol. 32, no. 3, February 1996, pp. 283–325.

NHZGB. Ningxia Huizu zizhiqu gaikuang bianxiezu, ed., *Ningxia Huizu zizhiqu gaikuang* (An Overview of Ningxia Hui Autonomous Region). Yinchuan: Ningxia renmin chubanshe, 1986.

NHZN. Ningxia Huizu zizhiqu nongyeting, ed., "Ningxia Huizu zizhiqu Yanchixian caoyuan diaocha baogao." In: Xumu shouyi xuehui, ed., *1963 Huilun wenji* (Abstracts of the Discussion Meeting of 1963). Internal Document, Xumu shouyi xuehui, 1964.

NHZT. Ningxia Huizu zizhiqu tongjiju, ed., *Ningxia Huizu zizhiqu guomin jingji tongji ziliao: 1949–1965* (Statistics of the National Economy of the Ningxia Hui Autonomous Region: 1949–1965). Classified Material, 1966.

Ningxia Huizu zizhiqu renmin daibiao dahui changwu weiyuanhui, "Ningxia Huizu zizhiqu caoyuan guanli tiaoli" (Rules and Regulations of Rangeland Management of the Ningxia Hui Autonomous Region). In: *Ningxia Daily*, 29 December 1994, p. 3.

Ningxia Huizu zizhiqu Yanchixian renmin zhengfu, ed., *"Ba wu" zongti guihua baogao —1991–1995: Ningxia Yanchixian shamohua tudi zonghe zhili gongcheng* ("Five Eight" Comprehensive Report of Regulations and Plans—1991–1995: Integrated Project for Soil Management against Desertification in Yanchi County, Ningxia), 1991.

Ningxia tongji nianjian (Ningxia Statistical Yearbook). Yinchuan, 1990.

Ningxiasheng dizhengju, ed., *Ningxia shinian kenwu jihuashu* (The Ten-Year Plan for Land Reclamation in Ningxia), 1942. Revised edition of the 1939 version.

Oakerson, Ronald J., "Analyzing the Commons: A Framework." In: Bromley, David W., ed., 1992.

Oi, Jean C., *State and Peasant in Contemporary China: The Political Economy of Village Government.* Berkeley: University of California Press, 1992.

Ostrom, Elinor, "The Rudiments of a Theory of the Origins, Survival, and Performance of Common-Property Institutions." In: Bromley, David W., ed., 1992.

Pang Jian, "Rural Income and Agricultural Marketing in Ningxia." In: Shen Changjiang and Jörg Steinbach, eds., 1993.

Potkanski, Tomasz, "Decollectivisation of the Mongolian Pastoral Economy (1991–92): Some Economic and Social Consequences." In: *Nomadic Peoples*, no. 33, 1993, pp. 123–135.

Ross, Lester, "Obligatory Tree Planting: The Role of Campaigns in Policy Implementation in Post-Mao China." In: Lampton, David, *Policy Implementation in Post-Mao China.* Berkeley: University of California Press, 1987.

Shen Changjiang and Jörg Steinbach, eds., *Improvement of Living Conditions in Rural Ningxia.* Berlin: Duncker & Humblot, 1993.

Shue, Vivienne, "Emerging State-Society Relations in Rural China." In: Delman, Jürgen; Christiansen, Fleming; and Östergaard, Clemens S., eds., *Remaking Peasant China.* Aarhus: Aarhus University Press, 1990.

Smil, Vaclav, "Land Degradation in China: An Ancient Problem Getting Worse." In: Blaikie, Piers, and Harold Brookfield, *Land Degradation and Society.* London: Methuen, 1987.

———, *China's Environmental Crisis: An Inquiry into the Limits of National Development.* Armonk, N.Y.: M.E. Sharpe, 1993.

Sun Minghe, "Huangse Yuhuo" (Yellow Temptation). In: *Science and Technology Daily*, 13 October 1993, pp. 1–4.

Van de Laar, Aart, *A Framework for the Analysis of Common Pool Natural Resources.* Institute of Social Studies, Working Paper No. 77, The Hague, 1990.

Wade, Robert, "The Management of Common Property Resources: Collective Action as an Alternative to Privatisation or State Regulation." In: *Cambridge Journal of Economics*, 1987, no. 11, pp. 95–106.

Wang Yiming, and Niu Hui'en, "Suspending Village: A Model of New Developed Area in Ningxia of China." In: *Journal of Arid Land Resources and Environment*, vol. 7, nos. 3–4, 1993.

Wang Yuesheng, *Guyuan diquzhi xumu ziliao changbian* (Guyuan Local Gazetteer, Essay on Animal Husbandry). Guyuan: Guyuan diqu difangzhi bangongshi, November 1987.

White, Gordon, *Riding the Tiger: The Politics of Economic Reform in Post-Mao China.* London: MacMillan, 1993.

Wu Zhongli, and Liu Qinbin, *Ningxia tongshi* (A History of Ningxia), vol. II. Yinchuan: Ningxia renmin chubanshe, 1993.

Yang Hongchun, "Ningxia Huizu zizhiqu caodi ruogan tedian ji qi liyong"(Some Special Traits of Grassland in Ningxia Hui Autonomous Region and Its Utilization). In: Xumu shouyi xuehui, ed., *1963 Huilun wenji* (Abstracts of the Discussion Meeting of 1963), Internal Document, 1964.

YXBWB. Yanchi xianzhi bianzuan weiyuanhui bangongshi, ed., *Yanchi xianzhi* (Local Gazetteer of Yanchi County), vol. III. Yanchi: Yanchi difangzhi bangongshi, 1983.

ZCX. Zhongguo caoyuan xuehui, ed., *The Rangeland Law of the People's Republic of China.* Zhongguo caoyuan xuehui, 1985.

Zhang Bo, *Xibei nongmushi* (A History of Agriculture and Animal Husbandry in the Northwest). Xi'an: Shaanxi kexue jishu chubanshe, 1989.

Zhang Guangzu, ed., *Yanchi xianzhi* (Local Gazetteer of Yanchi County). Yinchuan: Ningxia renmin chubanshe, 1986.

Zhang Xianzhu, ed., *Minguo Guyuan xianzhi* (Local Gazetteer of Guyuan during the Republic), vol. I. Yinchuan: Ningxia renmin chubanshe, 1991.

ZKNNZK. Zhongguo kexueyuan Neimeng Ningxia zonghe kaochadui, ed., *Ningxia shanqu wuxian: Hanzuo zhongzhiye de fazhan wenti* (Five Counties in the Mountainous Region of Ningxia: Development Problems of Dry Farming). Internal Document, 1963a.

————, ed., *Ningxia Huizu zizhiqu shengchanli fazhan yuanjing* (Perspectives for the Development of the Productivity of Ningxia Hui Autonomous Region). Internal Document, 1963b.

Part III

Political and Social Organization

9

Village Committees

The Basis for China's Democratization

Wang Zhenyao

The village committees in China are self-governing bodies at the basic level. Although they execute certain administrative functions, their members are rural commoners, not government officials. In 1993, there were 1,008,082 village committees, with a total membership of 4,281,748. Their main tasks were to develop public services and handle various administrative affairs within the villages. Article 111 of the Constitution of the People's Republic of China promulgated in 1982 stipulated that the chairman, vice-chairman and members of the neighbourhood committees and village committees should be elected by the local residents. The Organic Law on the Village Committees of the People's Republic of China (for trial implementation) issued on November 24, 1987, set forth that the chairman, vice-chairman and member(s) of the village committees (*cunmin weiyuanhui*) should be elected directly by the villagers for a term of three years. The trial law was a compromise between those who argued for greater village autonomy and those who felt that more guidance and supervision by the *xiang* authorities or CCP was needed (O'Brien 1994). A definitive version of the law has been under consideration for several years now, but not yet passed.

Direct elections of the village committees in mainland China started in 1988. The system of direct election of leaders by the villagers was without precedent in the history of Chinese politics, and should be seen as an important product of the rural economic reforms since 1978.

In the process of establishment and consolidation of the village committees, the villagers' representative assembly (*cunmin daibiao huiyi*, hereafter also called VRA) was spontaneously created in some places after 1984. Its purpose was to discuss matters and decide on important village affairs in a democratic way. The VRAs were a check on the 'executive' villagers' committees, and were promoted by the Ministry of Civil Affairs even if they were not mentioned in the

Organic Law. By 1994, they had been established in more than half of all villages. With the promotion of the direct elections of village committees and the establishment of the villagers' representative assemblies, there has been considerable progress in democratization in rural China. This, in turn, has laid a foundation for democratization throughout China.

I. Background: Fundamental Changes in the Rural Economic and Political Relationships

The direct election of the village committee members in the rural areas and the establishment of the villagers' representative assembly system had a long historical background. Most importantly, however, it has been rural economic reform that has thoroughly changed the rural economic, social and political relationships at the basic level.

In the first place, the household contract responsibility system with remuneration linked to output has led to profound changes in the rural economic system, and the resulting new pattern of economic relationships provided a fitting economic basis for the direct election of the village committees. The abolition of the people's commune system and the practice of the household contract responsibility system had three economic effects. It increased individual wealth, village economic complexity, and village control over resources.

The farmers' enthusiasm about production was stimulated to such a degree that the problem of inadequate food and clothing in the rural areas was basically solved. The economy along the coastal regions became quite developed. Everywhere, farmers built new homes, and increased their bank savings. Diets in North China changed from coarse grains such as maize, millet and sorghum to fine grains such as wheat and rice. The increased wealth of the farmers has enhanced their capacity for economic autonomy.

The household contract responsibility system has produced new ownership relations. Farmers now manage their own farms. The number of self-employed rural craftsmen, traders and entrepreneurs has increased greatly, resulting in an expansive private economy. But the collective village economy has rapidly developed as well. Finally, fully foreign-owned enterprises and joint ventures have appeared in many places. This co-existence of many forms of ownership and the competition among them made for very complex relationships between economic interests, and this has posed the need for a new mechanism for adjustment of various economic interests.

The household contract responsibility system has changed the pattern of distribution in the rural areas. Farmers and other rural residents have gained much more power over distribution of rural resources. In the past, the collective controlled the right of distribution, and farmers waited for the village collective and the government to distribute their share to them at the end of each year. At present, however, the government and collective levy taxes and charges; the money collected for the state is partly retained for use by the village collective. There is a direct confrontation between the interests of the farmers and the interests of the collective and the state. This kind of interest relationship has two results: (a) in most rural areas the collectives depend on the financial resources and labor of the farmers to build and repair public facilities such as roads and schools. Their village and township enterprises are not capable to shoulder these burdens; and (b) farmers are more concerned than before about the transparency of village affairs and village finance, since these sums are now collected from the farmers; it is only natural that they are very concerned about their proper use.

In the second place, since 1978, great changes have taken place in the rural social structure. Farmers now live in a more open atmosphere. A new generation of rural youth has grown up, and their social values tend to differ from the traditional values. The migration of farmers into big cities has led to a much greater mobility of rural laborers. This has, in turn, created a division of labor in the country. Rural residents may be divided into six social groups, based on the criteria of employment:

a. agricultural laborers engaged in crop cultivation and animal husbandry;
b. rural workers engaged in secondary and tertiary industries in village collective enterprises;
c. workers employed by private enterprises;
d. self-employed craftsmen and businessmen;
e. entrepreneurs of private enterprises (with more than 8 employees);
f. managers and staff in rural social and collective organizations.

To these may be added the rural teachers, and industrialists, and businessmen working in places other than their home towns. There are substantial social differences among these groups, which gives rise to conflicts of interest. Generally, agricultural laborers, self-employed craftsmen and businessmen are more concerned about the village committee's activities. They want to know why the village committee collects certain taxes, and how the proceeds are spent on village affairs. The entrepreneurs of private enterprises, and the managers and staff in rural organizations give much concern to the village committee's position. These people are the rural elite. They participate in the political campaigns in the village. Only democratic procedures carry enough authority to be able to balance the relationships among the different social groups.

In the third place, since 1978, the development of state politics and rural politics has led to fundamental changes in the rural political structure. These provided the political basis for the direct elections of the village committees in the rural areas. The state has entered into a period of strengthening democracy and the legal system. The household contract responsibility system gave farmers freedom. In 1984, the negative labels were lifted from the last 79,000 out of a previous twenty million so-called "four bad elements" (landlords, rich peasants, counter-revolutionaries and bad elements), so that the class status of all of them had changed. This symbolized the end of the political status system which had existed since the 1950 Land Reform. A younger generation of village heads has now come to the fore, and class struggle is no longer used as a means of enforcing social change upon the villages. All these changes have transformed the rural political relationships in a fundamental way. The new political relationships demand a direct and equal confrontation between the ideas and opinions of the villagers in the management of village affairs.

In the fourth place, the many problems which have emerged in rural society, such as social security and conflicts between village heads and farmers, have resulted in a build-up of social tensions. These tensions can only be relieved through democratic means, by mobilizing farmers to participate directly in management at the basic level. Some of the main social problems noted in rural areas are: the deterioration of social security in some areas; abuse of power by village heads; and messy financial management. Sometimes, problems between the village heads and farmers become so serious that the villagers appeal to the higher authorities to demand that justice be done. Such social problems are difficult to solve effectively by the government officials and village heads alone.

All these conflicts are the concern of the village committees because in the villages, only the village committee combines administrative duties with partial autonomy, so that it can play an intermediary role. According to the Organic Law, village committees should manage village land and collective property (art. 4), take care of public welfare, mediate disputes, and maintain public security (art. 2). At the same time, they are expected to support and make propaganda for government policies (such as birth control and education) (art. 5) and township government work (such as taxation) (art. 3). The fact that village committees' leaders must be elected by the villagers means that the rural elite can only obtain such a position if they gain the support from a majority of the villagers. The village committees have actually become the foundation of China's democratization.

II. The Progress of the Election of the Village Committees

The establishment of a sophisticated system of direct elections in the rural areas has the important objective of providing a system of self-government with roots in the daily life of the farmers. It is a sophisticated and gigantic social project which requires great effort. Neither the officials of the departments of civil affairs, which are in charge of local elections, nor the farmers previously had any experience in these matters. What is more, differences in social problems, and different attitudes and perceptions of the officials concerned have resulted in an uneven situation in regard to the direct election of village committees. Provincial and local political support for the process has varied. At the end of 1995, elections of village committees had been held in 30 provinces, autonomous regions and municipalities only once, but twice in 20 of them. In Fujian, Heilongjiang, Jilin, Liaoning and Sichuan Provinces, elections of village committees have already been held three times.

The progress of village committee elections in the rural areas of China can be divided into three stages. The first stage was from 1988 to 1989, during which trial implementation and elections in limited places were conducted. In the people's commune period, the system of electing commune members' representatives was required in the production brigades. In 1984, after village committees had been set up in many rural areas, local regulations about their organization were formulated in Beijing, Tianjin, Hebei, Inner Mongolia, Heilongjiang, Tibet, and Xinjiang, stipulating that they be elected directly. Elections were actually held in some places, e.g., Shandong and Sichuan. However, taking the country as a whole, elections of the village committees were not standard before 1988. In most places, village heads were appointed by township leaders instead of elected by the farmers.

In 1988, the provincial governments began to arrange for the elections of the village committees in accordance with the new trial law. Most took three measures: conducting trial implementation in order to gather experience; formulating provincial regulations for the implementation of the Organic Law on the Village Committees; and launching elections. In 1988, trial implementations were conducted in 1,093 counties throughout the country. In Hunan Province, the first trial implementation was conducted in 343 villages of 28 townships in March. A few months later, a second trial implementation was launched in over 200 townships. In Shandong and Hunan Provinces, detailed implementation plans were worked out. The main subjects of the trial implementation included the following:

a. publication and study of the relevant laws, in order to improve the villagers' understanding of the elections;

b. conduct of the elections of the village committees;

c. establishment of the system of the villagers' representative assembly;

d. formulation of village charters and rules for the activities of the village committees; and

e. training the members of the village committees.

In 1988, the Standing Committees of the Provincial People's Congresses of Fujian and Zhejiang approved their respective implementation methods of the organic law, and made specific regulations about the election system of the village committees. Similar implementation methods were formulated in Gansu, Guizhou, Hunan and Hubei the year after.

On the basis of trial implementations, formal elections of the village committees were conducted on a large scale in about half China's provinces in the second half of 1988 and 1989: by the end of the year, they had been completed in Liaoning, Fujian, Zhejiang, Jilin, Guizhou, Beijing, and Sichuan, and were still going on in Hunan, Hubei, Shandong, Tianjin, Jiangsu, Gansu, and Ningxia. In Liaoning Province, elections by competitive campaigning of the chairmen of the village committees were conducted in the nine counties (cities and districts) of Tieling city at the end of 1988, and the experiences gained were disseminated throughout the province in the spring of 1989.

It should be pointed out that in spite of many good practices found in the elections of the first-term village committees in many places since 1988, no specifically standardized election rules were formulated, due to inadequate experience on the part of the departments of civil affairs. In some places, local officials were worried that the elections might give rise to chaos and feuding between clans and factions in the rural areas. Therefore, they were not supportive of the elections. As a result, in many places elections were held just for show, with candidates frequently being appointed by town and township officials. Also, some farmers were pessimistic about the elections, believing that things would remain the same whether elections were held or not. Faced with these and other difficulties, the department of the Ministry of Civil Affairs which was in charge of the elections adopted the principle of first popularizing the elections on a larger scale, and improving the quality of the elections only later, i.e. the principle of "learning by doing." It required that elections of the village committees should be conducted throughout the country, and that their experiences would be summed up subsequently.

It is interesting to note that in the second half of 1989, there was a debate within the Communist Party whether or not to continue to hold direct elections of the village committees. In some places officials adopted a wait-and-see attitude. In this debate, senior officials such as the NPC Standing Committee Chairman Peng Zhen (who had promoted the village committees in their early phase) and Bo Yibo lent their full support to the development of democracy in the rural areas (White 1992).

The second stage was from 1990 to 1992 when the popularization of village self-government, partly through demonstration activities, was combined with a launching of elections of village committees throughout the country. The Ministry of Civil Affairs devised a policy of further spreading the elections on the one hand and improving their quality on the other, on the basis of a summing-up of local experiences. At the end of 1990, it decided to set up Laixi county in Shandong Province as a national demonstration county of village self-government. In addition, it required (backed up by Central Committee Document No. 19) that demonstration units be set up in each township, county, prefecture, and province as models for popularization of the elections of the village committees and establishment of the system of villages' representative assemblies. Experiences were summed up at the National Conference on the Demonstration of Village Self-government. From 1991 to 1992, the Ministry of Civil Affairs ran a three-term training class on the demonstration of village self-government which was attended by more than 500 officials in charge of the elections of the village committees, in order to achieve a standardisation of electoral procedures.

On the local level, over 30,000 people from all over the country visited Laixi county to observe the practice of democracy. This greatly encouraged rural villagers' participation. In 1990, the elections of the village committees were conducted together with the elections of the deputies to the County and Township People's Congresses in Qinghai, Hebei, Shandong, Guangxi, Ningxia, Xinjiang, Sichuan, Shanxi, and Shanghai. By the end of 1992, direct elections of the village committees had been held in almost all rural areas in China including Tibet; the only exception being Jiangxi Province, where (for reasons unknown) 30 percent of all villages never elected village committees. In every province, a certain percentage of so-called "paralyzed" villages remained, with a very low level or complete absence of village organization.

In 1991, the three-year term of the village committees elected in some provinces in 1988 expired, and the election of the second-term village committees began. The Jiangsu Provincial People's Congress ruled that the village committees should have multi-candidate elections. From 1990 to 1992, the Standing Committees of the People's Congresses of the following provinces formulated implementation methods: Hebei, Heilongjiang, Liaoning, Qinghai, Shaanxi, Tianjin, Shanxi, Sichuan, Jilin, Xinjiang, Ningxia, Shandong, Henan, Inner Mongolia and Anhui. Thus, local laws and regulations on the election of the village committees were worked out for most of the places in China.

During the first elections, competition for posts in the village committees was limited. In the elections of the second-term village committees farmers began to realize the importance of the elections, and different factions in the villages began campaigning to collect votes. In Fanshen village (Qiaotou township, Benxi city in Liaoning Province), the standing chairman of the village committee, Mr. Huang Xinran, did not want to campaign for himself, while the opposing faction made public speeches to gain more votes, so that Huang lost the election. Afterwards, he complained to the local department of civil affairs that pooling votes was an "unhealthy phenomenon." He began to have regrets when he was told that campaigning was natural in the election system, and declared that he would try again in the next election.

In some places, several elections had to be held due to the fierce competition. Some villages adopted moving ballot boxes. The opponents, however, were concerned that irregularities might occur with those boxes, so they sent several poll-watchers to follow them closely. At the end of the elections of the second-term village committees, many officials remarked that one could never be too careful about village committee elections, because farmers attached a far greater importance to them than to the election of deputies to the township and county people's congresses.

In spite of the progress in the second-term elections, there were several problems in regard to specific electoral procedures. For example, provinces and counties did not hold village elections at the same moment; within one province, counties held village elections in different years. No use was made of secret voting booths. Such technical questions had to be solved in order to guarantee the fairness of elections.

The third stage was from 1993 to 1996. In this period, the emphasis has been on the standardization of the electoral process and the improvement of the quality of the elections. By 1993, elections of the village committees had been held universally throughout the country. The guidelines for the elections shifted from making sure they were held to standardization of the electoral process and improvement of the quality of the elections. In summer, the Ministry of Civil Affairs held "the International Seminar on the Election System of the Village Committees in China," which was attended by experts and scholars from China and abroad, as well as by Chinese officials in charge of the local elections. Its theme was the perfection of the election system of the village committees. At the seminar, the issue of allowing household representatives to vote on behalf of their members, such as practised in Fujian Province, was addressed and generally disapproved of. Inspired by this, the officials from Fujian Province formulated new "Methods for the Election of the Village Committees in Fujian Province" in September 1993, which abolished the stipulations that allowed household representatives to vote for their household.

In May 1994, the International Republican Institute from the U.S. sent a mission to Fujian to observe the election of village committees. The mission made some valuable suggestions, such as how to arrange secret voting booths, how to seal the ballot boxes, etc. In August, the Ministry of Civil Affairs held an "International Seminar on the System of the Villages' Representative Assembly," which was again attended by Chinese and foreign experts and officials.

As far as the progress of the local elections is concerned, in 1993, second-term elections of village committees were held in Shanxi, Xinjiang, Hunan and Shanghai. In 1994 and 1995, third-term elections were conducted in Fujian, and second-term elections in several other provinces. The elections held in 1994 have been a rather exciting political process. In Hebei Province, an increasing number of villages had built up representative assemblies in previous elections, providing villagers with more opportunities to participate in the management of village affairs. The farmers had become gradually acquainted with democratic procedures, and showed enthusiasm for participation in the election. In addition, there were more cases of farmers' appeals for justice to the higher authorities. In May 1994, dozens of farmers from a village in Rongchen county in Hebei appealed to the Ministry of Civil Affairs for help in regard to problems encountered in the village committee election. The event was reported in the newspapers and on TV, and attracted wide public attention.

We may conclude that considerable progress has been made since 1988. The elections of the village committees have become training classes for villagers and Chinese officials in the practice of basic-level democracy.

III. Basic Modes and Results of the Elections

The election of the village committees is conducted at different paces in different parts of the country, and the modes of elections adopted are not uniform. Generally speaking, three main methods have been adopted, namely, campaigning, multi-candidate for one post, and semi-multi-candidate for one post. Below, we give some examples of each.

Election by Campaigning

In northeast China, election on the basis of campaigning is called *haixuan* "sea-campaigning," meaning completely free and open elections. In the elections held in 1988, it was practised mostly in Liaoning Province. In recent years, in addition to the counties where election by campaigning has been expressly allowed, the practice has also been adopted in some other places such as Xinzheng county of Henan Province, Qinggang county of Heilongjiang Province, and Lishu county of Jilin Province. According to statistics, campaigning is conducted in about 30 percent of all villages where village committees are elected. In the absence of unified standards for voting, provincial governments can make local electoral regulations. In Lishu county, every adult resident of the village is handed a blank sheet of paper on which he or she can secretly nominate any person for office. The posted results give a good idea of who the village's natural leaders are and how unpopular the incumbents might be. Secret elections were held whereby voters dropped their ballot slips into cardboard boxes in a secret voting booth. In the elections of 1993, the Shandong provincial government made a uniform requirement about the ballots, namely, that only the names of the candidates be printed on the ballots, without mentioning their intended specific posts in the committee, in order to guarantee that there would be campaigning and manipulation of the election would be avoided. If a voter felt that a given candidate would be an ideal chairman, he could draw a circle under the post "CHAIRMAN" behind the candidate's name. As a result, there was a fierce campaign among the candidates aspiring to the post of chairman.

The reasons for the campaigning are interesting to note. Let us take the case of Chen Jinman. When campaigning first appeared in the experimental district of Nanping city of Fujian Province at the end of 1988, more than 30 villagers from Tiantou village of Luxia township jointly recommended five people headed by Mr. Chen Jinman and Luo Shuicai as members of the village committee. In their open letter to the Leading Group for the Elections, they wrote: "the style and manner of the village heads in conducting their work have been intolerable. We are faced with serious problems. Reform has brought hope to our village. Here comes the election of the village committee. In order to change the situation in our village, we solemnly recommend five people including Mr. Chen Jinman to form the village committee." In the meantime, the five nominees drew up a three-year plan and posted it on the door of the village office building, calling for the approval and support of the local farmers. Also, they expressed their willingness to deposit 8,000 *yuan* as a pledge (3,000 *yuan* for the chairman, 2,000 *yuan* for the vice-chairman, and 1,000 *yuan* for each of the committee members). The event caused a stir in Luxia township. Some people disapproved, holding that this was the wrong kind of democracy and would result in chaos. Township officials were concerned, too. One of them said, "if we tolerate such things and let anyone who wants to be the village head succeed in his plan, how can we guarantee the completion of obligations to the state?" They wanted these events to be brought under control immediately. Faced with this situation, the city government first decided to conduct investigations. Finally, the Chinese Communist Party Committee, the municipal government, and the People's Congress of Nanping city all came to the same conclusions, namely that

a. the practice of the 30 villagers was natural and in full conformity with the gist of the Organic Law on the Village Committees;
b. the practice showed the farmers' concern about the future of the village and their sense of participation in the management of village affairs, which was precisely what the publicity activities had encouraged;
c. the election of village heads through competitive campaigns was helpful in finding able hands and promoted the development of basic-level democracy.

Therefore, the Nanping municipal government decided to seize this opportunity and allow the villagers to elect the village heads through election by competitive campaigning. As soon as the primary candidates were announced, the people who had nominated the five candidates took their three-year plan to each family and told them about the candidates, in the hope of winning their support. When the election was held, all five candidates recommended by the villagers won the election. Mr. Chen Jinman won 564 or 78 percent of the registered votes and became the chairman of the village committee. The Nanping municipal government summed up the positive experience of Tiantou village and disseminated it throughout the city's villages.

The candidates were willing to give financial pledges to the township government because this was the first time that a competitive campaign was conducted, and the candidates wanted to persuade the township officials. There was nothing about the practice in the laws or regulations, and in the second-term election, it had disappeared.

Campaigning made its first appearance in the nine counties and districts of Tieling city of Liaoning Province. In early 1988, in Hujia village of Tiefa city of Tieling, a Mr. Li Chunbao, supported by some farmers, wrote a letter to the municipal government in which he recommended himself as the chairman of the village committee. He gave his own family property of over 10,000 *yuan* as a pledge. The officials of Tiefa city agreed to make the village a test site for competitive campaigning. Soon, Kaiyuan city, which is also part of Tieling city, met with problems when the city government designated some quotas of their three-year plan to the villages. These quotas included economic development targets, social welfare, and promotion of education, etc. Quite a number of village heads were reluctant to accept the imposed quotas, claiming that they were much too difficult to be fulfilled. Thereupon, the municipal government of Kaiyuan city decided to allow competitive campaigning in the elections. As a result, the village heads elected through public campaigning carried out the various targets and quotas smoothly. Noting that the elections by public campaigning in Tiefa and Kaiyuan helped to promote the rural economy in this way, the Chinese Communist Party Committee and municipal officials of Tieling city decided to conduct elections through public campaigning in all rural areas.

In the election of the village committee held in Shenliu village of Linfen city, Shanxi Province in 1990, Mr. Wang Chengjiang, a self-employed businessman, asked the township heads if he could run in the election and compete with the current chairman of the village for the latter's post, and was given a positive reply. Encouraged by this, Mr. Wang Chengjiang gave a speech on how to run the village at a public meeting, and won the election by a majority vote.

The above examples show that two conditions are required for elections to be held through public campaigning, namely pressure or a request from the villagers, and the support of enlightened officials and their strict organization. In some cases, election by public campaigning was not practised in spite of farmers' requests, because of a lack of support from local leaders.

The modalities of public campaigning by villagers are rather strict. In Tieling, the candidate must register himself with the Leading Group for the Elections of the village first, and prepare an outline of how he will run the village, which is then communicated to the farmers. In Qinggang county in Heilongjiang and Lishu county in Jilin, a primary election round for the candidates is held, and those who win the primary must submit a plan of how they intend to run the village. In Nanping city in Fujian Province, the campaign speeches made by the candidates are given marks by the villagers, and those receiving the highest marks become the regular candidates. All contenders who want to participate in the campaign must prepare an outline of their policy plans first, and deliver it at a town meeting. During this process, the farmers watch the candidates closely, and the latter are not permitted to hear what other candidates are saying at the meeting. The candidates are taken to the town meeting in turn. There is no debate among the candidates. The villagers, having learned the views of each candidate, are free to ask the candidates about their policy plans.

As the ballot allows voters to propose candidates on their own initiative, open or covert competition before the election frequently occurs. For instance, in the 1994 election of the village committee held in Shexing village in Longyan city, Fujian, there was no apparent campaigning. An entrepreneur, Mr. Yang Zilie, organized a large number of women to go from door to door to tell people about his plans to lead the village. In this way he won the election and became chairman of the village committee, even without having been an official candidate. Many people who have launched election campaigns are reluctant to tell others they have campaigned at all, because there is no concept of campaigning in traditional Chinese culture and people are shy to admit that they want to become officials. As a matter of fact, the competition was fierce. Some people in Fujian said that when you heard the dogs in the village barking ferociously you knew that the campaigning had reached the point of highest intensity, with the candidates going from door to door collecting votes just before the election.

Election through campaigning is being adopted as an effective method of election in more and more rural areas. It is playing an important role in the perfection of the basic-level elections.

Multi-Candidate Election

Multi-candidate election is widely adopted in the election of the village committees in the rural areas. It means that voters can choose between more candidates than the number required to fill the positions of chairman, vice-chairman, and members of the village committee. In a multi-candidate election, the key lies in the determination of candidates. Four ways of nominating official candidates are in use in various parts of the country:

  a. nomination by more than ten registered voters;
  b. nomination by a village group;
  c. self-recommendation; and
  d. recommendation by the village Party branch.

However, the method of recommendation by the village Party branch is rarely used, in spite of the fact that well over one half of all candidates are Party members. For example, when the village Party branch in Rongcheng county of Hebei Province recommended candidates in some villages, the farmers appealed to the central government, arguing that the village Party branch should not recommend candidates because it enjoys the leading position. Otherwise, it would be a limited election instead of a free election. In order to avoid any direct conflicts between the village Party branch and farmers, nomination of candidates should best be undertaken by ten or more registered voters.

In Fujian Province, the official candidates are selected by the villagers' representative assemblies. In some places, the official candidates are ranked according to the number of voters who have nominated them. In Zhumadian prefecture in Henan, the official candidates are determined only after three rounds of discussions. Candidates are nominated by the villagers first, and then announced by the Village Election Leading Group according to the number of voters who have nominated the candidate. Then the villagers have to discuss the candidates again and make their recommendations. In some places, official candidates are selected through a primary election, while in other places, this is done through discussion and negotiations.

In Kengdong village of Linyi city, Shanxi, the former chairman and two members of the village committee all lost the election. The three newly elected people who replaced them all are self-employed business people, who are well versed in developing the village economy. In multi-candidate elections, because the existing village heads are usually from large clans or have a wide network of relationships, villagers sometimes nominate them as candidates out of fear of hurting their feelings, but then do not vote for them in the elections. According to a popular joke, a village head who had not done a very good job went around the village canvassing for votes. All people promised to vote for him. Then in the election he only got one vote. Many of his friends and relatives told him that it was their vote, but he knew that it was the vote he had cast himself. According to nation-wide statistics, in multi-candidate elections about 10 percent of the village heads have been voted out.

Quasi- Multi-Candidate Election

This method of election means that there is only one candidate for the post of chairman of the village committee, but more candidates than positions for the vice-chairman and members. The method is used in places where the authorities fear that the competition for the chairman of the village committee will be too fierce, or that the incumbent chairman might lose the election. In places which adopt this method, the election is generally not conducted well.

Uniform statistics about the result of the elections of the village committee are not available on a national scale. There are many regional differences. In terms of re-elections, approximately 20 percent of the village heads lose the elections in most places. In Shandong Province, 20 percent of the chairmen and 26 percent of the members of the village committees were not voted out in the 1993 elections. In the 1988 election of village committees in Qinggang county in Heilongjiang, 159 former chairmen of the village committees were reelected, or 71 percent, while 66 people or 29 percent were newly elected as chairmen. Three years later, 87 percent of the chairmen were elected for another term of office. Because personal abilities are much stressed in the elections, generally more than 10 percent of the elected chairmen of village committees are self-employed business people.

By 1994, villagers' representative assemblies had been established in more than half of all villages. Their coverage and sizes differ; in Liaoning, for example, there are 537,855 villagers' representatives, with an average of 34 per village, and in 1993, these assemblies called a total of 79,655 meetings, or an average of five per village. In Shandong, villagers' representative assemblies have been established in 74,700 or 85 percent of all villages, with a total of 2,785,199 villagers' representatives. In Jiangsu, there are 1,180,662 villagers' representatives, with an average of 33 for each village. In Hubei, there are villagers' representative assemblies in 15,692 villages, accounting for 57 percent of the total number of village committees. In Sichuan, villagers' representative assemblies are found in 40 percent of all villages, but this is 90 percent of the 17,622 villages with a village committee. Such figures show that although precise data on VRAs and village committees are recorded, they are not reported in a uniform way.

As for Communist Party affiliation, we have scattered local data. In Shandong, altogether 21,398, or one-quarter, of the 85,107 chairmen of the village committees are *not* Chinese Communist Party members. In Fujian, CCP members account for 51 percent of the 11,913 chairmen of the village committees. In Jiangsu, out of a total of 174,691 village committee members, 100,934 or 58 percent are CCP members. Based on these statistics, one may estimate CCP membership to range from 50 to 70 percent of the newly elected chairmen and members of the village committees. The percentage varies between places. In the absence of comprehensive research one can only speculate about the reasons for this: a high percentage of CCP membership among the village elite, a continued relevance of traditional political relations, the administrative experience of CCP members, and CCP block voting are possibilities which come to mind.

As for age, the average age of the elected members of the village committees in Fujian was 39 years. Of the 338,412 members of the village committees in Shandong, 213,460 were over 35 years old. The average age of the village committee members in Xinjiang was 38 years. Therefore, we may conclude that most of the village committee members are around 40 years old. In terms of education, members of the village committees with more than nine years of education accounted for 79 percent in Beijing, 78 percent in Liaoning, 77 percent in Fujian, 73 percent in Sichuan, but only 64 percent in Hunan and a mere 48 percent in Guangxi. As might be expected, the elections have already made a great difference for the authority of the new cadres in the local area. Although reportedly their attitude towards higher levels still does not give rise to any problems, they do give more notice to the opinions of the villagers.

In fact, the elections have hatched a new elite with firm roots in local society, which may be able to play an active role in the democratization of Chinese society. The methods of election of village committees show the progress of basic-level elections during the past decade. Together with a further reform of the rural economic system, a new political system—the system of democratic self-government—is being established in the rural areas of China.

IV. The Establishment and Development of the Villagers' Representative Assembly System

Since 1984, villagers' representative assemblies (VRAs) have been called spontaneously by farmers in Liaoning, Hebei and elsewhere to discuss important village affairs and solve complicated village problems. The system has increasingly been consolidated and exerts a growing influence in rural political life. The organizational structure of the VRA varies throughout the country. Generally speaking, one representative is elected from every group of ten to twenty households, with an average of 30 to 60 villagers' representatives for each village. In some places, the villagers' representatives have divided themselves into different working groups in charge of financial supervision, social welfare, ethical progress, rural planning, economic development, and civil conciliation and public security, for discussions about village affairs. The villagers' representative assembly is held once every two or three months, and discusses the major affairs of the village.

The subjects for discussion at the VRA may be listed as follows:

1) preparation of the annual industrial and agricultural production plans and the major measures for implementation;
2) adjustment of the production responsibility system in various forms and the signing of the various kinds of economic contracts;
3) drawing up the village charter;
4) financial management, including village annual revenue and expenditure, budgeting and final accounts; this may include approval of expenditures of over 500 *yuan* for non-productive purposes and expenditures of over 3,000 *yuan* for productive purposes;
5) construction and expansion of industrial and sideline production projects, water conservancy projects and various public welfare facilities;
6) collection, arrangement and use of taxes and levies for the state and/or retained for village use, village levies, and obligatory labor (or funds);
7) management and use of public and collective resources such as machinery, power, and water, as well as distribution and supply of means of production;
8) actual implementation of birth control programs;
9) formulation of village construction plans and the arrangement of household residential areas;
10) implementation of the allocation, increase, reduction or exemption of agricultural taxes;
11) methods of distribution of relief funds and materials;
12) all other important affairs which relate to the interests of the villagers.

As can be seen from the above official list, the VRA discusses and decides on all issues which fall within the sphere of the administrative village (*xingzhengcun*).

The villagers' representative assemblies have succeeded in playing an important role. To give two examples: in Hanjiazhuang village of Zhengding county in Hebei, different factions had fought with each other for a long time. The village was so poor that the village heads felt ashamed whenever they met their fellow-farmers. More than a hundred problems involving more than 200 households were unsolved. Across the county, the village was considered a "hardnut case." In 1978, a villagers' representative assembly was set up. Their representatives met to discuss village affairs and at this first meeting reached an unexpectedly unanimous decision: 20,000 yuan was to be collected from each family to build a running water system. The exciting thing, which was previously totally unimaginable, was that the funds were raised in a matter of days; the representatives themselves actually went to each family to collect the funds. The other remaining problems were also rapidly solved. In Yihe township of Pengshan county, Sichuan, the money collected for the state but partly retained for village use usually took several months to collect. Some villagers believed that village officials embezzled part of the funds, and therefore had not paid the taxes for several years. In 1993, this problem was addressed at the VRA, which gave full accounts of all items of expenditure; as a result of this openness, the taxes were fully collected within a fortnight. It is also worth noting that in 1993, this township decided to build a high quality, 4.6 km-long cement road with a total investment of 1 million yuan, for which funds had to be raised amounting to 20 yuan per person. After the issue had been discussed and approved at the VRA meeting, the sum was collected very quickly.

Without doubt, the villagers' representative assembly has become an important system of village self-government. It not only solves the many problems in the rural areas but also promotes democratic decision-making in village affairs.

V. Some Conclusions about Democracy in the Rural Areas

First, democracy means genuine representation of interests. In the elections of the village committees, farmers never raise any liberal slogans. What they are concerned about is whether the candidates will truly act on their behalf. Therefore, it can be said that basic-level democracy involves strong links of personal interests. A "democracy" which is divorced from the basic interests of the villagers will certainly not result in a healthy democratic system. In fact, even in countries with a multi-party system, voters choose their representatives in part because they are expected to improve living conditions. This shows that democracy must be closely combined with economic development, and enhancement of democracy cannot be pursued in isolation. If a democratic system is independent of economic and social development and is only a lofty ideal, then this system will not exert any influence on real events. Even worse, it may throw a country into chaos. The election of the village committees shows that every person who wants to stand for democratic election must ask him- or herself whether he or she is able to do anything for the well-being of the people and on behalf of the people.

Second, democracy is a gradual, accumulative process. We must avoid the extremes of thinking that a democratic system is either perfect or totally worthless. One cannot expect people to learn the practice of democracy immediately. The progress of the election of the village committees is a case in point. At the beginning, elections were not conducted in a satisfactory manner. This did not, however, discourage the officials of the relevant departments; instead, they gathered both positive and negative experiences in order to learn from them. For instance, since people were at first unfamiliar with the organization of village elections, many places just copied the methods for electing deputies to the county township people's congresses. Had it not been for the various political reforms implemented since 1979, the elections of village committees could not have had the present achievements. The Ministry of Civil Affairs has continued to promote village self-government in a gradual and accumulative manner, and this policy has proved to be correct. Any rash acts might block the progress of basic-level democratic self-government. Here also lies the problem of how to evaluate the work of one's predecessors who were also engaged in the promotion of democracy in some way. One cannot totally negate the work of other people and think oneself to be always correct. Instead, one should respect one's predecessors, proceed from reality, and learn from positive experiences. This is a basic requirement for those who promote democracy.

Third, the development of democracy requires training of common people and officials. Democracy is a system, a concept, as well as a habit. At the beginning, people may not be used to it. For example, during the election of the village committees, in some places one faction wanted to tear apart the ballot box and refused to recognize the election results on seeing that the candidate from the opposite faction had won the election. Of course, most farmers are good at exerting their democratic rights. But the improvement of people's qualities in democracy cannot take place overnight. Therefore, basic training should be given especially to the people who lack experience in democratic self-government, and the elections themselves are good opportunities for training. On the other hand, democracy also requires highly sophisticated administrative skills. If the government is not good at organizing democratic self-government, and lacks concrete procedures which guarantee the villagers' exercise of their democratic rights, then this will affect the progress of democracy. The experiences of the Ministry of Civil Affairs with its promotion of village self-government show that village self-government cannot be conducted well if the local departments of civil affairs lack the necessary knowledge for guiding village self-government. As soon as they become more versatile in the increasingly systematized knowledge of how to guide village committee elections, such elections will be greatly improved. The development of democracy goes hand in hand with the improvement of government guidance.

References

O'Brien, Kevin J. 1994. "Implementing Political Reform in China's Villages." *The Australian Journal of Chinese Affairs*, no. 32 (July 1994), pp. 1–32.

White, Tyrene. 1992. "Rural Politics in the 1990s; Rebuilding Grassroots Institutions." *Current History*, vol. 91, no. 566 (September 1992), pp. 275–276.

10

Networks, Groups, and the State in the Rural Economy of Raoyang County, Hebei Province

Frank N. Pieke

After 15 years of reforms in China, the contours of new types of local social organization that have sprung from the bosom of the Maoist state have become visible. After an initial period during which all intellectual energy was needed simply to keep up with the unfolding events, social scientists of China in the past six or seven years have begun to develop conceptual tools designed to understand the nature of the structural transformations taking place in China. Concepts such as "the transition to a market economy" (Nee 1989a, 1989b), "the emergence of civil society" (White 1993), and "the growth of local state corporations" (Oi 1992 and this volume) contradict each other on many points. But they all share a focus on new forms of social organization that connect families and individuals with higher levels of society, such as markets, associations, and the hierarchical structure of government and Party.

I agree that at this meso level, important changes of China's social structure have taken place and that it is here that we should continue to focus our efforts at analysis and interpretation.[1] Yet I want to caution against the reductionism (and often ethnocentrism) that comes with a too sweeping application of concepts such "market economy," "civil society," and "corporation." In my opinion, understanding the full complexity and variability of contemporary Chinese society is often impeded by treating market, civil society, and local state corporations as new social structures that exist independently from each other and from older structures, such as the family, the kin group, or the state apparatus. Concepts such as "market transition" only describe an aspect of reality; they should never be mistaken for structures that objectively exist, or prescriptions of what will necessarily happen in the future. Reifying structures only leads to futile debates about the "truth" of China's development, or at best to the misguided research question of how such imagined structures are connected together and interact.

The previous discussion should not be read as an argument against the concept of "structure" itself, but only serves as a warning against its often rigid and implicitly prescriptive interpretations in the current debates in the China field. To social actors and social scientists, in China as elsewhere, the world they live in does not present itself as composed of separate structures in which they occupy clearly proscribed roles. Instead, these structures can show one of two different faces to social actors and to social scientists. On the one hand, they are (parts of) spheres of action in which social actors interact to make optimal use of the economic, social, and cultural resources at their disposal. These spheres cannot be viewed independently from each other; actors operate in several of them at the same time and use their resources built up in one sphere to pursue their interests in others. On the other hand, families, state agencies, villages, and even temporary quasi-groups such as a collection of kinsmen or friends are themselves corporate actors with distinct interests, and strategies and resources to pursue them.[2]

In this chapter I will present the case of Raoyang, a rural county in Northern China. In Raoyang, as elsewhere in China, a market economy is growing, cooperative groups are being formed semi-independently from the state, and local governments gain more and more autonomy. However, this does not necessarily mean that Raoyang will become a full-blown market economy. Similarly, it is by no means certain that a fully independent civil society will emerge, or that local state corporations will completely sever the ties that bind them to higher levels of administration. Understanding social change in contemporary Raoyang requires that we look at these structures from an actional point of view, that is, both as spheres of action and as corporate actors.

Agricultural Development in Liuman Township

In the spring of 1994, I spent three months in Beiliuman, a village of approximately 450 households in Liuman township, Raoyang county, Hebei Province.[3] I was there as the tutor of a group of researchers who compared the development of agriculture in Liuman township with Niucun, a relatively backward township in the west of Raoyang county (Brandjes *et al.* 1994). Below are some of the results of this project, supplemented by my own interviews, conversations, and observations.

Raoyang is located in central Hebei on the North China plain, 235 kilometers south of Beijing. From the county it takes between five and eight hours by bus or truck to get to Beijing, Tianjin, or Shijiazhuang, the main urban and industrial centers in the Hebei area. Until recently, only Raoyang's main periodic market, Dayincun, located just north of Liuman, had good commercial relations with these centers, and more specifically with Tianjin. For this reason, the county government decided in 1985 that the scarce county funds for the development of rural industries (*xiangzhen qiye*) should be concentrated there. Other townships were deemed to have no competitive advantage in industry. They were told that they should concentrate on agriculture when "implementing the reforms" (*gao gaige*), a phrase which in the language of the Chinese Communist Party (CCP) stands for developing commercial activities. For years, this proved to be a hopeless task to Raoyang farmers and local cadres alike. Poor, far away from any potential customers, and with no especially sought-after specialized products, Raoyang had no ready entry into China's rapidly developing market economy. Relative remoteness, lack of capital, and county government policy therefore conspired to lock most of Raoyang, including Liuman township, into backwardness. Throughout most of the 1980s, Raoyang remained an agricultural county left behind by the reforms. It continued to be chiefly engaged in subsistence farming and the growth of underpriced bulk agricultural commodities, mainly grain and cotton, for the government's mandatory quota.

However, in 1986 a group of farmers in Liuman began to experiment with greenhouse vegetable production. Within three years and seemingly coming out of nowhere, Liuman township developed into a major producer of cucumbers and tomatoes that were sold on the structurally undersupplied vegetable markets of Beijing. In the 1990s, vegetable production gradually started spreading to other townships in Raoyang. Therefore, the description of Raoyang's development will begin with the story of its recent success at vegetable production as narrated by villagers and cadres in Liuman to outside officials, journalists, and foreign researchers.

Thanks to the production of greenhouse vegetables, Liuman households currently enjoy a standard of living unheard of only a few years ago, and much higher than the standard of living in most of the other townships in the vicinity. The vegetables that have made this possible, mainly cucumbers and tomatoes, are grown in simple unheated[4] greenhouses made of plastic sheets supported by a bamboo or steel frame. This type of greenhouse, originally developed in Japan, had been introduced in the suburban areas of Beijing in the late 1970s.

Like most other townships in Raoyang, Liuman had been a poor township mainly growing cotton, sorghum, corn, and wheat. Initially, Liuman remained backward after decollectivization in 1982. Although the local cadres were not oblivious to the hardship of their villagers, they saw no way out of it until in 1986, the Party secretary of Beiliuman, the main village of Liuman and seat of the township government, learned about greenhouse vegetable production through a complicated chain of kinship connections. The son of a fellow-villager was engaged to a daughter of a cousin of the Party secretary. The sister of this fellow villager had settled in Hongxing township in the southern suburbs of Beijing municipality where the local farmers had already been growing vegetables in plastic greenhouses for quite a few years. After hearing about the Hongxing greenhouses through his fellow-villager, the Party secretary and his cousin traveled to Beijing. Upon their arrival, the sister of their fellow-villager introduced them to a friend who was a local specialist in agricultural technology.

From their discussions, the three men concluded that there was good potential for greenhouse vegetable production in Liuman.

During the first season, the Party secretary, his cousin, their fellow-villager and two other relatives of the Party secretary took turns in going to Beijing every week to get advice from the specialist and buy the materials needed to build and operate their new greenhouses. Although each of the five households had its own greenhouse from the very beginning, they worked closely together during that first season, jointly drilling and using a well, taking turns going to Beijing, and buying inputs and selling outputs. After the first year, however, they ended their close cooperation. Henceforth, they only shared the well.

At that time, the cost of building a greenhouse was 5500 *yuan*. The money for the initial greenhouses was mostly borrowed from friends and relatives. The group also got a loan of 3000 *yuan* from the township credit cooperative. They could, however, not borrow the money themselves because the coop considered this too risky. Fortunately, they could use the name of Beiliuman village to obtain the loan thanks to the connections of the Party secretary. The latter's connections were also instrumental in mobilizing other types of support of the township leadership. The group received permission to use the township name to borrow money to drill the well necessary for the greenhouses. Furthermore, the township lent them 14 *mu* (1 *mu* is one-sixth of an acre) of land belonging to the township farm. This land was rent-free for the first three years. Five *mu* of the land went to the greenhouses, the rest was used for orchards.

During the first year, the initial group sold their vegetables to local small traders who picked up the produce by bike or with small vehicles. In 1987, the group signed a contract for one year with a city work unit that sent a truck every week. After that year, other city work units took over the role of this unit. The township leadership was again important here. They used their connections to get in touch with urban work units to pick up and market the vegetables. After a couple of years, the word about Liuman vegetables had spread sufficiently in Beijing, Shijiazhuang, and Tianjin for independent truckers to come to Liuman to purchase vegetables. As farmers got richer, some also pooled money to buy or rent a truck and take transport and marketing into their own hands.

As will be clear from the above, other families in Liuman quickly caught on to the success of this first group. In 1987, the Party secretary of Beiliuman was asked to organize a study class (*xuexiban*) for interested farmers. In that year, greenhouses had already been built in six out of the seven villages of Liuman township. Leaders from both Raoyang county and Hengshui prefecture came to Liuman to learn about greenhouse vegetable production. As a result, the pioneering Party secretary also went to other townships in Raoyang to instruct the farmers there. In the 1990s, Liuman became a local and even provincial model of agricultural development.

Thanks to the patronage of higher levels, the farmers in Liuman have had little problem building greenhouses. The support of the county and prefecture meant that the Agricultural Bank could provide loans to aspiring greenhouse farmers. In 1989, there were already more than 100 greenhouses in the township thanks to the support of the leadership and the entrepreneurial spirit of the farmers. Currently, almost all households in Liuman township own at least one greenhouse. Several families have already begun to diversify the money earned from vegetable production in other agricultural and non-agricultural enterprises, such as poultry raising, fruit growing, restaurants, and trucks. Recently, the village government had accumulated enough funds to start two small collective enterprises. Despite some very real and continuing constraints,[5] Liuman therefore seems to be in the midst of an economic take-off.

In both Liuman and Niucun, the other township we surveyed, almost all farmers cooperate in one way or the other with their fellow-villagers. Taken together, these grass-roots forms of cooperation have been indispensable in the transformation of the economy. Through a network of kin, neighbors, and friends, villagers get access to new markets and technologies, capital, and make the most efficient use of scarce resources at their disposal.

Households occasionally borrow draught animals or equipment they do not possess from other farmers in their village. Frequently, several farming households pool the expense of hiring a tractor, thresher, truck, or other relatively expensive machines. In other cases that typically involve more prosperous households, money is pooled to buy such machines. Another type of cooperation is illustrated by several poultry farmers in Luotun village who jointly contracted a technician for advice, with each household contributing 100 *yuan* per year. Friends and family are the most important source of interest-free loans. Under the current strict credit policy of the Agricultural Bank and the rural credit cooperatives, these loans are essential to most farmers who want to start a new enterprise.[6]

Furthermore, to get a loan from the bank or cooperative one usually needs the guarantee of a creditworthy individual. Family, friends and neighbors are also regularly consulted concerning improvements of production methods, pest control and the efficacy of new technologies. Apart from these almost daily interactions, some farmers who have recently specialized in a new type of crop or activity, such as fruit production or poultry farming, usually establish more focused contacts to obtain technical expertise from experienced farmers or agricultural specialists. Such informal contacts are the most important source of information in the absence of an effective extension system.

The irrigation group is by far the most important type of cooperation between farmers that has emerged after decollectivization.[7] Because a well can irrigate much more land than can be tilled by one farming household, farmers who wish to irrigate their land are forced to cooperate. Farmers with adjacent pieces of land jointly raise the money to drill a well and buy a pump plus diesel engine. The share in the investment of each farmer is usually determined by the number of people in the household. Irrigation groups are extremely common in Liuman and, as far as the land is irrigated, in Niucun as well. Naturally, the size of a group and the area irrigated by its well are determined by the water demand of the crops planted. Groups that grow greenhouse vegetables typically consist of 5 to 10 households irrigating a total of 8 to 15 *mu* of greenhouse land. Groups that irrigate fruit orchards are usually somewhat bigger, while the groups irrigating wheat typically consist of around 15 households.

Although I do not have sufficient evidence to prove this conclusively, many of the groups that share a well in the wheat fields in the Hutuo riverbed, especially those who inherited their well from the collectives, seem to be largely identical to work groups, the smallest unit during the collective period. This is because during decollectivization in 1982, much of this land was distributed by work teams (neighborhoods) rather than by brigades (villages). The work teams allocated the land to their constituent work groups, which in turn divided the land among the households. However, vegetable and fruit farming date from the years after decollectivization and the irrigation groups for these crops tend to be based mainly on friendship and kinship and on the adjacency of plots. But vegetable and fruit irrigation groups sometimes also have their roots in the social structure of the collective period, if only because members of work groups or teams were often also friends or kin.

A good example is provided by a large fruit orchard in Beiliuman planted in 1986. The fruit trees are divided into rows of about 150 trees each, with one row allocated to each adult worker. During the collective period, the ten-member households of this group were part of the same production team, but all households except three also happen to be close relatives. Although each household cultivates its own trees, sharing of labor, tools and information is considerably facilitated because of the kinship relation.

Naturally, the most important objective of irrigation groups is to share the investment and use of a well. Certain groups, however, also cooperate in other areas, especially when they, like in the example above, consist of good friends or relatives. Both in Liuman and in Niucun, fruit farmers sometimes share the cost of hiring an agricultural technician. In the winter, some groups of greenhouse vegetable farmers in Liuman raise cucumber seedlings together in order to decrease the expenses for heating. In Niucun, a group of greenhouse vegetable farmers who were old friends from school (*tongxue*) cooperate extensively, sharing new technologies and occasionally hiring trucks together to transport their vegetables to Beijing. Like the initial group of vegetable farmers in Beiliuman, irrigation groups seem to cooperate more when the farmers are still relatively inexperienced with a new type of enterprise. By cooperating, all member households gain better access to production technologies and markets, increasing their chance of success. Once the households feel more secure, they reduce their cooperation to sharing the water of their collective well.

Farmers, Cadres, and the State

In the preceding section we have seen how Raoyang farmers organize into cooperative groups that jointly own and operate irrigation wells, and use their social and political contacts to get access to scarce or expensive information, machines, labor and capital. They sell their products to specialized truckers who directly market the produce in Beijing and other large cities on the North China plain. Similarly, they obtain much of the necessary inputs, such as seeds, fertilizers, and pesticides, from private shops that have sprung up throughout the county, or at the traditional periodic markets that have witnessed a remarkable comeback with the onset of vegetable production. Farmers short of family labor hire day-laborers from neighboring Xian county, where vegetable farming has not yet caught on.[8]

A competitive and rapidly growing economic system has emerged that firmly ties Raoyang farmers into the regional economy without, so it seems, much formal organization or active involvement of local government. The farmers in Liuman themselves share this impression. They are justifiably proud of their achievements over the past seven years and point out that their entrepreneurial success has given them considerable immunity from the demands imposed by the state, such as grain and cotton quota and birth control. On the whole they cannot see or do not want to see that the vegetable boom from the onset would have been impossible, or at least a great deal more difficult, without the active involvement of village, township, and county. At an early stage, Liuman township permitted the township credit cooperative to lend to vegetable farmers, and later on allowed farmers to pay their grain quota in cash, enabling them to concentrate on vegetable farming. Similarly, cotton quota, much more assiduously enforced elsewhere, failed to make much impression on Liuman cadres and farmers.

Another example is provided by the implementation of the birth control policy. During our stay in Raoyang, a rather vicious campaign to enforce the single child policy was just underway. During the campaign it transpired that Liuman had the highest birth rate of all townships in Raoyang. This put a lot of pressure on Liuman cadres who had to balance at least a minimum compliance with the goals of the birth control policy with the farmers' wish for more children. Cadres thus had to pay a price for their share in the success of vegetable farming, by taking the heat for farmers' disregard of the single child policy.

Gradually, a symbiotic relationship between local cadres and the vegetable farmers of Liuman has grown. The county, township, and village cadres capitalize on the model status of Liuman to further their own standing in the state and Party hierarchy. Riding piggy-back on the success of vegetable farming, Raoyang county in 1994 received funding of over one million *yuan* from Hebei Province for agricultural modernization after agreeing to the status of a provincial grain and cotton base area, meaning that the county will have to fulfill higher quota than other counties for these two uneconomical crops. The one million *yuan* loan is thus earmarked for the development of cotton and grain production, but county officials were confident that they would be able to divert a substantial part of this money to vegetable production. It is thus to be expected that farmers who do not have the good fortune to live in Liuman, or one or two of the other townships targeted for further development of vegetable production, will be subjected to even more pressure than in the past to grow and deliver unprofitable cotton and grain. Somewhat speculatively, we can conclude that in Raoyang, market reforms have led and will continue to lead to greater income inequality. This is not a direct consequence of the market reforms themselves, however, but of the political economy of their implementation. Under the impact of the market, a specific pattern of interaction between farmers, the different levels of the state, and individual cadres has emerged that unequally distributes the gains and losses of the reform policies.

On the basis of fieldwork conducted in Beijing city in 1988 and 1989, I have described the result of increased local government autonomy and market reform with the term "capital socialism." Capital socialism points to the fact that under the reforms, local structures established under state socialism, such as city work units, have not disappeared but, on the contrary, explain much of China's spectacular economic growth over the past 15 years (Pieke 1995, 1996, chapter 4). Yet in view of the results of my subsequent fieldwork in Raoyang, I feel that the concept of capital socialism poses the danger of being read as a unilinear development model, in the same manner in which the theories of market transition, civil society, and local state corporatism have been applied, as pointed out in the beginning of this chapter. Yet capital socialism is still useful as a short-hand description for the devolution of state power and simultaneous persistence of the structures of state socialism, as long as it is understood that such structures have become part of a wide array of political economies throughout China.

Capital socialism thus points as much at the unities in diversities as it underlines the diversity in the apparent unity of contemporary China. Capital socialism is not intended as a theory of development or modernization. It serves only as a reminder that the old is very much new and alive in China today. Local social structures built up under "Maoism" have adapted to the new circumstances of the market and provide much of society's dynamism and structural stability, at least at the local level. They are, in other words, the inheritance from socialism and one reason why it is incorrect to say that the whole period 1949–1978 can be discarded as just a waste of time.

Under the umbrella of capital socialism, many different and often contradictory developments take place, sometimes in different areas but often also in one and the same locality. The debates about different models of economic development, such as the Wenzhou model, the Guangdong model, and the Jiangnan model, show that policy-makers and social scientists in China are acutely aware of the diversification of Chinese society. Local state corporatism, market transition, and civil society are but three of these developments that can take place within China's capital socialism.

Jean Oi's concept of local state corporatism (Oi 1992 and this volume) and my own analysis of "income creation" (*chuangshou*) by urban work units (Pieke 1995, 1996, chapter 4), are examples of how (seemingly) new structures can better be interpreted as just one aspect of a multifaceted capital socialism. Building on their organizational superiority and privileged access to state resources, villages and work units have entered the emerging market sphere. Under the flag of "rural enterprises" (*xiangzhen qiye*) in the countryside and *chuangshou* in the cities, rural governments and city work units have invested in a wide variety of economic activities quite often unrelated to their original role in the planned economy.

Market reform has thus neither eroded the local structures of state socialism, nor have state organizations been relegated to the role of facilitator and regulator as Victor Nee's market transition theory predicts (Nee 1989a, 1989b). The vitality of local governments and work units is one of the most important explanations of China's robust economic growth over the past 15 years. Yet it would be a mistake to think that the Chinese state has now neatly been divided into independent corporations, as Oi seems to suggest, that behave in much the same way as private enterprises or conglomerates of enterprises in a capitalist economy.

First, as Yang (1994) has pointed out, control over rural enterprises is often not exercised by the local government, but by individual cadres who mobilize networks, such as affinal kinsmen, that cross-cut the administrative divisions of local government. In these cases, local government is not only a corporation that acts as a unified social group, but also a sphere of action. Resources belonging to this sphere are used by the individuals, groups and networks that happen to control them. In other spheres, such as the market, the power of the state corporation and the authority of cadre position can be profitably mobilized to compete with actors on the market such as private enterprises and other state corporations. Local governments and work units are still part of the state bureaucratic structure. They therefore continue to have sectoral monopolies and privileged access to scarce resources: they have entered the market with a huge competitive advantage. Self-serving behavior, power abuse, and competition between state organs had been part and parcel of the planned economy before the reforms. The diminishing clout of higher authorities means, however, that the profits of such behavior can now more openly be retained by the local capital socialist corporations and their leaders and that competition between local corporations is more openly played out.

In Liuman, for instance, the township government has used its power to reap some of the rewards of the vegetable boom. With the spread of vegetable farming, Liuman had become the marketing center for vegetables for farmers from all over northern Raoyang. In 1991, the township government spent several hundred thousand *yuan* to build a large cold storage facility and market compound for vegetables. Unfortunately, this investment failed to yield the expected return.[9]

The farmers refused to pay the fees imposed by the township for use of the market. Under the pretense that the market area was too small, they continued to sell their produce to truckers just outside the compound. The cold storage facility was also hardly used because the farmers considered it uneconomical to pay for this service since selling their crops immediately yielded sufficiently high prices. To earn at least some money, the township rented part of the market area out to farmers on which to build their hothouses.[10] The market staff was put to work growing gourds on the remaining land. During our stay, the township authorities decided to counter farmers' non-compliance by a hard-nosed administrative measure. A new, larger market area just south of the cold storage facility was cleared and all trading outside of this area was forbidden. Henceforth, the farmers were forced to sell at this market and pay the fees imposed by the township.[11]

What is interesting about this case is that the investment found favor with no one. Farmers predictably were unhappy about the fees they had to pay, while village cadres resented the high interest payments on the loan taken by the township which were at the expense of local accumulation funds. Farmers and villages were thus made to pay for something they did not want. The county, too, was angry about the unilateral action of the township. According to them, the market was difficult to reach for trucks that came to purchase the vegetables, and should instead have been built just off the highway connecting Raoyang with Beijing and Tianjin. Although they would not say it, it was clear that in that case the county would have been responsible for the market and the main recipient of its revenues.

As the example of the Liuman cold storage and market area shows, local governments under capital socialism have become semi-independent actors in the market economy. Freed from some of the constraints of bureaucratic supervision they cater to the interests of the corporation and its personnel as much as they work for the common good of the rank-and-file members. Government power has become an asset to be used to compete with other capital socialist corporations and private enterprises.

The second point that has to be made concerning capital socialist corporatism is that the continuing statist character of local corporations has had another, opposite consequence apart from the use of government power to compete in the market sphere with the other social actors discussed above. Local governments and work units are not fully independent but continue to be tied to the hierarchical bureaucratic structure of the state. Both the application of higher level policy directives and the relative power of cadres of local governments and work units therefore continue to shape the behavior of capital socialist corporations. Viewed from this angle, the state apparatus re-emerges as a sphere of action in which local state corporations (but also, through connections or corruption of cadres, private individuals or enterprises) cooperate or compete. In Liuman, the relationship with higher levels had shaped a specific path of rapid economic development that, on the whole, suited the agendas of both local farmers and the various levels of government. The interaction between local, township, and county government could, however, also lead to conflict and economic stagnation.

During our stay in Raoyang, we also studied Niucun, one of the least developed townships in the county.[12] In Niucun township, Luotun village was particularly badly off. Located in the bed of the Hutuo river, Luotun's fields had been covered by several meters of sand during massive floods in 1954 and 1963, making them unsuited for the cultivation of the area's main crops of wheat, sorghum, and cotton.[13] As a result, Luotun had to depend on food aid from the national government for most of the collective period until the early 1980s.

With the reforms, the Maoist preoccupation with grain production gave way to more flexible agricultural policies. After Luotun village cadres had turned down the offer to relocate the population of the village to the surrounding areas, Niucun township cadres decided that the cultivation of peanuts would be the second best solution for Luotun. Peanuts, the principal cash crop in pre-reform Raoyang, have long been a bone of contention. In the early 1950s, enterprising local collectives wanted to grow more peanuts to earn cash and raise the farmers' incomes, running counter to the demands of the state for more grain and cotton (Friedman *et al.* 1991, pp. 126–127). The fact that Raoyang county recommended peanut growing to Luotun therefore carried an important symbolic meaning, as it signified an open refutation of Maoist preferences. The county provided loans and technical assistance to the Luotun farmers and, most importantly, allowed them to pay for their grain quota in cash earned from the sale of the peanut crop. Although still poor, Luotun farmers now could at least feed themselves.

In the late 1980s, however, Luotun village leaders became aware of other and more promising alternatives. Vegetable and fruit production was successfully embarked upon in surrounding townships such as Liuman, and a few wealthy farmers in Luotun started experimenting with these crops as well. Especially fruit production seemed promising given the relatively small amounts of irrigation water needed.[14] A plan to develop fruit orchards was drafted and submitted to the township and county authorities. These however turned the proposal down on the grounds that Luotun's flood-prone fields did not warrant the long-term investment in wells and orchards. They argued that Luotun should be grateful for their earlier efforts to start up peanut farming. Angrily, they put Luotun at the bottom of the county's and the township's priority list for agricultural investment.

This conflict between the village and higher levels of government was only the most recent of a series of confrontations. One of the key players in the conflict over the plan to plant fruit orchards in Luotun was the head of the Agricultural Development Office of Raoyang county. In the early 1980s, he had worked in Niucun as Party secretary and he was the one who had been responsible for first suggesting to evacuate Luotun and then, after the refusal of Luotun cadres and villagers to accept this, helping them to grow peanuts as an alternative. According to this official, Luotun is actually quite well off. Peanuts are a good and profitable crop and the village has much more land, 5 *mu* per head, than any other village in the county. The village cadres had no reason to complain and come up with unrealistic demands. He made no bones about his dislike for the Luotun cadres whom he considered stubborn and ungrateful for his efforts to start up peanut farming. Luotun's current bid for fruit orchards was to give him a slap in the face, and a confirmation that the Luotun leadership was no good and should be made to suffer for being so unreasonable.

However, more was at issue than the ruffled feathers of one county official. Apart from its own land, Luotun also leased low-grade sand-covered land in the riverbed from the surrounding villages for growing peanuts. This, the village leadership claimed, was actually land that had belonged to Luotun before collectivization in the 1950s but had been given to these other villages so that a roughly equal area of land per household could be distributed in all of the villages in the area. At the time, although this was not agreeable to the people in Luotun, it was considered at least somewhat reasonable because this land, all located in the riverbed, was of very good quality and Luotun villagers could still make a living on the remaining fields. But after the floods in 1954 and 1963 had covered the fields in the riverbed with sand the village suffered disproportionately: Luotun was the only village whose land was exclusively located in the riverbed. According to Luotun cadres, the village was therefore impoverished due to no fault of its own, and they greatly resented the fact that they now had to pay rent to other villages for land which they still thought of as their own.

Raoyang county officials however came up with a very different version of the same story. After the floods, the village had been given food aid for years, despite the fact that they had more land per household than any other village. In the 1970s special funds were allocated to the area for drilling wells,[15] and grain delivery quotas under the Maoist policy of "taking grain as the key link" (*yi liang wei gang*) were waived, all to no avail. Luotun cadres were just "lazy" and "always looking for handouts." Luotun therefore presents a very interesting case of a strong and long-standing animosity between a village and township and county governments. During the 1960s and 1970s, the conflict was bought off by the national state through direct national poverty-relief. Under the reforms the old issues resurfaced, again pitching the village and its cadres against the higher levels of government.

The refusal of the county and township to approve Luotun's plan for fruit production meant that the township credit cooperative was not given a separate budget to finance the loans, without which only very few Luotun farmers could drill wells, plant orchards, and buy food grain until the first fruit harvest five years later. Lacking financial resources of their own, Luotun villagers had no option but to dance to the tune of the higher authorities and remain relatively poor peanut farmers while the rest of Raoyang was allowed to prosper.[16]

The examples of Liuman and Niucun show that market forces and geographical conditions alone do not explain the type and degree of development. Rather, it is the perception of the market and nature of the government, cadres, and population, together with the balance of power between different levels of government and between government and farmers that determine where and in which direction economic development takes place. Perceptions and power relations in turn are shaped not only by policies (such as the agricultural development plan for Raoyang), past experiences, but also by the presence or absence of alternative organizational and financial resources that allow a greater or lesser degree of independence from higher levels of government.

Spheres of Action, Connections, and Competition

The reforms have given rise to a situation in Raoyang in which farmers and the different levels of government interact in complicated ways that cannot be captured by short hand descriptions such as "the emergence of civil society," "the growth of local level state corporations," or "the development of a market economy." The Beiliuman Party secretary who discovered and developed the potential of greenhouse vegetable production did so because national policy allowed and even required Chinese villages to diversify their economies: new economic activities had to be developed for the Chinese countryside deadlocked into the production of underpriced agricultural bulk products.

However, the Party secretary was also quick to understand that, if successful, vegetable production would yield not only prestige and profit but also more independence from the higher levels of the state for him and his village. Indeed, after only a couple of years of growing vegetables, the Party secretary resigned from his post that, by that time, had yielded sufficient competitive advantage for him to become the most successful vegetable farmer in Raoyang. Even after his resignation, however, he continues to use his political contacts and prestige when expedient to his farm and the other enterprises he is planning for himself and the other members of his family.

The behavior of the Party secretary was shaped by more than just the state bureaucracy, the emerging village corporation, and family enterprise. His connections with kin, friends, and cadres at the township were all mobilized when researching and developing greenhouse production. Connections of the township in turn were instrumental in getting access to the urban markets for the greenhouse produce. Finally, the success of Liuman was not only capitalized upon by the emerging local state corporation but was also incorporated into the agricultural development policies of Raoyang county and beyond.

The image of agricultural modernization in China, at least as it transpires from the Liuman case, is that of isolated agricultural technologies randomly tossed into different directions in rural China. Some technologies land in fertile soil, germinate and grow, leading to agricultural modernization of a very specific type that gradually spreads from the initial location to secondary sites in the neighborhood. This spread and further development will continue until the technology is either replaced by something better, or has depleted local resources, or until the area can no longer compete with other areas that have adopted the same or a similar technology and have gained one competitive advantage or the other, such as lower labor cost or closer proximity to the market. Judging from the Liuman case, the spread of such technologies seems to be predicated upon specific personal connections and definitely not on formal extension services or deliberate efforts at marketing or planning. Likewise, whether or not a technology takes root depends very much on who introduces the technology: his or her skills and knowledge together with his or her local networks and position in the local state structure.

To make sense of developments such as these, I have proposed in the introduction to shift our analytic efforts away from a preoccupation with social structure and the changes thereof: the way in which organizations, corporations, enterprises, families, and individuals have changed in nature, i.e., have come to play different roles and occupy new places relative to each other. Such an approach can help us understand certain aspects of contemporary Chinese society, but it obscures the ambiguity, fluidity, and contradictory nature that are at the core of the momentous changes currently underway.

Instead of problematizing change and trying to distill stable structures out of the ever-shifting reality of contemporary China it seems more fruitful to take continual change as a base line for analysis. The focus thus shifts to the processes and patterns underlying the actions of social actors, both individual and corporate, that produce change in some cases and a relative stability in others. Structures are spheres of social action and corporate social actors at the same time. Change in Chinese society, like all other societies, is an ongoing process without a clear point of departure or eventual outcome fueled by creative social actors. This process is multifaceted. Social actors simultaneously operate in several different spheres of social action, such as the market, the state apparatus, the local community, and networks of kin, friends, and political allies. These spheres of action therefore do not exist independently from each other; through the interactions social actors engage in, different spheres are brought into contact with each other and resources (status, money, power, connections, authority) accumulated in one sphere are applied in other spheres.

In the past, the state was the main sphere of social action; it mediated almost all external transactions even when the other party was located in a neighboring village. Now, the state's bureaucratized structure itself has changed and is moreover only one of many connections with the world, from nearby villages to big cities and even foreign countries. The less direct involvement of state organizations in affairs at the local level has made it both possible and necessary for individuals, communities, and organizations to diversify their relations with society beyond the village gate.

The case of Raoyang has shown that many different and often contradictory truths exist about the nature of contemporary Chinese society. Depending on the purpose and level of analysis, a social scientist highlights one or more of these truths. But the explanatory power of this analysis does not necessarily invalidate other truths. If we apply Victor Nee's market transition theory to Raoyang we could point at the greater independence and affluence of private farmers and other entrepreneurs. Similarly, local governments indeed play an active role in facilitating and regulating the further development of the market. Yet when viewed from another angle, the same local governments, by investing in collective enterprises, behave as the local state corporations described by Jean Oi that operate on the market and/or extract revenue from it. But local cadres are also members of Yang Minchuan's networks of friends and kin who use the authority of government position and the power of local state corporations for self-enrichment.

Finally, as shown in the foregoing, the various levels and organizations of the state are still tied to a bureaucratic hierarchy that continues to impose a fair degree of planning on the economy. The behavior of cadres is therefore in many ways still the same as it was before the reforms. They implement policies formulated at a higher bureaucratic level when necessary or expedient, but also stretch soft budget constraints and shield their constituency from unpopular policies.

In this chapter, I have argued that we should not stop after having delineated the structures of Chinese society. Especially when studying a society that is changing as rapidly as contemporary China, we should continue by asking what people make these structures do for them. In this way, we will not only eventually better understand, or at least appreciate, the richness and variety of Chinese society as it is experienced by the Chinese themselves. I sincerely hope that this will also help us become more aware of the theoretical and ideological assumptions that by necessity inform our understanding of China. If the price of this awareness is that we give up the search for the final truth about China, we should be glad to pay it.

Acknowledgment:

The author would like to thank Ellen Hertz, Tak-wing Ngo, and Yao Jianfu for their comments on a draft of this article.

Notes

1. Naturally, one could also concentrate on other aspects of the "nexus" (Duara 1988) that ties villages and families to the rest of society, such as kinship, migration, or religion. State, market and autonomous associations have, however, figured most prominently in the literature, which is why I am concentrating on them here.

2. I have discussed this theoretical point at greater length in Pieke (1996, chapters 1 and 2).

3. The recent history of Raoyang county until the early 1960s has been extensively studied by Friedman *et al.* (1991). Their study focuses on a model village in the south of the county, whereas the fieldwork reported here took place in two townships in the northeast (Liuman) and the northwest (Niucun).

4. Heating is only used in small separate greenhouses to raise seedlings for the first of the two crops of the year during a period of several weeks in March.

5. Major constraints are the continued availability of irrigation water and the almost total absence of a functioning agricultural extension system.

6. In 1994, only 15 per cent of the Raoyang farmers interviewed by us had received a loan from their local rural credit cooperative (Brandjes *et al.* 1994, p. 64). National data for 1986–1990 presented by Manoharan indicate that the Agricultural Bank of China and its local credit cooperatives extract much more money from individual farmers through their deposits than what they plow back into agriculture by means of individual loans (Manoharan 1992, tables I-A, I-B, and VI-A; see also Brandjes *et al.* 1994, pp. 57–62).

7. This is in line with the national trend (Vermeer, this volume).

8. With one *mu* of land requiring the full-time labor of at least one adult during most of the year, vegetable farming is extremely labor intensive. Indeed many farmers mentioned a shortage of family labor as their main constraint to a further growth in production. Although Raoyang farmers are very reluctant to hire outside labor, preferring instead to work themselves and the other members of their family to the bone, many nevertheless have to employ workers during certain peak periods of the crop cycle. At the time of the fieldwork, the going rate for a full day's work was 7 *yuan* plus lunch, or roughly US$1.00.

9. We had ample opportunity to verify the uselessness of this largest of Liuman's white elephants as we had been allocated rooms in the office building attached to the market compound. The rent and other fees paid probably amounted to the largest return on the investment to date.

10. Heated hothouses made of bricks, mud, plastic sheets and a bamboo or steel frame were a more expensive technology recently introduced in Raoyang. Some farmers had started to experiment with them to benefit from the much higher prices of vegetables in winter.

11. Depending on the size of the vehicle, this fee is 10 to 30 *yuan* for the farmers per cartload of vegetables. Trucks pay 70 to 100 *yuan*. The fine for trading outside the designated market area is between 200 and 500 *yuan*, plus the regular fee. Despite several attempts, I was never able to arrange interviews with township cadres about the very controversial issue of the new market area. I can therefore not explain why the township government went through the trouble of clearing this new market area instead of simply forcing the farmers to use the old one.

12. Interestingly enough, county level cadres tried to dissuade us from investigating this township. Instead, they wanted us to study a slightly less poor township where local cadres had little to complain about because their area had recently been singled out for county investment in irrigation and road construction.

13. In 1963, two dams were built upstream in the Hutuo river. After that, floods occurred only very infrequently. At the same time, however, almost all the water of the river was henceforth diverted to cities and counties upstream. Northern Raoyang was thus cut off from its source of surface water and required massive investment in the drilling of underground wells which many areas could only really afford in the 1980s. Raoyang's poverty therefore has as much to do with the politics of irrigation as with natural conditions and lack of capital.

14. Due to the sandy soils of Luotun, wells are difficult to drill and moreover often cave in, making them a more expensive and risky investment than in other areas.

15. The people who had dug these wells had apparently been more "red" than "expert," or else did not have the appropriate equipment. The wells, once dug, caved in soon afterwards and the investment was entirely lost.

16. To Luotun cadres, our research provided a more than welcome opportunity to vent their grievances against the county and hopefully to be heard by higher authorities in Shijiazhuang or Beijing. They thus had a powerful incentive to overstate the village's poverty. We therefore never took the word of the cadres as sufficient evidence and drew as much as possible from our interviews with Luotun farmers instead.

References

Brandjes, Pieter, *et al.* 1994. *Vegetable Boom and the Question of Sustainability in Raoyang County, North China.* Wageningen: International Center for Development-Oriented Research in Agriculture (ICRA).

Duara, Prasenjit. 1988. *Culture, Power, and the State: Rural North China, 1900–1942.* Stanford: Stanford University Press.

Friedman, Edward; Pickowicz, Paul G.; and Selden, Mark. 1991. *Chinese Village, Socialist State.* New Haven: Yale University Press.

Manoharan, Thiagarajan. 1992. "Credit and Financial Institutions at the Rural Level in China—Between Plan and Market." In Eduard Vermeer, ed., *From Peasant to Entrepreneur: Growth and Change in Rural China.* Wageningen: Pudoc, pp. 183–215.

Nee, Victor. 1989a. "A Theory of Market Transition: From Redistribution to Markets in State Socialism." *American Sociological Review*, vol. 54, pp. 663–681.

———. 1989b. "Peasant Entrepreneurship and the Politics of Regulation in China." In Victor Nee and David Stark, eds., *Remaking the Institutions of Socialism: China and Eastern Europe.* Stanford: Stanford University Press, pp. 169–207.

Oi, Jean. 1992. "Fiscal Reform and the Economic Foundation of Local State Corporatism in China." *World Politics*, vol. 45, pp. 99–126.

Pieke, Frank N. 1995. "Bureaucracy, Friends, and Money: The Growth of Capital Socialism in China." *Comparative Studies in Society and History*, vol. 37, no. 3 (July), pp. 494–518.

———. 1996. *The Ordinary and the Extraordinary: An Anthropological Study of Chinese Reform and the 1989 People's Movement in Beijing.* London: Kegan Paul International.

White, Gordon. 1993. "Prospects for Civil Society in China: A Case Study of Xiaoshan City." *The Australian Journal of Chinese Affairs*, no. 29, pp. 63–87.

Yang, Minchuan. 1994. "Reshaping Peasant Culture and Community: Rural Industrialization in a Chinese Village." *Modern China*, vol. 20, pp. 157–179.

11

Defining Cultural Life in the Chinese Countryside

The Case of the Chuan Zhu Temple

John Flower and Pamela Leonard

Many observers of contemporary China have noted the resurgence of economic and cultural life in the Chinese countryside.[1] Since agriculture began to be decollectivized in 1981, families are once again the basic unit of rural production, giving farmers more freedom to produce for the market and pursue sideline occupations, but the state still plays a strong role in the everyday lives of villagers. More than a decade of economic reforms and cultural liberalization have given rise to new forms of social relations, and to new "public" organizations thriving in the intersticial space between state and family. Remarkable rates of economic growth and the apparent success of the hybrid "socialist market economy" have focused much attention on rural collectives and "TVEs" (township village enterprises, *xiangzhen qiye*) as the engines of social change in the countryside. The appearance of "mass organizations" promoting villagers' collective interests outside the purely economic realm has also attracted scholarly interest. The debate over to what extent these (apparently) voluntary associations and (relatively) autonomous economic entities might constitute a nascent "civil society" has heated up, as the Chinese state seems to "recede" from a monopolistic hold on social life, and as rural Chinese take more of their affairs into their own hands.[2]

If some are optimistic that a new Chinese public sphere is growing out of the process of commoditization and the evolution away from state control, reasons to be skeptical of this sanguine view of rural development abound: As studies highlighting uneven economic growth and the increasing disparity between rich and poor areas in China suggest, the impact of TVEs is limited, leaving large areas of the Chinese hinterland outside the circle of "miraculous prosperity."

"Commoditization" itself is seen as a mixed blessing by many rural Chinese, bringing insecurity along with prosperity, and corroding the social ties of village life. Further, the notion that the state is "receding" in direct control of rural life overlooks the extractive practices that increasingly characterize state presence at the local level, and that antagonize villagers' resentment of the state. Even voluntary "non-government organizations" (NGOs) can be seen as new extensions of state control—as one Chinese scholar familiar with mass organizations sardonically observed, they are really "GONGOs": government organized non-government organizations.[3]

While the disjunction between these "two Chinas" might be attributed to the sheer size and diversity of China itself, it might also derive from the tendency to posit rigid dichotomies—state versus society, resistance versus accommodation—where social boundaries are in fact fluid and in a constant process of negotiation. Our experience living in a mountainous village in western Sichuan during 1991-1993 suggests that a local space between state organization and private interest is developing in the Chinese countryside, and that this space can be seen as a reaction to—and even against—the more global process of commoditization brought about by the accelerating pace of economic change.

We will argue that the case of a local temple revitalization movement that occurred during our fieldwork illustrates the way a spontaneous, voluntary organization in the Chinese countryside addressed the sense of moral "chaos" villagers felt in the face of dramatic economic, social and political change. The question of how this movement is defined will be central. On the one hand, some officials sought to castigate the movement as a return to feudal superstitious activities, while temple activists, on the other hand, labelled it as legitimate religious expression. While it is currently in vogue in academic discourse to see in such peasant actions the expression of "everyday forms of resistance" to, in this case, monopolistic powers of the state,[4] we will emphasize the way state-society interactions can be viewed as a relationship of mutual cooptation. More than a case of simple confrontation, we see these events as emphasizing the importance of local identity for villagers creating their own communal self-definition. Understanding the dynamics at play in the temple's spontaneous revitalization, and in the state's attempt to control and channel its meaning, is essential for understanding the way broader economic forces play out at the grassroots level.

The Political and Economic Backdrop

The village where we did fieldwork is located in an area that is considered poor by Chinese standards, a "mountain district" some three and a half hours by car from the provincial capital of Chengdu. The topography is one of steep mountain slopes, upland valleys and deep rocky gorges. There are terraced rice paddies in the valleys, but the main crop of the village is corn, planted by hand on the steep hillsides. The village has very little paddy land; farmers must purchase or trade corn for their rice each year. In the past twenty years, subsistence agriculture has been augmented by wage labor (mostly stone masonry) and sideline occupations such as raising dairy goats. While improvements in the standard of living were made sporadically since Liberation, decollectivization brought rapid progress as farmers were able to take fuller advantage of new hybrid variety crops, increased opportunities for wage earning, and the then new market for milk. Although it has always lagged behind the prosperity achieved in rural rice-growing regions and suburban villages close to large urban centers, the real gains made after decollectivization have actually begun to erode as inflation has begun to eat at stagnating incomes.

At the same time villagers began to feel the pressures of inflation, they also saw the tremendous economic boom in urban (especially coastal) areas, and the rise in waste and corruption that accompanied loosening government controls on the economy. Resentment of official corruption and of increased taxation—itself a product of a scramble for local revenues—began to crest after Deng Xiaoping's January–February 1992 "Southern Tour" to investigate the effect of the more liberal opening-up policies being tested in the coastal development zones such as Guangdong. Deng concluded that these market reforms were beneficial to the Chinese economy and that the benefits of this brand of "socialist market economy" should be made more widespread. Following his conclusions the government issued the important "number two document" (*erhao wenjian*) of 1992. This document opened the door for government work units to become financially more self-sufficient and even encouraged government employees to seek "second jobs." Its provisions also led to a restructuring of government to give more weight to township or *zhen* administrations. The effect was dramatic and forms the immediate backdrop to the Chuan Zhu temple revival.

In this area, the prefecture government (*diqu*, the level above county) interpreted the restructuring between county and township administrations as an opportunity to assume control of some of the tax base of the county government. The county government, as a result, had to decrease the incomes of its standard service employees by 25 percent. This was somewhat compensated for, however, by the fact that bureaus and individuals were now allowed to engage in business to make money. Due to these two changes, the employees of the county government service bureaus (the forestry bureau, the bureau of animal husbandry, the bureau of agriculture, etc.) almost overnight ceased to dedicate themselves to their former roles. Offices were increasingly empty and people spent more office time drinking tea, chatting, reading the paper and even playing cards. At the same time, many new enterprises were created to try to make the best of the new climate of liberalization, but rather than extending the productive base of the economy, they tended only to further divide up the existing market. New lottery stands, convenience stores and restaurants blossomed along the avenues of the county capital. Many units invested in real-estate and some even built luxury hotels. They also sought ways to use their official powers to generate special revenues. The capital for the investments came mostly from the public fund in a rather unregulated way, and so the general picture was one of a shift of resources from public welfare to private gain, of decreased opportunity for rural areas to increased corruption yielding benefits to some urban dwellers.

The political and economic changes that ensued from Deng's Southern Tour directly affected agricultural production. With the changeover in local township personnel, part of the general bureaucratic restructuring initiated by the shifting winds, there was a period of adjustment during which local infrastructure was poorly maintained. For example, the township failed to pay for routine repair of irrigation canals. Leakage from the canal resulted in water shortages when the rice shoots were planted and localized soil erosion on hillsides below the canal. The extensive and unregulated use of public funds to start new businesses resulted in a severe banking crisis; farmers' loans were called in and many villagers found themselves short of cash. Reorientation of government-owned factories interrupted the supply and affected the quality of basic inputs such as fertilizer and seed. A retaining wall was built in front of the village where we lived and along the public road following a severe flood in 1992, but due to corruption in the traffic bureau sand was substituted for cement and the first high water in the spring of 1993 obliterated the entire construction. The road was only sporadically passable during the milk season (approximately March to October) and as a result, at times farmers' milk could not be transported to the milk powder factory. Farmers rely on this milk money to purchase their basic rice rations. All of these examples point to what villagers see as an alarming trend toward "chaos." Mismanagement and corruption by government officials were commonly compared to the situation under the last years of Guomindang (Nationalist) rule. Many villagers complained about inflation and an increase in crime. Higher taxes and pressure to pay back government loans were also contributing factors to growing dissatisfaction. Against the background of an eroding standard of living, villagers saw the changes brought by the "socialist market economy" as, at worst, a threat to the infrastructure of government service on which they rely and to which they contribute ever higher taxes, and, at best, as an economic boom in which they could have no part.

During this period, from many parts of Sichuan we heard of numerous cases of angry confrontation between farmers and officials. Farmers were angry about the abuse of power and frustrated at the growing disparity brought by rampant corruption. At a township just a few miles away, farmers held a county official captive for twelve or more hours until they were given some credible assurance that a fund which had been collected from the sale of their farmlands had not been squandered in unauthorized speculation. The international press followed the actions of angry citizens in Renshou county in Sichuan as they took action against the imposition of too many ad hoc fees imposed by officials in the name of highway development.[5] While farmers in Sichuan at this time were clearly engaging in active resistance, we would like to detail a somewhat different kind of reaction to the new political and economic climate that also took place at this time—a creative reaction of community revival.

An Indigenous Public Concern: The Case of the Temple

The accelerated move toward a socialist market economy ushered in by "document number two" contributed to the expansion of the "public sphere" in a very unintended and concrete way: the proliferation of temples. Under the guise of "developing tourism" temples began to be (re)constructed all over the area of our fieldwork in 1992 and 1993. This trend grew especially strong just after the revival of the "Chuan Zhu temple" located in the township seat, and crested locally in the construction of a small nearby temple with a large placard above the entrance bearing the words: "tourist center." Ironically, an attempt by bureaucrats to coopt and channel the temple's activities provided local villagers with official sanction for expressing their own interests (hence the temple building boom) even as they subverted the intentions of the state and its agents.

When we first went to the local village temple devoted to the god Chuan Zhu in late 1991 it was deserted, save for some small old relics that to us had no apparent significance: a sword that had once been part of a statue, a shoe, some old bits of carving all set on a stone platform. Significantly, at about the time of Deng's Southern Tour, the local residents commissioned the carving of a wooden statue of Chuan Zhu and the temple was informally re-opened. It did not have official authorization from the government but was, rather, exclusively a spontaneous, bottom-up event.

Before Liberation, the Chuan Zhu temple held an annual festival on the twenty-fourth day of the sixth lunar month, a big event with people coming from neighboring villages to share a feast. On this day, the statue of Chuan Zhu was traditionally escorted to a second temple building located in the township, where he resided throughout the summer rainy season to protect the town from flooding. In June of 1992 there were no plans to celebrate the festival day, since the temple was still "unofficial," just starting to get organized. In any case, other circumstances arose. The local township government, disapproving of "feudal superstitious" behavior and no doubt aware that the temple was starting to bubble with activity, decided to destroy the new statue just two days before Chuan Zhu's festival day. This act began a series of "miraculous events" in the new life of the temple. First, two officials from the township government entered the temple and tried to burn the Chuan Zhu statue's clothes, but they would not light. Then they knocked off his head and carried off his mutilated remains to live in a groundfloor back-closet of the township government. The very next day, the day before Chuan Zhu's festival, a tremendous flood swept through the area (quite localized), destroying three houses in the village we lived in and several in the next. It also took out the local high school in the township proper and for the next year classes had to be held in the township government's own offices.

Chuan Zhu is the canonized identity of a historical figure, the "upright official" Er Lang of the early Han dynasty. His ability to "tame the dragon" refers to the construction of a vast and sophisticated irrigation system, still in use after two millennia, that transformed the Sichuan basin from flood-prone lowlands to the fertile and stable agricultural region it is today. Naturally enough, the flood on the eve of Chuan Zhu's festival day, following on the heels of his temple's desecration, only served to arouse more local interest in reviving the temple. Moreover, the fact that Chuan Zhu is a paragon of "upright officialdom" made the township government's suppression of the revival all the more galling, and set up an unflattering comparison for local officials. The act of suppression and the castigation of the temple's spontaneous revival as "feudal superstition" were a recognition of the inherent challenge the revitalization movement posed to the legitimacy of Party authority: a challenge in that it is "spontaneous" and uncontrolled, and a more subtle challenge in the form of an ideal of "good govern-. ment" that the authorities fell short of. This conclusion is supported by the simultaneous appearance of other "heterodox" phenomena, such as prophecies of impending doom and millenarian texts in the temple itself. For example, a hand-printed text passed around inside the temple called on the people to repent from evil ways and follow the goddess of mercy (Guanyin) for salvation in the terrible times to come.[6]

The accelerated change to a market economy has clearly made some people feel left out. It has also brought widespread disaffection from the government and both implicit and explicit rejection of Party leadership. In some of the more extreme examples, the challenge to authority is clear—and not lost on local officials who attempt to suppress "feudal superstition" as soon as it appears. We spoke with one official, the local township head (*xiang zhang*), for whom the central dynamic at play in production is the opposition of "superstition" (*mixin*) and "science" (*kexue*). He brought up as an example the idea of *fengshui* (geomancy):

> You can have the same 1 *mu* piece of land and get different production results. One person who is capable can get a lot out of it; another guy who is lazy and doesn't work hard produces very little. But instead of blaming himself, he blames the *fengshui* of the land!

The official's major complaint about peasants and their superstitions had to do with their resistance to new ideas—their conservatism and backwardness. He grew quite agitated, and in the space of three minutes of conversation produced this list of invectives against the peasants: stupid, conservative, superstitious, unscientific, lazy, backward thinking, unreceptive to new thinking and new methods, shortsighted, inbred ("lacking human quality"), and disobedient (*bu tinghua*)—especially this last, from his perspective.

Peasant "disobedience" was a common complaint from officials, and often connected to the persistence of "feudal superstition." The latter was a category reserved for forms of behavior that either fell outside of or directly challenged

Party control. Thus the spontaneous rebirth of the temple was suppressed, with literally disastrous results and bad feelings all around. But while the heavy-handed approach to the temple proved ineffective, especially against disaffected and disobedient villagers, there was an alternative approach to the problem: the temple could continue under the control of the Party. Officials did in fact adopt that strategy, but it involved the transformation of "superstition" into "religion," and the attempt to change the meaning of the temple from the spontaneous revival of popular religion and an assertion of local identity, to the acceptance of leadership by bureaucratized, state-sponsored Buddhism and the development of "tourism."

Redefinition and Control: A Meeting at the Temple

After the flood (but unconnected with it) there was a change of leadership at the township government, and the new Party secretary Gao arrived. Gao reversed the government's position toward the temple and decided to support it. Once the statue was returned to the temple, Gao went to inspect it, and when he leaned closer to look at Chuan Zhu's shoes, the statue fell on top of him. By the time word of this new "miraculous event" reached us, conventional wisdom had interpreted it as a happy portent: "Chuan Zhu performed the kowtow to Party secretary Gao in thanks for his support." Rumor also circulated that Gao's father and brother were both *daoshi* (Taoist priests) and so he was himself sympathetic to the temple.

In a public meeting called to organize a leadership structure for the temple, Gao's explanation for his support minimized his own initiative and grounded the decision in "orthodox" principles; namely, the leadership of the Party, the Party's official policy on religion, and (most interestingly) the Party's call to "develop the economy and develop tourism" in the "spirit of document number two":

> Today we come here to hold this cadre (*ganbu*) meeting [sic!]. The purpose is certainly not to practice superstition. Some people will say such nonsense, that we are holding a "feudal superstition activity," but we are acting in accordance with the Party's policy on religion. I want to emphasize this. Besides, we have a management group of seven people especially in charge of the temple's activities.
>
> First, I just want to say that building this temple is not my own personal decision. It has been agreed to by higher levels in the government. Moreover, there is management, leadership and discipline. First and foremost, there is to be absolutely no feudal superstition going on—no "spiritual possession" and no "black magic." If anyone is caught doing this, let it be known that I will severely punish them. Don't let this happen. Now, why is the township government supporting this temple ? Some rumors say that the government wants your money. I guarantee you that the government will not take one cent of your money; all the income from the temple will belong to the temple. Not only will the government not take money, it will add to the money you receive.

The temple has leadership and organization and the support of the Party, so don't be afraid. Now everyone should go out and make more friends; the more friends the faster the construction! So, through hard effort we can fulfill the responsibility given to us by the government. The things here, the land, the wood, all of it belongs to the nation (*guojiade*). All we need are for more people from outside to come here, more tourists, more friends, and we can improve the economic situation here. Economic construction is good for you; you should be "open" (*kaifang*). There's just one important rule: everything must be in accordance with the Party's policy on religion . . . Huang shifu and Jiu shifu [the Buddhist nuns put in charge of the temple] from Jin Feng Temple are both familiar with the policy on religion . . . You have the strong support of mayor Wan, who is a representative to the People's Congress. It's not just me, it's not just my crazy idea to build the temple; it's in accordance with policy.

In his speech, Gao repeatedly emphasized two themes: the temple must have (Party) leadership, and "superstition" would be "severely punished." In addition, developing the temple was legitimated as "developing tourism." "Following the Party's policy on religion" meant recasting the temple's identity to conform with state-sponsored Buddhism. These were the cornerstones of the authorities' attempt to give their own meaning to the temple's revival, to coopt it. Gao was particularly sensitive to the question of the temple's funding, since to this point the temple had been renovated through contributions of money, building materials and volunteer labor by local villagers. Many people held a cynical view of the government's belated involvement, and felt that the new ethic of "making money" would lead to government exploitation of their temple—and the cash and labor they put into it. Party secretary Gao tried to allay these fears by cutting a deal with local villagers: if they would desist from "feudal superstition" and accept the government's definition of the temple—that is, a tourist development zone with approved religious activity carried out under the clear leadership of the Buddhist bureaucracy—then the government would help provide money for both the temple's renovation, and for more economic development of tourism.

Gao's allies on the temple's leadership group tried other arguments to persuade locals to cooperate. The most active of these was a woman named Zheng from the United Front Department (*tongzhan bu*) of the county seat. Zheng was the spearhead of a movement to change the temple's identity from folk religion to Buddhism. In her speech following Gao, she appealed to many of the sentiments that had, in fact, motivated the spontaneous revival of the temple:

> Now we're all very clear; we will certainly follow the policy on religion in doing things. We will open up and do things correctly . . . Chuan Zhu temple (*Chuan Zhu si*) needs to attract people, if we attract people we can make money . . . This will be good for our economy . . . if the economy is good, the local peasants will have money. Then, when the township government wants you to pay taxes you don't have to be so mad about it . . . So building the temple is a good thing. It's good for the country (*guojia*); it helps the country by giving people faith and makes everyone better. So let's not be selfish.

We've all come here to make a better life, to give our grandchildren a better life. "If the will of heaven is not followed, the people's hearts will be uneasy" (*Tian xin bu shu, ren xin bu an*). Today's society has many bad things, like on the long distance buses when young men pull out knives and rob people, everyone says things are bad now. Look, one of the reasons we're here is to commemorate the good officials, like Er Lang [Chuan Zhu]; he was a good official. So this commemoration of them is a way to educate people, to tell them what "the good" is, and to "save" bad people, to have them come here and be turned into good people. If everyone has faith then this is good for maintaining peace in the family and the nation; it's beneficial to the family and the state.

Zheng's message, with its emphasis on faith as an antidote to social decay, echoed the attitudes of most of the villagers involved in the temple. The real difference between their points of view was that local people wanted to preserve the original identity of the *miaozi* (temple), while Zheng wanted to establish a *si* (Buddhist temple), and to absorb the Chuan Zhu temple into the broader Buddhist bureaucracy. To this end, Zheng courted a number of senior Buddhist nuns to persuade them to support and manage the temple. We asked one of these high-ranking nuns about the original religious identity of the temple. Was it Taoist, as locals say? She gave a look as though she had been assaulted by an offensive odor:

> This religion, that religion—these temples have no religion at all! Taoism, ha! . . . Taoism isn't really a religion, it is concerned with reality. Buddhism is more cultural and literate; that's why the state supports it . . .

She added that throughout history Buddhism had "led Taoism by its nose." She was quite openly contemptuous of both popular religion in general and of Taoism in particular. As interesting as her words was the way she said them; she had the precious and effete air of an aristocrat. She also gave off more than a whiff of corruption: "We ate so well at Wu Tai Shan [a famous convent in Shanxi], but these small temples—they really are just *too* awful!" She was treated with the deference due to an official, and she acted like one. Later we saw her being escorted to the temple by the leadership group and Party secretary Gao.

The state accepts Buddhism for a number of reasons, including the easily controlled organizational structure of the religion, its recognition as a "world religion," and its essentially passive moral message. Chinese religious policy allows for religious freedoms under the condition that religious activities remain unified under the Communist cause. Official documents have recognized the potentially constructive role religion can play in the cause of maintaining order and in attracting economic development.[7] The emphasis on unity resonates with traditional ideas of a single universe under one leadership. Thus bottom-up activism is tolerated, even welcomed, as long as it remains congruent with and controlled by the official government agenda.

The temple is a nascent "civil" institution in the Chinese countryside, independent of the state yet connected with it in a relationship of mutual cooptation. This relationship can only be understood in terms of the motivations underlying it, and in the context of the particular *timing* of the temple's revitalization. The phenomenon of "religious revival" was widespread in China during the reform period, and includes not only temple building but household-based rituals of ancestor worship and offerings to the "kitchen god," ritual offerings to the many "earth gods" (*tudi*) scattered in small shrines throughout the landscape, and, especially in southeast China, the re-opening of lineage halls and local festivals (e.g., Siu 1989b). In our area of fieldwork, furtive acts of individual worship— primarily the burning of incense and paper money at family altars, graves and *tudi* shrines—continued even through the collective period and began to be more openly practiced by the late 1980s, but, in our area, smaller local temples only began to reactivate in 1992.

In light of the fact that in other areas of China temple building also began earlier during the 1980s, the question of why the temple "revived" when it did is important. One possible answer is that market reforms spur temple reconstruction both in the sense that, traditionally, a certain level of prosperity gives rise to investment in prestige through donations to the community, and in the sense that temples and local festivals offer opportunities for developing the *guanxi* networks that underpin business, even at the expense of the ritual's consequent "vulgarization" (Siu 1989b, p. 127). Thus it seems to make sense that more economically developed areas such as southeast China would have earlier temple revivals, especially given the influence of returning emigrés from nearby Hong Kong and Taiwan. In more remote and poor locations, such as Sichuan, the time-lag in temple construction might reflect the time-lag in economic development. This explanation seems even more persuasive when put in the context of Deng's Southern Tour and "document number two," which aimed to spur economic growth in the hinterland by urging people to "learn from" the example of booming coastal regions like Shenzhen (next to Hong Kong).

The reconstruction of Chuan Zhu temple seems true to this pattern—except that the connection between market reform and temple building is exactly inverted; that is, the motivation behind rebuilding the temple was not for *guanxi* or economic reasons, but *against* the commoditization of relationships accompanying market reforms. One might safely conclude from this that market reforms can be linked to the timing of temple revivals, even if that linkage cannot tell us why any specific temple is undergoing revival—after all, China is a big place, with great variation in local conditions. That said, it is quite possible that the mixture of religious revival and economic motivation exhibited in the (well-studied) southeast of China is an exception rather than the rule; the hinterland is vast, and most of it a world apart from the freewheeling prosperity of villages in, say, Guangdong province. In fact, we argue that this disparity of wealth is one of the phenomena stemming from market reforms that feeds the fire of discontent in Sichuan, discontent expressed in the reactivation of local temples. This point is based on an important distinction in what we mean by a "temple," and this distinction, in turn, further explains the timing of temple building.

As the terms "local" and "reactivate" suggest, we are referring to temples which are *revitalized from the spontaneous initiative of local villagers*, as distinct from those primarily reconstructed at state initiative, developed as tourist centers. While the latter frequently house clerics and are visited by worshipping pilgrims as well as tourists, their religious activities are state-approved (overwhelmingly Buddhist, although Sichuan boasts some of China's most notable Taoist temples, especially Qingyang Gong in Chengdu, and the temples of Chingcheng Shan), and their significance is more redolent of a cultural-nationalistic invention of essence or heritage (*guoqing*) than religious. Local temples, by contrast, are centers of Chinese "popular religion" or "folk religion" (*minjian zongjiao*); or, less charitably and more frequently, of "feudal superstition" (*fengjian mixin*). As our analysis suggests, this is a crucial distinction of perspective that draws one into the larger debates surrounding cultural nationalism, modernization discourse, and issues of the interwoven identities of "peasants" and "intellectuals"—issues that this essay has only broached and cannot pursue. For the present discussion, it is important to understand that local temples are the assertion of a specific community's historical memory, and that a moral judgment of the present is both implicit and explicit in that assertion. Further, the tension between the classifications "feudal" (*fengjian*) and "folk" (*minjian*) mirrors the ambivalence in the state's interactions with local communities, and the top-down normative proscription of behavior enforced by state agents. For these reasons, the state perceived the temple as a threat and, until 1992, resisted the activities there—which underscores our contention that the timing of the temple's revival is crucial for understanding the motivations behind it.

While at the time of the earliest appearance of activity in the temple, in 1991, local officials felt that the threat of "feudal superstition" warranted a crackdown, by 1992 Party secretary Gao, "in the spirit of document number two," decided to channel the spontaneous initiative toward economic development. This decision was no doubt made easier by the critical mass of popular support for the temple reached after the flood, but it also reflects the "money-making fever" gripping the nation at that time, as well as Gao's sage estimation that the level of popular discontent in the countryside made it best to "follow from the will of the people" (*shun cong minyi*). This was precisely the point behind the temple's revival—getting the state to follow the will of the people. Even if the state's rationale of turning the temple into a money-making proposition was ironically symptomatic of the very trend the temple activists decried, it provided a point of mutual cooptation that both sides found accommodating.

It is important to note that local people did not express outrage at the stipulation that the government be involved in guiding the temple movement forward. On the contrary, there was a consensus welcoming government participation and a general spirit of accommodation from both directions. Locals welcomed well enough the Buddhist rituals Zheng organized, but suggested a separate building be constructed for the Buddhist "Goddess of Mercy" (Guanyin Pusa), and held firm that the temple's traditional name and identity not be forsaken.

The mood of accommodation may have been a product of mutual expectations of monetary advantage—the temple hoping to get a grant from the government for construction costs and the government hoping to reap rewards from potential tourism development, but there was another sphere in which they shared a common vocabulary of interest, if not exactly the same conclusions. This was the sphere of changing values. The officials for their part hoped that the revival would help put a check on soaring crime rates through the development of "spiritual civilization." Similarly, the farmers' general complaint was that everything nowadays is for love of money, not love of humanity, but through this one can see in the temple revival both a broad critique of changes in society and an implicit criticism of now-rampant official corruption. In a more positive sense, villagers created, in the temple, a sense of community, and they asserted their local identity despite the attempt by the state to absorb it into the "homogenized" realms of tourism and bureaucratic Buddhism.

Villagers' Reflections on the Temple

It would be misleading to suggest that the entire village community actively supported the temple's revival. Most people were simply too busy working to be involved in the activities outside of going to see the "excitement" of major festival days. Temple activists were mostly, though not exclusively, old people. But it would be equally misleading to characterize the revival as simple nostalgia. The temple served as a forum for expressing opinions about the changing world the villagers lived in, and for asserting values important to them.

A few villagers were even hostile toward the temple, seeing it as superstition or, more often, cynically dismissing it as another government scheme to make money. One middle-aged former grass-roots official with whom we spoke was particularly jaded about the government's involvement with the temple, and about the service religion rendered the government. First, in response to our question of who Chuan Zhu was, he compared the temple god to the "provincial Party secretary," and added the rather scornful observation that "he is supposed to be a god, but he was really a man!":

> They decided to open the temple when the local leadership changed. The Fourteenth Party congress called for "the development of culture," so they're going ahead with it. Old Deng is a smart guy; as soon as they started the reforms he also had them open up. It's basically a ruse to make money. Deng said, "ok, you want to see foreign movies? Pay for it; we'll take your money!" It's the same with this temple; they'll develop it and charge admission and make money from it—that's what "cultural development" is all about—a tactic to make money. ... Sure, it's a part of "building a spiritual civilization"

(*jingshen wenming*); but that really means informing people, controlling them. The *pusa* tells the people how to behave themselves; it's all very useful. . . . Your country has academic degrees (*xuewei*), we have authority (*quanwei*)— and a long history of authoritarianism. . . . Authority is important for public order and social stability.

While most people did not hold such a cynical view, there was a marked tendency to conflate the religious and the political. As mentioned above, Chuan Zhu's identity as an upright official made connections between him and officials today quite commonplace. In many cases, officials were judged on how they related to the temple. One man explained the connection to us during a festival held at the temple:

> The township head and Party secretary both came here today. They kowtowed, of course! They are officials, but they are still one of the people. It's important for an official to show that he is one of the people, the same as us. An official needs the support of the people. Officials and the people should have mutual respect. The peasants have culture, and there are intellectuals among the peasants. This kind of event, with musicians and people reading scripture shows that peasants have culture and knowledge.

This statement reveals both an ideal of good government and a strong sense of pride, an assertion of the essential worth of villagers who are often made to feel like second-rate citizens by officials, city people and intellectuals. Later, the man praised the new Party secretary and township head for their solidarity and respect for the people, shown by their respect for Chuan Zhu, and complained about the old officials (who had tried to suppress the temple) and their unfair and disrespectful practice of withholding taxes (*kou shui*) from peasant incomes.

We heard many complaints about Party officials and their mismanagement of the temple. The main thrust of these criticisms was not against the Communist Party, but rather against Party members today who fell short of villagers' idealization of the Party—they were "not real Party members." During the city god's festival day at the temple we overheard a woman loudly complaining about an official who ignored the temple:

> I said to him, "you're a Communist Party member! You shouldn't just sit around all day! You should come get involved (*lai guan*). Party member or not I'll box your ears if you don't come! Party member, ha!

On the same occasion, another woman said she had encountered resistance in her production team about coming to the temple:

> They opposed me coming here, but I said "you can't stop me." They opposed me because they say it's "superstition," but they should be more clear about what superstition is! This is China's religious belief . . .

Here she was interrupted by a man, "they're Party members, Party members don't believe in anything . . ." She replied: "But this is religious belief."

This, of course, is the crucial question of cultural definition: are the temple's activities superstitious or religious?[8] As we have seen, state approval of the temple is qualified; spontaneous revival of popular religion must conform to state standards and be carried out under the leadership of the Party. But local villagers make no such distinction. For them, religious belief is an important anchor against the winds of change; religion provides values to believe in when all around them they see the chaos wrought by people who seem to believe in nothing.

Conclusion

In the post-Mao period, China has been in a process of accelerating change. With the *de facto* end of communism as a total legitimating ideology, China is in the throes of a crisis of belief and intense value change. As controls on the economy and on cultural life have been lifted, long-suppressed forms of behavior and expression have begun to reappear to fill the vacuum of values. The case of the Chuan Zhu temple illustrates villagers' reactions to changes in the economy, in government, and in society. Through the temple, villagers sought to restore "harmony" between the values of authority, justice and freedom, and to assert local identity against efforts by the state to control the definition of culture.

The spontaneous self-organization of the temple is clearly an important example of a "public sphere" emerging in the countryside between the state and the household and outside the market. Villagers who supported the temple were expressing their dissatisfaction with the chaos and social decay of the changing world around them. Through the temple they criticized corruption, injustice and the lack of values and principles in society. They put forward their ideal of just and good government and the correct relationship toward authority. The temple was also an important source of local pride, identity and cultural expression, and villagers resisted the pressures to give up this local identity. In this sense, the temple revival underscores Richard Madsen's idea that "the associations of civil society are not just interest groups, but communities. And communities are historically constituted, they are 'communities of memory'." (1993, p. 192).

As an institution recreated from memory, the temple fulfilled some of the functions it had served in pre-Liberation times, especially that of being the center of a sense of local community. The importance of the idea that the temple is a place villagers go simply to have some fun should not be underestimated. As Weller (1994) observes, the bustling excitement (or what he terms "heat and noise" [*renao*]) of Chinese popular religion forms a thick brew of potential meanings, saturated with a plurality of possible interpretations. The Chuan Zhu temple exemplifies this interplay of contested meanings. We have isolated an interpretation of the temple as an expression of community identity to highlight the local way villagers encounter forces that are often described in global terms—commoditization, "scientific progress," resistance or "subversion" of state control. Just as the level of economic development varies enormously from locality to locality in China, the reactions of local villagers to the transformations wrought by commoditization vary. In a similar way, for every conflict that precipitates into open resistance, as in the tax revolt in Renshou county, we believe there are many cases of negotiation-through-mutual cooptation that mediate between community interests and those of the state.[9] For over a quarter of a century in post-revolution China, the power of the state in managing public affairs was overwhelming. Thus alternative networks must still be seen as nascent. Rowe (1989, p. 183) has made the point that in late Qing China societal forces responded more adroitly than did bureaucratic ones to the changing social and economic forces tearing at the social fabric. In the current era of rapid change, there is much to be gained by encouraging such impulses at the grassroots, and great care is required to ensure that agents of the state, working within a dominant state rhetoric which casts the villagers' political and religious impulses as ignorant and backward, do not excessively impair these initiatives. Too often the differences in "interest" between local communities and state agents are veiled by the processes of co-optation we have sought to describe. But co-optation cuts both ways; farmers sought both engagement with and independence from the state in their assertion of moral order against chaos. Moreover, as the case of the temple illustrates, the co-optation of spontaneous "civil" organizations by the state is not necessarily rejected by the grassroots, nor does co-optation mean that civil society is somehow negated; in fact, villagers were *more* able to express their interests *after* the state attempted to take over the temple revival, both in terms of using the legitimation of state approval for "tourist development" to build more temples, and by using the temple as a forum for expressing their values to the government leadership.

The divergent interests of farmers and state agents points to a gap more fundamental than corruption or exploitation: the gap of values between urban and rural dwellers. Chinese intellectuals, in promoting their own agenda for development in the countryside, tend to dismiss local interests, confident that their own methods are modern, progressive, rational, efficient and thus superior to those of the feudal, superstitious and backward peasant (Cohen 1993). In at least this sense of negative reference to "the peasant," state agents and intellectuals in China have common cause. In our area of fieldwork, at any rate, sanguine predictions of an increasing urbanization and "rationalization" of the countryside not only ring false, but are based on interests and values that may be widely held by intellectuals and state agents, yet are alien and even hostile to the farmers.

Thus, it is not surprising that in the case of the temple revival we see farmers were expressing their own sense of the limitations of the rhetoric of rationality. The orthodoxy of rational economic development has left their interests largely ignored. Non-government networks such as the temple offer a certain flexibility and responsiveness to popular thinking absent in the formal government structures, and it is only through increased understanding of the needs and desires at the grassroots that ultimately successful political and economic structures can be created.

Perhaps most importantly, the case of the Chuan Zhu temple suggests that we look beyond the economy when trying to understand the emerging space between social organization and private interest. The temple serves many important social functions. Contributions to the temple are a way of showing "face" and establishing status in the community. The donations of labor and materials to build and maintain the temple make it an outlet for community voluntarism. Finally, and most important for villagers, the temple is an institution for passing on knowledge (in this case, moral knowledge) to succeeding generations. The Chuan Zhu temple is the kind of community institution that was suppressed under the years of Maoist rule, and the resulting social structure of today is scattered, atomistic and lacking any focal point. In this sense, the revival of popular religion can be seen as the spontaneous resurgence of community, a development that should be encouraged.

Notes

1. Anthropologists Potter and Potter (1990), Siu (1989a and 1989b) and Kim (1991) have debated the social and economic significance of what they have each observed in their fieldwork: a resurgence of religious and cultural life in post-Mao China. In addition, Vivienne Shue (1990) has emphasized the (re)development of horizontal ties in new rural economic structures which, she argues, are replacing the "cellular" formations of the Maoist period.

Both of us treat the temple revitalization at some length in our Ph.D. theses: Pamela Leonard (1994) from the perspective of landscape, historical memory and environmental consciousness, John Flower as part of an analysis of values and cultural identity in a comparative study of villagers and urban intellectuals (forthcoming).

A discussion of the debate over the significance of the "resurgence of tradition" in the Chinese countryside is beyond the scope of this paper. It should be evident, however, that our interpretation differs substantially from that of Helen Siu, who states that " . . . the contemporary popular rituals express a lack of faith in both the supernatural and material power structures, and a pervasive sense of alienation among the practitioners. These cultural fragments paradoxically show the extent to which popular beliefs have been affected by the Marxist state." (1989a, p. 300). Nor do we wholly subscribe to the view of Sulamith and Jack Potter that religious beliefs and practices constitute a "fundamental continuity too powerful to be altered by efforts to induce change that have merely scratched the surface of social life." (1990, p. 269). While we tend to follow the Potters in emphasizing the persistence of traditional values and historical continuities, our aim is to demonstrate how old ideas have been reconstituted to speak to new realities; to use Vitebsky's terms, it is not a survival but a revival (1992, p. 240).

2. Cf. Wakeman (1993), Rowe (1993), Madsen (1993) and Yang (1994).

3. Liang Congjie, founder of the Chinese environmental group "Friends of Nature," quoted in *Environmental Defense Fund* newsletter (March 1995).

4. A theoretical approach pioneered by James Scott (1985). A very useful discussion of the tendency to over-read "resistance" in peasant actions in current anthropological discourse is found in Weller (1994) who develops his argument based on ethnographic data on religion from Taiwan.

5. Sun (1993) and Sung (1993).

6. The text (entitled: *Guanyin pusa jiu dong yuwen*) began with the story of a woman from Hunan who believed in Guanyin and faithfully recited scripture (*nian jing*). She died but seven days later Guanyin brought her back to life and out of hell because of her piety. The story goes on to describe a time when the good will be separated from evil by two successive years (1992 and 1993) of disaster and calamity, including: epidemic diseases, famine, poisonous snakes, mad dogs and tigers, great storms, poisonous water, apocalyptic wars, bandits and the unleashing of demons and monsters from hell to attack people night and day. The text portended that evil people will be the victims of this onslaught, even the wealthy, the high, the mighty, and the learned will not be spared: warriors and generals will be consumed, physicians will not be able to cure their own diseases. Finally, eighteen concentric pits will devour the evil people, and they will be ground between millstones and transformed into monsters. The apocalypse will heighten to a crescendo of disaster, with those not dying at first finding themselves destroyed in the end by progressively debilitating disease, and the second year of disaster more ferocious than the first.

7. James Thrower of Aberdeen University has made a formal study of religious policy in China (unpublished) focusing on document number 19 of 1978 (3rd plenum of the 11th congress) published in English in 1982. See James Thrower, "Article 36 and 'Document 19': Religion and the State in Contemporary China with Particular Reference to Islam in the Xinjiang-Uighur Autonomous Region." Document 19 was written for cadres at all levels. Section three reviews failures and successes of the PRC's religious policy of the past, noting in particular Leftist errors of the Cultural Revolution and it makes a call to bring all religious believers together for building a powerful Communist state. Section 10 names three great world religions which have international networks useful for international development. The document makes explicit that "religious activities" as opposed to "superstitious activities" are legal as long as their organization maintains the principle of remaining under the leadership of the Chinese Communist Party.

8. Anagnost (1987) examines the discourse concerning "feudal superstition," religion and "science" in Chinese newspaper accounts. A thoughtful article on the stance of social scientists (Chinese and Western) toward superstition and religion in China is Feuchtwang and Wang (1993).

9. We have also explored this theme in the context of gift-giving practices in a livestock development project which took place in Sichuan at this same time (Flower and Leonard, forthcoming).

References

Anagnost, Ann. 1987. "Politics and Magic in Contemporary China." *Modern China*, vol. 13, no. 1 (January), pp. 40-61.

Cohen, Myron L. 1993. "Cultural and Political Inventions in Modern China: The Case of the Chinese 'Peasant'." *Daedalus*, vol. 22, no. 2 (Spring).

Feuchtwang, Stephan, and Wang Mingming. 1993. "The Politics of Culture or a Contest of Histories: Representations of Chinese Popular Religion." *Dialectical Anthropology*, vol. 16, pp. 251-272.

Flower, John, and Leonard, Pamela (forthcoming). "Community Values and State Cooptation: An Ethnographic View of Civil Society in the Sichuan Countryside." In Chris Hann and Elizabeth Dunn, eds., *Civil Society: Challenging Western Models*. London: Routledge.

Kim, Kwang-ok. 1991. "Socialist Civilization and Resurgence of Tradition in China." Paper presented at ASA Conference in Cambridge, England.

Leonard, Pamela. 1994. *The Political Landscape of a Sichuan Village*. Ph.D. thesis, University of Cambridge.

Madsen, Richard. 1993. "The Public Sphere, Civil Society and Moral Community: A Research Agenda for Contemporary China Studies." *Modern China*, vol. 19, no. 2, pp. 183-98.

Potter, Sulamith, and Potter, Jack. 1990. *China's Peasants: The Anthropology of a Revolution.* Cambridge: Cambridge University Press.

Rowe, William T. 1989. *Hankow: Conflict and Community in a Chinese City, 1796-1895.* Stanford, CA: Stanford University Press.

———. 1993. "The Problem of Civil Society in Late Imperial China." *Modern China*, vol. 19, no. 2, pp. 139-157.

Scott, James. 1985. *Weapons of the Weak: Everyday Forms of Peasant Resistance.* New Haven: Yale University Press.

Shue, Vivienne. 1990. "Emerging State-Society Relations in Rural China." In Jürgen Delman, Clemens Stubbe Østergaard, and Fleming Christiansen, eds., *Remaking Peasant China: Problems of Rural Development and Institutions at the Start of the 1990s.* Aarhus, Denmark: Aarhus University Press.

Siu, Helen F. 1989a. *Agents and Victims in South China: Accomplices in Rural Revolution.* New Haven: Yale University Press.

———. 1989b. "Recycling Rituals: Politics and Popular Culture in Contemporary Rural China." In Perry Link, Richard Madsen, Paul G. Pickowicz, eds., *Unofficial China: Popular Culture and Thought in the People's Republic.* Boulder, CO: Westview Press.

Sun, Lena H. 1993. "China's Peasants Hit Back; Rising Rural Unrest Alarms Beijing." *Washington Post*, June 20, 1996, p. A1, col. 5.

Sung, Kuo-Cheng. 1993. "Peasant Unrest in Szechuan and Mainland China's Rural Problems." *Issues and Studies*, vol. 29, no. 7, pp. 129–132.

Thrower, James (n.d.). "Article 36 and 'Document 19': Religion and the State in Contemporary China with Particular Reference to Islam in the Xinjiang-Uighur Autonomous Region."

Vitebsky, Piers. 1992. "Landscape and Self-Determination among the Eveny: The Political Environment of Siberian Reindeer Herders Today." In Elisabeth Croll and David Parkin, eds., *Bush Base: Forest Farm: Culture, Environment and Development.* London: Routledge, pp. 223–247.

Wakeman, Frederic. 1993. "The Civil Society and the Public Sphere Debate." *Modern China*, vol. 19, no. 2, pp. 108-38.

Weller, Robert P. 1994. *Resistance, Chaos and Control in China: Taiping Rebels, Taiwanese Ghosts and Tiananmen.* Seattle: University of Washington Press.

Yang, Mayfair. 1994. *Gifts, Favors and Banquets: The Art of Social Relationships in China.* Ithaca, NY: Cornell University Press.

(n.a.). 1995. "China's First Environmental Leader Talks to EDF." In the March issue of the newsletter of the *Environmental Defense Fund*, New York.

Index

Irrigation management *(continued)*
   district organization and, 146–52
   development of (1980–1992)
      quality decline in, 140–41, 144–45,
         162–63, 165n7
      quality increase in, 141–45, 163,
         165n7
   district organization and, 138–39,
      166n8
      Chinese Communist Party (CCP) and,
         145–46, 148–49
      decollectivization and, 146–52
      Hunan Province, 145–46
      Sanyuan County, 148–49, 166n13
      Shandong Province, 149
      Shanxi Province, 149–50
      state control and, 145–52
   equipment management and, 155–58,
      167n18
      Shandong Province, 156, 167n19
   facility construction and, 137, 153–55,
      164, 165n1
   funding for, 139, 160–62
      state investment and, 136–37, 140–41,
         165n5
   Household Contract Responsibility
      System (HCRS) and, 137–38
   modernization of, 136–37
   provision of services and, 158–60
   state control and, 83–84, 137–38,
      153–55, 163–65
      district organization and, 145–52
   state subsidization and, 84, 151–52, 162,
      163
   user fees and, 83–84, 137, 139, 160–62
      enforcement of, 84, 162
      free-riders and, 84
      Water Fee law (1985), 84, 160, 162,
         163, 164
   water conservation and, 84, 136–38, 140,
      152–55
   See also Common property resource
      management (CPRM);
      Groundwater management (Yao
      Ba); Rangeland management
      (Ningxia)

Jae Ho Chung, 136
Japan
   comprehensive cooperatives and, 33
   state control and, 22

Jiangsu Province
   township-village enterprises (TVEs)
      of, 27
   villages of, 63, 65, 70, 71
      committees and, 244, 245, 251–52
Jilin Province, village committees and,
   243, 245, 247, 249
Johnson, G., 119

Kornai, J., 27, 31

Land distribution, 62–63
   groundwater management (Yao Ba) and,
      178–79
   Household Contract Responsibility
      System (HCRS) and, 18–19
   mutual aid and, 35–36
LAPCs. *See* Lower Agricultural
   Producers' Cooperatives
Leonard, P., 55
Liaoning Province, village committees
   and, 243, 244, 245, 247, 248–49,
   251, 252
Lieberthal, K., 221
Lineage relations
   township-village enterprises (TVEs) and,
      119, 125–26
   villages and, 56–57, 59–60
Lin Qingsong, 118, 119
Liuman township. *See* Hebei Province,
   Raoyang County
Li Yutang, 217
Local government
   collective ownership of township-village
      enterprises (TVEs)
      Household Contract Responsibility
         System (HCRS) and, 96–98
      pooling of risks/capital and, 99–100
      rapid rural industrialization and, 95–96,
         98–101, 107
      relations with county and, 100–107,
         108n15
   county
      Agricultural Bank and, 104–5,
         108n19
      bureaucratic services of, 102–4
      coordinating role of, 101–2
      investment and credit and, 104–5,
         108n19
      production materials provision and,
         102